NATURAL SCIENCES IN AMERICA

ORNITHOLOGY

BY

ROBERT RIDGWAY

ARNO PRESS
A New York Times Company
New York, N. Y. • 1974

Reprint Edition 1974 by Arno Press Inc.

Reprinted from a copy in The Museum
  of Comparative Zoology, Harvard University

NATURAL SCIENCES IN AMERICA
ISBN for complete set: 0-405-05700-8
See last pages of this volume for titles.

Manufactured in the United States of America

Publisher's Note: This volume was reprinted
from the best available copy.

————————◆————————

Library of Congress Cataloging in Publication Data

Ridgway, Robert, 1850-1929.
    Ornithology.

    (Natural sciences in America)
    Reprint of v. 4, pt. 3 (1877) of the Report of the
U. S. Geological Exploration of the Fortieth Parallel
published 1870-80 by the Govt. Print. Off., Washington.
        1. Birds--United States. I. United States.
Geological Exploration of the Fortieth Parallel.
Report. II. Title. III. Series.
QL682.R52 1974   598.2'973   73-17839
ISBN 0-405-05761-X

UNITED STATES GEOLOGICAL EXPLORATION OF THE FORTIETH PARALLEL.

CLARENCE KING, Geologist-in-charge.

PART III.

ORNITHOLOGY.

BY

ROBERT RIDGWAY.

TABLE OF CONTENTS TO PART III.

SMITHSONIAN INSTITUTION,

WASHINGTON, D. C., *November* 18, 1876.

SIR: I transmit herewith a report on the ornithology of the route explored by the United States Geological Exploration of the Fortieth Parallel, based upon field-work from June, 1867, to August, 1869, inclusive, the time during which I had the honor to serve in the capacity of zoölogist to the expedition; the region investigated being that directly between Sacramento City, California, and Salt Lake City, Utah, including a few points directly to the eastward of the last-mentioned locality.

The ornithological specimens preserved, and deposited in the National Museum, at Washington, number 1,522, of which 769 are skins, and 753 nests and eggs. This may seem a small collection proportioned to the time employed in its formation, but the making of protracted field-observations and the elaboration of notes therefrom were deemed of greater importance than the amassing of a large duplicate collection. Moreover, almost equal attention was given to other branches of zoölogy, particularly to reptiles and fishes, large series of which, representing very completely the fauna of the country, were placed, according to instructions, in the hands of specialists for identification.[1]

The unusual facilities most generously afforded by you, and your kind encouragement at all times, aided very materially the successful operations of the zoölogist; so that whatever is creditable in the results attained by his labors, the merit is mainly due to yourself. Another friend deserves special mention in this connection for his valued assistance—Mr. H. G. Parker, of Carson City, Nevada (at the time of the writer's connection with the expedition Superintendent of Indian Affairs for that State), whose frequent and gratuitous services contributed greatly to the completeness of the natural history collections.

---

[1] The reports on these collections have not been received.

In the preparation of this report, the valued facilities afforded by the Smithsonian Institution were availed of, through the courtesy and kindness of Professor Joseph Henry, the Secretary of the Institution; among the many advantages thus secured being frequent access to a splendid working library and an unrivaled collection of North American birds. The author wishes also to express himself as particularly indebted to Professor Spencer F. Baird, Assistant Secretary of the Smithsonian Institution and Curator of the National Museum, for invaluable assistance kindly rendered throughout the progress of the work.

I have the honor to be,

Very respectfully, your obedient servant,

ROBERT RIDGWAY.

CLARENCE KING, Esq.,
United States Geologist,
In charge of U. S. Geological Explorations, 40th Parallel

GENERAL REPORT.

DESCRIPTION OF THE ROUTE.

The investigations on which the following report is based, were made almost wholly within the limits of that vast interior region of continental drainage known as the Great Basin, between the parallels of 39° and 42° north latitude, collections having been made at but one outlying locality, the vicinity of Sacramento City, California. As observations were extended along the entire course of travel, however, from San Francisco to points in Utah eastward of Salt Lake City, we shall not confine our treatise to the limited region noted, but shall describe each of the main points where observations were made and notes taken, in regular sequence.[1]

All the way from Panama to San Francisco several species of pelagic birds followed our vessel, the Black-footed Albatross (*Diomedia nigripes*) and White-headed Gull (*Blasipus heermanni*) being daily companions until we entered the "Golden Gate." No land-birds made their appearance, however, until, when off the coast of Mexico, between Acapulco and Cape St. Lucas, a solitary Mourning Dove (*Zenædura carolinensis*) made its appearance one day about noon, and, although flying around the vessel for nearly an hour, did not alight, but finally disappeared to the eastward, where no land was in sight.

---

[1] We reluctantly omit, as too far beyond the geographical province of our subject, some notes on the Isthmus of Panama, where, however, no North American birds were seen, excepting some waders, observed in the pools along the railroad, among which were the Purple Gallinule (*Gallinula martinica*) and the Little White Egret, or Snowy Heron (*Garzetta candidissima*). In the Bay of Aspinwall several Man-o-war Hawks (*Tachypetes aquila*) were observed sailing in circles overhead, much in the manner of Swallow-tailed Kites (*Elanoides forficatus*); and in the Bay of Panama, on the opposite (Pacific) side, Brown Pelicans (*Pelecanus fuscus*) were particularly numerous, and noticeable from their occupation of plunging from the air into the water after their prey.

Arrived in California, no peculiarly western bird was observed until we reached Sacramento City; since, after landing at San Francisco, only Purple Martins (*Progne subis*) and Cliff Swallows (*Petrochelidon lunifrons*), which swarmed about old buildings on certain streets, were seen, while the only notes of other species heard were the familiar songs of caged Canary Birds. The journey up the Sacramento River was equally disappointing in this respect, since, though we kept a vigilant look-out from our post of observation on the hurricane deck of the steamer, none but familiar eastern species, most of which were water-birds (Coots, Florida Gallinules, and various species of ducks), were seen, the only land-birds being an occasional Belted Kingfisher (*Ceryle alcyon*) perched on an overhanging willow. During the first day at Sacramento, however, we became familiarized with several of the species peculiar to the western portion of the continent, but as this locality brings us to the commencement of our observations in the field, we shall begin a *resumé* of the subject in another chapter.

1867.—The first camp of the survey was established at Sacramento City, California, on the 6th of June, from which date collections were made until July 4th, when the plains to the eastward and the Sierra Nevada were crossed into Nevada. It is much to be regretted that no opportunity was afforded for making collections along this route, especially in the western foot-hills and in the pine-region of the western slope, since a number of additional species and many valuable observations were thus lost to the collection and archives of the exploration. After entering Nevada, the Big Bend of the Truckee was selected for the first working-camp, and there we remained from July 24th until August 18th; a portion of the time being devoted to an excursion to Pyramid Lake, which was reached by descending the river in a *batteau*, the party returning on horseback, after about a week's absence. During this trip the main island in the lake was visited. Our investigations from the main camp also included several visits to the dry cañons of the Virginia Mountains, about eight miles to the westward, across a very sandy *mesa*. This camp was abandoned on the 25th of August, when we started across the desert for Humboldt Lake; but upon reaching the latter place the writer became a victim of malarial fever, which for weeks interfered very materially with the prosecution of his duties. We next proceeded up the Humboldt River to Oreana, where a camp was fixed near the town, but our stay was short on account of the spread of the fever in a very malignant form, compelling the entire party to seek healthier water and purer air in the high mountains to the eastward. A camp was accordingly made in Wright's Cañon, on the western slope of the West Humboldt Mountains, a locality which proved to be well adapted for a collecting-ground. This camp was deserted, however, about the middle of September, for one on the eastern slope of the same range, for which the town of Unionville, in Buena Vista Cañon, was selected. This proved to be the best locality, for birds, yet visited. We left this place about the last of October, and moved westward again, along the same route, toward winter-quarters. At the Humboldt Marshes, on the 31st of October, several new species were added to the collection during the single evening of our stay, but no further collections were made until again at the Truckee Meadows, where we remained from November 7th until the 21st of the same month; and from which place an excursion to the Pea-vine Mountains, near the Sierra Nevada, was made on the 20th inst., in company with Mr. H. G. Parker. From this camp we repaired to Carson City, and remained there until the 5th of December, when, after first spending one day in the pine forests of the Sierra near Genoa, we revisited the Truckee Reservation near Pyramid Lake, through facilities extended by Mr. Parker, who accompanied the writer and assisted him in making his collections. This trip was made via the Carson River to below Fort Churchill, whence the desert was crossed to the Big Bend of the Truckee; but in returning the river was followed to the Meadows (at Glendale), thence to Hunter's Station, and across the valley to the Steamboat Springs, and over the Virginia Mountains, to Virginia City and Carson.

1868.—Winter-quarters at Carson City were left early in May, for the Truckee Reservation. which was reached on the 14th inst. Large collections were made here, the most important being from the island and "pyramid" in the lake, which we were enabled to visit through the kindness of Mr. Parker, who placed his handsome yacht "Nettie" at our service, and assisted us to secure large numbers of the previously very rare eggs of several species of water-fowl breeding on these islands. Early in June we repaired to Virginia City, and thence to Austin, in the Toyabe Mountains, which were reached on the first of July. Collections and valuable notes were made by the way, especially at the Carson River, seven miles above Fort Churchill (June 23d), Fort Churchill (June 24th), Nevada Station (June 25th), Soda Lake, on the Carson Desert, (June 27th), Sand Springs, (June 29th), Fairview Valley, (June 29th), and Edward's Creek (June 30th). At Austin we remained only a few days, when, departing for Ruby Valley, we arrived there July 13th, and camped at the base of the mountains, some four miles northward of Fort Ruby. Toward the last of August we left this place and proceeded northward along the foot of the East Humboldt Mountains, pitching camps of a few days' duration at intervals of the journey. Crossing the range through the pass known as Secret Valley, near Fort Halleck, we approached the upper portion of the Humboldt River, and in continuing northward camped on several of the streams flowing from the lofty Clover Mountains into the Humboldt. The month of September was principally spent in traveling northward to the Humboldt "Wells," thence through Thousand Spring Valley to the Goose Creek Mountains, crossing which we entered the southern portion of Idaho at the "City of Rocks," the most northern locality reached; from whence our course directed eastward toward Salt Lake City, where we arrived early in October. At intervals during the pursuance of the route traced, small collections were made, when opportunity permitted; the principal stations being—"Overland Ranche," Ruby Valley, (August 26–29), "Camp 22," Ruby Valley, (September 4–5), Secret Valley (September 6–8), Dearing's Ranche, Upper Humboldt Valley (September 10–12), Trout Creek, Upper Humboldt Valley, (September 16–20), Thousand Spring Valley (September 21–24), "City of Rocks," southern Idaho (October 3), and Deep Creek, northwestern Utah (October 5).

1869.—On the 20th of May of this year, collecting was begun at Salt Lake City, and continued until June 21st, when we proceeded to Parley's Park, about twenty-five miles to the eastward, in the Wahsatch Mountains. In the meantime, Antelope, Stansbury, and Carrington Islands, in the Great Salt Lake, were visited. On the 2d of July an excursion was made, in company with the botanists of the expedition, eastward to the western spurs of the Uintah Mountains; there we remained from the 3d until the 8th instant, when we returned to the main camp in Parley's Park *via* the Provo

Cañon, Utah Lake, and Salt Lake City. Work was continued at main camp until August 16th, when collections and notes were packed and our field-work ended.

PHYSICAL FEATURES OF THE GREAT BASIN.

While the region traversed by the survey after its equipment embraces the entire distance from Sacramento City, California, to points in Utah eastward of the Salt Lake Valley, the actual field-work began only at the eastern base of the Sierra Nevada, and was thus entirely confined to the interior area of continental drainage known to geographers as the Great Basin, and which we shall frequently refer to in the following pages by this name, as well as by that of the "Interior," a convenient synonymous term. This vast area corresponds almost strictly in its geographical boundaries with the "Middle Province" of zoölogists. The route of the expedition was mainly across the middle portion of the Great Basin proper, so that the fauna encountered was that typical of the Middle Province.

In few regions is the influence directed on the distribution of birds by that of the plants so manifest to the observer as in the one under consideration; and as vegetation is influenced so materially by configuration of the surface, conditions of the soil, elevation, etc., a brief description of the physical features of the country embraced within the limits of our trip is necessary to the intelligent understanding of the nature of the Middle Province avifauna, and the manner in which it is divided into bands of restricted range, according to conditions of environment. Such an excellent description of the field of our investigations has been given by Mr. Watson, the botanist of the expedition, that we cannot do the subject greater justice than to quote the following from "Geographical Notes," on pages xiii–xvii of the Botanical Report:[1]—

---

[1] Professional Papers of the Engineer Department, U. S. Army, No. 18. Report of the Geological Exploration of the Fortieth Parallel, made by order of the Secretary of War according to acts of Congress of March 2, 1867, and March 3, 1869, under the direction of Brig. and B'vt Major-General A. A. Humphreys, Chief of Engineers, by Clarence King, U. S. Geologist. Volume V, Botany. By Sereno Watson, aided by Prof. Daniel C. Eaton and others. Submitted to the Chief of Engineers, and published by order of the Secretary of War under authority of Congress. Illustrated by a Map and Forty Plates. Washington: Government Printing Office, 1871.

This region constitutes the northern portion of what was at first designated as the "Great Basin," the high plateau, without outlet for its waters, separated on the north by low divides from the valley of the Snake River and continuing southward until it merges into the desert of the Lower Colorado. Geologically considered, however, as well as botanically, the term is now properly made to include the whole similar arid stretch of country northward to the plains of the Columbia, in latitude 48°.

The lofty and unbroken range of the Sierras bounds this section of the Basin on the one side by its steep eastern slope, entering Nevada at only a single point, where it throws over the border a high flanking-spur, the Washoe Mountains. On the opposite side lies the broad and nearly equally elevated system of the Wahsatch, broken through by the Bear, Weber, and Provo Rivers, which head among the peaks of the adjoining Uintahs. The intervening space, 460 miles broad in latitude 42°, but narrowed by the convergence of the opposing mountains to about 200 miles in latitude 37°, is for the most part occupied by numerous short and somewhat isolated minor ranges, having a general north and south trend, and at average distances of about twenty miles. The bases of these ranges are usually very narrow, even in the most elevated, rarely exceeding eight or ten miles in breadth, the slopes abrupt and the lines of foot-hills contracted, the mesas grading at a low and nearly uniform angle into the broad uninterrupted valleys. Over the larger portion of the territory, and especially in Nevada, the combined areas of the valleys and the area occupied by the mountains and accompanying foot-hills are very nearly equal. The main depressions within this region are two, one at the base of the Sierras at a level of about 3,850 feet above the sea, into which flows all of drainage there is from the whole northern half of Nevada and from the eastern slope of the Sierras, the other the "Great Salt Lake Basin," at an altitude 400 feet greater, close upon the base of the Wahsatch and receiving the waters from that range above latitude 40° and from the northeastern portion of the Uintahs. Into the first flow the Truckee, Carson, Quinn's, and Humboldt Rivers. The Truckee is a clear, cold stream, which issues from Lake Tahoe in the Sierras, and after a rapid descent breaks through the Virginia Mountains and turning north soon empties into Pyramid and Winnemucca Lakes. These are much the deepest of all the lakes of the Basin, being hemmed in by mountains, and are moderately saline. The Carson River also rises in the Sierras farther to the south, but after leaving the base of the mountains is a less rapid stream and gradually becomes somewhat alkaline. Inclining more to the eastward it forms a small shallow lake on the border of Carson Desert, and thence issues in a number of devious channels, and is finally spent in an extensive "sink" or alkaline mud-plain of some twenty or thirty miles in diameter. Of a like character are the "Mud Lakes," lying north of Pyramid Lake and fed by Quinn's River, which has its source in southeastern Oregon. Beyond the limits of the survey to the south are Walker's and some other smaller lakes, supplied by streams from the Sierras, but all strongly saline.

From this western depression the general level of the country rises gradually to the eastward very nearly to the border of Nevada, where the valleys have an altitude of about 6,000 feet. Here in the northeastern part of the State the Humboldt River takes its rise, by far the most important river of the Basin, not only as the longest but as opening a passage for three hundred miles to the Central Pacific Railroad through the mountain ranges, that would otherwise have proved a serious obstruction. It is nowhere a large stream, receives few affluents, and in some parts of its course is very tortuous. It at length spreads out into Humboldt Lake, shallow and subalkaline, and from this the little remaining surplus water finds its way in a manner similar to the Carson River into the same sink.

The descent of 2,000 feet from eastern Nevada into the Great Salt Lake Basin is almost immediate, nearly the whole northwestern portion of Utah being an alkaline desert, broken by fewer mountain or hill-ranges, and but little above the level of the lake. The lake itself is for the most part very shallow, in no place over 50 feet in depth, the waters a concentrated solution of salt. As with all these sheets of water the shore-line and consequent area vary greatly in different years.

The intermediate ranges of the Basin are very similar to each other in character. They vary in altitude from one to 6,000 feet above the valleys, culminating in occasional peaks scarcely ever so rugged that they cannot be ascended from some direction upon mules. They are cut up by numerous ravines or "cañons," which are narrow, very rarely with an acre of interval or surface approaching to a level, the sides sometimes rocky or precipitous, more frequently sloping to the summits of the lateral ridges. In geological structure these ranges are more or less complicated, showing rocks of all ages from the azoic to the glacial period, here metamorphic rocks, quartzites, slate, and limestones, there an outburst of granite or syenite, volcanic rocks of often the most diverse and picturesque colors, or broad table-lands of lava overflow. The erosion and decomposition of these various rocks have filled the valleys to a monotonous level with a detritus of gravel, sand or silt, and given to them that accumulation of alkaline salts which is so marked a peculiarity of the country.

With few exceptions, also, these mountains are for most of the year wholly destitute of water, with but small rivulets in the principal cañons, frequently with only scanty springs here and there at their bases, irrigating a few square yards of ground. Even where the mountain supply is sufficient to send a stream into the valleys it is usually either soon entirely evaporated, sinks into the porous soil, or becomes demoralized with alkali and is "lost" in the mud of the plain. The lowest portion of nearly every valley is occupied by some extent of alkali flat, where in the winter season the water collects and the softened clay-like mud is bottomless and impassable. As the moisture evaporates under the heat of coming summer the level naked surface becomes hard and pavement-like, or covered with a snowy incrustation or deposit of salt or carbonates. The springs and wells even are often more or less saline, and thermal springs are not rare.

The chief exceptional ranges in northern Nevada, which from their greater altitude receive heavier snowfalls in winter, retained through the year in greater or less quantity in the more sheltered depressions of the higher peaks, and which in summer are subject to more abundant rains, are the West Humboldt Mountains, 100 miles east of the California State line, the East Humboldt Mountains, 75 miles from the Utah line, and the Toyabes, nearly intermediate between the two. Star Peak is the highest point of the first range, with an altitude of nearly 10,000 feet, but with little deposit of snow and the vegetation of the summit scarcely sub-alpine. Several constant streams here flow from the principal eastern cañons and reach the middle of the valley, where they supply irrigation for as many small ranches. The Toyabe Range, especially in its southern portion, is higher, several of its peaks having an altitude of from 10,000 to 12,000 feet, with more snow and fuller streams. The waters of the eastern slope are spent in Smoky Valley. On the western side lies Reese River, flowing northward toward the

Humboldt, of which it is a reputed tributary. In the upper portion of its course of 150 miles it is reënforced to some extent by the drainage of the Shoshone Mountains, a rather high range west of the Toyabes, but as it nears Humboldt Valley it diverges into side-channels and seldom has volume sufficient to reach the main river itself.

The East Humboldt Mountains are by far the most stern and alpine of all these ranges, the main peaks between 11,000 and 12,000 feet in height, precipitous and ragged, the deeper cañons evidently scooped out by glaciers, gemmed with snow-fed lakes beneath the peaks and carrying full streams into the valleys. The southern portion, however, below Frémont's Pass, is less rugged and of different geological structure, mainly of nearly horizontal strata of limestone. The cañons here, often mere gorges, with close precipitous walls, are perfectly dry on the eastern slope, the melting snows sinking almost immediately, but reappearing at the base in bold ice-cold springs. The water from these springs and streams reunites to form Ruby and Franklin Lakes, bodies of nearly fresh water, very shallow, and largely occupied by a dense growth of "Tule" (*Scirpus validus*). As usual in these ranges the western slope is much the more gentle, with a broader line of foot-hills. The streams upon this side form the South Fork of the Humboldt. The 'Clover Mountains' of the Catalogue form the northern extremity of this range, isolated by a depression known as Seeret Valley, but of equal height and similar character.

Such is a general description of the country as far east of the foot of the Wahsatch in Utah. These mountains, upon a broad base of nearly fifty miles in width, and with an irregular crest-line 10–12,000 feet high, have a system of long, deep, well-watered cañons, often exceedingly rocky, and sometimes cleft like a gateway to the valley level, with perpendicular mountain-walls on each side, but usually opening out at some part of their course into meadow-like basins or "parks." The prevalent western winds deposit their moisture, which they have gathered in the traverse of the Basin, in abundant snows in winter and at other seasons in frequent and occasionally heavy rains. The upper cañons and mountain slopes are to some extent timbered, much more generally so than in any of the ranges westward, and the naked peaks above have a truly alpine vegetation. The Uintahs, which connect immediately with the Wahsatch and extend eastward on the line of the 41st parallel for a distance of one hundred and fifty miles to Green River, where they meet the outspurs of the Rocky Mountains of Colorado, have more of the character of those mountains, with broad open cañons and extended lines of foot-hills, the peaks overtopping those of the Wahsatch, glacier-scored and polished at the northern base, but the declivity upon the opposite side stretching southward beyond the limits of vision in a high plateau broken only by the deeply-worn channels of numerous rapid streams, tributaries of the Uintah and Green Rivers.

LOCAL AVIFAUNÆ OF THE GREAT BASIN.

We have gone thus into detail with regard to the more prominent characteristic features of the Great Basin for the reason that the distribution of the birds depends so much upon that of the vegetation; and as we know that the latter is separated into several quite distinct groups, whose distribution depends upon altitude, humidity, proportionate amount of alkaline salts in the soil, and other causes, we may easily correlate the bird-fauna into corresponding sections.

The boundaries between local floras of entirely different character are usually so abrupt in the Great Basin that often a single step will lead from one to the other; thus, the upper limit of the "pine belt" on the mountains marks a given line where the trees disappear almost immediately, and these begin almost as suddenly at the lower edge of the zone; narrow belts of mountain mahogany, western cedar, or cedar and piñon together, may follow in the order given, but there is usually no marked straggling of these trees where they meet the sage-brush, as if disputing possession of the ground. The sage-brush reigns supreme from the base of the foot-hills to the brink of the mesa, or over the elevated plain extending from the foot of the mountains to the narrow valleys of the streams, where only the steep, nearly naked bluffs separate the squalid growth of the higher level from the more thrifty growth of the same plants, first with grease-wood intermingled, which occupies the outer portion of the valley-floor; then follows the green-sward of salt-grass in the moister portion of the valley, while nearer the river are thickets of low willows, or in exceptionally rich valleys buffalo-berry and other shrubs, with cotton-wood trees interspersed. In a like manner the luxuriant shrubbery of the mountains is usually restricted to the margin of the brooks in the bottom of the cañons or ravines, where often the slopes so nearly meet that scarcely room is left for a trail. Such are the main features of the distribution of vegetation in this region, subject, of course, to numerous and sometimes, but not often, complicated local modifications.

The strict correlation between the birds and plants in this matter of distribution was a fact immediately noticed, and the more firmly impressed toward the close of our long period of observations in the field; each locality of particular vegetation being inhabited by its own peculiar set of birds with almost unvarying certainty. In order to familiarize the reader with the local causes which govern the distribution of the birds within the Great Basin the accompanying arrangement of the more distinct types of localities is given, followed by lists of the species of birds characteristic of each. It is of course to be understood that by *characteristic* we do not mean that a bird is found in the sort of locality to which it is assigned, and nowhere else, but simply that such a place is where it is most abundant, or most likely to be found; and also, that the arrangement presented is based upon the distribution of the species during the breeding-season.

There are, however, certain species whose distribution seems to be in nowise connected with vegetation, the considerations which influence their range being the presence of water, of rocks, or of earth-banks; but these form a small proportion of the summer residents, most of them being the water-fowl, and of these many might be assigned to the meadow series, since they nearly all resort to the meadows to breed.

The main natural subdivisions of the avifauna of the Interior, as above determined, are the following :—

I. *Arboreal Avifauna.*
  1. Birds of the pine-region, or higher coniferous forests. (18 species.)
  2. Birds of the cedar or nut-pine groves. (9 species.)
  3. Birds of the aspen groves or copses. (7 species.)
  4. Birds of the cañon shrubbery. (7 species.)
  5. Birds of the wooded river-valleys. (25 species.)

II. *Terrestrial Avifauna.*
  6. Birds of the sage-brush. (10 species.)
  7. Birds of the mountain meadows, or parks. (9 species.)
  8. Birds of the lowland meadows. (8 species.)

III. *Mural Avifauna.*
  9. Species strictly saxicoline. (2 species.)
  10. Species saxicoline only in nesting habits. (5 species.)
  11. Species nesting in earth-banks. (3 species.)

IV. *Aquatic Avifauna.*
  12. Water birds. (41 species.)

1. *Birds of the pine-region, or higher coniferous woods.*—Compared with the general extent of the Interior, the wooded portions are exceedingly limited, the only approach to a continuous forest encountered being that clothing the eastern slope of the Sierra Nevada, and the more scant and interrupted forests of the Wahsatch and Uintahs, on the opposite side of the Basin. Between these two distant forest-clad mountain systems no true forests exist, only a few of the loftier ranges supporting an extensive tree-growth on their higher summits, forming islands, as it were, in a sea of desert.

Woods of Coniferæ form by far the greater part of the sylva of the Great Basin, and though differing somewhat in their character have much the same bird-fauna wherever they exist, the only decided difference with locality being the replacing of species of one side by representative forms on the opposite side. On the Sierra Nevada these forests are much more extensive than anywhere to the eastward. and the growth far larger and more dense, consisting chiefly of *Pinus ponderosa*, but with which are mixed *Abies grandis*, *A. menziesii*, *A. douglasii*, *Libocedrus decurrens*, and perhaps some other trees. Of these species, only the latter did not occur to the eastward, where, on the higher ranges, as the East Humboldt, Wahsatch, and Uintahs, *Pinus balfouriana*, *P. flexilis*, *Abies englemanni*, *A. amabilis* (?), and *Juniperus virginianus* occurred as additional species.

The birds peculiar to these dark woods are far less numerous than those found only in the more open and sunny groves of the river valleys, but eighteen species being noted as peculiar to them, exclusive of those restricted to one side of the Basin. The strictly pinicoline species are the following:—

1. Cinclus mexicanus. *Not arboreal.*
2. Regulus calendula.
3. Parus montanus.
4. Sitta aculeata.
5. Sitta canadensis.
6. Sitta pygmæa.
7. Certhia americana.
8. Dendrœca auduboni.
9. Pyranga ludoviciana.
10. Loxia leucoptera.
11. Carpodacus cassini.
12. Chrysomitris pinus.
13. Picicorvus columbianus.
14. Contopus borealis.
15. Empidonax difficilis.
16. Sphyrapicus thyroideus.
17. Canace obscura.
18. Bonasa umbelloides.

The representative and peculiar species of the opposite mountain systems are as follows:—

Representative species.

Sierra Nevada.	Wahsatch and Uintahs.
1. Junco oregonus.	1. Junco caniceps.
2. Cyanura frontalis.	2. Cyanura macrolopha.

Peculiar species.[1]

1. *Turdus ustulatus.*	[None.]
2. *Sphyrapicus ruber.*	
3. Picus albolarvatus.	

---

[1] Of these species the two in italics are represented in the eastern ranges by closely allied forms, *T. swainsoni* and *S. nuchalis*, but they are not inhabitants of the pines, the former being confined to the cañon shrubbery and the latter to the aspen groves.

2. *Birds of the cedar or nut-pine groves.*—These groves are generally found on the lower slopes and foot-hills of the desert ranges, between elevations of about 5,000 and 7,000 feet, and occur even in the most barren and arid districts. In general, two species, the western cedar (*Juniperus occidentalis*) and the nut-pine, or piñon (*Pinus monophyllus*), are mixed together, but often only one species, the former, is the sole constituent of these groves, this being usually the case on the more barren mountains in the absolutely waterless districts; the latter, on the other hand, prevailing on those ranges which have copious streams in the cañons. These trees are of low, compact habit and unshapely form, their height rarely exceeding 15 feet, while the branches are characteristically crooked and the trunks short, rugged, and twisted.[1] Along the upper edge of this belt occur, more or less plentifully, trees of the "mountain mahogany" (*Cercocarpus ledifolius*), equally stunted and scraggy, but with scant, deciduous foliage. These monotonous groves are seldom inhabited by many birds, but, on the other hand, are often so nearly devoid of animal life that an entire day may be spent among the gnarled and stunted trees without a single living thing being seen, or a sound heard except the far-away croak of a solitary raven from some distant hills. Sometimes, however, the profound silence is broken for a moment by the chattering of a Gray Titmouse (*Lophophanes inornatus*) or the twittering of a straggling troop of the diminutive "Fairy Titmice" (*Psaltriparus plumbeus*), while the intruder may be suddenly startled by the piercing whistle of a little Chipmunk (*Tamias quadrivittatus*). Occasionally, a solitary *Myiadestes townsendi* flies silently by, and more frequently a flock of querulous Piñon Jays (*Gymnokitta cyanocephala*) sweeps overhead, when all is again silent. In case these woods occur on

---

[1] On the foot-hills or lower slopes of the Wahsatch these woods are represented by the dwarf-oak "scrub"—the western cedar having disappeared far to the westward. This scrub consists of a dense growth of oak bushes about 5–15, rarely 20, feet high, the species being considered by botanists a dwarf form of *Quercus alba*. The birds inhabiting these oaks are much the same as those found in the cedar and nut-pine groves, with the exception of *Gymnokitta cyanocephala* and *Myiadestes townsendi*, the first of which appears to be peculiar to the cedars, while the other occurs elsewhere only in the high coniferous woods. In addition to these species, *Helminthophaga virginiæ*, *Pipilo megalonyx*, and *Cyanocitta woodhousii* may be regarded among the most characteristic species of the oak thickets.

the foot-hills and lower slopes of the higher and more fertile ranges, they may be occasionally visited by several species from the pine-region higher up, or from the adjacent cañon shrubbery. The following, however, are particularly characteristic of the cedar and nut-pine groves:—

1. Myiadestes townsendi.
2. Sialia arctica.
3. Lophophanes inornatus.
4. Lanivireo plumbeus.
5. Collurio excubitoroides.
6. Spizella arizonæ.
7. Scolecophagus cyanocephalus.
8. Gymnokitta cyanocephala.[1]
9. Empidonax obscurus.

3. *Birds of the aspen groves and copses.*—The aspens (*Populus tremuloides*) occur only on the higher, well-watered ranges, commonly in the upper cañons, in moist and sheltered situations just below the fields or patches of perpetual snow. The slender trees composing these groves or copses are seldom large, never, except perhaps on certain of the more eastern ranges, exceeding 30 or 40 feet in height, and usually not more than half so tall. They are of straight, clean habit, however, with a smooth whitish-green bark, and are carpeted underneath by a varied herbaceous growth, among which beautiful ferns are sometimes conspicuous. The characteristic birds of the aspens are not numerous, the following being all that were noted:—

1. Turdus migratorius.
2. Progne subis.
3. Helminthophaga celata.
4. Empidonax obscurus.
5. Empidonax hammondi.
6. Picus gairdneri.
7. Sphyrapicus nuchalis.

Several of the above, or all with the exception of the last three, and *Helminthophaga celata*, are rather to be considered as species of general and variable range, since they may sometimes be found in very considerable abundance in other wooded localities.

4. *Birds of the cañon shrubbery.*—Several of the higher ranges of the Interior receive sufficient precipitation, or retain throughout the summer snow enough near their summits, to supply the main ravines and cañons with constant streams of water; and these nourish a thrifty or often luxuriant shrubby growth along their banks, where many species of birds resort,

---

[1] This species we believe to be entirely peculiar to these woods, its food apparently consisting exclusively of the seeds and berries of the nut-pine and cedar.

as their favorite haunt. These shrubs are of various species, different ones of which predominate in different localities, the more common kinds being *Cornus pubescens*, upon the berries of which many birds feed almost exclusively in the fall, *Sambucus glauca, Prunus demissa, Ribes irriguum, Alnus incana*, and, more rarely, *Cratægus rivularis*, while in many localities species of *Salix* are also a common component of the thickets along the cañon streams.[1] The birds particularly characteristic of this section are:—

1. Psaltriparus plumbeus.
2. Geothlypis macgillivrayi.
3. Hedymeles melanocephalus.
4. Cyanospiza amœna.

5. Melospiza fallax.
6. Cyanocitta woodhousii.
7. Empidonax pusillus.

In addition to these, *Turdus swainsoni*,[2] *Galeoscoptes carolinensis, Setophaga ruticilla*,[3] and *Passerella schistacea* were found in the Wahsatch region.

5. *The Birds of the wooded river-valleys.*—As a rule, the valleys of the rivers in the Great Basin are destitute of trees, like the adjacent mesas; but in the "western depression" are two notable exceptions in the Truckee and Carson Rivers, both of which are bordered along the lower portion of their course by inviting groves or scattered clumps of large and beautiful cottonwood trees (*Populus monilifera*) and dense copses of a smaller species, *P. trichocarpa*. The buffalo-berry (*Shepherdia argentea*) and willows (*Salix*, species) form the greater part of the shrubbery, but they are associated with numerous other woody plants. In the possession of these features the lower portions of the valleys of both the above-named streams share in common, but the timber along the latter is less regularly distributed, although in places equally extensive.

Localities so inviting as these being extremely rare and distant from each other, it follows as a natural consequence that the birds are found greatly multiplied both in species and individuals in these restricted oases.

---

[1] In the East Humboldt Mountains, but more especially in the Wahsatch, other species, belonging to the Rocky Mountain region, are added, the number being small in the first-named range, but in the latter very considerable, and embracing several eastern species. In the cañons of the Wahsatch, for instance, are found *Betula occidentalis, Rhus aromatica, R. glabra, Acer grandidentatum, Negundo aceroides*, and *Sambucus racemosa*. [See Watson, Botanical Report, p. xxxvii.]

[2] Found also as far west as the East Humboldt Mountains, in September.

[3] Noticed only in the lower portion of the cañons, and more commonly in the valleys, as was also the case with *Galeoscoptes carolinensis*.

Indeed, to realize how attractive the river-valleys must be to the feathered tribe, one has but to cross the almost limitless desert on either side, with a scorching sun overhead and little else than glaring, heated sand beneath his feet, and after thus suffering all day come suddenly to the verge of one of these lovely valleys, with the fields and groves of verdure close by, while the refreshing breeze brings to the ear the rippling of cooling waters and the glad voices of the birds! The merry little Wood-Wrens (*Troglodytes parkmanni*) gabble and chatter among the trunks and massive branches of the old cotton-wood trees; black-and-orange orioles (*Icterus bullocki*) and crimson-headed linnets (*Carpodacus frontalis*) whistle plaintively or chant a cheerful ditty as they sport among the leafy branches, while from the willows or the more open thickets is heard the mellow flute-like song of the Black-headed Grosbeak (*Hedymeles melanocephalus*).

The birds most characteristic of the wooded river-valleys are the following:—

1. Sialia mexicana.
2. Troglodytes parkmanni.
3. Dendrœca æstiva.
4. Geothlypis trichas.
5. Icteria longicauda.
6. Myiodioctes pusillus.
7. Tachycineta bicolor.
8. Vireosylvia swainsoni.
9. Carpodacus frontalis.
10. Chrysomitris tristis.
11. Cyanospiza amœna.
12. Pipilo oregonus.
13. Icterus bullocki.
14. Pica hudsonica.
15. Tyrannus carolinensis.
16. Tyrannus verticalis.
17. Myiarchus cinerascens.
18. Contopus richardsoni.
19. Empidonax pusillus.
20. Coccyzus americanus.
21. Nephœcetes borealis.
22. Chætura vauxi.
23. Otus wilsonianus.
24. Falco sparverius.
25. Zenædura carolinensis.

6. *Birds of the sage-brush.*—The term "sage-brush" is the western vernacular for that shrubby growth which prevails over the valleys, mesas, and desert mountain-slopes of the Great Basin to the utter exclusion of all other vegetation, except in isolated and extremely restricted places. One species, the "everlasting sage-brush" (*Artemisia tridentata*), composes by far the larger part of that growth, "covering valleys and foot-hills in broad stretches farther than the eye can reach, the growth never so dense as to seriously obstruct the way, but very uniform over large surfaces, very rarely reaching to the saddle-height of a mule, and ordinarily but half that

altitude." The species just mentioned is not the exclusive component of the "sage-brush" however, for quite a number of other shrubs, belonging to many genera and several widely-different orders, are mingled with it in varying abundance, according to the nature of the soil, some prevailing on the most arid or sandy places, and others thriving best where the soil is strongly alkaline. Those additional to the species given above, are mainly the following, named in the order of their abundance: *Obione confertifolia* ("grease-wood"), *O. canescens, Sarcobatus vermiculatus, Linosyris viscidiflora, Grayia polygaloides, Halostachys occidentalis, Linosyris graveolens* ("broom-sage"), *Artemisia trifida, A. spinescens, Eurotia lanata, Purshia tridentata, Ephedra antisyphilitica,* and *Tetradymia canescens.* [See Botanical Report, p. xxvi.] The genera named above belong to the following orders: *Artemisia, Linosyris,* and *Tetradymia* to the Compositæ; *Obione, Sarcobatus, Grayia,* and *Eurotia* to the Chenopodiaceæ; *Purshia* to the Rosacæ, and *Ephedra* to the Gnetaceæ. The general aspect of these plants is quite the same, however, in the different species, all having a similar scraggy, stunted appearance, with dull-grayish foliage in which there is but the slightest suspicion of green, and a characteristic, disagreeable, pungent odor; and in the utter absence of other shrubs over areas hundreds of square miles in extent, they constitute a most miserable apology for vegetation.

The most numerous animals of these arid wastes are the various species of lizards, which are startled at every step as one walks along, and run nimbly to one side—some kinds disappearing like a flash, so swift are they, while the larger species in their flight scatter the fine gravel and sand so as to make it fairly rattle. These reptiles were most numerous in the western depression, and it was found that they abounded most on the burning deserts, farthest from water.

The birds characteristic of the sage-brush are not numerous, either as to species or individuals, but several of them are peculiar to these districts; the characteristic or peculiar species are these:—

1. Oreoscoptes montanus.
2. Amphispiza nevadensis.
3. Amphispiza bilineata.
4. Spizella breweri.
5. Chondestes grammaca.

6. Eremophila alpestris.
7. Antrostomus nuttalli.
8. Chordeiles henryi.
9. Speotyto hypogæa.
10. Centrocercus urophasianus.

7. *Birds of the mountain-meadows or "parks."*—On the higher ranges of the Interior, the gentle slopes of the upper cañons support the richest or most varied vegetation of the entire region; especially is this the case when they incline so gently as to form broad and nearly level meadows on either side of the main stream, with pine forests and snow-fields on the higher ridges and a copious volume of water in all the brooks and rivulets. Here the streams are bordered for their whole length with a luxuriant shrubbery, the bushes consisting of numerous species, and overtopped here and there by occasional trees of the narrow-leafed cotton-wood (*Populus angustifolia*), sometimes of 50 or 60 feet in height. The higher slopes are densely matted with low but vigorous bushes of "laurel" (*Ceanothus velutinus, C. sorediatus*, and, in some ranges, *Arctostaphylos glauca*), with coriaceous, shining, deep- or dark-green foliage. The greater portion of these upper slopes, however, are mainly covered with a rank herbaceous growth, composed of very numerous species, and in season brilliant with a variety of flowers of beautiful or showy appearance, among which the blue spikes or panicles of **Lupinus** and **Pentstemon**, the orange-red bracts of *Castilleia*, and the lovely scarlet blossoms of *Gilia aggregata* are among the most conspicuous. Species of *Geranium* are also very prevalent in places, while, in many localities, low bushes of *Symphoricarpus montanus* are scattered through the herbage.

The birds most characteristic of these flowery slopes are not numerous, but among them are several fine singers, whose clear and musical voices are among the pleasant memories of these salubrious spots. The following are the most characteristic species:—

1. Zonotrichia intermedia. (*Western ranges.*)
2. Zonotrichia leucophrys. (*Eastern ranges.*)
3. Passerella schistacea.
4. Pooecetes confinis.
5. Melospiza lincolni.
6. Pipilo chlorurus.
7. Stellula calliope.
8. Selasphorus platycercus.
9. Trochilus alexandri.

8. *Birds of the lowland-meadows.*—The lowland meadows include the bright sward of "salt-grass" (*Brizopyrum spicatum*, var. *strictum*) of the low river-valleys, the "bunch grass" (*Poa tenuifolia* and *Eriocoma cuspidata*), scattered over the foot-hills, the patches of "rye-grass" (*Elymus condensatus?*)

near the entrance to the cañons, and also the sedge and *tule* marshes, in
the neighborhood of the lakes and rivers. The birds most characteristic of
the meadows are all mostly peculiar to them, being seldom if ever found in
other localities. Besides the land-birds here enumerated, a multitude of the
water-fowl resort to the meadows during the breeding-season, but these are
best given in a separate list. The most characteristic birds of the meadows
are the following:—

1. Telmatodytes paludicola .... *Marshes.*
2. Coturniculus perpallidus .... *Dry meadows.*
3. Passerculus alaudinus .... *Wet meadows.*
4. Agelæus phœniceus .... *Marshes.*
5. Xanthocephalus icterocephalus .. *Marshes.*
6. Sturnella neglecta .... *Everywhere except in marshes.*
7. Pediœcetes columbianus .. .. *Dry meadows.*
8. Grus canadensis .... *Wet meadows.*

9–11. *Mural Avifauna.*—This group is a rather heterogeneous one,
part of the species being saxicoline, while others nest in vertical banks of
earth; and of the former only two species keep altogether among the rocks,
the others merely breeding there, the greater part of their time being spent
in obtaining their food in other localities.

They may be grouped as follows:—

a. Species strictly saxicoline.

1. Salpinctes obsoletus.   } *Modifying their habits in neighborhood of settlements.*
2. Catherpes conspersus.   }

b. Species saxicoline only in nesting habits.

3. Tachycineta thalassina.—(*In other districts said to be arboreal.*)

4. Petrochelidon lunifrons.   }
5. Hirundo horreorum.   } *Habits modified in settled districts.*
6. Sayornis sayus.   }
7. Panyptila saxatilis.   }

c. Nesting in earth-banks.

8. Cotyle riparia.
9. Stelgidopteryx serripennis.
10. Ceryle alcyon.

To group "*b*" of this list might be added such species as *Aquila canadensis* and *Falco polyagrus*, since these species usually build their eyries on

the narrow ledges or in niches on the face of cliffs, but their nesting-habits are too variable. The same objection might be urged in regard to *Tachycineta thalassina*, since in some localities this species nests in hollow trees, but along our route we found it to be everywhere strictly saxicoline.

12. *Aquatic birds.*—This group includes the vast multitude of waterfowl, both waders and swimmers; these inhabit chiefly the valleys, the following being the species which breed in the interior:—

1. Ægialitis vociferus.
2. Ægialitis nivosus.
3. Steganopus wilsoni.
4. Recurvirostra americana.
5. Himantopus mexicanus.
6. Numenius longirostris.
7. Tringoides macularius.
8. Rhyacophilus solitarius.
9. Tringa bairdi.
10. Tringa minutilla.
11. Ereunetes pusillus.
12. Falcinellus guarauna.
13. Falcinellus thalassinus.
14. Ardea herodias.
15. Herodias egretta.
16. Nyctiardea nævia.
17. Botaurus minor.
18. Ardetta exilis.
19. Rallus virginianus.
20. Porzana carolina.
21. Porzana jamaicensis. ?
22. Branta canadensis.
23. Anas boschas.
24. Chaulelasmus streperus.
25. Dafila acuta.
26. Spatula clypeata.
27. Querquedula discors.
28. Querquedula cyanoptera.
29. Nettion carolinensis.
30. Mareca americana.
31. Aix sponsa.
32. Erismatura rubida.
33. Larus californicus.
34. Sterna regia.
35. Sterna fosteri.
36. Hydrochelidon lariformis.
37. Pelecanus erythrorhynchus.
38. Graculus floridanus.
39. Podiceps occidentalis.
40. Podiceps cristatus.
41. Podiceps californicus.

In the preceding lists of the species characterizing special faunal subdistricts of the Great Basin, we have included mainly those which are common to the entire breadth of the Province. Other species, which might properly be assigned to these lists with respect to their habitats, are excluded, from the fact that they belong to only one side or the other of the Basin. The western series was lost almost immediately after our departure from the Sierra Nevada, very few being found even so far to the eastward of that range as the West Humboldt Mountains. The eastern series, however, presented itself much more gradually, additional species being met with in each successive high range to the eastward, the first of them appearing on the lofty Toyabe Mountains, while a more decided accession of Rocky Mountain and Eastern forms was noticed on the Ruby and East Humboldt ranges, where, however, the number was far less than that encountered on the Wahsatch and in the Salt Lake Valley.

DESCRIPTION OF LOCALITIES WHERE COLLECTIONS OR OBSERVATIONS WERE MADE.

1. *Vicinity of Sacramento City, California* (June 6–29, 1867.)—The period of our stay at Sacramento being the midst of the dry season, when the valleys of California are parched by the excessive and protracted drought, the bird-life was found to be comparatively scant, and, as in the Interior, though not to so great an extent, confined within the very restricted limits where the vegetation was nourished by the presence of water—either that of natural streams or that derived from artificial irrigation. But even there the abundance of the birds was due to the number of individuals of each kind, rather than of the species themselves. Away from the vicinity of the city, the country at the time of our sojourn presented a scorched appearance, the rolling plains being destitute of rivulets or pools, all the surface-moisture having been long since extracted by the excessive and prolonged heat; the ground itself was baked to a tile-like hardness except where ground to dust, and what remained of the grass and herbage was burnt to a dingy yellow, while the scant foliage of the scattered oaks was desiccated to a russet-brownness. In the moister locations, near the river, the aspect of the landscape was more inviting, however, for green meadow-lands prevailed, with woods of good-sized trees along the river bank (among which the western plane tree, *Platanus racemosa*, was conspicuous from its white branches), with a pleasing variety of oak, willow, and cotton-wood copses, interspersed with cultivated farms, with here and there isolated large cotton-wood trees left in the fields for shade. Extensive marshes, connected with the river, were filled with tall rushes, or *tule* (*Scirpus validus*), and other aquatics, many of them being hemmed in by skirting jungles of willows and other shrubs, having a dense, often impenetrable, undergrowth. Waste places were overspread by a rank growth of wild chamomile, or dog-fennel (*Maruta cotula*), and large thistles, the latter standing chiefly in the fence-corners, where they presented to the

44. Butorides virescens.............................. ......*Abundant.*
45. Nyctiardea nævia....................................*Common.*
46. Gallinula galeata....................................*Abundant.*
47. Fulica americana.................. ....*Abundant.*
48. Anas boschas ....*Abundant.*
49. Chaulelasmus streperus............................*Abundant.*
50. Querquedula cyanoptera ....*Abundant.*
51. Aythya —— sp.?....................................*Abundant.*
52. Larus —— sp.?..................................*Abundant.*
53. Sterna forsteri?....................................*Abundant.*
54. Hydrochelidon lariformis..........................*Abundant.*

Having alluded to the close similarity between the bird-fauna of the vicinity of Sacramento City and that of a locality of corresponding latitude in the Mississippi Valley, we select from the above list the species not belonging to the latter locality, they being as follows:—

1. Vireo pusillus.
2. Carpodacus frontalis.
3. Spizella breweri.
4. Cyanospiza amœna.
5. Hedymeles melanocephalus.
6. Pipilo oregonus.
7. Agelæus tricolor.
8. Icterus bullocki.
9. Tyrannus verticalis.
10. Sayornis nigricans.
11. Contopus richardsoni.
12. Calypte annæ.
13. Trochilus alexandri.
14. Colaptes mexicanus.
15. Speotyto hypogæa.
16. Querquedula cyanoptera.

Twelve of the above species are repesented east of the Rocky Mountains by species so similar in appearance or habits that, to the common observer, they might readily pass for the same birds. These representative species are the following:—

Western representatives.	*Eastern representatives.*
Vireo pusillus, *representing*......	Vireo belli.
Spizella breweri, *representing*	Spizella pallida.
Hedymeles melanocephalus, *representing*......	Hedymeles ludovicianus.
Cyanospiza amœna, *representing*...............	Cyanospiza cyanea.
Pipilo oregonus, *representing*..................	Pipilo erythrophthalmus.
Icterus bullocki, *representing*..................	Icterus baltimore.
Tyrannus verticalis, *representing*	Tyrannus carolinensis.
Sayornis nigricans, *representing*............ ...	Sayornis fuscus.
Contopus richardsoni, *representing*............	Contopus virens.
Trochilus alexandri, *representing*....	Trochilus colubris.
Colaptes mexicanus, *representing*....	Colaptes auratus.
Querquedula cyanoptera, *representing*.........	Querquedula discors.

It will thus be observed that the general *facies* of the avian-fauna of the two remote regions is so similar that out of a total of 54 species noted at Sacramento, only 4 are unrepresented in the eastern locality![1]

2. *From the Sacramento River to the foot-hills of the Sierra Nevada* (July 4–5).—This route lay across a rolling plain, of a character similar to that described before, except that the monotony of the dusty landscape was more frequently relieved by groves of low, spreading oaks, while occasional spots near springs or along running streams were quite refreshing from the cool shade they afforded. Such places were usually the site of a ranche, and called to mind a country-place in one of the less-thickly wooded portions of the Eastern States, the oak trees which, almost exclusively, composed the groves being exceedingly similar in size and general appearance to the white oak (*Quercus alba*). Among these trees sported the California and Nuttall's Woodpeckers (*Melanerpes formicivorus* and *Picus nuttalli*), whole troops of chattering Yellow-billed Magpies (*Pica nuttalli*), and an occasional screeching Valley Jay (*Cyanocitta californica*). The other species seen in these groves were the Ash-throated Flycatcher (*Myiarchus cinerascens*), Lewis's Woodpecker (*Melanerpes torquatus*), Black-capped Chickadee (*Parus occidentalis*), House Wren (*Troglodytes parkmanni*), Common Crow (*Corvus americanus*), Barn Owl (*Strix pratincola*), Mottled Owl (*Scops asio*), and Red-breasted Hawk (*Buteo elegans*); while on the plains, the Horned Lark (*Eremophila chrysolæma*), Burrowing Owl (*Speotyto hypogæa*), and Turkey Buzzard (*Rhinogryphus aura*) were observed. Nearly all these

---

[1] The winter fauna would, of course, be considerably different from that observed by us, on account of accessions from the ranks of species which spend the summer in the mountains or farther northward, as well as by the absence of some of the summer visitors. An esteemed correspondent, Mr. Gilbert R. Lansing, of San Francisco, has furnished a list of birds collected by him at Sacramento in March, 1873, which includes the following species not in our enumeration of summer birds:—

1. Chamæa fasciata. March 23.	5. Cyanocitta californica.
2. Hesperiphona vespertina. March 16.	6. Zonotrichia intermedia.
3. Junco oregonus.	7. Zonotrichia coronata. March 23.
4. Corvus carnivorus.	8. Melospiza guttata. March 16.

Of the above, specimens were sent of Nos. 1, 2, 6, 7, and 8.

species were noticed from the very beginning of the open country, on the outskirts of the city, to the first foot-hills of the Sierra Nevada.

3. *The Sierra Nevada* (July 6–12).—The rolling plains became so gradually modified into more pronounced undulations, and these so imperceptibly into decided hills, that there was no abrupt change noticeable in either the fauna or the flora. With the first pine trees, however, were observed the Robin (*Turdus migratorius*), the California Bluebird (*Sialia mexicana*), and Brown Creeper (*Certhia americana*); while among the thick chaparral of the ravines and hill-sides the following species were seen for the first time:—

a. Western foot-hills (July 6–7).

1. Psaltriparus minimus.
2. Polioptila (cærulea?)
3. Chrysomitris lawrencii.

4. Pipilo crissalis.
5. Lophortyx californicus.

These species were not seen near the summit, but were gradually left behind as we ascended the now steeper slopes and entered a denser forest, where large and lofty coniferæ became exclusive. The three species previously mentioned, however, continued with us during the journey. As was the change from the plains to the foot-hills a very gradual one, so did the mixed woods and chaparral of the latter, in which deciduous trees and shrubs abounded, become as imperceptibly transformed into denser and loftier forests, where coniferæ first greatly prevailed and then constituted the entire sylva. The change was indeed so gradual that we could detect no well-defined point where there was a marked difference in the birds observed; one species after another being left behind, while one by one new ones made their appearance, so that it was found impossible to fix a boundary-line between two regions. The "Mountain Jay" (*Cyanura frontalis*) was met with long before we lost sight of the "Valley Jay" (*Cyanocitta californica*), and the "Valley Quail" (*Lophortyx californicus*) was common, and leading its young, in ravines, beside which the pines resounded with the screams of the Mountain Jay and Nutcracker (*Picicorvus columbianus*) and the tapping of pinicoline Woodpeckers (*Sphyrapicus ruber* and *Picus albolarvatus*).

b. The western slope.

At an altitude of about 5,000 feet, all the species characteristic of the foot-hills were lost sight of, the Louisiana Tanager (*Pyranga ludoviciana*) and Audubon's Warbler (*Dendrœca auduboni*) made their first appearance, the Mountain Jay and Nutcracker and the Woodpeckers above mentioned became more numerous, while the dark ravines below the road echoed with the carols of Townsend's Solitaire (*Myiadestes townsendi*) and the Oregon Thrush *Turdus ustulatus*), and the chattering of the Dippers (*Cinclus mexicanus*).

c. The summit (July 9).

At an altitude of about 7,000 feet snow lay, even at this season of the year, in situations protected from the sun. The pine forests continued, but were more interrupted, with occasional park-like openings, in one of which, known as the "Summit Meadows," we established our camp. Snow-capped peaks were in sight on every hand, while around the borders of the broad meadow snow-banks lay, protected by the shade of the majestic pines; and a strange sight it was to see, almost touching the snow, beds of flowers which, in variety of form and splendor of coloring, might vie with the choicest to be seen in our gardens or conservatories; while the park itself was so overspread by a plant bearing bright-yellow blossoms, that this was the prevailing color of the surface. Scattered over this meadow were clumps of low spreading dwarf-willow bushes, from the tops of which numerous White-crowned Sparrows (*Zonotrichia intermedia*) were singing beautifully during the evening, and now and then throughout the night. The other more conspicuous birds of this charming spot were the Common Robin (*Turdus migratorius*), the California Bluebird (*Sialia mexicana*), and the Oregon Snow-bird (*Junco oregonus*).[1]

---

[1] Owing to the unsatisfactory nature of our opportunities for studying the avifauna of this interesting and exceedingly rich district, our notes are necessarily meager. It is therefore with great pleasure that we avail ourself of the experience of Mr. E. W. Nelson, of Chicago, who made collections on the western slope of the Sierra Nevada, chiefly in the vicinity of Nevada City. We quote from Mr. Nelson what is of direct interest in this connection: [See Proc. Boston Soc. Nat. Hist., Vol. XVII, Jan. 20, 1875, pp. 355–365. "Notes on Birds observed in portions of Utah, Nevada, and California." "IV. Notes on Birds observed in the vicinity of Nevada City, Cal., between

d. The eastern slope (July 10–12).

The descent from the summit down the eastern slope was much more rapid than had been our ascent of the other side. The forest, however, continued much the same, but the trees were appreciably smaller, becoming more so as we descended. The only new bird detected during our hurried

---

August 15 and December 15, 1872."] "This locality has an intermediate situation between the lofty peaks and the foot-hills of the Sierra Nevadas, and is in the midst of the gold-mining region. My visit being in the last of the dry season, when the vegetation is dried up by the hot sun, probably many of the spring and early summer residents had gone farther down, where the farms are more numerous and less parched than the uncultivated hills surrounding Nevada.

In November, while collecting twenty miles farther down, we found many species abundant which were rare at Nevada; among which may be mentioned, *Sturnella neglecta, Zonotrichia coronata,* and *Glaucidium californicum,* which assembled in numbers around our camp-fires every night and serenaded us with their curious notes; [*Note.*— Mr. Henshaw suggests that this owl may have been *Scops flammeola,* which has this habit, while the *Glaucidium* is diurnal and crepuscular.] also, *Lophortyx californicus, Oreortyx pictus,* and many others, were observed on the cultivated flats, which were rare at Nevada." We give below a full list of the species found by Mr. Nelson at Nevada City, those which we did not see in ascending the western slope in July being distinguished by an asterisk :—

  1. Turdus migratorius. *Aug.–Oct.*
  2. Turdus ustulatus. *Common; Aug.–Nov.*
*3. Oreoscoptes montanus. *Oct.; two pairs.*
  4. Sialia mexicana. *Last of Sept.–last of Nov.*
  5. Regulus calendula. *Last Sept.–first Dec.*
*6. Chamæa fasciata. *Nov.; one pair.*
*7. Lophophanes inornatus. *First Oct.–Nov.*
*8. Parus occidentalis. *Nov.; high mountains.*
*9. Psaltriparus minimus. *Oct.–Dec.; very abundant.*
10. Certhia americana. *Aug.–Dec.*
*11. Thryomanes spilurus. *Aug.–Nov.*
*12. Troglodytes parkmanni. *Oct.; one spec.*
*13. Helminthophaga ruficapilla. *Last Sept.; one spec.*
14. Dendrœca æstiva.
*15. Dendrœca nigrescens. *Sept.–1st Nov.; common.*
16. Dendrœca auduboni. *Abundant after Oct. 1st.*
*17. Geothlypis macgillivrayi. *Sept.; two specs.*
*18. Myiodioctes pusillus. *Last Sept.; one spec.*
19. Pyranga ludoviciana. *Oct.; rare.*
20. Hirundo horreorum. *Aug.–Sept.*
*21. Carpodacus californicus. *First two weeks in October; common.*
22. Chrysomitris pinus. *Last Sept.–first Nov.*
*23. Chrysomitris psaltria. *Aug.–Sept.; very abundant.*

trip was a solitary Rock Wren (*Salpinctes obsoletus*) perched upon a boulder, in a rather open region, soon after passing the summit of the Pass.

4. *Glendale, or Truckee Meadows* (July 16–20; November 7–21. *Altitude 4,372 feet*).—The Truckee Meadows, so called from the fact that hay

24. Passerculus alaudinus. *Oct. 1st.*
*25. Melospiza heermanni. *Not common.*
26. Junco oregonus. *Aug.–last Nov.*
27. Spizella arizonæ. *Abundant.*
*28. Spizella breweri. *Sept.–Oct.; abundant.*
*29. Zonotrichia coronata. *Last of October; common.*
*30. Chondestes grammaca. *Aug.–Oct.; very abundant.*
*31. Passerella townsendi. *Aug.–last Oct.; abundant.*
32. Hedymeles melanocephalus. *Aug.–last Sept.*
33. Pipilo oregonus. *Aug.–middle Nov.*
34. Pipilo crissalis. *Oct. 1st; one spec.*
*35. Pipilo chlorurus. *Common.*
36. Sturnella neglecta. *Common.*
37. Icterus bullocki. *Oct.; one spec. (♀).*
38. Scolecophagus cyanocephalus. *First November.*
39. Corvus americanus (given as *C. caurinus*, but probably not). *Last Nov.; 1 flock.*
40. Cyanura frontalis. *Very abundant.*
41. Cyanocitta californica. *Very abundant.*
*42. Sayornis nigricans. *Aug.–last Nov.; common in Sept.*
43. Contopus richardsoni. *Sept.; rare.*
44. Empidonax pusillus. *Last Sept.; one spec.*
45. Antrostomus nuttalli. *Last Oct.; one spec.*
*46. Calypte annæ. *Aug.–middle Oct.; common.*
*47. Geococcyx californianus. *Rare; not seen.*
*48. Hylatomus pileatus. *Not common.*
49. Picus albolarvatus. *Common until last Nov.*
*50. Picus nuttalli. *Common.*
51. Picus harrisi. *Rare.*
*52. Picus gairdneri. *Common until last Nov.*
53. Sphyrapicus ruber. *Oct.–Dec.; common.*
*54. Melanerpes formicivorus. *Very common.*
*55. Melanerpes torquatus. *Middle Oct.–Dec.*
56. Colaptes mexicanus. *Abundant.*
*57. ? Scops asio. *Not seen.*
*58. Glaucidium gnoma. *Rare.*
*59. Nisus fuscus. *Common from Aug.–Dec. 1st.*
60. "Buteo, sp." [*Probably B. borealis calurus or B. swainsoni*].
*61. Haliaëtus leucocephalus. *Nov.; one spec.*
62. "Cathartes, sp." [*Probably Rhinogryphus aura Oct.*].
*63. Columba fasciata. *Oct.; one flock.*
64. Zenædura carolinensis. *Common until middle Nov.*

for the Virginia City market is the chief production of the settlement, lie on the eastern side of the valley, between the Sierra Nevada and the Comstock, or Virginia Mountains, the first of the desert ranges. Through the middle portion of these extensive meadows the Truckee River courses, its banks being fringed with dense thickets of rather tall willows, growing about fifteen feet high. During the summer these luxuriant meadows were the abode of numerous water-fowl, while in the thickets Magpies (*Pica hudsonica*) and smaller birds were abundant. The species found in this locality were the following:—

1. Telmatodytes paludicola.
2. Dendrœca æstiva.
3. Geothlypis trichas.
4. Icteria longicauda.
5. Pyranga ludoviciana.
6. Hirundo horreorum.
7. Petrochelidon lunifrons.
8. Stelgidopteryx serripennis.
9. Cotyle riparia.
10. Vireosylvia swainsoni.
11. Collurio excubitoroides.
12. Passerculus alaudinus.
13. Pooecetes confinis.
14. Melospiza heermanni.
15. Chondestes grammaca.
16. Hedymeles melanocephalus.
17. Cyanospiza amœna.
18. Pipilo oregonus.
19. Xanthocephalus icterocephalus.
20. Agelæus phœniceus.
21. Sturnella neglecta.
22. Icterus bullocki.
23. Pica hudsonica.
24. Empidonax pusillus.
25. Chordeiles henryi.
26. Ceryle alcyon.
27. Colaptes mexicanus.
28. Circus hudsonius.
29. Zenædura carolinensis.
30. Ægialitis vociferus.
31. Recurvirostra americana.
32. Himantopus mexicanus.
33. Rhyacophilus solitarius.
34. Tringoides macularius.
35. Botaurus minor.
36. Porzana carolina.
37. Anas boschas.
38. Chaulelasmus streperus.
39. Mareca americana.
40. Dafila acuta.
41. Spatula clypeata.
42. Querquedula cyanoptera.
43. Nettion carolinensis.

*65. ? Canace obscura. ["*Canace canadensis*, var. *franklini*." Probably *C. obscura*, which is abundant on the Sierra Nevada.]

*66. Oreortyx pictus. *Abundant after Oct. 1st.*

67. Lophortyx californicus. *Abundant.*

68. Ægialitis vociferus. *Oct.*

*69. Gallinago wilsoni. *Nov.; two specs.*

*70. Branta canadensis. *Nov.*

*71. Anas boschas. *Not seen.*

*72. Pelecanus erythrorhynchus. *Oct.; one flock passing over.*

The more noteworthy of the above species are *Chamœa fasciata*, *Sayornis nigricans*, and *Calypte annœ*, which would hardly have been supposed to occur so high up among these mountains.

22 P R.

In November, the following additional species were found, while many of the above were wanting:—

Anthus ludovicianus.	Colaptes (?) [a yellow-shafted species,
Turdus migratorius.	probably C. auratus.]
Cinclus mexicanus.	Falco columbarius.
Spizella monticola.	Archibuteo sancti-johannis.
Eremophila alpestris.	Gallinago wilsoni.
Agelæus gubernator.	Columba fasciata. ?[1]
Corvus carnivorus.	Branta hutchinsi.
Corvus americanus.	Podilymbus podiceps.

The most abundant of these were *Anthus ludovicianus, Agelæus phœniceus, A. gubernator, Archibuteo sancti-johannis,* and *Branta hutchinsi.*

5. *Big-Bend of the Truckee (altitude, 3,995 feet; July 24–August 18.)*—After emerging from its deep, narrow gorge through the Virginia Mountains, the Truckee River bends abruptly to the left, and flows toward the northwest into Pyramid Lake, about thirty miles distant. The vicinity of our camp at this place proved a rich locality for birds, for the narrow valley of the river was very fertile, supporting a rich and varied vegetation, while the arid sage-brush plain stretched off on one side to the Humboldt Desert, and in the opposite direction to the Virginia Mountains. Only the very few birds characteristic of the desert could exist upon the surrounding sandy wastes, and, as a consequence, the fertile valley was rich in the number of species and individuals crowded within the narrow limits embraced between the steep earth-walls. Along the bank of the river, and surrounding the sloughs connected with the stream, were exceedingly dense willow-jungles, the sloughs themselves being filled with rushes, flags, and other aquatic plants; but most of the valley consisted of meadow-land, interspersed with velvety swards of "salt-grass" and acres of beautiful sun-flowers (*Helianthus giganteus*), studded with fine large cotton-wood trees (*Populus monilifera* and *P. trichocarpa*), which were here and there grouped into delightful groves, sometimes unincumbered, but generally with a shrubby undergrowth, amongst which the "buffalo-berry" (*Shepherdia argentea*) was conspicuous. No birds, excepting Mourning Doves

---

[1] A single specimen of what was probably this species was observed, flying over, on the 19th of November.

(*Zenædura carolinensis*), were breeding at the time of our sojourn; nor was the fauna particularly interesting, except from the occurrence of swarms of the Rufous Hummer (*Selasphorus rufus*) among the sun-flowers, and of several pairs of the Eastern Kingbird (*Tyrannus carolinensis*), which appeared to have bred in the cotton-wood trees, a few individuals of *Coccyzus americanus* and *Myiodioctes pusillus*, and several families of *Sialia mexicana*, being the only other birds of note which came under our observation.

6. *Truckee Reservation, near Pyramid Lake* (August 10–16, 1867; December 9–19, 1867; May 15–June 6, 1868).—Investigations along the lower portion of the Truckee Valley extended from the shore of Pyramid Lake several miles up the river, and embraced several trips across the desert *mesa* to the northern end of the Virginia range, fronting on the southern shore of the lake, besides occasional visits to the islands within the lake. The fertile valley of the river received the principal attention, however, on account of the abundance of its birds; and, as respects the character of the locality where our observations were mostly made, there was no material difference from the surroundings of our former camp at the Big-Bend, twenty-five miles above, except that the valley was considerably broader and the cotton-wood groves proportionately more extensive. During our sojourn here, from May 15th to June 6th, one hundred and two species were observed in the valley of the river, most, if not all, of them breeding in the locality. The following are the species observed:—

1. Turdus ustulatus.................................*One specimen.*
2. Oreoscoptes montanus.........................*Common.*
3. Troglodytes parkmanni.........................*Abundant.*
4. Telmatodytes paludicola.......................*Abundant.*
5. Dendrœca æstiva................................*Abundant.*
6. Geothlypis trichas...............................*Common.*
7. Icteria longicauda...............................*Common.*
8. Pyranga ludoviciana.............................*Common.*
9. Hirundo horreorum..............................*Common.*
10. Tachycineta bicolor.............................*Abundant.*
11. Tachycineta thalassina.........................*Common.*
12. Progne subis....................................*Rare.*
13. Stelgidopteryx serripennis....................*Abundant.*
14. Cotyle riparia...................................*Abundant.*
15. Petrochelidon lunifrons........................*Abundant.*
16. Vireosylvia swainsoni..........................*Abundant.*

17. Collurio excubitoroides ....Common.
18. Carpodacus frontalis........................Common.
19. Chrysomitris tristis........................Rare.
20. Passerculus alandinus ....Common.
21. Pooecetes gramineus ....Rare.
22. Melospiza heermanni ....Abundant.
23. Amphispiza bilineata ....Common.
24. Amphispiza nevadensis ....Abundant.
25. Spizella arizonæ........................Abundant.
26. Spizella breweri........................Abundant.
27. Chondestes grammaca ....Abundant.
28. Hedymeles melanocephalus........................Common.
29. Cyanospiza amœna ....Rare.
30. Pipilo oregonus ....Common.
31. Pipilo chlorurus ....Rare.
32. Molothrus ater ....Rare.
33. Agelæus phœniceus ....Abundant.
34. Xanthocephalus icterocephalus ....Abundant.
35. Sturnella neglecta ....Abundant.
36. Icterus bullocki ....Abundant.
37. Pica hudsonica......................Abundant.
38. Tyrannus verticalis......................Abundant.
39. Myiarchus cinerascens ....Rare.
40. Sayornis sayus......................Rare.
41. Contopus richardsoni ....Abundant.
42. Empidonax pusillus......................Abundant.
43. Chordeiles henryi ....Common.
44. Nephœcetes borealis......................Rare.
45. Chætura vauxi ....Common.
46. Trochilus alexandri......................Abundant.
47. Ceryle alcyon ....Common.
48. Picus harrisi......................Common.
49. Colaptes mexicanus......................Abundant.
50. Bubo subarcticus......................Common.
51. Otus wilsonianus......................Common.
52. Circus hudsonius ....Abundant.
53. Falco sparverius......................Abundant.
54. Falco nævius ....One pair.
55. Buteo calurus ....Common.
56. Buteo swainsoni......................Common.
57. Haliaëtus leucocephalus......................Rare.
58. Pandion carolinensis......................Rare.
59. Rhinogryphus aura......................Abundant.
60. Zenædura caroliuensis ....Extremely abundant.
61. Ægialitis vociferus ....Common.
62. Recurvirostra americana ....Common.
63. Himantopus mexicanus ....Common.

64. Steganopus wilsoni ....*Rare.*
65. Tringa americana ....*Rare.*
66. Tringa bairdi ....*Rare.*
67. Tringa minutilla ....*Abundant.*
68. Ereunetes pusillus...............................*Abundant.*
69. Rhyacophilus solitarius ....*Rare.*
70. Tringoides macularius ....*Common.*
71. Numenius longirostris ....*Common.*
72. Symphemia semipalmata.............................*Rare.*
73. Ardea herodias.............................*Abundant.*
74. Herodias egretta ....*Rare.*
75. Nyctiardea nævia ....*Rare.*
76. Botaurus minor ....*Common.*
77. Ardetta exilis.............................*Rare.*
78. Falcinellus thalassinus ....*Rare.*
79. Grus canadensis.............................*Rare.*
80. Rallus virginianus ....*Rare.*
81. Porzana carolina ....*Common.*
82. Fulica americana.............................*Very abundant.*
83. Branta canadensis.............................*Common.*
84. Anas boschas ....*Abundant.*
85. Chaulelasmus streperus.............................*Abundant.*
86. Mareca americana ....*Abundant.*
87. Querquedula discors.............................*Rare.?*
88. Querquedula cyanoptera ....*Common.*
89. Dafila acuta ....*Rare.*
90. Spatula clypeata ....*Common.*
91. Aythya vallisneria.............................*Rare.*
92. Aix sponsa ....*Rare.*
93. Lophodytes cucullatus ....*Rare.*
94. Erismatura rubida.............................*Rare.*
95. Pelecanus erythrorhynchus.............................*Very abundant.*
96. Graculus floridanus.............................*Abundant.*
97. Larus californicus ....*Very abundant.*
98. Sterna regia ....*Rare.*
99. Sterna forsteri ....*Rare.*
100. Podiceps occidentalis ....*Abundant.*
101. Podiceps californicus ....*Common.*
102. Podilymbus podiceps ....*Common.*

In the above list are the following species which were not observed
during the preceding July and August at the Big Bend:—

1. Turdus ustulatus.
2. Carpodacus frontalis.
3. Molothrus pecoris.

4. Nephœcetes borealis.
5. Chætura vauxi.
6. Trochilus alexandri.

All of these were undoubtedly breeding, except the first, a mountain bird, of which only a single individual was seen, probably the last lingering one from the spring migration. It is also a noteworthy fact that *Tyrannus carolinensis*, *Myiodioctes pusillus*, and *Selasphorus rufus*, found at the Big Bend in July and August, were not observed in the lower portion of the valley in May and the early part of June.

As the above list embraces only those species found within the valley proper of the river, including the marshes at its mouth, other localities produced additional species; thus, on the mesa stretching from the valley to the Virginia Mountains, *Eremophila alpestris*, *Antrostomus nuttalli*, *Speotyto hypogæa*, and *Centrocercus urophasianus* were found.

This locality was visited the previous winter, when the fauna was quite different, the following species, not in the summer-list, having been observed:—

1. Regulus calendula..... .... *Abundant.*
2. Anthus ludovicianus .... *Very abundant.*
3. Dendrœca auduboni.............................. *Abundant.*
4. Sialia arctica .... *Rare.*
5. Troglodytes pacificus............................. *Rare.*
6. Certhia americana................................ *Rare.*
7. Zonotrichia intermedia........................... *Abundant.*
8. Junco oregonus .... *Abundant.*
9. Spizella monticola .... *Common.*
10. Falco columbarius................................ *Rare.*
11. Archibuteo sancti-johannis...................... *Rare.*
12. Cygnus (buccinator?)............................ *Abundant.*
13. Anser albatus .... *Abundant.*
14. Branta hutchinsi................................. *Abundant.*
15. Branta nigricans................................. *Rare.* ?
16. Aythya americana............................... *Common.*
17. Aythya vallisneria............................... *Common.*
18. Fulix marila.................................... *Abundant.*
19. Fulix affinis.................................... *Abundant.*
20. Fulix collaris .... *Abundant.*
21. Bucephala albeola.............................. *Abundant.*
22. Bucephala americana........................... *Abundant.*
23. Mergus americanus............................. *Common.*
24. Mergus serrator................................ *Common.*
25. Erismatura rubida.............................. *Common.*
26. Larus delawarensis............................. *Common.*

Besides the land-birds marked as abundant in the above list, the other more characteristic winter residents were *Amphispiza nevadensis*, *Melospiza heermanni*, and *Pipilo oregonus*. *Turdus migratorius*, *Troglodytes parkmanni*, *Ceryle alcyon*, *Nettion carolinensis*, and *Mareca americana* were also among the winter residents.

7. *Islands of Pyramid Lake* (August, 1867, and May, 1868).—The two islands investigated ornithologically are the main island and the one known as "The Pyramid," from the latter of which the lake receives its name. The former is about ten miles distant from the mouth of the Truckee River and about two miles from the nearest point on the eastern shore. Its shores are, for the most part, abrupt and precipitous, though not high, there being but two convenient landing-places, each a pointed beach of sand extending far out into the water. The island is about three miles in circuit, while in the middle it rises into two bold peaks, each about five hundred feet in height. In May, 1868, we found the limited shore near the southern beach thickly covered with remarkably large grease-wood bushes, on the top of each of which, at the height of about five feet from the ground, was the immense, elaborate nest of a pair of Great Blue Herons (*Ardea herodias*). Not a hundred yards distant, in an oven-like recess in the face of the precipitous rock forming the shore, and inaccessible, was the deserted eyrie of a Bald Eagle (*Haliaëtus leucocephalus*); on the elevated portion of the northern beach several hundreds of Pelicans (*P. erythrorhynchus*) were breeding; on a rocky plateau between the northern peak and the shore an immense colony of Gulls (*Larus californicus*) had their nests, while swarms of Violet-green Swallows (*Tachycineta thalassina*) were passing into and out of the crevices of the high cliffs near by. "The Pyramid" is close to the eastern shore, and appears as a huge rock of very regular pyramidal shape, rising about three hundred feet above the surface of the lake. Its base is a nearly perfect triangle, each side being a sheer precipice from the water to the height of a hundred and fifty feet, while only one of the three corners was found to be easily accessible from the boat. Tempted by the sight of numerous nests near the top, among them being one belonging to a pair of Falcons (*F. nævius*), which flew, clamoring, around, we ascended this corner, and, after a careful climb without looking about, reached the almost

pointed summit. The view toward the water was a frightful one. In no direction could be seen more than the upper third of the rock, and thus the only one possible path by which we had ascended was lost to view. Looking down into the depths of the deep-blue water, three hundred feet below, we could see the pointed ends of similar pyramidal rocks submerged many feet below the surface, and only visible from this height. The descent was finally accomplished by exercising the utmost caution in selecting the path, in which indispensable aid was furnished by our boat-men, who, having watched us ascend, often directed us when we were at a loss which way to proceed. The only species breeding on this isolated cliff were the Great Blue Heron and Peregrine Falcon, there being of the latter but one pair in the vicinity.

Along the neighboring shore were many rocks of peculiar form and structure, styled by our geologists "tufa-domes;" these usually had rounded or domed tops, and were thickly incrusted with calcareous-tufa, while beneath they were honey-combed with winding passages and deep grottoes. Among these rocks several birds were nesting, conspicuous among which were the Barn Swallow, Say's Pewee, and the "House Finch" (*Carpodacus frontalis*), the nests of the latter, placed on shelves of projecting rock inside of caverns, affording another, and very remarkable, instance of the ease with which this species accommodates itself to circumstances in selecting a site for its nest.

8. *Comstock or Virginia Mountains, near Pyramid Lake* (December 24–27, 1867).—From the south end of Pyramid Lake a wide cañon leads up into these mountains, and this was ascended for a considerable distance on three occasions—twice in December and once in June. The slopes of this cañon were dotted with scattered cedar and piñon groves, and in many places were covered with bunch-grass meadows, while along the stream was the fringe of shrubbery usual to the banks of mountain-streams in the Great Basin. In December, *Myiadestes townsendi* was found in the cedar groves, while *Oreortyx pictus* was common in the open portions.

9. *Washoe Valley* (April 25–May 9, 1868).—This valley is one of the most beautiful in Nevada. Its form is that of an amphitheater inclosed

on all sides by mountains, the lofty, snow-capped. and pine-clad Washoe spur of the Sierra Nevada on the west, and the high desert range known as the Comstock or Virginia Mountains on the east, with ranges of elevated hills connecting the two on the north and south sides of the valley. Entering this park from the south, Washoe Lake is seen, shining like silver, to the right, while the steep slopes of the dark-green Sierra form an abrupt wall on the left, the pine forests projecting, in places, upon the grassy valley in beautiful groves, destitute of undergrowth and carpeted by a clean green-sward. In these groves Purple Finches (*Carpodacus cassini*) sweetly warbled, and the Robins sang their mellow carols, while Magpies and Woodpeckers (*Pica hudsonica* and *Melanerpes torquatus*) sported among the trees. Higher up in one of these groves, where alder thickets grew along the stream, the Thick-billed Sparrow (*Passerella megarhyncha*) delighted us with its rich and powerful song, while Blue Jays (*Cyanura frontalis*) and Woodpeckers (*Picus albolarvatus* and *Sphyrapicus thyroideus*) were seen on every hand. After leaving these pine groves and crossing the valley to the edge of the lake, we noticed numbers of Terns (*Sterna regia*, *S. fosteri*, and *Hydrochelidon lariformis*) flitting and hovering over the water, while the surface of the lake itself was dotted with swimming-birds, among which were identified the Coot (*Fulica americana*), Grebes (*Podiceps occidentalis* and *P. californicus*), besides several of the commoner ducks.

10. *Steamboat Valley* (January 3–5, 1867; May 9, 1868).—On account of an accident to our vehicle while returning from Pyramid Lake, we were obliged to stop at the way-side hotel in this valley for repairs. The delay, however, was compensated by the pleasure of making some desirable additions to our collection. The ground was covered with snow, so that many birds flocked to the neighborhood of the buildings for food, and from among these were obtained specimens of *Eremophila alpestris, Sialia arctica, Colaptes mexicanus, C. "hybridus"* (one specimen), and *Pica hudsonica ;* while from a willow thicket in the meadow near by were secured a pair of *Otus wilsonianus.*

Another portion of this valley, the narrow cañon of a stream flowing from Washoe Peak, we passed through on the 9th of May, 1868, after leaving Washoe Valley, and observed, for the first time that spring, *Dendrœca æstiva*, *Cyanospiza amœna*, and *Icterus bullocki*.[1]

11. *Carson City, Nevada* (November 25–December 4, 1867; January 13–April 29, 1868).—Carson City (altitude 4,700 feet) constituted a central point from which investigations radiated to localities of very dissimilar character; the pine-forests of the Sierra Nevada to the west, ånd the scant groves of low gnarled cedars and piñon on the otherwise bare ranges to the eastward; the grassy valley of the Carson River, with its thickets of small willows; the cultivated fields, and the general open waste of sage-brush plain.

a. Pines of the Sierra Nevada.

The pine-forests of the eastern slope of the Sierra Nevada had originally extended from the timber-line, near the summits of these high mountains, down to their very base, ceasing abruptly where the valley began, except in a few places where they stood out in scattered groves upon the edge of the gentle slope at their foot; and, although composed of trees far less tall and massive than those on the western slope, were yet quite as dense and continuous, where left untouched by the hand of man. But,

---

[1] The dates of arrival of spring birds in western Nevada, in 1868, were as follows, so far as noted :—

Along the shore of Washoe Lake.

1. Fulica americana............................May 9.
2. Sterna regia ....May 9.
3. Hydrochelidon lariformis ....May 9.

In Steamboat Valley.

4. Dendrœca æstiva.............................May 9.
5. Cyanospiza amœna............................May 9.
6. Icterus bullocki ....May 9.

Along the Truckee, at Truckee Meadows.

7. Geothlypis trichas..........................May 10.
8. Icteria longicauda..........................May 10.
9. Pyranga ludoviciana ....May 10.

In the lower Truckee Valley.

10. Carpodacus frontalis........................May 13.
11. Amphispiza bilineata ....May 13.
12. Rhyacophilus solitarius.....................May 13.
13. Hedymeles melanocephalus ....May 14.

unfortunately, the most accessible portions of this forest had been almost completely destroyed by the incessant cutting of timber to supply the market of western Nevada. These woods were composed of several species of pines and spruces, but the *Pinus ponderosa* was the prevailing growth. We have no notes respecting the size of the largest timber, but probably few trees exceeded 150 feet in height, and we saw none of more than four feet in diameter. The undergrowth was in places very dense, and consisted mainly of a shining-leafed evergreen *Ceanothus* and other bushes of similar appearance. Owing to the distance to the base of the mountains and the difficulty of ascending to the dense pine timber of the higher portions of the mountains, we seldom penetrated farther than to the edge of the uncut forest, where the characteristic birds of the pines were found to be abundant. The most common species were the Mountain Jay (*Cyanura frontalis*), Clarke's Nutcracker (*Picicorvus columbianus*), Nuthatches (*Sitta aculeata* and *S. pygmæa*), Mountain Chickadees (*Parus montanus*), and, in the early spring, *Carpodacus cassini*. The winter residents of the pines, besides those named above, were the following:—

Sialia mexicana	*Common.*	Colaptes mexicanus	*Common.*
Certhia americana	*Common.*	Bubo subarcticus	*Common.*
Regulus satrapa	*Rare.*	Falco sparverius	*Common.*
Lophophanes inornatus	*Common.*	Nisus cooperi	*Rare.*
Picus harrisi	*Common.*	Aquila canadensis	*Common.*
Picus albolarvatus	*Common.*	Archibuteo sancti-johannis	*Abundant.*
Picoides arcticus	*Rare.*	Buteo calurus	*Common.*
Sphyrapicus thyroideus	*Common.*	Oreortyx pictus	*Common.*
Sphyrapicus nuchalis	*One spec.*		

In the spring, besides *Carpodacus cassini*, the following species were added to the list:—

Pipilo chlorurus (*ravines*) .... April 25.
Melanerpes torquatus (*scattered pines*) .... April 25.
Cyanocitta californica (*foot-hills*) .... April 29.
Melospiza lincolni (*foot-hills*) .... April 29.
Myiadestes townsendi (*pine forests*) .... May 4.

b. Cedar and piñon groves of the desert mountains.

The scant groves of stunted cedars and piñon on several ranges to the eastward are the only approach to woods on the desert mountains. In these scattered groves the two trees above named are mingled, their relative abundance varying with the locality, one or the other of them sometimes alone constituting the entire growth, the greater sterility of the soil being indicated by the prevalence of the *Juniperus*. These trees are usually diminutive, rarely exceeding fifteen feet in height, while their average is hardly more than ten or twelve feet; their trunks are usually large in proportion, however, and twisted and gnarled into an unsightly shape. In such woods, near Carson City, we found only the Blue Nutcracker (*Gymnokitta cyanocephala*), *Sialia arctica*, *Pica hudsonica*, *Lophophanes inornatus*, and *Oreortyx pictus*, with an occasional *Spizella breweri*, *Collurio excubitoroides*, and *Colaptes mexicanus*, with now and then a straggling flock of *Psaltriparus plumbeus*, the latter, however, most usually seen in the ravines. The *Empidonax obscurus* was an additional summer resident, arriving about April 20.

c. *The meadows and sage-brush plains.*

The plain upon which Carson City is situated consists of the usual sage-brush waste, changing, however, to meadows along the foot of the Sierra Nevada, where the soil is watered by brooks and rivulets from the mountains. The winter residents of this section were: *Anthus ludovicianus*, *Collurio excubitoroides*, *Plectrophanes lapponicus*, *Eremophila alpestris*, *Amphispiza nevadensis*, *Sturnella neglecta*, *Speotyto hypogæa* in the sage-brush and meadows of the plain, and *Turdus migratorius*, *Sialia mexicana*, *Regulus calendula*, *Troglodytes parkmanni*, *Collurio borealis*, *Zonotrichia intermedia*, *Junco oregonus*, *Spizella monticola*, and *Pipilo oregonus* among the more bushy fields at the base of the Sierra. Besides the foregoing, *Corvus carnivorus* and *Pica hudsonica* were abundant about the slaughter-houses, while *Xanthocephalus icterocephalus* and *Scolecophagus cyanocephalus* frequented the vicinity of corrals. In the spring, the following species were added to this fauna:—

Sayornis sayus (*about buildings*)...................................March 12.
Salpinctes obsoletus (*rocky places*)...............................March 20.
Oreoscoptes montanus (*sage-brush*)................................March 24.
Tachycineta bicolor (*about buildings*)............................March 25.
Passerculus alaudinus (*meadows*).................................March 28.
Pooecetes confinis (*sage brush and meadows*)..............April 1.

Rhinogryphus aura (*everywhere*)......................April 2.
Hirundo horreorum (*about barns*).....................April 8.
Spizella breweri (*sage brush*)..........................April 9.
Stelgidopteryx serripennis (*ravine banks*)..............April 15.
Progne subis (*about buildings*)........................April 23.
Zenædura carolinensis (*everywhere*)....................April 23.
Chondestes grammaca (*sage-brush*)....................May 3.
Petrochelidon lunifrons (*about barns*)................May 4.

d. Valley of Carson River.

The prominent characteristics of the valley proper of the Carson River consisted of meadow-lands, with dense willow thickets near the river. In the latter, the winter birds were the following species: *Turdus migratorius, Regulus calendula, Certhia americana, Troglodytes parkmanni, T. hyemalis, Dendrœca auduboni, Zonotrichia intermedia, Melospiza heermanni, Passerella schistacea, Pipilo oregonus, Pica hudsonica, Picus harrisi, Colaptes mexicanus,* and *Otus wilsonianus.* The marshes were inhabited by *Telmatodytes paludicola, Melospiza heermanni, Circus hudsonius,* and *Botaurus minor.* The water-fowl of the valley were, *Branta canadensis, B. hutchinsi, Anas boschas, Aythya americana, A. vallisneria, Bucephala americana, B. albeola, Fulix marila, F. collaris, Erismatura rubida, Podiceps occidentalis, P. californicus,* and *Podilymbus podiceps;* while along the streams were found *Ægialitis vociferus* and *Cinclus mexicanus,* with the addition of *Tringoides macularius* after April 29.

12. *Virginia City, Nevada,* (January 5, 6, and June 10–20, 1868).— Virginia City is situated on the southern slope of Mount Davidson, one of the highest peaks of the Virginia or Comstock range, about midway between the base and summit of the mountain, at a total altitude of near 6,200 feet. The surrounding mountains are of an arid nature, the nearest timber being the few cotton-woods along the bank of the Carson River, several miles distant. The birds observed in the town or its vicinity were exceedingly few in number, those occurring during the breeding-season being species which build their nests in caves, old buildings, or similar places. The most common species was the House Finch (*Carpodacus frontalis*), which was abundant about all old buildings, even in the most populous portions of the city; while the Rock Wren (*Salpinctes obsoletus*) was

to be found about every abandoned shaft or dilapidated building. *Sialia arctica* was also frequently seen on the houses, particularly in the outskirts of the town, and nested in the eaves or in any suitable place, in company with the House Finch. All the Swallows were extremely rare, but one individual, a solitary Purple Martin (*Progne subis*), having been seen or heard during the time of our residence, although it is said to be common at times. During winter time, all these birds disappear, by descending to the milder valleys, excepting the *Sialia*, which itself leaves during severe storms. Snow Birds (*Junco oregonus*) and Sparrows (*Spizella monticola* and *Zonotrichia intermedia*) resort to the door-yards for crumbs, and on one occasion (January 6, 1868) we observed a large flock of Gray-headed Purple Finches (*Leucosticte littoralis*) gleaning over the snow in the outskirts of the city.

13. *Carson River, seven miles above Fort Churchill* (June 23, 1868).—The valley of the river was here heavily wooded with cotton-woods (*Populus monilifera* and *P. trichocarpa*), with the usual undergrowth of willows, buffalo-berry bushes, etc. Near by, a range of hills fronted the river in a bold cliff of basaltic rock, while the general surroundings were the usual sage-brush plains, hills, and mountains. The birds observed here were the following:—

Turdus migratorius.
Sialia mexicana.
Salpinctes obsoletus.
Catherpes conspersus.
Troglodytes parkmanni.
Dendrœca æstiva.
Icteria longicauda.
Petrochelidon lunifrons.
Collurio excubitoroides.
Carpodacus frontalis.
Chondestes grammaca.
Cyanospiza amœna.
Pipilo oregonus.
Amphispiza bilineata.

Amphispiza nevadenses.
Sturnella neglecta.
Icterus bullocki.
Contopus richardsoni.
Myiarchus cinerascens.
Tyrannus verticalis.
Picus harrisi.
Colaptes mexicanus.
Antrostomus nuttalli.
Nephœcetes borealis.
Falco sparverius.
Buteo swainsoni.
Tringoides macularius.

Nephœcetes borealis was the most abundant species, flying over the cotton-wood trees in the morning in immense numbers. *Antrostomus nuttalli* and *Icteria longicauda* both sang throughout the night.

14. *Fort Churchill, Carson River*[1] (June 24, 1868).—In general character the valley at this point resembled the place just described. The species observed here were as follows:—

Troglodytes parkmanni.
Sialia mexicana.
Dendrœca æstiva.
Icteria longicauda.
Myiodioctes pusillus.
Vireo swainsoni.
Amphispiza bilineata.
Amphispiza nevadensis.
Spizella breweri.
Cyanospiza amœna.
Pipilo oregonus.

Sturnella neglecta.
Scolecophagus cyanocephalus.
Tyrannus verticalis.
Myiarchus cinerascens.
Contopus richardsoni.
Picus harrisi.
Colaptes mexicanus.
Falco sparverius.
Buteo swainsoni.
Buteo calurus.

All these species seemed to be breeding, but, owing to the fact that the valley was mostly inundated from a late freshet, it was found to be impossible to explore the locality for nests.

15. *Nevada Station* (June 25, 1868).—This place was merely a stage-station in the midst of an inhospitable desert, upon which a few stunted grease-wood bushes constituted the only vegetation in the immediate vicinity. The only birds seen about the station were the ever-present Mourning Doves (*Zenædura carolinensis*) and a single pair of *Sayornis sayus*, the latter having a nest in one of the out-buildings. The former was particularly abundant about a hill of calcareous tufu, containing many caverns, some distance from the house, the *Salpinctes obsoletus* being also common there. On the plain, only *Eremophila alpestris*, *Amphispiza bilineata*, and *Rhinogryphus aura* were found.

16. *Soda Lake, Carson Desert* (June 27, 1868. *Altitude*, 3,906 *feet*).—This most remarkable spot consisted of a cistern-like depression in the midst of the desert, containing a nearly circular lake of about a mile in circuit, and with nearly vertical walls seventy-five, or perhaps a hundred, feet high. Seen from the top of this wall the water appeared very clear, while the bottom was distinctly visible far out toward the center, where the depth seemed to be immense, since the floor of pure white borate of soda ended abruptly, after which the water was a deep, dark blue. Springs of fresh

[1] Altitude, 4,284 feet.

water issued from the walls at several places, and upon their borders the vegetation was excessively luxuriant, in consequence of protection from winds by their great distance below the general surface of the desert, as well as the constant moisture of the spot; this vegetation consisted chiefly of tall *tule,* rank grasses and sedges, and rose-briers. Elsewhere, the entire country was a sandy waste, with a scant growth of the ordinary desert shrubs, which within the walls of the lake were more thrifty than elsewhere. The most abundant bird of this place was a very small, and clamorous, grebe (perhaps *Podiceps californicus*), which kept out of gunshot from the shore; next in numbers were the Avocets (*Recurvirostra americana*), multitudes of which ran along the beach, scooping up the dead insects which blackened the water around the margin of the lake; mixed with these were a few Stilts (*Himantopus mexicanus*). A few pairs of Gulls (*Larus californicus*), which were nesting on a large rock away out in the lake, completed the list of water-birds of this locality. Among the land-birds we noticed only the *Oreoscoptes montanus, Amphispiza bilineata,* and a remarkable species, probably *Phœnopepla nitens,* which we tried in vain to secure.

A few rods distant was another somewhat similar, but smaller and shallower, lake, where large numbers of Avocets and a few Stilts were breeding on the numerous islands of borax in the shallow water.

17. *Sand Springs Station* (June 29, 1868).—This locality is in the midst of the desert, the country being extremely barren, with an immense hill of shifting sand near the station. Only the ordinary desert birds were found here, the following being the species: *Amphispiza bilineata, Eremophila alpestris, Corvus carnivorus, Zenædura carolinensis,* and *Rhinogryphus aura.*

18. *Fairview Valley* (June 29, 1868).—This locality presented the usual characteristics of a sage-brush valley, with no conspicuous or interesting features. The entire region was so dry that water for the use of the station had to be hauled in wagons the distance of twelve miles. The only birds observed were the following: *Amphispiza bilineata, A. nevadensis, Chondestes grammaca, Eremophila alpestris,* and *Speotyto hypogæa.*

19. *Edwards Creek* (June 30, 1868).—At this camp, where there was no shrubbery along the stream other than a more thrifty growth of sage-brush

and grease-wood than that elsewhere upon the plain, only the following species of birds were observed: *Oreoscoptes montanus*, *Spizella breweri*, and *Speotyto hypogæa*.

20. *Humboldt Marshes, near the "Sink"* (*Altitude*, 3,893 *feet;* August 26–October 31, 1867).—Although a week was spent at this camp, the state of our health permitted the use of but one day for collecting, which is much to be regretted, since we have never seen another locality where water-fowl so abounded. The writer was a victim of malarial fever, which was only aggravated by the nature of the surroundings. The marshes were miles in extent and almost entirely covered by a dense growth of *tule*, except where the river meandered through, now and then expanding into a small lake. These marshes were surrounded by a bare plain, consisting in the winter season of mud, but at this time baked perfectly dry and hard by the heat of the sun, except in the more depressed portions, which were covered by a deep deposit of snow-white "alkali." From these extensive flats, desert plains lead away to the barren mountains on either side, whose summits are bare and rugged eruptive rocks, of weird forms and strange colors. Upon the whole, the entire region was one of the most desolate and forbidding that could be imagined, and in these respects is probably not surpassed by any other portion of the land of "alkali" and the "everlasting sage-brush." The effluvium from the putrid water and decaying vegetation of the marshes was at times sickening, while at night the torments of millions of the most voracious mosquitoes added to the horrors of the place.[1] The land-birds of this desolate locality were very few, a solitary raven, hoarsely croaking, being now and then seen winging his way to or from the distant mountains, an occasional Desert Lark (*Eremophila chrysolæma*) in the scanty sage-brush or on the bare plain, or a few Savanna Sparrows in the salt-grass of the meadows, comprising all that were seen. The water-fowl, however, were extremely numerous, and consisted of many species, of which the following were identified: *Tringa bairdi, T. minutilla, Ereunetes pusillus, Symphemia semipalmata, Recurvirostra americana, Himantopus mexicanus, Falcinellus*

---

[1] The reader may be surprised, if not incredulous, when told that the mosquitoes and other insects sometimes came in such swarms about the candles in the camp as to extinguish the lights in a few moments!

23 P R

thalassinus (extremely abundant), *Fulica americana, Erismatura rubida, Sterna regia,* and *S. forsteri.* This, however, is but a small proportion of the species inhabiting these marshes, since without a boat we had no means of invading the haunts of the more wary kinds. On the 31st of October the same place was again visited, and several birds not seen during our summer stay were noted. Crows (*Corvus americanus*) were walking about the door-yard with the familiarity of domesticated birds; a Falcon (*Falco polyagrus*) was seen to dash into a flock of tame pigeons belonging to the station, while from an Indian we obtained the fresh skin of a Lesser Snow-Goose (*Anser albatus*).

21. *Humboldt River, at Oreana* (August 30–September 3. *Altitude,* 4,036 *feet*).—At this place the valley of the Humboldt was, as usual, destitute of trees, the only woody vegetation near the river being the thick clumps of small willows on the points and around the sloughs. The greater portion of the valley consisted of meadows of salt-grass, but back toward the mesa this gradually gave way to an unusually tall and vigorous growth of grease-wood and sage-brush. In the latter, the most common bird was the *Oreoscoptes montanus,* another abundant species being *Amphispiza nevadensis;* on the meadows, *Xanthocephalus icterocephalus, Molothrus ater, Agelæus phœniceus,* and *Sturnella neglecta;* in the willows, *Melospiza fallax, Dendræca æstiva, Vireosylvia swainsoni,* and *Collurio excubitoroides;* Swallows, particularly *H. horreorum,* were common in the air, while large flocks of the Green Ibis, or "Black Curlew" (*Falcinellus thalassinus*), were almost constantly passing up and down the river, now and then alighting to feed for awhile in a slough hidden among the willows. This camp was finally abandoned on account of a severe form of malarial fever having attacked nearly the entire party, the disease having been contracted at our previous camp—the Humboldt marshes.

22. *Wright's Cañon, West Humboldt Mountains* (September 3–13, 1867. *Altitude,* 4,881 *feet*).—Wright's Cañon was supplied with a brook, which, though of considerable volume during the rainy season, was intermittent through the dry summer months. The water ran briskly at night and in the cool hours of morn and evening, but during the hotter

portion of the day could be found only in pockets of the rocks, the bed of the stream, or cool nooks completely shaded by overhanging bushes. Bordering this stream, in its entire extent, the vegetation was luxuriant, compared to that of other sections, the shrubbery consisting principally of a thick growth of a small cornel (*Cornus pubescens*), from six to ten feet high, often canopied by the trailing stems and delicate foliage of a species of *Clematis*. There were also clumps of wild roses and a few willows, interspersed at intervals with patches of elder (*Sambucus glauca*) and thickets of choke-cherries (*Prunus andersoni* and *P. virginianus*). No woods were in sight, but on the slopes of the cañon were small, scattered cedars (*Juniperus occidentalis*), while a few isolated small aspens were distributed far apart along the stream. During midday the water of the brook being confined to small pools where shaded by the overhanging shrubbery, or in "pockets" of the rocks in the bed of the stream, the birds resorted to these little reservoirs to refresh themselves in the shade of the thickets or by bathing in the cool water. The characteristic birds of this cañon were Woodhouse's Jay (*Cyanocitta woodhousii*), Little Titmouse (*Psaltriparus plumbeus*), and Swainson's Vireo (*Vireosylvia swainsoni*). Besides these, the following species were found: *Salpinctes obsoletus*, *Icteria longicauda*, *Myiodioctes pusillus*, *Amphispiza bilineata*, *Pipilo chlorurus*, *Troglodytes parkmanni*, *Zonotrichia intermedia*, *Hedymeles melanocephalus*, *Lanivireo cassini*, *Geothlypis macgillivrayi*, *Pica hudsonica*, *Ectopistes migratoria* (!), and *Sayornis sayus*. The most abundant birds of the locality were the *Psaltriparus*, *Vireosylvia*, *Myiodioctes*, and *Zonotrichia*, above mentioned, the specimen of *Ectopistes* being the only one observed during the entire exploration.

23. *Buena Vista Cañon, West Humboldt Mountains* (September 17–October 23. *Altitude, 5,169 feet*).—The general aspect of this locality was that of Wright's Cañon, on the opposite side of the range, except that its stream was constant and much larger, with a wider extent of level land on each side, and correspondingly more extensive shrubbery, which, at the same time, was more vigorous and varied. This consisted chiefly of a thick growth of buffalo-berry bushes, willows, and wild-rose briers in the lower portion of the cañon, and higher up of choke-cherry and rose bushes, mixed with extensive copses of small aspens. The slopes on each side

were sparingly covered with scattered groves of "cedar," piñon, and "mountain mahogany," while the summits of the mountains were for the most part bare and rocky, but not sufficiently high to retain snow during summer, their elevation ranging from 8,000 to 10,000 feet. The birds found at this locality during our stay were the following:—

Turdus migratorius	Abundant.	Passerculus alaudinus	Common.
Cinclus mexicanus	Common.	Pipilo oregonus	Rare.
Regulus calendula	Common.	Pipilo megalonyx	Common.
Regulus satrapa	Rare.	Scolecophagus cyanocephalus	Very abund't.
Sialia arctica	Abundant.		
Salpinctes obsoletus	Abundant.	Agelæus phœniceus	Common.
Psaltriparus plumbeus	Abundant.	Agelæus gubernator	Rare.
Anthus ludovicianus	Rare.	Icterus bullocki	Rare.
Helminthophaga celata	Abundant.	Sturnella neglecta	Common.
Helminthophaga lutescens	Rare.	Pica hudsonica	Abundant.
Dendrœca auduboni	Abundant.	Cyanocitta woodhousii	Common.
Myiodioctes pusillus	Abundant.	Corvus carnivorus	Common.
Lanivireo solitarius	Rare.	Eremophila alpestris	Common.
Lanivireo cassini	Rare.	Sayornis sayus	Common.
Carpodacus frontalis	Common.	Empidonax obscurus	Rare.
Zonotrichia coronata	One specimen.	Colaptes mexicanus	Common.
Zonotrichia intermedia	Very abund't.	Colaptes auratus?	One specimen.
Junco oregonus	Very abund't.	Nisus cooperi	Rare.
Melospiza fallax	Very abund't.	Zenædura carolinensis	Rare.
Melospiza guttata	Very rare.	Centrocercus urophasianus	Rare.

The most abundant of these was the *Scolecophagus cyanocephalus.*

24. *Toyabe Mountains, near Austin* (July 2–5, 1868).—On the western slope of this lofty range, near its northern extremity, at an altitude of about 6,500 feet, our camp was established in a cañon adjoining the outskirts of the above-named town. The cañons and principal ravines in this neighborhood were well watered by brooks and rivulets, whose course was followed by shrubbery from their sources to the valleys. At the heads of these cañons extensive copses of small aspens and choke-cherry bushes prevailed, while 2,000 feet below, or near our camp, thrifty bushes of *Symphoricarpus montanus* were the predominating growth. Corresponding in altitude with the aspens, were scant groves of stunted mountain mahogany, growing upon the summits or ridges of the mountains; but on the lower slopes a thin wood of cedar and piñon prevailed. In sight, to the south-

ward, the magnificent snow-capped peaks of the higher portion of the range were seen to be timbered with pine and fir forests, but no opportunity was afforded to visit these.

The species observed in the neighborhood of our camp were the following: In the lower portions of the cañon, *Pipilo chlorurus* among the snow-berry bushes, *Pooecetes confinis* on the weed-clad and grassy slopes, *Spizella breweri, Cyanospiza amœna, Antrostomus nuttalli, Oreoscoptes montanus, Eremophila alpestris, Chondestes grammaca, Amphispiza nevadensis,* and *Sturnella neglecta* in the sage-brush—from the valley-level to 2,000 feet above camp; *Empidonax obscurus* and *Vireosylvia swainsoni* in the aspen copses; *Hedymeles melanocephalus, Icterus bullocki,* and *Pipilo megalonyx* in the shrubbery along the streams; *Tyrannus verticalis, Myiarchus cinerascens, Spizella arizonæ, Scolecophagus cyanocephalus,* and *Gymnokitta cyanocephala* in the cedar and piñon groves, while *Turdus migratorius* occurred in all wooded localities; *Sialia arctica, Hirundo horreorum, Tachycineta thalassina, Petrochelidon lunifrons,* and *Salpinctes obsoletus* nested about out-buildings or in old mining-shafts, while species of indiscriminate distribution were *Rhinogryphus aura, Buteo calurus, B. swainsoni, Archibuteo (ferrugineus?), Aquila canadensis, Chordeiles henryi, Collurio excubitoroides, Corvus carnivorus,* and *Zenœdura carolinensis.* It was here that we met with the first specimen of *Panyptila saxatilis,* a solitary individual having been observed to pass swiftly over one of the higher hills.

25. "*Camp* 19," *Ruby Valley and Ruby Mountains* (July 12–September 5.) *Altitude of Camp,* 6,300 *feet.*—This camp was the base of extensive researches in all directions, both the mountains upon whose foot-slope we were encamped and the valley below us being included within the field of investigation. The valley was of the same character that sage-brush valleys usually are, except that its depressed center was occupied by an extensive marsh, known as "Ruby Lake," the receptacle of the numerous springs of pure, cold water which burst from the base of the limestone mountains on the western side of the valley. This marsh is so filled with tule that the meandering channels of clear water can only be seen from the mountains, from which they appear as narrow silver threads in the dark-green rush-

meadows. The birds observed in the valley adjacent to this camp were the following species: In the sage-brush, *Oreoscoptes montanus*, *Chondestes grammaca*, *Spizella breweri*, *Amphispiza nevadensis*, *Antrostomus nuttalli*, *Chordeiles henryi*, and *Zenædura carolinensis;* on the meadows, *Passerculus claudinus*, *Coturniculus perpallidus*, and *Grus canadensis:* in the brier thickets, *Geothlypis trichas;* and in the marshes, *Telmatodytes paludicola*, *Xanthocephalus icterocephalus*, *Fulica americana*, *Anas boschas*, and *Sterna forsteri*. The mountains above this camp are exceedingly complicated in their varied characteristics and in the distribution of their bird-life. The main cañons, at right-angles with the trend of the range, become contracted in their lower portion, where their sides consist of vertical limestone cliffs, many of which are 200 to 300 feet in height; similar cliffs also crop out, in places, near the summit of the range, standing singly, like immense walls, from each side of which the slopes lead down to the bottom of the cañons. The altitude of the valley at the base of the mountains is about 6,000 feet above sea-level, while the summits of the range are from 9,000 to upwards of 12,000 feet high. The cañons here support nearly all the shrubbery and herbaceous vegetation, while only the spurs and higher slopes are wooded. The lower portion of the streams within the cañon is followed by the usual shrubbery of cañon streams, which here consisted chiefly of choke-cherry, snow-berry (*Symphoricarpus*), and service-berry (*Amelanchier canadensis*) bushes, the remainder of the cañon, where not occupied by rocks, being covered with the ordinary sage-brush plants. About half way to the summit, however, the cliffs cease, the cañon sides gradually become less abrupt and wider apart, and at this elevation the gently-inclined slopes are overspread with a luxuriant meadow in which various plants with showy flowers abound. The sage-brush still predominates, however, until the lower edge of the side-slopes of the "saddles" between the peaks of the range are reached, when the vegetation is transformed into a garden, as it were, so numerous and showy are the flowers, among which the scarlet Castilleias and Gilias, and blue Pentstemons and Delphineums are most conspicuous, from the circumstance that they give the prevailing hues to the meadows. These flowery slopes reach up to the fields of snow, which are found in all shaded spots, and, at a proper elevation, even in places constantly exposed to the sun. The woods of this range begin at the base of the "spurs" between the cañons, and continue, in successive belts, to the timber-line, as follows: From the valley level, thick and extensive woods, composed exclusively of cedar and piñon, extend for 2,000 or 2,500 feet, when they gradually give way to more scant groves of mountain mahogany (*Cercocarpus ledifolius*), which, however, scarcely extend higher than 3,500 feet above the valley. Beyond this altitude no trees of these species are met with, for on the higher peaks they are replaced by forests of pines (*Pinus flexilis* and *P. balfouriana*), with an undergrowth of hardy shrubs. These pine trees are not tall, the highest not exceeding thirty or forty feet, but they have trunks of comparatively large size; and it was observed that when growing in situations where exposed to the wind, which here constantly blows from one direction, all the branches of these trees are bent away from the wind, or, indeed, grow only upon that side, while the shrubs underneath are pressed flat to the ground in the same direction. During our investigations among these mountains, the following species were observed, between July 12 and the 5th of September:—

Shrubbery of cañon streams.

Icteria longicauda.........*Rare.*
Geothlypis macgillivrayi...*Abundant.*
Myiodioctes pusillus.......*Rare.*
Dendrœca æstiva..........*Common.*
Melospiza fallax ....*Rare.*
Hedymeles melanocephalus.*Common.*

Cyanospiza amœna.........*Common.*
Pipilo megalonyx. ....*Very rare.*
Pipilo chlorurus....... ...*Common.*
Icterus bullocki...........*Common.*
Empidonax pusillus.......*Common.*

Lower woods.

Turdus migratorius........*Common.*
Parus montanus...... ....*Rare.*
Psaltriparus plumbeus.....*Rare.*
Psaltriparus melanotis? ...*One specimen.*
Troglodytes parkmanni... *Common.*
Helminthophaga virginiæ..*Common.*
Dendrœca nigrescens......*Common.*
Pyranga ludoviciana.......*Common.*
Lanivireo plumbeus.......*Common.*
Vireosylvia swainsoni .....*Common.*
Collurio excubitoroides.....*Common.*
Carpodacus cassini (Aug. 10)*Abundant.*
Loxia leucoptera (Aug. 12).*One specimen.*
Spizella arizonæ .... *Very abund't.*

Icterus bullocki. ....*Common.*
Scolecophagus cyanocepha-
lus...................*Common.*
Picicorvus columbianus....*Rare.*
Gymnokitta cyanocephala..*Rare.*
Cyanocitta woodhousii.....*Rare.*
Tyrannus verticalis........*Abundant.*
Myiarchus cinerascens.....*Common.*
Contopus richardsoni......*Common.*
Empidonax obscurus......*Common.*
Chordeiles henryi.........*Abundant.*
Picus harrisi. ....*Rare.*
Colaptes mexicanus ....*Rare.*
Zenædura carolinensis.....*Abundant.*

Alpine woods.

Turdus migratorius..	Common.	Chrysomitris pinus........	Abundant.
Sialia arctica.......	Abundant.	Spizella arizonæ	Common.
Carpodacus cassini........	Abundant.	Pipilo chlorurus........	Common.

Cliffs and rocky places.

Salpinctes obsoletus.......	Abundant.	Falco polyagrus	Common.
Catherpes conspersus......	Common.	Falco nævius	Rare.
Tachycineta thalassina	Abundant.	Falco sparverius	Abundant.
Hirundo horreorum........	Common.	Aquila canadensis..	Common.
Petrochelidon lunifrons....	Very abund't.	Buteo calurus.......	Common.
Sayornis sayus............	Rare.	Buteo swainsoni	Common.
Panyptila saxatilis	Very abund't.		

Open meadows.

Pooecetes confinis.	Common.	Trochilus alexandri........	Common.
Chondestes grammaca....	Common.	Selasphorus platycercus ...	Very abund't.
Stellula calliope..........	Abundant.		

26. *Overland Ranche, Ruby Valley* (August 28–September 3).—The characteristics of both valley and mountains were quite different from those at "Camp 19," although both were a continuation of the same. The limestone formations of the southern portion of the range had become transformed to steeper and more rugged granite peaks, the highest of which towered to an altitude of about 12,000 feet, while, owing to their granitic structure and extreme ruggedness, their slopes and spurs were almost destitute of vegetation. The cañons, however, supported a luxuriant growth of shrubs and other plants, with here and there small copses or groves of aspen and narrow-leafed cotton-wood (*Populus angustifolia*), the copses and thickets having usually an undergrowth of briery rosaceous shrubs, but these, in places, were replaced by a carpeting of beautiful ferns. Unlike localities farther southward in this valley, this shrubbery was continued across the valley, on the borders of the stream, to the meadows which extend to the shores of Franklin Lake. The meadow-lands of the valley had become transformed by cultivation into broad fields of grain, more than a thousand acres of the valley being thus reclaimed. The lake, which occupied the more depressed portion of the valley, was simply an enlargement of Ruby Lake, containing in its central portion a wide expanse of open water, in which thousands of water-fowl dwelt secure from the gunner—

the lack of a boat rendering them inaccessible. During the short season
of our stay at this locality the following species were identified:—

In the marshes and meadows.

Geothlypis trichas .... *Common.*	Grus canadensis .... *Common.*
Passerculus alaudinus..... *Very abund't.*	Botaurus minor.......... *Common.*
Coturniculus perpallidus .. *Common.*	Falcinellus guarauna.. ...*Abundant.*
Dolichonyx oryzivorus ....*Abundant.*	Fulica americana ....*Abundant.*
Xanthocephalus icterocepha-	Branta canadensis .... *Common.*
lus ....*Abundant.*	Anas boschas........... *Common.*
Agelæus phœniceus..... ...*Abundant.*	Sterna forsteri.. .... *Common.*
Sturnella neglecta.........*Abundant.*	Hydrochelidon lariformis ..*Abundant.*
Circus hudsonius........ .. *Common.*	Podiceps cristatus .... *Common.*

Along the stream.

Ægialitis vociferus........*Abundant.*	Tringoides macularius..... *Common.*
Gallinago wilsoni......... *Common.*	

In the sage-brush.

Spizella breweri ....*Abundant.*	Oreoscoptes montanus ....*Common.*
Chondestes grammaca..... *Common.*	Zenædura carolinensis.....*Abundant.*
Pooecetes confinis .... *Common.*	

In the cañon.

Turdus migratorius . ....*Abundant.*	Melospiza fallax .. .. *Common.*
Turdus swainsoni .... *Common.*	Cyanospiza amœna ....*Common.*
Trolodytes parkmanni... . *Common.*	Pipilo chlorurus ....*Common.*
Dendrœca æstiva ....*Common.*	Icterus bullocki.... ...*Common.*
Dendrœca occidentalis ... . *Rare.*	Cyanocitta woodhousii ....*Rare.*
Dendrœca townsendi...... *Rare.*	Tyrannus verticalis ....*Abundant.*
Myiodioctes pusillus .... *Common.*	Contopus richardsoni...... *Common.*
Geothlypis macgillivrayi ..*Common.*	Empidonax pusillus....... *Common.*
Geothlypis trichas ....*Rare.*	Empidonax hammondi ....*Common.*
Icteria longicauda .... *Rare.*	Selasphorus platycercus ...*Abundant.*
Vireosylvia swainsoni ....*Abundant.*	Ceryle alcyon............*Rare.*
Loxia americana . ...*Common.*	Nisus cooperi.............*Rare.*
Loxia leucoptera ....*Common.*	

All of the species in the latter list were found along the entire length
of the stream, from the lower end of the shrubbery away out in the valley
to the upper portion of the cañon, with the exception of *Dendrœca occidentalis,*
D. townsendi, Loxia leucoptera, and *Empidonax hammondi,* which we found
only in the aspen copses, far up the cañon. *Turdus migratorius, T. swainsoni,*
Loxia americana, and *Selasphorus platycercus* were also more abundant high
up the cañon than elsewhere.

On the foot-hills of the range, on each side the cañon, were a few scattered mountain mahogany and cedar trees, and among these we found *Helminthophaga virginiæ*, *Contopus borealis*, *Empidonax obscurus*, and *Picicorvus columbianus*.

. A decided step toward a different faunal district, besides the addition of *Dolichonyx oryzivorus*, *Podiceps cristatus*, *Turdus swainsoni*, *Dendrœca townsendi*, *D. occidentalis*, *Loxia americana*, *L. leucoptera*, *Empidonax hammondi*, and *Contopus borealis* to our list of birds, was the circumstance that the large white-tailed hare, *Lepus campestris*, replaced the black-tailed *L. callotis*, which, up to this time, had been the only one observed.

Species of general distribution observed at this locality were as follows:

Rhinogryphus aura	Common.	Hirundo horreorum	Common.
Aquila canadensis	Common.	Scolecophagus cyanocephalus.	Abundant.
Buteo swainsoni	Common.	Colaptes mexicanus.	Common.
Archibuteo sancti-johannis	Common.	Corvus carnivorus	Common.
Collurio excubitoroides	Common.	Zenædura carolinensis	Abundant.

27. "*Camp 22*," *Ruby Valley* (September 4–5, 1868).—The surroundings of this camp were much the same as those at the Overland Ranche, except that the valley was uncultivated, while the foot-hills were higher; besides, we had left the marshes behind. The stream was bordered with willows entirely across the valley, while in a marshy spot stood quite an extensive grove of very tall willows and alders. In the latter, considerable numbers of *Loxia americana* and *L. leucoptera* were found, besides *Dendrœca æstiva*, *Empidonax pusillus*, and *Contopus richardsoni*, while *Gallinago wilsoni* was abundant on marshy ground, where was also a small black Rail, supposed to be *Porzana jamaicensis*. In the sage-brush were *Collurio excubitoroides*, *Oreoscoptes montanus*, *Spizella breweri*, *Pooecetes confinis*, and *Chondestes grammaca*, while along the stream we found *Passerculus alaudinus* and *Melospiza fallax*. In an elevated park, at the head of the main cañon in the foot-hills, the following species were observed: *Empidonax hammondi*, *Contopus richardsoni*, *Chrysomitris pinus*, *Canace obscura*, *Ceryle alcyon*, *Colaptes mexicanus*, *Buteo swainsoni*, *Falco sparverius*, *Zenædura carolinensis*, *Selasphorus platycercus*, *Pooecetes confinis*, *Chondestes grammaca*, *Spizella breweri*, and *Pipilo chlorurus*.

28. *Secret Valley, East Humboldt Mountains* (September 6–8, 1868).—
Secret Valley is a small park nestled among high hills, with the East Humboldt Mountains proper on the west, and the equally lofty portion of that range known as the "Clover Mountains" to the eastward. The higher slopes of this valley, especially near the sources of the streams, were clothed with by far the most varied and extensive vegetation we had yet seen east of the Sierra Nevada. The aspens along the streams were from 40 to 70 feet high, some of them being 1½ to 2 feet in diameter; while in places they were so numerous as to form considerable groves. Accompanying these aspens, were dense thickets of varied and luxuriant shrubbery, tall alders and willows predominating in the swampy spots, while the slopes were covered with a nearly impenetrable growth of "laurel" bushes (*Ceanothus velutinus*). On the ridges the mountain mahogany formed groves, while in the lower valleys *Amelanchier canadensis*, or service berry, grew in great abundance, furnishing food for many species of birds. The birds observed at this place were the following: Among the aspens, *Melanerpes torquatus, Colaptes mexicanus, Turdus migratorius, Chrysomitris pinus, Loxia americana, L. leucoptera, Contopus richardsoni*, and *Empidonax hammondi.* In the shrubbery along the streams, *Selasphorus rufus* (!), *S. platycercus, Turdus swainsoni, Troglodytes parkmanni, Geothlypis trichas* (lower portions), *G. macgillivrayi, Myiodioctes pusillus, Dendrœca œstiva, D. townsendi, Empidonax hammondi, Helminthophaga ruficapilla, H. lutescens, H. celata, Vireosylvia swainsoni, Chrysomitris tristis, Melospiza fallax, Zonotrichia intermedia, Cyanospiza amœna*, and *Pipilo chlorurus*. In the sage-brush, *Oreoscoptes montanus, Collurio excubitoroides, Eremophila alpestris, Pooecetes confinis, Chondestes grammaca, Spizella breweri, Sturnella neglecta, Zenœdura carolinensis*, and *Centrocercus urophasianus*. Among the mahoganies, *Empidonax obscurus* was the most common species. *Salpinctes obsoletus* was found in all rocky places, particularly on the ridges; a single individual of *Ceryle alcyon* was seen along the brook, while *Corvus carnivorus, Buteo calurus, Circus hudsonius*, and *Falco polyagrus* were species of irregular distribution.

29. *Dearing's Ranche, Upper Humboldt Valley* (September 10–14).—
After crossing the East Humboldt range through the pass called Secret

Valley, we found the country along the western base of the Clover Mountains to be similar to the upper portion of Ruby Valley in its general characteristics. As along the eastern base of the East Humboldt range, the streams from the main cañons were of considerable volume, while their bordering shrubbery continued with them across the valley to the river. The shrubbery along the main streams of the Upper Humboldt valley was more extensive and vigorous, however, the cotton-woods and aspens being more numerous, and constituting extensive groves, other spots being occupied by dense thickets of thorn-apple (*Cratægus rivularis*), wild-cherry (*Prunus andersoni?*), and willows (*Salix*, species). At this place the following species were observed:—

Turdus migratorius......... *Common.*	Passerella schistacea ...... *Common.*
Turdus swainsoni... .. .. *Common.*	Corvus carnivorus........ *Common.*
Regulus calendula..... ..... *Common.*	Pica hudsonica........... *Common.*
Troglodytes parkmanni...... *Common.*	Contopus richardsoni...... *Common.*
Sitta canadensis .... *Common.*	Empidonax hammondi..... *Common.*
Helminthophaga celata.......*Abundant.*	Ceryle alcyon.. ....*Rare.*
Helminthophaga lutescens... *Rare.*	Colaptes mexicanus....... *Common.*
Dendrœca æstiva .... *Common.*	Melanerpes torquatus..... *Rare.*
Dendrœca auduboni........ *Abundant.*	Picus gairdneri......... *Rare.*
Myiodioctes pusillus..... ....*Abundant.*	Otus wilsonianus ....*Rare.*
Ampelis cedrorum.... ...... *Common.*	Falco sparverius .... *Common.*
Vireosylvia swainsoni . .....*Abundant.*	Falco columbarius........ *Rare.*
Lanivireo solitarius..... ... *Common.*	Circus hudsonius........... *Rare.*
Pyranga ludoviciana......... *Common.*	Nisus cooperi. .... *Rare.*
Zonotrichia intermedia......*Abundant.*	Nisus fuscus.............. *Common.*
Melospiza fallax..............*Abundant.*	Buteo calurus............ *Rare.*
Spizella breweri.............*Abundant.*	Buteo swainsoni........... *Rare.*
Cyanospiza amœna.......... *Common.*	Aquila canadensis......... *Rare.*
Pipilo chlorurus .... *Common.*	Rhinogryphus aura....... *Rare.*
Scolecophagus cyanocephalus.*Abundant.*	Zenædura carolinensis.....*Abundant.*

30. *Trout Creek, Upper Humboldt Valley* (September 16–20, 1868).— This locality was very similar to the last, a large brook, with an accompanying growth of shrubbery and thickets of small trees, extending across the valley from the Clover Mountains to the Humboldt River, the plain itself being covered by the usual sage-brush plants; but the upper portion, next to the lower foot-hills of the mountains, was clothed with rye-grass meadows, interspersed with willow and aspen copses. In these rye-grass meadows

the Sharp-tailed Grouse (*Pediæcetes columbianus*) was very abundant. The principal species met with along this creek were, besides that above-named, the following:—

Turdus guttatus	*One specimen.*	Passerculus alaudinus	*Abundant.*
Parus septentrionalis	*Rare.*	Empidonax obscurus	*Common.*
Zonotrichia intermedia	*Abundant.*	Sphyrapicus nuchalis	*Rare.*
Junco oregonus	*Abundant.*	Picus harrisi	*Rare.*
Melospiza fallax	*Abundant.*	Picus gairdneri	*Rare.*
Melospiza lincolni	*Abundant.*	Antrostomus nuttali	*Common.*
Pipilo chlorurus	*Common.*		

31. *Clover Mountains* (September 19, 1868).—On the above date, a trip was made to near the summit of the main peak of this range by following Trout Creek from our camp up the cañon to its head, returning by another cañon to the southward. The summit of this peak is very lofty, rising considerably above the timber-line, or to an altitude of near 12,000 feet. Large fields of perpetual snow lay in the ravines and behind masses of rock, and in several places below the bare summit were quite extensive pine woods. Nothing of interest, ornithologically, resulted from this exceedingly laborious day's work, however, only the usual species being observed. The commoner species of the alpine woods were *Sitta canadensis*, *Parus montanus*, and *Junco oregonus*, while at the head of one of the cañons, where pines and aspens were intermingled, *Canace obscura* was very abundant.

32. *Holmes's Creek, near Thousand Spring Valley* (September 22–26. *Altitude, about 6,000 feet*).—Observations at this camp were confined chiefly to a small valley nestled among a range of low hills separating the valley of the upper Humboldt from Thousand Spring Valley. Around a spring, which supplied the camp with water, grew a thicket of tall willows and aspens, while along the rivulet from this spring grew willow bushes. Elsewhere, only the ordinary sage-brush plants flourished. In the thickets above mentioned, *Dendrœca townsendi*, *Sphyrapicus nuchalis*, and *Nyctale acadica* were obtained.

33. "*City of Rocks*,"[1] *Southern Idaho* (October 2, 1868).—The hills

[1] This locality derives its name from a remarkable valley among the mountains close by, where immense piles of granite, rising from the floor of the valley, vaguely represent a city of castles, domes, and mosques.

about this locality were extensively covered with unusually luxuriant woods of cedar and piñon, among which *Gymnokitta cyanocephala* and *Cyanociita woodhousii* were more abundant than we had ever seen them elsewhere. *Corvus carnivorus* and *Centrocercus urophasianus* were also abundant.

34. *Deep Creek, Northwestern Utah* (October 5, 1868).—At this point of our route, the nearly level sage-brush plain was intersected by a narrow valley considerably below the general level, through which flowed, with a sluggish current, a very narrow but remarkably deep creek, a tributary of the Great Salt Lake. The banks of this creek were lined with rushes, while in the valley itself were willow thickets. The principal birds observed here were the following:—

Amphispiza nevadensis.
Zonotrichia intermedia.
Melospiza fallax.

Melospiza lincolni.
Telmatodytes paludicola.
Geothlypis trichas.

35. *Vicinity of Salt Lake City, Utah*[1] (May 20–June 1, and June 14–21, 1869).—Owing to its diversified character, the vicinity of Salt Lake City proved exceedingly favorable to the objects of the exploration; the scrub-oaks of the hill-sides, the luxuriant and varied shrubbery along the stream in City-Creek Cañon, the meadow-lands, both wild and cultivated, between the city and the lake, the tule sloughs along the Jordan River, and the extensive marshes about the lake-shore, having each their peculiar species besides those found in the sage-brush, and others of general distribution. The species noted in the vicinity of Salt Lake City during the months of May and June were those given in the annexed list, most, if not all, of them having been found breeding in the neighborhood. The asterisk placed in one or more columns after the name of a species indicates its center of abundance, the columns representing the following types of localities:—

1. Sage-brush plains and mesas.
2. Meadows, chiefly toward the lake.
3. Tule sloughs and marshes near Jordan River.
4. Open ponds, shore of the lake, etc.
5. Thickets along the streams, valley, and lower part of City Creek Cañon.
6. Scrub-oaks, slopes of City Creek Cañon.
7. Rocky places, City Creek Cañon.
8. Of general distribution.
9. Mountain mahoganies and scattered cedars on lower spurs of mountains.

---

[1] Altitude about 4,000 feet.

	1.	2.	3.	4.	5.	6.	7.	8.	9.
1. Turdus migratorius					*	*			*
2. Turdus auduboni					*				
3. Turdus swainsoni					*				
4. Oreoscoptes montanus	*								
5. Galescoptes carolinensis					*				
6. Cinclus mexicanus					*				
7. Sialia arctica								*	*
8. Troglodytes parkmanni								*	
9. Telmatodytes paludicola			*						
10. Dendrœca æstiva								*	
11. Helminthophaga virginiæ						*			
12. Geothlypis trichas		*							
13. Geothlypis macgillivrayi						*			
14. Icteria longicauda					*				
15. Setophaga ruticilla					*				
16. Pyranga ludoviciana									*
17. Progne subis								*	
18. Petrochelidon lunifrons							*	*	
19. Hirundo horreorum							*	*	
20. Tachycineta thalassina							*	*	
21. Tachycineta bicolor								*	
22. Cotyle riparia								*	
23. Stelgidopteryx serripennis								*	
24. Vireosylvia swainsoni					*				
25. Lanivireo plumbeus						*			*
26. Carpodacus cassini									*
27. Carpodacus frontalis								*	
28. Chrysomitris tristis					*				
29. Chrysomitris psaltria					*				
30. Chrysomitris pinus									*
31. Passerculus alaudinus		*							
32. Coturniculus perpallidus		*							
33. Zonotrichia leucophrys						*			
34. Melospiza fallax					*				
35. Amphispiza bilineata	*								
36. Spizella breweri	*								

	1.	2.	3.	4.	5.	6.	7.	8.	9.
37. Spizella arizonæ						*			*
38. Chondestes grammaca	*								
39. Hedymeles melanocephalus					*				
40. Cyanospiza amœna					*	*			
41. Pipilo megalonyx						*			
42. Pipilo chlorurus						*			
43. Dolichonyx oryzivorus		*							
44. Molothrus ater								*	
45. Xanthocephalus icterocephalus			*						
46. Agelæus phœniceus			*						
47. Scolecophagus cyanocephalus									*
48. Sturnella neglecta		*							
49. Icterus bullocki						*			
50. Cyanocitta woodhousii						*	*		
51. Corvus carnivorus								*	
52. Tyrannus verticalis								*	
53. Tyrannus carolinensis								*	
54. Myiarchus cinerascens									*
55. Sayornis sayus								*	
56. Contopus richardsoni								*	
57. Empidonax pusillus						*			
58. Antrostomus nuttalli	*								
59. Chordeiles henryi	*							*	
60. Panyptila saxatilis							*		
61. Selasphorus platycercus						*			
62. Trochilus alexandri						*			
63. Ceryle alcyon								*	
64. Melanerpes erythrocephalus								*	
65. Colaptes mexicanus								*	
66. Speotyto hypogæa	*								
67. Circus hudsonius		*							
68. Falco polyagrus								*	
69. Falco sparverius								*	
70. Buteo swainsoni								*	
71. Zenædura carolinensis								*	
72. Centrocercus urophasianus	*								

	1.	2.	3.	4.	5.	6.	7.	8.	9.
73. Pediœcetes columbianus	*								
74. Ægialitis vociferus								*	
75. Ægialitis nivosus				*					
76. Recurvirostra americana				*					
77. Himantopus mexicanus				*					
78. Steganopus wilsoni				*					
79. Ereunetes pusillus				*					
80. Tringa minutilla				*					
81. Tringoides macularius								*	
82. Symphemia semipalmata				*					
83. Numenius longirostris		*		*					
84. Falcinellus guarauna				*					
85. Ardea herodias				*					
86. Herodias egretta				*					
87. Botaurus minor		*	*	*					
88. Grus canadensis		*	*	*					
89. Rallus virginianus		*	*	*					
90. Porzana carolina		*	*	*					
91. Fulica americana			*	*					
92. Anas boschas		*	*	*					
93. Dafila acuta		*	*	*					
94. Chaulelasmus streperus		*	*	*					
95. Mareca americana		*	*	*					
96. Spatula clypeata		*	*	*					
97. Querquedula cyanoptera		*	*	*					
98. Querquedula discors		*	*	*					
99. Nettion carolinensis		*	*	*					
100. Erismatura rubida		*	*	*					
101. Graculus floridanus				*					
102. Sterna regia			*	*					
103. Sterna forsteri			*	*					
104. Hydrochelidon lariformis			*	*					
105. Podiceps occidentalis			*	*					
106. Podiceps californicus			*	*					
107. Podilymbus podiceps			*	*					

24 P R.

36. *Antelope Island, Great Salt Lake* (June 4–8, 1869).—Antelope Island. the largest of the islands in the Great Salt Lake, appears as a long range of barren mountains, rising from the water. The island is about fifteen miles in length, by about three in width at the broadest part, while its longitudinal axis culminates in a broken rocky ridge, the highest peak of which is, perhaps, some 1,500 to 2,000 feet above the surface of the lake. Some years ago, when the Salt Lake Valley was first settled by the Mormons, this island was indeed a part of the mainland, a strip of low ground then connecting it with the shore. The gradually increased annual rain-fall, brought about by the careful cultivation of the country by the early settlers, first by artificial irrigation, but in time aided by more and more frequent showers, wrought, among other notable changes in the character of the country, a great difference in the level of the lake, which grew higher, year by year, until the isthmus above mentioned became entirely submerged. The entire island presents the usual desert aspect, through the general absence of water, save at one place on the eastern shore, where springs of pure, fresh water irrigate the soil. This spot had been selected by representatives of the Mormon church as the site of a ranche; and it was here that our camp was established. In the thrifty orchard of this thriving little farm were found, nesting, the Cat-bird (*Galeoscoptes carolinensis*), Redstart (*Setophaga ruticilla*), Traill's Flycatcher (*Empidonax pusillus*), Bullock's Oriole (*Icterus bullocki*), and Warbling Vireo (*Vireosylvia swainsoni*); while about the buildings a pair of Mountain Blue-birds (*Sialia arctica*) had their abode, as did also several pairs of the House Finch (*Carpodacus frontalis*). The former were feeding a family of full-fledged young, and were the first of this species we ever saw at so low an altitude during the breeding-season, although they were observed later, under similar circumstances, in Salt Lake City.

In the sage-brush, *Oreoscoptes montanus*, *Amphispiza bilineata*, *Spizella breweri*, *Chondestes grammaca*, *Carpodacus frontalis*, *Eremophila chrysolœma*, *Collurio excubitoroides*, *Zenædura carolinensis*, *Agelæus phœniceus*, and *Ægialitis vociferus* were nesting; while, in a wet meadow, *Passerculus alaudinus*, *Agelæus phœniceus*, and *Numenius longirostris* had young. The only additional species noticed among the mountains, were *Cyanospiza amœna* and *Pipilo megalonyx*, in a ravine, and *Corvus carnivorus*, about the rocky peaks.

37. *Stansbury Island, Great Salt Lake* (June 12, 1869).—This island, like the one just described, was formerly connected with the mainland at its southern extremity; but it is now far out in the lake. No water could be found upon it, and consequently the birds were very scarce. The only species obtained was *Galeoscoptes carolinensis*, of which a single individual, probably a straggler, was secured.

38.—*Carrington Island, Great Salt Lake* (June 17, 1869).—The writer did not visit this island, but two members of the party, Messrs. Watson and Davis, who were there, brought with them on their return eggs of *Recurvirostra americana*, *Branta canadensis*, and *Larus californicus*, and reported various other water-fowl as breeding upon this island and a smaller one near by.

39. *"Rabbit Island," Great Salt Lake* (June 11, 1869).—This island was, at the time of our visit, merely a remnant of that portion of the southern shore of the lake which is now submerged. It consisted of merely a low knoll, occupying scarcely an acre in extent, and was named by our party "Rabbit Island" on account of the large numbers of hares (*Lepus callotis*) which were found on it. The latter were so numerous that when our boat landed they were seen rushing frantically around, several of them leaping into the water in their efforts to escape. The surface of this small island was covered with a thrifty growth of sage-brush and grease-wood, in which several pairs of *Oreoscoptes montanus* and *Spizella breweri* had their nests. A single nest of *Mareca americana*, containing ten eggs, was also found beneath a grease-wood bush.

40. *Parley's Park, Wahsatch Mountains, Utah* (June 23–July 2, and July 16–August 16, 1869)—This locality is an elevated park, or broad valley, lying at the eastern base of the main chain of the Wahsatch, and 25 miles distant from Salt Lake City. From the latter it was approached by the cañon of Jordan Creek, a considerable brook, whose sources are among the mountains surrounding this park, while along the eastern side

flowed Silver Creek, a tributary of the Weber. The average altitude of this park is about 6,500 feet, while some of the neighboring peaks of the main range rise 4,000 feet or more higher, and on whose bare, rocky summits spots of snow linger all the summer in the sheltered places. The general character of this park is that of a luxuriant meadow, parts of it under cultivation, the hill-sides being covered with a thick scrub of dwarf-oaks (*Quercus alba*, var.?), while the higher slopes are covered by a dense forest of Coniferæ, composed of several species (*Pinus flexilis*, *P. ponderosa*, *P. contorta*, *Abies menziesii*, *A. englemanni*, *A. douglassi*, *A. grandis*, *A. amabilis*, and *Juniperus virginiana*). The higher portions of the ravines are occupied by shady groves of tall aspens (*Populus tremuloides*), while bordering the lower portions of the streams grow scattered trees of the narrow-leafed cotton-wood (*Populus angustifolia*), and luxuriant shrubbery, of varied species. Indeed, the desert character of the country to the westward of the Great Salt Lake was here almost entirely wanting. As a natural consequence of increased prevalence and luxuriance of vegetation, the birds were much more numerous than we had found them at any previous camp, and while we found eastern trees and shrubs replacing their western representatives, or added as new elements to the western sylva, we also found many birds of the Eastern Region as common here as at any point in the Atlantic States. Such species were the Cat-bird (*Galeoscoptes carolinensis*) Swainson's Thrush (*Turdus swainsoni*), Redstart (*Setophaga ruticilla*), and White-crowned Sparrow (*Zonotrichia leucophrys*). A species of the plains, or the Campestrian Province (*Calamospiza bicolor*), was also here met with for the first time, while several birds characteristic of the Rocky Mountains proper were more or less common, as *Turdus auduboni*, *Helminthophaga virginiæ*, *Passerella schistacea*, *Junco caniceps*, and *Cyanura macrolopha*. In this beautiful park three species of Humming-birds were found, viz: *Selasphorus platycercus*, *Stellula calliope*, and *Trochilus alexandri*, the flowery meadows of the upper portion of the cañons being especially attractive to these "feathered gems."

The following is a complete list of the species found at this locality during the period indicated above, their distribution being explained by the annexed columns :—

	Sage-brush.	Meadows.	Marshes and brooks.	Shrubbery along streams.	Higher flowery slopes.	Scrub-oaks.	Aspen groves.	Coniferous woods.	Rocks, banks, etc.
1. Turdus migratorius					*		*	*	
2. Turdus swainsoni				*					
3. Turdus auduboni								*	
4. Galeoscoptes carolinensis				*					
5. Sialia arctica						*		*	*
6. Cinclus mexicanus									
7. Regulus calendula								*	
8. Parus montanus								*	
9. Sitta aculeata								*	
10. Sitta canadensis								*	
11. Sitta pygmæa								*	
12. Certhia americana								*	
13. Troglodytes parkmanni				*		*	*		
14. Telmatodytes paludicola			*						
15. Eremophila alpestris	*								
16. Helminthophaga celata							*	*	
17. Helminthophaga virginiæ						*			
18. Dendrœca æstiva				*					
19. Dendrœca auduboni							*		
20. Dendrœca nigrescens						*			
21. Geothlypis macgillivrayi				*					
22. Geothlypis trichas			*						
23. Icteria longicauda				*					
24. Myiodioctes pusillus				*			*?		
25. Setophaga ruticilla				*			~		
26. Pyranga ludoviciana						*?	*?	*	
27. Progne subis							*		
28. Petrochelidon lunifrons									*
29. Hirundo horreorum									*
30. Tachycineta bicolor							*		
31. Tachycineta thalassina							*		
32. Cotyle riparia									*
33. Stelgidopteryx serripennis									*
34. Vireosylvia swainsoni				*		*?	*		

	Sage-brush.	Meadows.	Marshes and brooks.	Shrubbery along streams.	Higher flowery slopes.	Scrub-oaks.	Aspen groves.	Coniferous woods.	Rocks, banks, etc.
35. Lanivireo plumbeus						*			
36. Collurio excubitoroides	*					*			
37. Carpodacus cassini							*	*	
38. Carpodacus frontalis				*			*		*
39. Chysomitris tristris				*					
40. Chysomitris psaltria				*					
41. Chysomitris pinus							*	*	
42. Passerculus alaudinus		*	*						
43. Pooecetes confinis		*			*				
44. Coturniculus perpallidus		*							
45. Melospiza lincolni					*				
46. Melospiza fallax				*					
47. Junco caniceps								*	
48. Spizella arizonæ					*	*			
49. Spizella breweri	*								
50. Zonotrichia leucophrys					*				
51. Chondestes grammaca	*								
52. Passerella schistacea				*					
53. Calamospiza bicolor		*							
54. Hedymeles melanocephalus				*					
55. Cyanospiza amœna				*					
56. Pipilo megalonyx				*		*			
57. Pipilo chlorurus					*				
58. Molothrus ater		*		*					
59. Agelæus phœniceus		*	*						
60. Xanthocephalus icterocephalus			*						
61. Icterus bullocki					*				
62. Sturnella neglecta	*	*							
63. Scolecophagus cyanocephalus					*		*		
64. Corvus carnivorus									*
65. Cyanocitta woodhousii					*	*			
66. Cyanura macrolopha								*	
67. Picicorvus columbianus								*	
68. Tyrannus verticalis					*				

	Sage-brush.	Meadows.	Marshes and brooks.	Shrubbery along streams.	Higher flowery slopes.	Scrub-oaks.	Aspen groves.	Coniferous woods.	Rocks, banks, etc.
69. Tyrannus carolinensis				*					
70. Myiarchus cinerascens				*		*			
71. Contopus borealis								*	
72. Contopus richardsoni				*		*	*		
73. Empidonax obscurus						*	*		
74. Empidonax difficilis								*	
75. Empidonax pusillus				*					
76. Antrostomus nuttalli	*								
77. Chordeiles henryi	*					*			
78. Trochilus alexandri				*	*				
79. Stellula calliope				*	*				
80. Selasphorus platycercus				*	*				
81. Ceryle alcyon			*						
82. Picus harrisi							*	*	
83. Picus gairdneri							*	*	
84. Sphyrapicus nuchalis				*			*		
85. Sphyrapicus thyroideus								*	
86. Colaptes mexicanus				*		*	*	*	*
87. Bubo subarcticus				*		*	*	*	
88. Falco polyagrus	*								*
89. Falco sparverius				*		*	?	?	*
90. Circus hudsonius		*	*						
91. Nisus cooperi				*		?	*		
92. Nisus fuscus				*		*	*		
93. Buteo calurus								*	
94. Buteo swainsoni					*	*			
95. Archibuteo saucti-johannis								*	*
96. Aquila canadensis								*	*
97. Rhinogryphus aura									
98. Zenædura carolinensis	*			*		*			
99. Canace obscura					*	*	*	*	
100. Bonasa umbelloides						*?	*		
101. Centrocercus urophasianus	*								
102. Pediœcetes columbianus	*	*							

	Sage-brush.	Meadows.	Marshes and brooks.	Shrubbery along streams.	Higher flowery slopes.	Scrub-oaks.	Aspen groves.	Coniferous woods.	Rocks, banks, etc.
103. Ægialitis vociferus			*						
104. Gallinago wilsoni		*	*						
105. Ereunetes pusillus			*						
106. Actodromus minutilla			*						
107. Symphemia semipalmata			*						
108. Tringoides macularius			*						
109. Rhyacophilus solitarius			*						
110. Numenius longirostris		*	*						
111. Grus canadensis		*	*						
112. Porzana carolina			*						
113. Porzana jamaicensis?			*						
114. Fulica americana			*						
115. Anas boschas		*	*						
116. Querquedula cyanoptera		*	*						

41. *Pack's Cañon, Uintah Mountains* (July 3–8, 1869).—This cañon is the valley of a considerable stream, flowing from the higher regions of one of the western peaks of the Uintah range into the Weber River, *via* Kamas Prairie. In its upper portion both valley and mountains are densely covered with a coniferous forest, while along the banks of the stream the extensive and vigorous growth of shrubbery consists of many species. The birds found in this locality were, in part, the following:—

Turdus migratorius.
Turdus swainsoni.
Galeoscoptes carolinensis.
Cinclus mexicanus.
Geothlypis macgillivrayi.
Dendrœca nigrescens.
Helminthophaga virginiæ.
Setophaga ruticilla.
Pyranga ludoviciana.
Chrysomitris tristis.
Chrysomitris psaltria.

Chrysomitris pinus.
Melospiza fallax.
Cyanura macrolopha.
Picicorvus columbianus.
Selasphorus platycercus.
Antrostomus nuttalli.
Chordeiles henryi.
Canace obscura.
Zenædura carolinensis.
Tringoides macularius.

42.—*Kamas Prairie, Utah* (July 9, 1869).—Kamas Prairie is a grassy valley, lying between the western spur of the Uintahs and the rolling eastern foot-hills of the Wahsatch. We noticed there the ordinary species of meadow localities, with the addition of *Actiturus bartramius*, which seemed to be quite common.

43. *Provo River, Utah* (July 10–11, 1869).—We followed this river, from the valley in which Heber City is situated, to Provo, near the shore of Utah Lake, through the deep and picturesque cañon cleft between two high peaks of the Wahsatch range. Among the dense and extensive willow thickets along this river we first found *Turdus fuscescens* and *Parus septentrionalis* (the former in great abundance), and the Magpie again numerous. The other species noticed along this river were, mainly, the following: *Galeoscoptes carolinensis* (abundant), *Setophaga ruticilla* (abundant), *Zenædura carolinensis* (abundant), *Dendrœca œstiva*, *Melospiza fallax*, *Icterus bullocki*, etc.

GENERAL REMARKS ON THE AVIFAUNA OF THE GREAT BASIN.

The total number of species of birds observed during the exploration is 262, of which only 24 were not seen east of the western slope of the Sierra Nevada; thus leaving a total of 238 species noticed in the Great Basin, including the approximate slopes of the Sierra Nevada and Wahsatch ranges, which form the boundary of the district on the west and east. This number includes both winter and summer birds, as well as the transient species, or those which merely pass through in the spring and fall; the latter were comparatively very few, however, since the complicated topography of the country afforded such a diversity of climate, with variations of altitude, that extreme northern and southern species passed the summer at different elevations on the same mountain ranges. Although the Great Basin forms a natural "Province" of the Western Region, the Sierra Nevada and main Rocky Mountain ranges forming its longitudinal boundaries, the mountains form much less of an actual barrier to the distribution of the species than might be supposed, as is clearly attested by the occurrence of a large proportion of the Californian species on the eastern slope of the former, down to the very verge of the desert, and the presence of so many eastern birds on the Wahsatch and other extreme western ranges of the latter system. It is, therefore, evident that not the mountains, but the deserts, check the species in their range away from their centers of distribution. It was also noticed that the species having a general range throughout the Interior were those particularly characteristic of, if not peculiar to, the Basin Province, and that their distribution was regulated less by mere topographical features than by other local conditions, the presence or absence of water and vegetation being the main agents.

As stated in the chapter on the local avifaunæ of the Great Basin (see pp. 316–328), certain groups of birds not only characterize particular zones of vegetation, but, also, isolated spots of a particular description, no matter at what altitude. An excellent example in illustration of this case is afforded by the humming-birds of the Interior, which are found wherever flowers grow in profusion, either in the valleys or on the mountains; they abound most on the upper slopes of the cañons, where numerous flowering plants bloom in such abundance as to form natural gardens; but on one day, in August, we observed an individual of *Selasphorus platycercus* in the door-yard of a ranche, in Ruby Valley, the altitude of which was between 6,000 and 7,000 feet, while a few hours later, as we stood on the summit of one of the lofty peaks of the East Humboldt range, at an elevation of about 12,000 feet above sea-level, and far above the fields of perpetual snow, an individual of the same species flew rapidly by, bound for the slopes of an adjoining cañon. The extreme vertical range of this species was thus shown to be nearly 6,000 feet, or more than one mile! In all cases where farms had been established in the valleys, humming-birds were noticed in the door-yards, though had not careful cultivation, with the aid of artificial irrigation, produced these oases in the desert, it is needless to say these birds would not have been seen there. Other cases in point are those of the birds frequenting the cañon shrubbery, which have a vertical range almost equal to that of the humming-birds, the same species following the streams from the valleys up to the snow-fields, provided the shrubbery continues so far. Certain birds which frequent woods, of whatsoever kind, are almost sure to be found wherever trees occur; thus *Colaptes mexicanus* or *Picus harrisi* may be observed the same day among the cotton-woods of the lowest valleys, less than a hundred feet above sea-level (as in California), and in the alpine woods, 10,000–12,000 feet above the sea.

Independent of these local modifications of the fauna, as controlled by conditions of environment, important changes were noticed in proceeding eastward, which are of a truly geographical nature. Thus, although the character of the country changed completely with the termination of the coniferous forests of the eastern slope of the Sierra Nevada, the change in the fauna was by no means so abrupt. New forms of course immediately made their appearance, or even predominated in number of species and individuals, over those we had met with before, but still many of the latter were not lost sight of completely until we had penetrated many miles into the desert country, but reappeared on the higher ranges of the western depression. This was particularly the case with the West Humboldt Mountains, where *Lanivireo cassini*, *Pipilo oregonus*, *Melospiza guttata*, *Zonotrichia coronata*, and *Ayelæus gubernator* were found in the fall, all being birds of the Pacific Province; while on the desert ranges, within sight of the Sierra, *Oreortyx pictus* was more or less plentiful. Along the eastern base of the Sierra Nevada, near Carson City, *Cyanocitta californica*—the "Valley Jay" of California—was found in place of *C. woodhousii*, which was the only species from the West Humboldt Mountains eastward, and the form characteristic of the Middle Province.

As we approached the eastern border of the Basin we met with species characteristic of the Eastern Region or the Rocky Mountain District of the Middle Province, as gradually as on the western side we had left the Californian forms behind; each successive high range introducing a larger number to the list. But even in this district, where so many eastern forms were met with, there was still a sprinkling of the extreme western element, which, however, seemed to have reached nearly to its eastern limit in the upper Humboldt valley or the neighboring mountains, where such birds as *Turdus guttatus*, *Helminthophaga lutescens*, *Dendrœca occidentalis*, *D. townsendi*, and *Selasphorus rufus* were noticed *as autumnal migrants*.

It seems to be a general rule, that western birds have a tendency to extend eastward during their fall migrations, thus spreading over the whole of the Western Region at this season, though in summer their habitat may be confined strictly to the area of Pacific-coast drainage. This circumstance we have previously alluded to, in these words:—[1]

"Another very remarkable peculiarity of the Wahsatch region, which I wish particularly to mention in this connection, is the fact that in the case of representative species or races, the Eastern or Rocky Mountain forms breed there, while the more Western forms replace them in winter. Thus, *Zonotrichia leucophrys* and *Junco hyemalis*, var. *caniceps*, are the only species of these two genera which breed on the Wahsatch, and they nest there very numerously; but in the fall their place is taken by the western *Z. leucophrys*, var. *gambeli* [=*intermedia*] and *J. hyemalis*, var. *oregonus*, which are unknown in summer. *Lanivireo solitaria*, var. *plumbea*, breeds there, while var. *solitaria*, coming from the northwestward, replaces it in autumn. The same is the case with *Turdus pallasi*, var. *auduboni* (summer resident), and var. *nanus* (autumnal migrant); and apparently the case also with *Helminthophaga virginiæ* (summer), and *H. ruficapilla* (autumn)."[2]

The eastern species occurring within the Basin were found to have reached their maximum in the Salt Lake Valley and adjacent country to the eastward, but, as was the case with the western series, some of them had intruded so far within the western domain as to reach the opposite side. Thus, *Tyrannus carolinensis* was not rare *during the breeding-season* in the lower Truckee Valley, almost at the foot of the Sierra Nevada. *Ectopistes migratoria* was obtained in the West Humboldt Mountains, although the only individual seen was a young one, and evidently a straggler. In the East Humboldt Mountains, *Turdus swainsoni*, *Helminthophaga ruficapilla*, and

---

[1] Proc. Essex Inst., Vol. V, Nov., 1873, pp. 170, 171. ["Notes on the Bird Fauna of the Salt Lake Valley and the adjacent portions of the Wahsatch Mountains."]

[2] Other examples of species which have an extreme western or northwestern distribution during the breeding-season, but which migrate in fall both eastward and southward, are, *Helminthophaga lutescens*, *Dendrœca occidentalis*, *D. townsendi*, and *Selasphorus rufus*, found as far east as the Clover Mountains, with the addition of *Lanivireo cassini*, *Melospiza guttata*, *Pipilo oregonus*, *Zonotrichia coronata*, and *Agelœus gubernator*, which in September and October were obtained in the West Humboldt range. The most plausible explanation of this eastward migration would appear to be found in the supposition that nearly, if not all, these migrants were from the Valley of the Columbia River, whose main tributary, the Snake River, heads almost directly north of the Great Salt Lake; the birds of the Columbia basin would naturally follow the valleys of these upper tributaries as the route offering the least obstacle to their southward passage, many species which do not breed eastward of the lower Columbia thus regularly reaching the eastern border, if not the whole extent, of the Great Basin. Whether their return northward is by the same route, remains to be determined.

Dolichonyx oryzivorus were more or less common in the fall. In the Wahsatch district, including the Salt Lake Valley, were *Turdus fuscescens*, *Galeoscoptes carolinensis*, *Setophaga ruticilla*, and *Zonotrichia leucophrys* as abundant summer residents, and *Melanerpes erythrocephalus* as a summer straggler; while on Kamas Prairie, between the Wahsatch and the Uintahs, *Actiturus bartramius* was common in July.

Another result of our investigations was the discovery of the fact that several species, supposed to be peculiarly eastern, are in reality among those which inhabit the entire breadth of the continent. Among these were *Coccyzus americanus*, which was found both at Sacramento, California, and in the Truckee Valley, in June and July, and *Coturniculus passerinus*, which was as abundant in the vicinity of Sacramento as at any eastern locality; also, *Spizella monticola*, heretofore supposed to be of casual or accidental occurrence in the West, but which was found to be an abundant winter resident in suitable localities. There was also seen at two places in the western depression—the West Humboldt Mountains (October) and the Truckee Valley (November)—a *Colaptes*, which was probably the eastern *C. auratus*, though it may possibly have been *C. chrysoides* of the Gila and Saint Lucas districts, since it is certain that the individuals in question were not the form intermediate between *C. auratus* and *C. mexicanus*, known as *C. "hybridus."*[1]

Somewhat of an anomaly was noticed in the distribution of several species in the region indicated, in their abundance on the two opposite

---

[1] In addition to these species, the following are known to occur westward of the main divide of the Rocky Mountains:—

1. Dendrœca blackburniæ; Ogden, Utah, Sept.—*Allen.*
2. Dendrœca coronata; Fort Bridger, Wyoming.—*Baird.*
3. Seiurus noveboracensis; Fort Bridger, Wyoming.—*Baird.*
4. Cistothorus stellaris; Utah Lake; breeding.—*Henshaw.*
5. Vireosylvia olivacea; Ogden, Utah, September.—*Allen.* ["More or less common"]; Fort Bridger, Wyoming.—*Baird.*
6. Junco hyemalis; Iron Springs, Utah, October 4.—*Henshaw.*
7. Melospiza palustris; Washington, Utah, October 23.—*Henshaw.*
8. Quiscalus æneus; Fort Bridger, Wyoming—*Baird.*
9. Empidonax minimus; Fort Bridger, Wyoming.—*Baird.*
10. Rallus elegans; Ogden, Utah, September.—*Allen.*
11. Ibis alba; Ogden, Utah, September.—*Allen.* ["Said to be frequent in summer."]
12. Anas obscura; Rush Lake, Utah, November.—*Yarrow.*

mountain ranges and their apparent absence from the entire intervening territory. Such was particularly conspicuous regarding *Sialia mexicana* and *Lophophanes inornatus*, which, if occurring at all in the Basin proper, were so rare that they were not noticed. An apparent explanation of this exceptional range is the general absence of suitable localities over the greater portion of this vast area; but the circumstance that the species named were still wanting on the Wahsatch and Uintahs, where the conditions of environment are in every way favorable, would seem to suggest other causes. The partial or entire absence of certain woodland species from the sufficiently extensive forests of the higher interior ranges was indeed a subject of continual speculation, since they were searched for in vain, after leaving the Sierra Nevada, until the Wahsatch or Uintah woodlands were reached, when many of them reappeared, while others did not, although they are known to occur in the same latitudes on the main Rocky Mountain ranges. Besides the species named above, we may mention *Scops flammeola, Glaucidium gnoma*, and *Columba fasciata*, which are common to the two widely-separated districts named, but which have not yet been recorded from any intermediate locality; while other species, found both on the Sierra Nevada and Wahsatch, were found to be either extremely rare or apparently not existing at all on any ranges between. These species are the following: *Regulus calendula. Parus montanus, Sitta aculeata, S. pygmœa, Certhia americana*, and *Sphyrapicus thyroideus*. All of these, it may be observed, are of pinicoline habits.

It seems to us that the most reasonable explanation of the abundance of these birds on the Sierra Nevada and Rocky Mountains, and their rarity in or absence from the intervening region, is to be found in the fact that the two great mountain systems named approximate closely along the northern and southern borders of the United States, thus allowing short and scarcely interrupted passage from one to the other, without being obliged to cross the wide expanse of desert which intervenes along the line of our route.

The following tables are intended to show more briefly the changes noticed in the bird-fauna during our transit of the Basin, as well as the main local peculiarities noted by the way :—

SPECIES OF THE GREAT BASIN NOT OBSERVED IN CALIFORNIA.

Species.	Range within the Basin.
1. Turdus auduboni	Eastern side.
2. Oreoscoptes montanus	Entirely across.
3. Sialia arctica	Entirely across.
4. Psaltriparus plumbeus	Entirely across.
5. Psaltriparus melanotis	Eastern side; straggler.
6. Salpinctes obsoletus	Entirely across.
7. Catherpes conspersus	Entirely across.
8. Helminthophaga virginiæ	Eastern side.
9. Lanivireo plumbeus	Eastern side.
10.? Phænopepla nitens	Western side.
11. Carpodacus cassini	Entirely across.
12. Junco caniceps	Eastern side.
13. Amphispiza bilineata	Entirely across.
14. Amphispiza nevadensis	Entirely across.
15. Melospiza fallax	Entirely across, except western border.
16. Passerella schistacea	Eastern side, chiefly.
17. Calamospiza bicolor	Eastern side; straggler.
18. Pipilo megalonyx	Entirely across, except western border.
19. Pipilo chlorurus	Entirely across.
20. Gymnokitta cyanocephala	Western side.
21. Pica hudsonica	Entirely across.
22. Cyanura macrolopha	Eastern side.
23. Cyanocitta woodhousii	Entirely across.
24. Sayornis sayus	Entirely across.
25. Empidonax obscurus	Entirely across.
26. Empidonax hammondi	Entirely across.
27. Panyptila saxatilis	Eastern side.
28. Selasphorus platycercus	Eastern side.
29. Stellula calliope	Entirely across.
30. Sphyrapicus nuchalis	Entirely across.
31. Sphyrapicus thyroideus	Entirely across.
32. Colaptes hybridus	Entirely across.
33. Colaptes auratus?	Western side.
34. Canace obscura	Entirely across.
35. Bonasa umbelloides	Entirely across.
36. Pediœcetes columbianus	Entirely across.
37. Centrocercus urophasianus	Entirely across.
38. Falcinellus guarauna	Eastern side.
39. Falcinellus thalassinus	Western side.

SPECIES OF THE EASTERN REGION FOUND IN THE BASIN.

1. Turdus swainsoni	Eastern side.
2. Turdus fuscescens	Eastern side.
3. Galeoscoptes carolinensis	Eastern side.

Species.	Range within the Basin.
4. Helminthophaga celata	Eastern side.
5. Setophaga ruticilla	Eastern side.
6. Lanivireo solitarius	Entirely across.
7. Zonotrichia leucophrys	Eastern side.
8. Dolichonyx oryzivorus	Eastern side.
9. Tyrannus carolinensis	Entirely across.
10. Melanerpes erythrocephalus	Eastern side.
11. Ectopistes migratoria	West Humboldt Mts.; straggler.
12. Actiturus bartramius	Eastern side.
13. Querquedula discors	Entirely across.

LOCALITIES WHERE CERTAIN SPECIES WERE FIRST MET WITH IN JOURNEYING EASTWARD.

Eastern slope of Sierra Nevada.

1. Oreoscoptes montanus. July.
2. Sialia arctica. December–April 25.
3. Carpodacus cassini. March 21–April 4.
4. Salpinctes obsoletus. Summer resident.
5. Catherpes conspersus. Constant resident.
6. Amphispiza nevadensis. Constant resident.
7. Amphispiza bilineata. Summer resident.
8. Spizella monticola. Winter resident.
9. Passerella megarhyncha. From April 25 through summer.
10. Passerella schistacea. February and March; scarce.
11. Pipilo chlorurus. Summer resident.
12. Scolecophagus cyanocephalus. Winter resident in valleys, breeding on mountains.
13. Gymnokitta cyanocephala. Constant resident.
14. Pica hudsonica. Constant resident.
15. Sayornis sayus. Summer resident.
16. Empidonax obscurus. Summer resident.
17. Antrostomus nuttalli. Summer resident.
18. Chordeiles henryi. Summer resident.
19. Picoides arcticus. Winter resident; rare.
20. Sphyrapicus thyroideus. Constant resident.
21. Sphyrapicus nuchalis. Casual (April 4).
22. Falco polyagrus. Constant resident.
23. Canace obscura. Constant resident.
24. Centrocercus urophasianus.

Truckee Valley (below Virginia Mountains).

1. Troglodytes hyemalis. December.
2. Tachycineta thalassina. Summer resident.
3. Tyrannus carolinensis. Summer resident.

4. Nephœcetes borealis. Summer resident.
5. Chætura vauxi. Summer resident.
6. Selasphorus rufus. August; excessively abundant.
7. Steganopus wilsoni. May; rare.

West Humboldt Mountains.

1. Psaltriparus plumbeus. September–October.
2. Lanivireo cassini. September 9–25.
3. Lanivireo solitarius. September.
4. Melospiza guttata. One specimen; October 3.
5. Zonotrichia coronata. One specimen; October 7.
6. Cyanocitta woodhousii. September–October.
7. Ectopistes migratoria. One specimen: September 10.
8. Colaptes auratus. ? One specimen: October.

Soda Lake, Carson Desert.

1. ? Phænopepla nitens. June 27; rare.

Toyabe Mountains (near Austin).

1. Panyptila saxatilis. July 4; one specimen.

Ruby Mountains (eastern slope).

1. Psaltriparus melanotis. ? One specimen; August 4.
2. Dendrœca nigrescens. Summer resident.
3. Helminthophaga virginiæ. Summer resident.
4. Lanivireo plumbeus. Summer resident.
5. Loxia leucoptera. One specimen; August 12.
6. Selasphorus platycercus. Summer resident.
7. Stellula calliope. Summer resident.

East Humboldt Mountains (eastern slope).

1. Turdus swainsoni. September 1–11.
2. Dendrœca townsendi. September 8–24.
3. Dendrœca occidentalis. August 29.
4. Helminthophaga ruficapilla. September 6.
5. Empidonax hammondi. September 5–8. [Also found on eastern slope of the Sierra Nevada.]

Here were seen the most eastern individuals of *Selasphorus rufus*, a pair having been observed, and the male secured, September 8.

Ruby Valley (west side, near Franklin Lake).

1. Dolichonyx oryzivorus. August and September.
2. Falcinellus guarauna. August and September.

From here northward, *Lepus callotis* was found to be replaced by *L. campestris.*

25 P R

Upper Humboldt Valley (west of Clover Mountains).

1. Turdus guttatus. September 16.
2. Sitta canadensis. September 10.
3. Ampelis cedrorum. September 10.
4. Picus gairdneri. September 12–17.
5. Nisus fuscus. September 10.
6. Pediœcetes columbianus. September 16.

Thousand Spring Valley.

1. Nyctale acadica. September 24; one specimen.

Vicinity of Salt Lake City (including shores and islands of the lake, City Creek Cañon, etc.).

1. Galeoscoptes carolinensis. Common summer resident.
2. Setophaga ruticilla. Common summer resident.
3. Chrysomitris psaltria. Rare summer resident.
4. Pipilo megalonyx. Abundant summer resident.
5. Melanerpes erythrocephalus. One specimen, June.
6. Ægialitis nivosus. Very abundant summer resident.

Parley's Park (Wahsatch Mountains).

1. Junco caniceps. Common summer resident.
2. Zonotrichia leucophrys. Common summer resident.
3. Calamospiza bicolor. One specimen, July 30.
4. Cyanura macrolopha. Common resident.
5. Bonasa umbelloides. Rare resident.

Kamas Prairie.

1. Actiturus bartramius. July.

Provo Cañon.

1. Turdus fuscescens. Very abundant summer resident.
2. Parus septentrionalis. Summer resident.

CATALOGUE OF THE SPECIES COLLECTED OR OBSERVED.[1]

Turdidæ. Page.

*1. Turdus migratorius, L............ 391
2. Turdus guttatus (Pall.).......... 393
*3. Turdus auduboni, Baird......... 394
*4. Turdus ustulatus, Nutt.......... 395

Turdidæ— Continued. Page.

*5. Turdus swainsoni, Caban........ 397
*6. [Turdus fuscescens, Steph.]....... 398
*7. Galeoscoptes carolinensis (L.). ... 399
*8. Oreoscoptes montanus (Towns.)... 399

[1] For the sake of convenience, we adopt a strictly binomial nomenclature, even in case of forms which are unquestionably mere geographical races. Species distinguished by an asterisk are those which were observed during the breeding-season; those in italics were seen only in California, while those not in the collection are inclosed in brackets.

REPORT PROPER.

[EMBRACING BIOGRAPHICAL AND OTHER NOTES ON THE SPECIES OBSERVED.]

FAMILY TURDIDÆ—THRUSHES.

TURDUS MIGRATORIUS.[1]

Robin-Thrush; American Robin.

Turdus migratorius, LINN., S. N., I, 1766, 292.—BAIRD, B. N. Am., 1858, 218; Cat.
  N. Am. B., 1859, No. 155; Rev. Am. B., 1864, 28.—COOPER, B. Cal., I, 1870,
  7.—COUES, Key, 1872, 71, fig. 13; Check List, 1873, No. 1; B. N.W., 1874, 1.
Turdus migratorius var. *migratorius*, B. B. & R., Hist. N. Am. B., I, 1874, 25, pl. II,
  fig. 3.—HENSHAW, 1875, 143.

The Common Robin was not found at Sacramento in June, nor was
it seen anywhere in the Sacramento Valley until we neared the foot-hills of

---

[1] For obvious reasons, we have abstained from burdening this report with numerous references, and have confined the citations to the more important *general* works,
including, of course, the original description of the species, and the first authority for
the binomial combination as adopted. Those desiring other references are advised to
consult Dr. Coues's " Birds of the Northwest," and Mr. Henshaw's report, cited below,
where may be found in the very complete synonymatic tables almost any reference
required. The general works quoted in this report are the following:—

(1.) "BAIRD, B. N. Am., 1858."—Vol. IX, Pacific R. R. Reports.—Birds: by Spencer
F. Baird, Assistant Secretary Smithsonian Institution, with the coöperation of John
Cassin and George N. Lawrence. Washington, D. C., 1858.

(2.) "BAIRD, Catal. N. Am. B., 1859."—Catalogue of North American Birds,
chiefly in the Museum of the Smithsonian Institution. [First octavo edition.] Washington: Smithsonian Institution [Smithsonian Miscellaneous Collections, No. 108], 1859.

(3.) "BAIRD, Rev. Am. B."—Review of American Birds, in the Museum of the
Smithsonian Institution. Part I. Washington: Smithsonian Institution [Smithsonian
Miscellaneous Collections, No. 181], 1864–1866. [Edition with indices, published 1872.]

(4.) "B. B. & R., Hist. N. Am. B."—History of North American Birds, by S. F.
Baird, T. M. Brewer, and R. Ridgway [etc.], 3 vols. Boston: Little, Brown & Co., 1874.

(5.) "COUES, Key."—Key to North American Birds [etc.]. By Elliott Coues,
Assistant Surgeon United States Army. Salem: Naturalists' Agency, 1872.

(6.) "COUES, Check List."—Check List of North American Birds. By Dr. Elliott
Coues, U. S. A. Salem: Naturalists' Agency, 1874.

(7.) "COUES, B. N.W."—Birds of the Northwest [etc.]: Miscellaneous Publica-

the Sierra Nevada, where the first individuals of the species were noticed among the scattered pines which formed the outposts of the continuous forest of the mountains. From the Sierra Nevada eastward, however, it was continually met with in all wooded localities, the aspen groves of the higher cañons being its favorite resort during the summer, while in winter it descended to the lower valleys, and passed the season among the willows or cotton-woods and attendant shrubbery along the streams. In the vicinity of Carson City it was extremely abundant from the middle of March until the middle of April, and assembled in large flocks among the scrubby thickets of dwarf-plum bushes along the base of the Sierra. In August they were quite plentiful in the valley of the Truckee, below the "Big Bend," being attracted thither by the abundance of fruit of the buffalo-berry bushes (*Shepherdia argentea*), which at this time formed an important portion of their food; and later in the season they were observed feeding on service-berries (the fruit of *Amelanchier canadensis*) along the foot-hills of the eastern ranges.

In their manners and notes we could not detect the minutest difference between the western and eastern Robins, although climatic or other geographical influences have perceptibly modified their plumage.[1] In all respects it seems the same bird, the song and other notes being identical.

tions, No. 3, U. S. Geological Survey of the Territories, F. V. Hayden, U. S. Geologist-in-charge. Washington: Government Printing Office, 1874.

(8.) "COOPER, Orn. Cal., I."—[Reports Geological Survey of California. J. D. Whitney, State Geologist.] Ornithology. Vol. I. Land Birds. Edited by S. F. Baird, from the manuscript and notes of J. G. Cooper. Published by authority of the Legislature. Cambridge: [Printed by Welch, Bigelow & Co.,] 1870.

(9.) "HENSHAW, 1875."—Report upon Geographical and Geological Explorations and Surveys west of the One Hundredth Meridian, in charge of First Lieut. Geo. M. Wheeler, Corps of Engineers, U. S. Army [etc.]. Chapter III, Vol. V.—Zoology. Washington: Government Printing Office, 1875.

[NOTE.—In the *History of North American Birds*, *Birds of the Northwest*, and other recent publications, occasional reference is made to a "Zoology of the 40th Parallel [in press]," or "Rep. 40th Parallel [in press]." It is to be understood that these citations do *not* apply to the present report, but to the original one, stereotyped in 1870, but suppressed on account of unavoidable delay in its publication. In its present form the report is substantially the same, but the changes necessary to bring it up to date render the citations of pages and names frequently inapplicable.]

[1] The western birds of this species may be distinguished as a geographical race, for which the name *Turdus migratorius propinquus*, Ridgway, is proposed. See [*Bulletin of the Nuttall Ornithological Club*, Vol. II, January, 1877, p. 9.]

List of specimens.[1]

226. ♂ *ad.;* Camp 19, West Humboldt Mountains, Nevada, October 4, 1867. $10\frac{3}{8}$—16—$5\frac{5}{16}$—$4\frac{5}{16}$—$\frac{7}{16}$—$1\frac{1}{8}$—$4\frac{1}{2}$—$1\frac{3}{4}$. Bill, brownish-black, more yellowish-brown along commissure, and on lower mandible; iris, brown: tarsi and toes, brownish-black.

269, ♂ *ad.;* Truckee meadows, Nevada, November 8. 11—$16\frac{7}{8}$—$5\frac{1}{2}$—$4\frac{1}{2}$—$\frac{7}{8}$—$1\frac{1}{4}$—$4\frac{3}{8}$—$1\frac{7}{8}$. Upper mandible, dilute yellowish horn-color; tip and culmen, blackish; lower, more yellowish; gonys and tip, black; iris, brown; tarsi and toes, deep black.

358, ♀ *ad.;* Truckee Valley, December 16. $10\frac{3}{8}$—$15\frac{1}{2}$—$5\frac{1}{2}$—$4\frac{1}{2}$—$\frac{7}{8}$—$1\frac{1}{8}$—$4\frac{1}{4}$—2. Same remarks.

359, ♂ *ad.;* same date and locality. $10\frac{1}{8}$—$16\frac{1}{4}$—$5\frac{1}{2}$—$4\frac{1}{2}$—$\frac{27}{32}$—$1\frac{1}{8}$—$4\frac{1}{4}$—2. Bill, nearly uniform blackish; yellowish on upper edge of lower mandible; iris, brown; interior of mouth, deep yellow-orange; tarsi and toes, intense black.

803, nest and eggs (4); Truckee Valley, June 6, 1868. Nest in cotton-wood tree.

820, nest and eggs (4); Toyabe Mountains, 7,500 feet altitude, July 3, 1868. Nest in a copse along stream, about six feet from ground, in choke-cherry bush.

851, nest and eggs (4); Camp 19, East Humboldt Mountains, July 22. Nest on piñon tree, about fifteen feet from ground. (8,000 feet altitude.)

1265, 1266, 1267, 1268, nest and eggs; 1269, single egg; Parley's Park (Wahsatch Mountains), Utah, June 23, 1869. Nests in cotton-woods along a stream.

1287, nest and eggs (4); Parley's Park, June 25. Bushes along stream.

1301, nest and eggs (2); Parley's Park, June 27. Nest in aspen.

1338, nest and eggs (4); Parley's Park, June 28. Willows along stream.

1367, nest and eggs (3); Uintah Mountains (Pack's Cañon), Utah, July 3, 1869. Nests in thorn-apple bushes along stream.

1368, nest and eggs (3); same locality and date.

1395, nest and eggs (4); Parley's Park, July, 1869.

TURDUS GUTTATUS.

Hermit Thrush.

α. guttatus—Dwarf Hermit Thrush.

Muscicapa guttata, PALL., Zoog. Rosso-As., I, 1811, 465. [*Juv.*]

Turdus nanus, AUD., Orn. Biog., V, 1839, 201, pl. cci (doubtful whether this form!). BAIRD, Birds N. Am., 1858, 213; Cat. N. Am. Birds, 1859, No. 150; Review, 1864, .—COOPER, Orn. Cal., I, 1870, 4.

Turdus pallasi var. *nanus*, COUES, Key, 1872, 72; Check List, 1873, No. 4 b.—B. B. & R., Hist. N. Am. B., I, 1874, 20, pl. I, fig. 7.

Turdus pallasi. b. *nanus*, COUES, B. Northwest, 1874, p. 3.—HENSHAW, 1875, 146.

But one individual of the Dwarf Thrush was met with, this one being secured. It is probably more or less common, however, during the migra-

[1] In the enumeration of specimens certain figures require explanation. The first number denotes the current number of the specimen as registered in the Field Catalogue. The measurements are as follows, in regular sequence: (1), length; (2), ex-

tions, particularly in the fall, in all suitable localities embraced within the country traversed by the expedition. The specimen in question was obtained on Trout Creek, a tributary of the Humboldt River, and when observed was perched on a low twig in a willow copse, silently watching us as we reclined on the grassy bank of the brook. It uttered no note whatever, and exhibited no fear at our presence.

List of specimens.

928, ♀ *ad;* Trout Creek, Upper Humboldt Valley, Nevada, September 16, 1868. 6¹¹⁄₆—10¹³⁄₆—2⁵⁄₆. Bill, black; basal half of the lower mandible, lilaceous-white; interior of the mouth, rich yellow; iris, dark bister; tarsi and toes, pale purplish-brown— the toes darkest, the tarsi paler along their posterior edge.

β. auduboni—Rocky Mountain Hermit Thrush; Audubon's Hermit Thrush.

> *Merula silens,* SWAINS., Phil. Mag., I, 1827, 369 (not *Turdus silens,* VIEILL. 1823 = *T. fuscescens*). *Turdus silens,* BAIRD, B. N. Am., 1858, 213, 922; Cat. N. Am. Birds, 1859, No. 149a.
> *Turdus auduboni,* BAIRD, Rev. Am. Birds, 1864, 16.
> *Turdus pallasi* var. *auduboni,* COUES, Key, 1872, 72; Check List, 1873, No. 4a. —B. B. & R., Hist. N. Am. B., I., 1874, 21, pl. I, fig. 8.—HENSHAW, 1875, 144.
> *Turdus pallasi.* b. *auduboni,* COUES, Birds N.W., 1874, 3.

The large Mountain Thrush was first met with in the Wahsatch range, where it inhabited chiefly the deep ravines of the pine region. The first specimen seen was shot May 26, in City Creek Cañon, near Salt Lake City; but this was probably a mere straggler from the higher portions of the mountains. In its manner of flight, which is gliding and noiseless, this Thrush greatly resembles Townsend's Solitaire (*Myiadestes townsendi*), the resemblance being increased by the pale ochraceous band across the base of the remiges, which shows as a very conspicuous feature on both birds when flying. The haunts of this bird were so difficult of access from our

---

pause of wings when fully stretched; (3), length of wing from tip of the longest primary to the carpal joint; (4), the same measurement to the metacarpo-phalangeal articulation; (5), length of the culmen (not including the cere, and if the bill is curved, the chord, and not the arc, of the curve); (6), length of the tarsus *in front;* (7), length of the tail to the base of the coccyx; (8), length of the tail to the tip of the longest upper coverts. If a measurement is wanting, *its place is supplied by an interrogation point, the order being invariably the same.* All measurements, and notes on color of eyes, etc., are from fresh specimens, before skinning.

camp, and its manners so reserved, that we could not learn much regarding its habits, nor did we hear its song. The latter, however, is probably little different from that of the eastern bird, *T. guttatus pallasi.*

List of specimens.

1051, ♂ *ad.;* City Creek Cañon (near Salt Lake City), Wahsatch Mountains, Utah, May 26, 1869. 7¾—12¾. Bill, black; basal half of lower mandible, dull yellow; iris, brown; tarsi and toes, pale brown.

1487, ♀ *juv.;* Parley's Park, August 5, 1869. 7½—12½. Bill, black, the lower mandible purplish basally; interior and angle of the mouth, yellow; iris, dark brown; tarsi and toes, lilaceous-white; claws, brown.

1488, ♂ *juv.;* same locality and date. 7⅞—13. Same remarks.

1489, ♂ *juv.;* same locality and date. 7⅝—12½. Same remarks.

1498, ♀ *ad.;* Parley's Park, August 10. 7½—12. Bill, black; basal half of lower mandible, whitish; interior of mouth, deep yellow; iris, brown; tarsi and toes, very pale brownish flesh-color.

1499, ♂ *juv.;* 7⅞—12⅝. 1500, ♂ *juv.;* 7—12¾. Same date and remarks.

TURDUS USTULATUS.

Olive-backed Thrush.

α. ustulatus—Oregon Thrush; Russet-backed Thrush.

Turdus ustulatus, NUTT., Man., I, 1840, 400 ("*cestulatus*").—BAIRD, B. N. Am., 1858, 215, pl. 81, fig. 1; Cat. N. Am. B., 1859, No. 152; Rev. Am. B., 1864, 18.— COOPER, Orn. Cal., 4 (part).

Turdus swainsoni var. *ustulatus,* COUES, Key, 1872, 73; Check List, 1873, No. 5 b.—B. B. & R., Hist. N. Am. B., I, 1874, pl. I, fig. 2.

Turdus swainsoni. c. *ustulatus,* COUES, B. N.W., 1874, 4.

Turdus nanus, COOPER, Orn. Cal., I, 4 (part).

The Russet-backed or Oregon Thrush, which we consider a mere geographical form of the same species as Swainson's Thrush, or at most a very closely related species, was first met with in the pine-region of the Sierra Nevada, on the western slope of that range, at an altitude of about 4,000 or 5,000 feet above the Sacramento Valley. It inhabited there the deep ravines, where the undergrowth was extremely dense and overtopped by a thick growth of gigantic Coniferæ, extending in a vast unbroken forest for hundreds of miles over the mountains to the North and South. Eastward of that range it was met with but once, a single individual having been obtained, on the second of June, in the Truckee Valley, not far from the eastern base of the Sierra Nevada, the individual in question being no doubt a last lingering one, since no others were observed after that date, all having departed for the mountains to the westward. The species is known to migrate in winter southward along the Pacific slope as far as Costa Rica, but its summer-home is chiefly among the forest-clad mountains and wooded valleys from California to British Columbia and Sitka.

The song of this Thrush much resembles that of the *T. swainsoni*, but is different in some important respects, conspicuous among which is its finer quality. Its modulation is quite correctly expressed by Mr. Nuttall [*Manual of the Ornithology of the United States and Canada*, I, 1840, p. 401], who describes it as resembling the syllables "*wit-wit, t'villia-t'villia*"; but to convey to the reader even the slightest idea of its tone and effect would be the vainest endeavor. We heard the enchanting songs of these birds under circumstances calculated to make a lasting impression. It was in the midst of the dense and lofty forests of the Sierra Nevada, about half way up the western slope, that we rested for the Sabbath from our journey across the mountains. Hemmed in and overshadowed by giant forest trees, we halted, with rippling and sparkling brooks from the snow-fields far above dashing through the ferns and varied herbage, the roadside bedecked with the gay and lovely flowers so characteristic of Californian glades, while below yawned the depths of a dark ravine, through which dashed and roared a mountain torrent. In the tall pines, overhead, skulked the noisy Jays and Nutcrackers (*Cyanura frontalis* and *Picicorvus columbianus*), mingling their discordant notes with the twittering of the wood-peckers, who sported about the branches of the dead trees. But certain outbursts of rarest melody, heard at intervals from the dark recesses of the deep ravine, drew the attention of every one in camp; notes of exceeding simplicity, yet full of tenderest expression and thrilling effect, far finer than the softest and sweetest notes of the flute. These harmonious carols would be taken up first by one, then by another, musician, then answered from a distant portion of the dell. It was long before the author of these wild melodies could be seen, but patient search revealed a little brown bird, afterward determined to be this species, shyly flitting into the gloomy maze of foliage at our approach.

List of specimens.

779, ♀ ad.; Truckee Reservation, Nevada, June 2, 1868. 7⅝—12—3¼. Bill, black, basal half of lower mandible, pale brownish-lilac; iris, sepia; tarsi, dilute lilaceous-brown; toes, darker.

β. swainsoni—Swainson's Thrush; Olive-backed Thrush.

Turdus swainsoni, CABANIS, Tschudi's Fauna Peruana, 1844-'46, 188.—BAIRD, B. N. Am., 1858, 216; Cat. N. Am. B., No. 153; Rev. Am. B., 1864, 19.—COOPER, Orn. Cal., 6.—COUES, Key, 1872, 72; Check List, 1873, No. 5.—B. B. & R., Hist. N. Am. B., I, 1874, 14, pl. I, fig. 4.—HENSHAW, 1875, 147.

Turdus swainsoni. a. swainsoni, COUES, B. N.W., 1874, 4.

After leaving the Sierra Nevada, not a single individual of any species of the smaller Thrushes was met with until we arrived at the East Humboldt Mountains, in eastern Nevada, where the Olive-backed Thrush was encountered, in considerable numbers, in the eastern cañons of that range. It was during the season of their southward migration, and it is uncertain whether they came from the northward, or whether they had bred in the cañons where they were observed. During the ensuing spring and summer they were found in still greater abundance among the Wahsatch Mountains, on the opposite side of the Salt Lake Basin, in the thickets bordering the cañon streams, particularly in the elevated "parks," thus occupying a region intermediate between that of the Rocky Mountain Hermit Thrush (*T. auduboni*) of the pine-region, and that of the Tawny Thrush (*T. fuscescens*) of the lower valleys.

The song of this species is simple and brief, but very sweet, though less so than that of either *T. fuscescens* or *T. ustulatus*.

List of specimens.

886, ♂ ad.; East Humboldt Mountains, Nevada, September 1, 1868. 7¼—12¼ —3⅜. Bill, black, the basal half of lower mandible, pale lilaceous-brown; interior of mouth, rich yellow; iris, dark brown; tarsi and toes, dilute lilaceous-brown, with a slight plumbeous cast—the tarsi whitish on the posterior edge.

918, ♂ ad.; East Humboldt Mountains, September 11. 7½—11½—3⁵⁄₁₆. Same remarks as to preceding.

1262, nest and eggs (4); Parley's Park (Wahsatch Mountains), Utah Territory, June 23, 1869. Nest on bush near stream; female shot on nest.

1271, ♀ *ad.* 7¼—11½. Bill, black, basal half of lower mandible, lilaceous; interior of mouth, deep yellow; iris, brown; tarsi, pale brown; toes, darker.

1296, 1297, nest and eggs (4); 1298, nest; 1299, single egg; Parley's Park, June 27. Nests in willows along the stream.

1302, nest and eggs (4); Parley's Park, June 27. Nest in clump of willows near stream.

1339, nest and 1 egg; Parley's Park, June 27. Nest in willows. (Contained also three young.)

1404, nest; Cash Valley, Utah, July, 1869. [J. C. Olmstead.]

Turdus fuscescens.

Tawny Thrush; Wilson's Thrush.

Turdus fuscescens, STEPHENS, Shaw's Gen. Zool., X, 1817, 182.—BAIRD, B. N. Am.,
1858, 214; Cat. N. Am. B., 1859, No. 151.—COUES, Key, 1872, 73; Check List,
1873, No. 6; B. N.W., 1874, 5.—B. B. & R., Hist. N. Am. B., I, 1874, 9, pl. I,
fig. 5.—HENSHAW, 1875, 148.

The Tawny Thrush, although essentially an eastern species, was found to be more or less common in the Wahsatch district of Utah, where it inhabited only the vicinity of the streams in the lower valleys. It was extremely abundant along the Provo River, especially just above the *debouché* of that stream through its picturesque cañon between two lofty snow-clad peaks of the main range of the Wahsatch Mountains; and it was also seen in the valleys of the Bear and Weber Rivers, farther northward. In all these localities it frequented the dense willow-thickets in the immediate vicinity of the rivers, where it was extremely difficult to discover, and next to impossible to secure specimens after they were shot.

We never tired of listening to the thrilling songs of these birds, for they were truly inspiring through their exceeding sweetness and beautiful expression. The modulation of their notes was somewhat similar to that expressed by the syllables *ta-weél-ah, ta-weél-ah, twil'-ah, twil'-ah*, the latter portion subdued in tone, thus seeming like an echo of the first. In the valley of the Provo it was not unusual to hear a dozen or more of these exquisite songsters uniting in their rivalry, the most favorable time being the afternoon and evening. Considerable resemblance in tone to the song of the *T. ustulatus* was noted, but it was observed that the modulation was distinctly different.

GALEOSCOPTES CAROLINENSIS.

Cat-bird.

Muscicapa carolinensis, LINN. S. N., I, 1766. 328.

Mimus carolinensis, BAIRD, B. N. Am., 1858. 346; Cat. N. Am. B., 1859, No. 254.—
COOPER, Orn. Cal., I, 23.—COUES, Key, 1872, 74; Check List, 1873, No. 9;
B. N.W., 1874, 8.

Galeoscoptes carolinensis, CABANIS, Mus. Hein., I, 1850, 82.—BAIRD, Review, 1864,
54; B. B. & R., I. 1874, 52, pl. III, fig. 5.—HENSHAW, 1875, 152.

Like many species considered to be characteristically eastern, the Cat-bird is likewise one of the most abundant summer residents of the Wahsatch region. Indeed, we found it not uncommon on the large islands in the Great Salt Lake, specimens being shot in an orchard on Antelope Island in the month of June, while another was obtained, during the same month, on Stansbury Island, where few other birds were found. Among the mountains it was more abundant, its favorite haunts being the shady thickets along the streams which descend the cañons or course across the meadow-like "parks." It was thus an associate of the Olive-backed Thrush and the Redstart (*Setophaga ruticilla*), but while it did not ascend to as high an altitude as the former, we found the latter with it only in the lower portions of its range. No differences from the eastern birds of the same species were detected, in either manners or notes.

List of specimens.

1105, ♂ ad.; Antelope Island, Great Salt Lake, Utah, June 4, 1869. (Too badly mutilated for measurement.)

1163, ♀ ad.; Stansbury Island, Great Salt Lake, June 12. 8⅝—11. Bill and feet, black; iris, brown.

1263, 1264, nests; Parley's Park (Wahsatch Mountains), Utah, June 23. Nest in willows along stream.

1323, nest and eggs (2); Parley's Park, June 28. Nest in willows.

1384, nest and eggs (4); Provo River, Utah, July 10, 1869. Nest in willow-thicket.

OREOSCOPTES MONTANUS.

Sage Thrasher; Mountain Mocking-bird.

Orpheus montanus, TOWNSEND, Journ. Ac. Nat. Sci., Philad., 1837, 192.

Oreoscoptes montanus, BAIRD, B. N. Am., 1858, 347; Cat. N. Am. B., 1859, No. 255;
Review, 1864, 42.—COOPER, Orn. Cal., 12.—COUES, Key, 1872, 74; Check List,
1873, No. 7; B. N.W., 1874, 7.—B. B. & R., I, 1874, 32, pl. III, fig. 6.—HEN-
SHAW, 1875, 149.

Before beginning our account of this interesting species, we pause to protest against the name "Mountain Mocking-Bird," the appellation usually given it in books. This name is objectionable from the fact that it is doubly a misnomer, and therefore likely to convey an entirely erroneous idea of its distribution and song. A more appropriate term would be that of "Sage Thrasher," which is descriptive of both its habitat, and its relationship to the better-known species of the sub-family to which it belongs.

The Sage Thrasher is a widely-distributed species, since it occurs throughout that extensive portion of the West where the "everlasting sage-brush" forms the prevailing growth. It seems to be strictly governed in its range by the growth of these plants, and is consequently chiefly an inhabitant of the valleys and mesas, rarely extending farther up the mountains than the foot-hills, to the commencement of the juniper or mahogany woods. It is a migratory species, arriving from the South, in the latitude of Carson City, about the 20th of March, and departing in October or November. Its presence has been noted at but few Mexican localities, but it winters in such great numbers along our southern border that its abundance in northern and central Mexico at this season may be taken for granted.

At Carson City, very favorable opportunity was afforded for observing the habits of this interesting species during the breeding-season. The males began singing about the 24th of March, or immediately after their arrival, but their notes were then subdued, while their manners were reserved in the extreme. They soon became numerous in the sage-brush around the outskirts of the city, and were often seen perched upon the summit of a bush, turning the head from side to side in a watchful manner, even while singing; when approached, disappearing by diving into the bush, and, after a long circuitous flight near the ground, reappearing some distance in the rear of the pursuer. This peculiar, concealed flight we found to be a constant habit of the species. As the pairing-season approached, with the advance of spring, the songs of the males became greatly improved, both in strength and quality; their manners also became changed, for they had lost their former shyness. About the 10th of April, the males were engaged in eager rivalry, each vying with the other as he sang his sweetest notes, his wings being at intervals raised vertically so as to almost touch over the back, and quivering with the ecstacy that agitated the singer. The first eggs were laid about the 20th of April, the nests having been commenced a week or more earlier; and by this time the males had become perfectly silent, their main occupation being that of sentinel on guard for the approach of an intruder. In fact, we know of no oscine bird so completely mute as the present one during the period of incubation, and throughout the summer and fall, at which time one unacquainted with their habits earlier in the season might think they had no voice. Even when a nest is disturbed, the parent birds do not protest, but merely run anxiously about the meddler, in the manner of a Robin, now and then halting, and with outstretched necks closely observing his actions. When the young are hatched, however, they become more solicitous, and signify their concern by a low *chuck*.

The song of this bird possesses no remarkable attributes, but it is extremely pleasing when heard under favorable circumstances. It is most deficient in power and energy, being comparable to the subdued, subtile warbling of the Ruby-crowned Kinglet (*Regulus calendula*) rather than to the vigorous songs of the Brown Thrasher (*Harporhynchus rufus*) or Mocking-bird (*Mimus polyglottus*), its nearer kindred. It is not, however, lacking in sweetness or variety, while at times it is characterized by considerable vivacity.

List of specimens.

144, ♂ *ad.;* Camp 17, Valley of the Humboldt River (Oreana), August 31, 1867. $9—12\frac{1}{4}—4—3\frac{5}{16}—\frac{11}{16}—1\frac{1}{8}—3\frac{1}{2}—2$. Bill, black, basal half of lower mandible, pale pinkish-gray, with a faint yellowish tinge; rictus and interior of mouth, deep yellow; iris, gamboge-yellow; tarsi, grayish olive-green; toes, darker, their soles deep yellow.

145, ♂ *juv.;* Camp 17, Aug. 31, 1867. $9—12\frac{1}{4}—3\frac{31}{32}—3\frac{1}{4}—\frac{11}{16}—1\frac{1}{8}—3\frac{9}{16}$—(?). Bill, black; basal half of the lower mandible, yellowish-ash, with a lilac cast; *interior, and angle of the mouth, greenish or ashy yellow;* iris, lemon-yellow; tarsi, dark greenish horn-yellow. deepest greenish along the posterior edge; toes, nearly black, their soles yellow; claws, black.

152 ♀ *juv.;* (same locality and date). $8\frac{5}{8}—12\frac{1}{4}—4—3\frac{5}{16}—\frac{11}{16}—1\frac{1}{8}—3\frac{1}{2}$—(?). Bill, dull black; basal half of lower mandible, pinkish ashy-white; interior and angle of the mouth, yellow; iris, greenish-yellow; tarsi, dark yellowish horn-green; toes, darker, their soles yellow.

451, ♂ *ad.;* Carson City, Nevada, March 24, 1868. $9—12\frac{1}{2}—4\frac{3}{16}—3\frac{1}{4}$. Bill, black, becoming pinkish ashy-brown on basal half of lower mandible; *interior of the mouth* (except corneous portions), *lilaceous flesh-color;* iris, chrome-yellow; tarsi, yellowish-olive, with a tinge of sepia-brown; toes, blackish sepia, straw-yellow beneath.

452 ♂ *ad.;* $8\frac{13}{16}—12\frac{5}{8}—4\frac{1}{8}—3\frac{1}{4}$.

453, ♂ *ad.;* 8¾—12⅜—4 1/16—3 5/16. Same remarks, etc.

517, eggs (4); Carson City, April 24. Nest in brush-heap, in cemetery.

518, eggs (5); Carson City, April 24. Nest in sage-bush, about 18 inches from ground.

519, eggs (4); Carson City, April 24. Nest on ground beneath sage-bush.

520, eggs (3); Carson City, April 24. Nest in sage-bush, about two feet from ground.

521, eggs (3); Carson City, April 24.

554, 555, nest and eggs (5); Carson City, April 28. Nests in brush-heaps, in cemetery.

821, eggs (3); Austin, Nevada, July 3, 1868. Nest in small bush of *Symphoricarpus montanus*, about two feet from ground.

1123, 1124; single eggs, from nests containing young. Antelope Island, Great Salt Lake, June 7, 1869.

1125, nest; Antelope Island, Great Salt Lake, June 7, 1869. Nest in sage-bush, situated as usual.

1135, nest and eggs (3); Antelope Island, June 8.

1153, nest; Antelope Island, June 8. Nest in sage-bush.

1158, nest and eggs (4); "Rabbit Island" (near Stansbury Island), Great Salt Lake, June 11. Nest in grease-wood bush, near shore.

Family SAXICOLIDÆ—Stone-Chats.

Sialia mexicana.

California Blue-bird.

Sialia mexicana, Swains., Fauna Bor. Am., I, 1831, 202.—Baird, B. N. Am., 1858, 223; Cat. N. Am. B., 1859, No. 159; Review, 1864, 63.—Cooper, Orn. Cal., 28.—Coues, Key, 1872, 76; Check List, 1873, No. 17, B. N.W., 1874, 14.— B. B. & R., Hist. N. Am. B., I, 1874, 65, pl. v, fig. 2.—Henshaw, 1875, 161.

The Western Blue-bird is known to have a range nearly co-extensive with the limits of the Western Region, it being abundant throughout the main ranges of the Rocky Mountains, north to Colorado, and also in the same parallels of latitude, or even farther northward, on the Pacific coast. Yet we lost sight of this species entirely after we left the eastern water-shed of the Sierra Nevada, and never saw nor heard of it in the Wahsatch or Uintah Mountains, notwithstanding the latter country appeared equally adapted to the requirements of the species. The last individuals seen, as we journeyed eastward, were a few families of young birds, with their parents, in the wooded valley of the Truckee River, near the Big

Bend. Although these birds appeared to have been bred at that locality, and though we saw an equally small number in the similar valley of the Carson River in the breeding-season, the center of abundance of the species, so far as the Interior is concerned, seemed to be the pine-region of the Sierra Nevada, where they were observed in summer from the lower limit of these forests up to an altitude of more than 6,000 feet, or near the summit of Donner Lake Pass, where these Blue-birds, the Robin, the Oregon Snow-bird, and the Western White-crowned Sparrow (*Zonotrichia intermedia*) were the characteristic or dominant species.

This beautiful Blue-bird seemed to be a perfect counterpart of the eastern species (*S. sialis*) in its habits, while it resembled it closely in appearance; but we listened in vain for that lovely warbling which so justly renders the latter bird a universal favorite; neither did we hear it utter any note comparable to the plaintive call of the eastern bird, so often heard in autumn. This lack of sweetness of voice is, however, somewhat compensated by its superior beauty of plumage, for the richness of its coloring is decidedly superior to that of its eastern representative.

List of specimens.

413, ♂ *ad.;* Carson City, Nevada, February 21, 1868. 7—13—4½—3$\frac{11}{16}$. Bill, tarsi, and toes, deep black; interior of mouth, chrome-yellow; iris, bister.

414, ♂ *ad.;* same locality and date. 7⅛—13⅛—4½—3¾. Same remarks.

428, ♂ *ad.;* San Francisco, California; H. G. Parker. ("Oaks.") "7—13—(?) —3¾." Same remarks.

469, ♂ *ad.;* Carson City, March 28. 6⅞—12½—4$\frac{5}{16}$—3$\frac{9}{16}$. Same remarks.

SIALIA ARCTICA.

Rocky Mountain Blue-bird.

Sialia arctica, SWAINS., Fauna Bor. Am., II, 1831, 209, pl. 39.—BAIRD, B. N. Am.,
    1858, 224; Cat. N. Am. B., 1859, No. 160; Review, 1864, 64.—B. B. & R.,
    Hist. N. Am. B., I, 1874, 67, pl. V, fig. 4.—COOPER, Orn. Cal., 29.—COUES,
    Key, 1872, 76; Check List, 1873. No. 18; B. N.W., 1874, 14.—HENSHAW,
    1875, 162.

This is the characteristic Blue-bird of the Interior, and it is most numerous where the other species is rarest. Its favorite haunts are the higher portions of the desert ranges of the Great Basin, where there is little water, and no timber other than the usual scant groves of stunted cedars, piñon, or mountain mahogany. In these elevated regions it is abundant during summer, and even remains in winter, except when violent storms or severe cold drive it to the more clement valleys, where it may be seen, either singly or in considerable but scattered flocks, whenever a snow-storm prevails on the mountains. At such times we have seen both this species and the other one (*S. mexicana*) together in the fields around Carson City, and remarked the striking difference in their manners; the *S. mexicana* being often observed perched upon a fence-post or a willow-bush, descending to the ground only to pick up some insect, and immediately returning to its post of observation, while the individuals of *S. arctica* were usually seen flitting restlessly over the ground, now and then, but rarely, an individual alighting for a moment on some prominent object, as a fence-post or telegraph-wire. The visits of this species to the lower valleys are only occasional, however, for as soon as a storm in the upper regions subsides, they return to their own haunts; and when spring has fairly set in they are seen no more, while the "Valley Blue-bird" remains during the summer. In June, the "Mountain Blue-bird" was observed to be common in Virginia City, Nevada, where it nested in the manner of the Eastern species, in suitable places about buildings in the town, the old mills and abandoned shafts of the mines being its favorite haunts, which it shared with the House Finch (*Carpodacus frontalis*) and the Rock Wren (*Salpinctes obsoletus*). But while it thus commended itself to the hospitality of the people by its familiarity, it was never heard to utter any note except a weak chirp, when startled from its perch. It was also common under similar circumstances at Austin, in the Toyabe Mountains, while on the higher portions of the West Humboldt, Ruby, and East Humboldt Mountains it was still more abundant. On the Ruby Mountains it was found in July and August only in the upper portion of the timber-belt, or at an altitude of 9,000 to 11,000 feet, where it nested both among the rocks and in the deserted holes of woodpeckers among the stunted pines, cedar, or mahogany trees. In the West Humboldt Mountains it was observed that they seldom if ever alighted on the bushes in the bottom of the cañon, although they constantly frequented the adobe houses of the deserted town near by.

This species is usually much more shy than either the eastern Blue-bird or its western representative, being at all times, according to our experience, a rather difficult bird to procure. In the fall, they rove about in restless companies over the barren slopes, scattering among the low cedars, only the straggling or lingering individuals permitting a near approach. Their manners during the winter season are most interesting to witness, for they seem to enjoy the playing of the snow-flakes, as they hover in the air over some object on the ground which attracts their attention; then, after alighting to examine it more closely, they flit off to a tall weed-stalk, never thinking, apparently, to enter the cosy copses where the Snow-birds have taken refuge.

A subject of interesting and profitable speculation is the influence of spreading civilization upon the habits of animals in their native haunts. In all well-settled districts, the Purple Martins, the Barn Swallows, and the Chimney Swifts have forsaken the hollow trees and caves as nesting-places, and availed themselves of the superior accommodations and protection afforded by civilized man and his surroundings, with a readiness that is indeed remarkable. The Blue-birds and certain Wrens, even in the most recently-settled sections of the country, are gradually, but rapidly, making the same revolution in their habits, and so are many others of our native birds, too numerous to mention; and every one knows how the Cliff Swallows have abandoned the precipices of mountainous districts and overspread the entire country, even to places remote hundreds of miles from the original haunts of the species, when they discovered how well suited for their nests were the eaves of barns and churches. The present species is one of this class whose habits are undergoing such modification, for although it is naturally a bird of the high mountains, we noticed that at Salt Lake City they were quite numerous, although, were the locality unreclaimed from its primitive state, they would not have been found there except during their vertical migrations, influenced by changes in the climate. Even on Antelope Island, in the Great Salt Lake, a few pairs were seen about the buildings of the ranche.

List of specimens.

228, ♂ ad.; West Humboldt Mountains, Nevada, October 4, 1867. 7¹¹⁄₁₂—14—5—4⅝—1—1⅓—3¼—1⁷⁄₁₆. Bill, deep black; interior of mouth, light naples-yellow; iris, hazel; tarsi and toes, black.

229, ♂ *ad.;* same locality and date. $7\frac{5}{16}$—$13\frac{1}{2}$—$4\frac{7}{8}$—4—$\frac{1}{2}$—$1\frac{3}{8}$—3—$1\frac{1}{4}$. Interior of mouth, delicate light greenish-yellow.

243, ♀ *ad.;* West Humboldt Mountains, October 8. $7\frac{3}{16}$—$13\frac{3}{16}$—$4\frac{1}{2}$—$3\frac{3}{4}$—$\frac{1}{2}$—$\frac{3}{4}$—$2\frac{13}{16}$—$1\frac{1}{4}$. Same remarks.

244, ♀ *ad.;* same date. 7—$12\frac{5}{8}$—$4\frac{7}{16}$—$3\frac{11}{16}$—$\frac{1}{2}$—$\frac{3}{4}$—$2\frac{13}{16}$—$1\frac{1}{4}$. Same remarks.

375, ♂ *ad.;* Truckee Bottom, December 21. $7\frac{1}{4}$—$13\frac{5}{8}$—$4\frac{3}{4}$—$3\frac{11}{16}$. Iris, vandyke-brown.

376, ♂ *ad.;* same locality and date. $7\frac{3}{16}$—$13\frac{1}{4}$—$4\frac{3}{4}$—$3\frac{11}{16}$. Same remarks.

399, ♂ *ad.;* Steamboat Valley, Nevada, January 4, 1868. 7—$13\frac{3}{8}$—$4\frac{3}{4}$—$3\frac{5}{16}$. Same remarks.

416, ♂ *ad.;* Carson City, Nevada, March 5. $7\frac{1}{2}$—$13\frac{5}{8}$—$4\frac{13}{16}$—$3\frac{5}{16}$.

467, ♂ *ad.;* Carson City, March 28. $7\frac{1}{4}$—$13\frac{1}{2}$. Same remarks.

468, ♀ *ad.;* same locality and date. $7\frac{1}{4}$—$13\frac{1}{4}$. Same remarks.

533, ♂ *ad.;* Washoe Valley, Nevada, April 25. $7\frac{3}{4}$—14. Same remarks.

862, ♂ *juv.;* East Humboldt Mountains, Nevada, August 6, 1868.

1103, ♀ *juv.;* Antelope Island, Great Salt Lake, June 4, 1869.

1108, ♂ *ad.;* Antelope Island, Great Salt Lake, June 5, 1869. $7\frac{1}{4}$—$13\frac{7}{8}$. Bill, tarsi, and toes, pure black; iris, brown; interior of mouth, rich yellow.

1508, ♂ *juv.;* $7\frac{1}{4}$—$13\frac{5}{8}$. 1509, ♂ *juv.;* $7\frac{1}{4}$—$13\frac{1}{4}$. 1510, ♀ *juv.;* 7—13. 1511, ♀ *juv.;* $7\frac{1}{4}$—$13\frac{1}{4}$. Parley's Park (Wahsatch Mountains), Utah, August 14, 1869.

FAMILY CINCLIDÆ—WATER OUZELS.

CINCLUS MEXICANUS.

Dipper; Water Ouzel.

Cinclus mexicanus, SWAINS., Phil. Mag., I, 1827, 368.—BAIRD, Review Am. B., 1864, 60.—B. B. & R., Hist. N. Am. B., 1874, I, 55, pl. v, fig. 1.—COOPER, Orn. Cal., 25.—COUES, Key, 1872, 77; Check List, 1873, No. 10; B. N.W., 1874, 10.—HENSHAW, 1875, 159.

Hydrobata mexicana, BAIRD, B. N. Am., 1858, 229; Cat. N. Am. Birds, 1859, No. 164.

This remarkable bird, so characteristic an element of the western avifauna, was found in all localities where the summer rains or melting snows on the mountains were sufficient to supply the cañons with rushing streams. It was noticed to be abundant only where the torrents were impetuous and the country generally forest-clad, and was therefore most frequently seen on the Sierra Nevada and among the western ranges of the Rocky Mountain system, as the Wahsatch and Uintahs, being rarely observed in the intermediate area of the Great Basin, although it was encountered at intervals on the higher of the intervening ranges. The habits and manners of this bird are most strikingly peculiar, it being one of the very few Passeres which are strictly aquatic. Its movements while walking in the shallow water, or as it stands upon a rock in the bed of a stream, remind one very much of the "Teeters" or "Tilt-ups" (*Tringoides* and *Rhyacophilus*), for, whether moving or stationary, its body tilts up and down with an incessant motion. It is more often observed, however, flying rapidly along a stream, with a buzzing flight, following with the greatest ease the tortuous windings of its course without in the least checking its speed; or dashing swiftly through the spray or foam of a water-fall. Its flight is usually accompanied by a sharp chattering, especially when one is chased by another, as is often the case during the breeding-season; and when they alight they descend by a sudden drop, much after the manner of the "Gutter Snipes" (*Gallinago*). Nor are their movements confined to the surface of the water or its neighborhood, for they have been observed to dive into the aqueous element and perform various and dextrous evolutions in its depths, as they pursue their insect-food, propelling themselves by the rapid beating of the wings, in the well-known manner of Grebes and other water-fowl.

We heard the song of this bird on but one occasion, in October, at Unionville, Nevada. It was a pleasing warble, but not sufficiently distinctive, at least on that occasion, to admit of particular description.

List of specimens.

230, ♂ *ad.;* West Humboldt Mountains, Nevada, October 4, 1867. $7\frac{1}{4}$—$11\frac{1}{4}$—$3\frac{11}{16}$—$2\frac{7}{8}$—$\frac{5}{8}$—1—$1\frac{15}{16}$—$\frac{3}{8}$. Upper mandible, horn-color, darker terminally; lower, paler, dull light yellowish basally; iris, burnt-umber; tarsi and toes, clear, glossy, livid white, with a sepia tinge between the scutellæ and on joints of toes.

231, ♀ *ad.;* (mate of preceding). $7\frac{3}{8}$—$11\frac{1}{8}$—$3\frac{3}{4}$—$2\frac{3}{4}$—$\frac{9}{16}$—1—$2\frac{1}{16}$—$\frac{1}{4}$. Same remarks.

248, *ad.;* West Humboldt Mountains, October 11. $7\frac{11}{16}$—$11\frac{1}{2}$—$3\frac{13}{16}$—$3\frac{1}{8}$—$\frac{5}{8}$—1—2—$\frac{3}{8}$. Same remarks.

300, ♀ *ad.;* Truckee River (east of Sierra), November 19. $7\frac{7}{8}$—$11\frac{5}{8}$—$3\frac{3}{4}$—$2\frac{11}{16}$—$\frac{13}{16}$—$1\frac{1}{8}$—2—$\frac{1}{4}$. Bill, plumbeous-black; extreme basal portion of lower mandible, and small space on upper below nostril, brownish-white; iris, bright hazel; tarsi and toes, clear, bright, lilaceous-white; divisions of scutellæ, and sides of toes, abruptly, sepia.

324, *ad.;* 325, *ad.;* near source of American River, California, November. [H. G. Parker.]

1378, ♂ *juv.;* Pack's Cañon, Uintah Mountains, Utah, July 7, 1869. $7\frac{5}{8}$—$12\frac{1}{4}$. Upper mandible, and tip of lower, dark plumbeous; lower mandible, *salmon-orange*, this color tinging the upper at the base, and along commissure; iris, grayish-brown; tarsi and toes, whitish-lilaceous; under side of toes, dusky, the pellets yellow.

FAMILY SYLVIIDÆ—TRUE WARBLERS.

MYIADESTES TOWNSENDI.

Townsend's Ptilogonys.

Ptiliogonys townsendi, AUDUBON, Orn., Biog., V, 1839, 206, pl. 419, fig. 2.
Myiadestes townsendi, CABANIS, Weigm. Archiv, I, 1847, 208.—BAIRD, Birds N.
    Am., 1858, 321; Cat. N. Am. B., 1859, No. 235; Review, 1866, 429.—COOPER,
    Orn. Cal., 134.—COUES, Key, 1872, 117, fig. 57; Check List, 1873, No. 121;
    Birds N.W., 1874, 93.—B. B. & R., Hist. N. Am. Birds, I, 1874, 409, pl.
    XVIII, figs. 5, 6.—HENSHAW, 1875, 231.

We first met with this curious species on the western slope of the Sierra
Nevada, in a dense pine forest, at an altitude of about 5,000 feet. The
first individual seen was one which had a nest near by, as was apparent
from its anxious manner, for as we walked along the embankment of a
mining-sluice it flitted before us, now and then alighting upon the ground,
and, with drooping and quivering wings, running gracefully, in the manner
of a Robin, then flying up to a low branch, and, after facing about, repeat-
ing the same maneuvers—evidently trying to entice us away from the spot.
So much were its actions like those of various Thrushes under similar
circumstances that not once did we suspect the species, although perfectly
familiar with it in museums, but immediately concluded that a new species
of Thrush had been found. Indeed, many times afterward, when an individual would be seen to glide noiselessly before us, in the characteristic
manner of the Thrushes, displaying the ochraceous mark across the wing,
was the same illusion entertained. Patient watching and a careful search
finally revealed the nest, which was built in the upper bank of the sluice,
a foot or two above the water, and in a recess of the rocks. The nest was
bulky for the size of the bird, being nearly as large as that of *Harporhynchus
rufus*, which it nearly resembled, and was composed externally of coarse
sticks, laid in a mass upon the floor of the cave. It contained four half-
fledged young, and was consequently left undisturbed.

The species was afterward seen, at various times, among the cedar
groves of the interior ranges, but it was nowhere common. It appeared to
feed largely on the berries of the *Juniperus occidentalis*, and lived mostly
among these trees, where, as observed, it combined the manners of the
Thrushes and Blue-birds. Its song was not heard, or else it was confounded

with that of *Turdus ustulatus*, dozens of which were singing at the first locality mentioned above.

List of specimens.

377, ♂ ad.; Virginia Mountains, near Pyramid Lake, December 21, 1867.   9—13½—4¾—4—⅝—¾—4½—2¾. Bill, tarsi, and toes, deep black; iris, dark brown.

POLIOPTILA CÆRULEA. ?

Blue-gray Gnatcatcher.

Motacilla cærulea, LINN., S. N., I, 1766, 43.

Polioptila cærulea, SCLATER, Proc. Zool. Soc. Lond., 1855, 11.—BAIRD, B. N. Am., 1858, 380; Cat. N. Am. B., 1859, No. 282; Review, 1864, 74.—B. B. & R., Hist. N. Am. B., I, 1874, 78, pl. VI, fig. 5.—COOPER, Orn. Cal., 35.—COUES, Key, 1872, 78; Check List, 1873, No. 23; B. N.W., 1874, 17.—HENSHAW, 1875, 166.

In the chaparral of the western foot-hills of the Sierra Nevada, we observed, in July, a species of this genus, in considerable plenty. To all appearance it was the same species as that found in the East, but as no specimens were obtained we cannot be positive that the individuals in question were not *P. plumbea*. They were certainly not *P. melanura*, which would have been recognized by its black crown.

REGULUS CALENDULA.

Ruby-crowned Kinglet.

Motacilla calendula, LINN., S. N., I, 1766, 337.

Regulus calendula, LICHT., Verzeichn., 1823, No. 408.—BAIRD, B. N. Am., 1858, 226; Cat. N. Am. B., 1859, No. 161; Review, 1864, 66.—B. B. & R., Hist. N. Am. B., I, 1874, 75, pl. V, fig. 9.—COOPER, Orn. Cal., 33.—COUES, Key, 1872, 78; Check List, 1873, No. 21; B. N.W., 1874, 15.—HENSHAW, 1875, 164.

While the Golden-crowned Kinglet was extremely rare, the Ruby-crown was directly the opposite, for it was a common winter resident in all the lower valleys, while in early spring it became abundant to such an extent as to exceed all other birds in numbers. During the coldest portion of the winter they dwelt among the willows along the river-banks, where the dense cover afforded them a suitable shelter from the cold winds, and a cosy retreat at night.   As spring advanced, they spread themselves over the foot-hills and up the ravines of the mountains, gradually working upward, until the commencement of the summer found them in the pine-forests, where they remained during the season, again descending to the valleys when the cold weather began. At Carson City they were most numerous in April, and at that time the thickets along the foot-hills were literally alive with these restless, sprightly little creatures, who hopped briskly among the budding branches, nervously twitching their wings in their characteristic manner, the males now and then warbling their low, soft song, so liquid and indescribably sweet, at the same time displaying the red patch ordinarily concealed beneath the overlying feathers of the crown.

List of specimens.

225, ♀ *ad.;* West Humboldt Mountains, Nevada, October 3, 1867. $4\frac{1}{4}$—$6\frac{3}{4}$—$2\frac{3}{4}$—$1\frac{15}{16}$—$\frac{3}{8}$—$\frac{5}{8}$—$1\frac{3}{4}$—$1\frac{3}{8}$. Bill, horn-black; iris, brown; tarsi and toes, brownish-yellow, the latter, deep yellow beneath. [*No red on the crown.*]

371, ♂ *ad.;* Truckee Bottom, near Pyramid Lake, December 25. $4\frac{1}{2}$—7—$2\frac{5}{8}$—$1\frac{5}{8}$—$\frac{5}{16}$—$\frac{3}{4}$—$1\frac{3}{4}$—1. Bill, deep black; iris, very dark brown; tarsi, brownish-black; toes, deep brownish-yellow, purer yellow beneath.

REGULUS SATRAPA.

Golden-crowned Kinglet.

Regulus satrapa, LICHT., Verzeichn., 1823, No. 410.—BAIRD, B. N. Am., 1858, 227;
    Cat. N. Am. B., 1859, No. 162; Review, 1864, 65.—B. B. & R., I, 1874, 73, pl.
    V, fig. 8.—COOPER, Orn. Cal., 32.—COUES, Key, 1872, 78, fig. 19; Check List,
    1873, No. 22; B. N.W., 1874, 16.

This sprightly little bird, so common in our eastern groves and orchards in early spring and in the autumn, and, except the Hummers, the most diminutive of all our species, was very rarely observed by us in the Great Basin. A very few individuals, however, were noticed in the cañons of the West Humboldt Mountains, among the thick bushes along the streams. It is probably nowhere a common bird in the Interior.

FAMILY PARIDÆ—TITMICE or CHICKADEES.

LOPHOPHANES INORNATUS.

Gray Titmouse.

Parus inornatus, GAMBEL, Pr. Ac. Nat. Sci. Phila., 1845, 265.
Lophophanes inornatus, CASSIN, Ill. B. Cal., Tex., etc., 1853, 19.—BAIRD, B. N.
    Am., 1858, 386; Cat. N. Am. B., 1859, No. 237; Review, 1864, 78.—B. B. & R.,
    I, 1874, 20, pl. VI, fig. 3.—COOPER, Orn. Cal., 42.—COUES, Key, 1872, 80, fig.
    22; Check List, 1873, No. 28; B. N.W., 1874, 20.—HENSHAW, 1875, 167.

In the pine forests of the eastern slope of the Sierra Nevada, especially in their lower portion, and among the cedar and piñon groves on the desert ranges immediately adjacent to the eastward, the Gray Titmouse was a rather common species; but it did not seem to be abundant anywhere. Its manners and notes were quite the same as those of the eastern species (*L. bicolor*), but weaker and less varied, though still retaining the vehement character of utterance apparently common to all the birds of this genus.

List of specimens.

272, ♀ *ad.*; cedars of Pea-vine Mountains, near the Sierra Nevada, November 14, 1867. 6—$8\frac{3}{4}$—3—$2\frac{1}{2}$—$\frac{17}{32}$—$\frac{11}{16}$—$2\frac{9}{16}$—$1\frac{3}{16}$. Bill, plumbeous, deepening into horn-black terminally; iris, umber; tarsi and toes, plumbeous-ash.

PARUS MONTANUS.

Mountain Chickadee.

Parus montanus, GAMBEL, Pr. Ac. Nat. Sci. Phila., I, 1843, 259.—BAIRD, B. N. Am., 1858, 394; Cat. N. Am. B., 1859, No. 294; Review, 1864, 82.—B. B. & R., Hist. N. Am. B., I, 1874, 95, pl. VII, fig. 5.—COOPER, Orn. Cal., 46.—COUES, Key, 1872, 81; Check List, 1873, No. 32; B. N.W., 1874, 22.—HENSHAW, 1875, 169.

The distribution of this species seems to be governed entirely by that of the coniferous woods; consequently, we found it in all pine forests, as well as the more extensive of the piñon and cedar woods on the interior ranges. It was much less numerous on the Wahsatch and Uintah Mountains than on the Sierra Nevada, however, as indeed were nearly all species of pinicoline habits. This species is quite a counterpart of the Carolina Chickadee (*P. carolinensis*) in manners and notes, although it differs so much in size and markings; and we consider it as much more closely allied to that species than to the common Black-cap (*P. atricapillus*). In its notes we could discover no difference from those of *P. carolinensis* beyond the noticeable fact that the ordinary ones were louder and more emphatically enunciated, while the spring song, so pleasing in *P. carolinensis*, and sounding like a clear, fife-like whistling of the syllables *tsip'adee, tsip'adee, tsip'adee*, was appreciably more feeble and less musical.

List of specimen.

333, ♂ *ad.;* $5\frac{5}{8}$—$8\frac{5}{8}$—$2\frac{3}{4}$—$2\frac{1}{2}$—$\frac{3}{8}$—$\frac{5}{8}$—$2\frac{5}{8}$—$1\frac{1}{2}$. 334, ♀ *ad.;* $5\frac{5}{8}$—$8\frac{3}{4}$—$2\frac{13}{16}$—$2\frac{1}{2}$—$\frac{7}{16}$—$\frac{5}{8}$—$2\frac{1}{2}$—$1\frac{1}{4}$. 335, ♂ *ad.;* $5\frac{9}{16}$—$8\frac{5}{8}$—$2\frac{7}{8}$—$2\frac{1}{2}$—$\frac{3}{8}$—$1\frac{1}{16}$—$2\frac{1}{2}$—$1\frac{5}{8}$. Carson City, Nevada, November 27, 1867. Bill, plumbeous-black; iris, deep hazel; tarsi and toes, dull plumbeous.

450, ♂ *ad.;* Carson City, March 21, 1868. $5\frac{7}{16}$—$8\frac{5}{8}$—3—$2\frac{1}{2}$. Bill, black; iris, burnt-sienna; tarsi and toes, plumbeous-black.

Parus atricapillus.

Black-capped Chickadee.

β. septentrionalis—Long-tailed Chickadee.

Parus septentrionalis, Harris, Pr. Ac. Nat. Sci. Philad., 1845, 300.—Baird, B. N. Am., 1858, 389; Cat. N. Am. B., 1859, No. 289; Review, 1864, 79.

Parus atricapillus var. *septentrionalis,* Allen, Bull. Mus. Comp. Zool., III, 1872, 174.—Coues, Key, 1872, 81; Check List, 1873, No. 31a; B. N.W., 1874, 21. —B. B. & R., I, 1874, 99, pl. VII, fig 2.—Henshaw, 1875, 170.

Parus septentrionalis var. *albescens,* Baird, B. N. Am., 1858, p. xxxvii; Cat. N. Am. Birds, 1859, No. 289a.

γ. occidentalis—Western Chickadee.

Parus occidentalis, Baird, B. N. Am., 1858, 391; Cat. N. Am. B., 1859, No. 291; Review, 1864, 81.—Elliot, Illustr. Am. B., I, pl. VIII.—Cooper, Orn. Cal., 45.

Parus atricapillus var. *occidentalis,* Coues, Key, 1872, 81; Check List, 1873, No. 31c.—B. B. & R., Hist. N. Am. B., I, 1874, 101, pl. VII, fig. 3.

The common Black-capped Chickadee was apparently wanting in all portions of the western depression of the Great Basin, and even on the eastern side it was so extremely rare that none were seen except in the valley of the Provo River, where but a few families, with their full-grown young, were met with. They kept in the willow thickets, and seemed very gregarious, in marked contrast to the Mountain Chickadee (*P. montanus*) and that eastern species, the Southern Black-cap, or Carolina Chickadee (*P. carolinensis*). Their notes were also very different, the usual utterances being a sort of twittering, resembling but little the distinct and sharp notes of the species named.

List of specimens.

1392, ♀ *juv.;* $5\frac{5}{16}$—$7\frac{3}{4}$. 1393, ♂ *juv.;* $5\frac{5}{16}$—$7\frac{3}{4}$. 1394, ♂ *juv.;* $5\frac{1}{4}$—$8\frac{3}{8}$. Provo River, Utah, July 11, 1869. Bill, black; interior of mouth, yellow; iris, dark brown; tarsi and toes, fine ashy-blue.

PSALTRIPARUS MINIMUS.

Least Titmouse.

Parus minimus, TOWNSEND, Journ. Ac. Nat. Sci. Philad., 1837, 190.

Psaltriparus minimus, BONAP., Comp. Rend., 1854, 62.—BAIRD, B. N. Am., 1858, 397; Cat. N. Am. B., 1859, No. 298; Review, 1864, 84.—COOPER, Orn. Cal., 48.—COUES, Key, 1872, 82; Check List, 1873, No. 35.

Psaltriparus minimus var. *minimus*, B. B. & R., Hist. N. Am. B., I, 1874, 109, pl. VII, fig. 9.

Of this delicate little bird we had but a mere glimpse, while passing through the western foot-hills of the Sierra Nevada. It was there seen in small straggling companies, among the brushwood of the ravines, appearing much like the *P. plumbea* of the Interior in its manners and notes.

PSALTRIPARUS PLUMBEUS.

Lead-colored Titmouse.

Psaltria plumbea, BAIRD, Pr. Ac. Nat. Sci. Philad., 1854, 118.

Psaltriparus plumbeus, BAIRD, B. N. Am., 1858, 398; Cat. N. Am. B., 1859, No. 299; Review, 1864, 79.—COOPER, Orn. Cal., 49.—COUES, Key, 1872, 82; Check List, 1873, No. 36; B. N.W., 1874, 23.

Psaltriparus minimus var. *plumbeus*, B. B. & R., Hist. N. Am. B., I, 1874, 110, pl. VII, fig. 10.—HENSHAW, 1875, 171.

Of late years, the known range of this species has been greatly extended by the more recent field-observations of the Government surveys. It was at first supposed to be one of those birds characteristic of the southwestern portion of the country, but it is now known to have a range co-extensive with the Middle Province, having been obtained by the naturalists of Dr. Hayden's survey as far to the northeastward as Green River and Bitter Creek, Wyoming Territory, while Captain Charles Bendire, U. S. A., found it a winter resident at Camp Harney, in eastern Oregon. How much farther northward it may extend is not known, but its range in that direction is probably limited by the Columbia Valley. We met with this species on several occasions from the very base of the Sierra Nevada eastward to the Wahsatch Mountains, but the localities where it occurred in abundance were few and remote from each other, while its habits are so erratic that it was seldom met with twice at one place. In the cañons of the West Humboldt Mountains it was very numerous in September. It was found there in ever-restless companies, continually twittering as they flew from bush to bush, at which time the flocks became greatly scattered, the individuals straggling, or "stringing out," one behind another. In all their movements they were remarkably restless, in this respect even surpassing the Gnat catchers (*Polioptilæ*), to which they bear considerable resemblance in their movements and appearance. In November many of these birds were seen in company with the Gray Titmice (*Lophophanes inornatus*) among the cedars on the Pea-vine and Virginia Mountains, and adjacent ranges in western Nevada, and in the spring one or two flocks, supposed to be this species, were observed in the gorge of the Carson River, near Carson City. On the eastern side of the Great Basin a few individuals in City Creek Cañon, near Salt Lake City, comprised all that were seen.

Among the numerous specimens killed in September, we noticed that many had the iris blackish, while in others it was clear light sulphur-yellow, and in some intermediate, or yellowish outwardly, and brownish next the pupil. A close examination, however, of these specimens, showed that this difference apparently depended on age, those having the darkest eyes being unmistakably young birds, while those in which the iris was clear yellow were all old birds, as was readily detected by the difference in the texture of their plumage. Even the youngest specimens had a yellowish outer ring to the iris, concealed by the eyelids, so that it seems that this color gradually spreads from the outside to the pupil, with advancing age, until, when fully mature, the iris becomes wholly clear light yellow.

List of specimens.

171, ♂ *juv.;* West Humboldt Mountains, Nevada, September 7, 1867. $4\frac{1}{8}$—6—2—$1\frac{11}{16}$—$\frac{5}{16}$—$\frac{9}{16}$. Bill, black; *iris, sepia-black, very narrow outer yellowish ring;* tarsi and toes, black.

184, ♀ *ad.;* West Humboldt Mountains, September 11. $4\frac{1}{4}$—$5\frac{7}{8}$—2—$1\frac{11}{16}$—$\frac{1}{4}$—$\frac{9}{16}$—$2\frac{3}{8}$—$1\frac{3}{8}$. Bill, black; *iris, light yellow;* tarsi and toes, black.

185, ♂ *juv.;* $4\frac{1}{8}$—6—2—$1\frac{11}{16}$—$\frac{1}{4}$—$\frac{9}{16}$—$2\frac{1}{16}$—1. Iris, light yellow, *brownish next pupil.*

250, *ad.;* West Humboldt Mountains (east side), October 12, 1867. $4\frac{9}{16}$—6—$2\frac{1}{4}$—$1\frac{3}{16}$—$\frac{1}{4}$—$\frac{9}{16}$—$2\frac{1}{4}$—$1\frac{3}{8}$. Bill, tarsi, and toes, deep black; iris, sulphur-yellow.

PSALTRIPARUS MELANOTIS.?

Black-eared Titmouse.

Parus melanotis, HARTLAUB, Rev. Zool., 1844, 216.
Psaltriparus melanotis, BONAP., Comp. Rend., 1854, —.— BAIRD, B. N. Am., 1858,
 386, pl. LIII, fig. 3; Cat. N. Am. B., 1859, No. 297; Review, 1864, 84.—B. B.
 & R., Hist. N. Am. B., I, 1874, 108, pl. VII, fig. 8.

On the 4th of August, 1868, we saw near our camp, on the eastern
slope of the Ruby Mountains, what was unquestionably a bird of this
species, since the black patch on the ear-coverts was distinctly visible. Its
restless movements made ineffectual our attempt to shoot it, and before we
were prepared for another shot it disappeared among the cedar trees, and
could not be found again. This we believe is the first known instance of
its occurrence within the limits of the United States, though it has been
obtained near our border, and is a common bird of the high mountain
portions of northern Mexico; but it probably occurs in greater or less
numbers, in suitable places, throughout our southern Rocky Mountains.

FAMILY SITTIDÆ—NUTHATCHES.

SITTA CAROLINENSIS.

White-bellied Nuthatch.

β. aculeata—Slender-billed Nuthatch.

Sitta aculeata, CASSIN, Pr. Ac. Nat. Sci. Philad., 1856, 254.—BAIRD, B. N. Am.,
 1858, 375, pl. xxxiii, fig. 3; Cat. N. Am. B., 1859, No. 278; Review, 1864,
 86.—COOPER, Orn. Cal., 54.
Sitta carolinensis var. *aculeata*, ALLEN, Bull. Mus. Comp. Zool., 1872, 174.—COUES,
 Key, 1872, 83; Check List, 1873, No. 38a; B. N.W., 1874, 24.—B. B. & R.,
 Hist. N. Am. B., I, 1874, 117, pl. VIII, fig. 2 (bill only).—HENSHAW, 1875, 173.

Being strictly a pinicoline species, this Nuthatch was observed in
abundance only on the Sierra Nevada, being comparatively rare on the
Wahsatch and Uintah mountains, while none were seen in the intervening
region, not even among the most extensive cedar and piñon woods. In
its manners it is a counterpart of the eastern form, but its notes are markedly different, being much weaker, and some of them of another character

altogether. It is with hesitation that we refer this bird to *S. carolinensis*, as a geographical race.

List of specimens.

439, ♂ *ad.;* Carson City, Nevada, March 10, 1868.   6—10$\frac{7}{8}$—3$\frac{3}{4}$—3.   Bill, pure blackish-plumbeous, basal half of lower mandible, opaque, bluish, or milky-white; iris, very dark bister; tarsi and toes, sepia-black.

448, ♂ *ad.;* Carson, March 21.   6$\frac{1}{8}$—10$\frac{1}{4}$—3$\frac{3}{4}$—3.   Same remarks.

449, ♀ *ad.;* (mate of preceding.)   5$\frac{7}{8}$—10$\frac{5}{8}$—3$\frac{11}{16}$—3.   Same remarks. Tarsi and toes, sepia-slate.

487, ♀ *ad.;* Carson, April 3.   6—11—3$\frac{3}{4}$—3.   Same remarks.

491, ♂ *ad.;* Carson, April 4.   6—10$\frac{3}{4}$—3$\frac{11}{16}$—3.   Same remarks.

SITTA CANADENSIS.

Red-bellied Nuthatch.

Sitta canadensis, LINN., Syst. Nat., I, 1766, 177.—BAIRD, B. N. Am., 1858, 376; Cat. N. Am. B., 1859, No. 279; Review, 1864, 86.—B. B. & R., Hist. N. Am. B., I, 1874, 118, pl. VIII, figs. 7, 8.—COOPER, Orn. Cal., 54.—COUES, Key, 1872, 83, fig. 27; Check List, 1873, No. 39; B. N.W., 1874, 25.—HENSHAW, 1875, 174.

An inhabitant in summer of the pine woods exclusively, this species was met with, at that season, only in the thickest or most extensive coniferous forests, such as those on the Sierra Nevada, Wahsatch, and Uintah ranges. In all localities where observed it was much less common, however, than either *S. aculeata* or *S. pygmæa*, but wherever found made its presence known by the loud, penny-trumpet *toot*, so peculiar and so characteristic of the species. Unlike the other two species, this one appears to make more or less of a vertical migration, since in September we found it common in the aspen groves along the streams in the upper Humboldt Valley. Later in the same month it was also common among the pines of the lofty Clover Mountains, at an altitude of near 11,000 feet.

List of specimens.

914, ♀ *ad.;* Camp 24, head of Humboldt Valley, September 10, 1868.   4$\frac{5}{3}$—8$\frac{3}{16}$— (?)—2$\frac{1}{4}$.   Bill, uniform blackish-plumbeous, basal half of lower mandible, abruptly, bluish white; iris, umber-brown; tarsi, dull wax-green; toes, more yellowish.

SITTA PYGMÆA.

Pigmy Nuthatch.

Sitta pygmœa, VIGORS, Zool. Beechey's Voy., 1839, 29, pl. 4.—BAIRD. B. N. Am., 1858, 378; Cat. N. Am. B., 1859, No. 281; Review, 1864, 88.—B.B. & R., Hist. N. Am. B., I, 1874, 120, pl. VIII, fig. 10.—COOPER, Orn. Cal., 55.—COUES, Key, 1872, 83, fig. 27; Check List, 1873, No. 41; B. N.W., 1874, 25.—HENSHAW, 1875, 175.

This curious little Nuthatch was always a companion of the larger species (*S. aculeata*), the same local conditions being favorable or unfavorable to their presence. They appear to live together on the best of terms, since we have often seen individuals of each pass and re-pass one another as they searched the same branch or trunk. The manners of this diminutive Nuthatch partake in their general nature of those common to the genus, and present no marked peculiarities worthy of note. It is extremely noisy, its shrill notes being uttered almost continually, whether the bird is engaged in creeping among the branches or in flying from the top of one tree to that of another; and although one may be making a din greater than that of any other bird in the forest, it is generally hard to discover him, on account of his diminutive size. The notes of this species greatly resemble in their high pitch the "peet" or "peet-weet" of certain Sandpipers (as *Tringoides* and *Rhyacophilus*), but they are louder and more piercing. When once paired, these birds seem to possess a strong attachment to their mates, since on one occasion, after a female had been killed, the male made loud and continued complaint, and after being followed from tree to tree, was finally shot from the same one where his mate had been secured.

List of specimens.

410, ♂ *ad.;* Carson City, Nevada, February 19, 1868. $4\frac{1}{2}$—$8\frac{1}{8}$—$2\frac{3}{4}$—$2\frac{3}{16}$. Bill, slate-black, basal half of lower mandible (abruptly), milk-white; iris, very dark vandyke-brown; tarsi and toes, plumbeous-black.

411, ♀ *ad.;* mate of preceding. $4\frac{3}{8}$—$7\frac{3}{4}$—$2\frac{5}{8}$—$2\frac{3}{16}$. Same remarks. White of bill with delicate bluish tinge.

488, ♀ *ad.;* Carson, April 3. $4\frac{3}{8}$—8—$2\frac{5}{8}$—$2\frac{1}{2}$. Same remarks.

492, ♂ *ad.;* Carson, April 4. $4\frac{9}{16}$—8—$2\frac{11}{16}$—$2\frac{3}{16}$. Same remarks.

27 P R

FAMILY CERTHIIDÆ—CREEPERS

CERTHIA FAMILIARIS.

Brown Creeper.

β. americana.

Certhia americana, BONAP., Comp. & Geog. List, 1838, 11.—BAIRD, B. N. Am.,
   1858, 372, pl. 83, fig. 2; Cat. N. Am. B., 1859, No. 275; Review, 1864, 89.
Certhia familiaris var. *americana*, B. B. & R., Hist. N. Am. B., I, 1874, 125, pl.
   VIII, fig. 11.—HENSHAW, 1875, 177.
"*Certhia familiaris*," COUES, Key, 1872, 84, fig. 28; Check List, 1873, No. 42; B.
   N.W., 1874, 26.
"*Certhia mexicana*," COOPER, Orn. Cal., I, 1870, 58.

The distribution of this species corresponds with that of *Regulus calendula*, the pine forests being its home in summer, while in winter it performs
a partial migration to the timbered portions of the lower valleys, or to the
lower edge of the coniferous belt.   It was first observed among the western
foot-hills of the Sierra Nevada, where it was seen early in July, at the very
commencement of the pine forest.   In winter it was more or less common
among the cotton-woods in the lower portion of the valleys of the Truckee
and Carson Rivers, but eastward of those localities it was not again met
with at any season, except on the Wahsatch and Uintah Mountains, where
it was a rather common summer resident in the pine-region.

List of specimens.

349, ♀ *ad.*; Truckee Reservation, near Pyramid Lake, December 7, 1867. $5\frac{9}{16}$—
7—$2\frac{1}{2}$—$2\frac{1}{16}$—$\frac{9}{16}$—$\frac{1}{2}$—$2\frac{5}{8}$—$1\frac{7}{8}$.   Upper mandible, black; lower, dilute brownish-white,
with pinkish tinge; iris, hazel; tarsi and toes, dilute horn-color.

FAMILY TROGLODYTIDÆ—WRENS.

SALPINCTES OBSOLETUS.

Rock Wren.

Troglodytes obsoletus, SAY, Long's Exped., II, 1823, 4.
Salpinctes obsoletus, CABANIS, Wiegm. Archiv, 1847, 323.—BAIRD, B. N. Am.,
   1858, 357; Cat. N. Am. B., 1859, No. 264; Review, 1864, 110.—B. B. & R.,
   Hist. N. Am. B., I, 1874, 135, pl. VIII, fig. 3.—COOPER, Orn. Cal., 65.—
   COUES, Key, 1872, 85; Check List, 1873, No. 45; B. N.W., 1874, 27.—HEN-
   SHAW, 1875, 179.

The Rock Wren is by far the most common and generally distributed
species of the family in the Western Region, since the prevailing character

of that country is so well suited to its habits. It was first met with near the summit of the Donner Lake Pass of the Sierra Nevada, but this was on the eastern slope, and in a district where the pine forests were interrupted by considerable tracts of open country, of a more or less rocky nature. Eastward of this point, as far as we journeyed, it was found in suitable localities on all the desert ranges. Its favorite resorts are piles of rocks, where it may be observed hopping in and out among the recesses or interstices between the bowlders, or perched upon the summit of a stone, usually uttering its simple, guttural notes. It is not strictly rupicoline, however, for along the eastern base of the Sierra Nevada, where the pine forest reaches to the very base of the mountains, it was common in cleared tracts where there was much rubbish of old stumps, prostrate logs, and piles of brush, seeming as much at home there as among the rocks. At that place the males were occasionally observed to fly up to a naked branch of some dead tree, and remain there while they sang their simple trill. This species also freely accepts of the accommodations and protection afforded by man, for in many towns, notably those among the mountains, it nests about the old buildings and inside the entrance to mining-shafts, displaying as much familiarity and confidence as the little House Wren, or Bewick's Wren. It is an exceedingly unsuspicious little bird, if unmolested, always greeting an intruder to its haunts by its cheerful note of *tureé*, while it bows and scrapes most politely at each utterance; but if too closely observed, or pursued, it manages, by hopping through the interstices, to keep always on the opposite side of the rock-pile, while it changes the note of welcome to an admonishing, guttural *turrrr*. In its general appearance, except color, and in many of its movements, the Rock Wren bears a somewhat close resemblance to the Carolina Wren (*Thryothorus ludovicianus*) of the Eastern Region, being of almost exactly the same size and shape; the notes, too, are somewhat similar in their general nature, particularly the ordinary ones, which have the same guttural character; but the song is a simple monotonous trill, very much like that of the Snow-birds (*Junco*), and though often varied indefinitely, lacks any particular merit, from want of power and sweetness, while it is in no wise comparable to the superb whistling song of the species above mentioned.

At Carson City the Rock Wren was migratory, not making its appear ance during the season of our stay until the 20th of March, and first singing on the 30th of that month.   Indeed, we saw it nowhere during the winter, and thus infer that it makes a complete migration southward.

List of specimens.

163, ♂ *ad.;* $6\frac{5}{16}$—$9\frac{1}{16}$—$2\frac{7}{8}$—$2\frac{7}{16}$—$1\frac{1}{16}$—$\frac{3}{4}$—$2\frac{1}{4}$—$1\frac{13}{16}$.   164, ♀ *ad.;* 6—9—$2\frac{7}{8}$—$2\frac{7}{16}$—$1\frac{1}{16}$—$1\frac{1}{16}$—$2\frac{3}{16}$.   West Humboldt Mountains (Camp 18), September 4, 1867.   Upper mandible, uniform slaty horn-color, with lilaceous cast; end of the lower mandible similar, fading on middle portion into ashy-lilac—pale-yellowish basally and on angle of mouth; iris, olive; tarsi and toes, deep black.

253, ♂ *ad.;* West Humboldt Mountains (Camp 19), October 23. 6—9—$2\frac{13}{16}$—$2\frac{7}{16}$—$1\frac{1}{16}$—$\frac{3}{4}$—$2\frac{3}{8}$—$1\frac{11}{16}$.   Upper mandible, purplish-slaty; lower, pale slaty-lilaceous, darker terminally, more pinkish at base; iris, olivaceous-drab; tarsi and toes, slate-black.

458, ♂ *ad.;* Carson, March 25. 6—9—3—$2\frac{1}{4}$.   Bill, uniform slate, lower mandible, paler; iris, grayish-umber; tarsi and toes, black.

478, ♂ *ad.;* Carson City, Nevada, March 30, 1868. $5\frac{7}{8}$—9—$2\frac{7}{8}$—$2\frac{5}{16}$.   Bill, uniform plumbeous-slate, lower mandible, paler, except terminally; iris, grayish-umber; tarsi and toes, black.

486, ♂ *ad.;* Carson City, April 3. $6\frac{1}{4}$—$9\frac{1}{4}$—$3\frac{1}{16}$—$2\frac{1}{4}$.   Bill, uniform dull-slate, basal half of lower mandible, slaty bluish-white; iris, raw-umber; tarsi and toes, deep black.

CATHERPES MEXICANUS.

White-throated Wren.

β. *conspersus—Cañon Wren.*

Catherpes mexicanus, BAIRD, B. N. Am., 1858, 356; Cat. N. Am. B., 1859, No. 263;
    Review, 1864, 111.—COOPER, Orn. Cal., 66.—COUES, Key, 1872, 85; B. N. W.,
    1874, 28. [Not *Thryothorus mexicanus,* Swains.]
Catherpes mexicanus var. conspersus, Ridgway, Am. Nat., 1872, 2.—B. B. & R.,
    Hist. N. Am. B., I, 1874, 139, pl. VIII, fig. 4.—COUES, Check List, 1873, No.
    46, p. 125.—HENSHAW, 1875, 131.

Somewhat similar to the common Rock Wren (*Salpinctes*) in its distri- bution and habits, this remarkable species differs in many noteworthy respects, the principal of which are its appearance and notes.   We found it everywhere more rare than the other species, and apparently confined to the more secluded portions of the mountains, where it frequented rocky gorges and the interior of caves more often than the piles of loose rocks on the open slopes.   It was generally observed to be rather shy, and prone to elude pursuit by retreating to the deeper recesses of the rocks, now and then slyly peeping from some crevice but an instant, and then very unexpectedly reappearing at some distant place. While thus engaged, or while hopping about. examining each crevice for a spider or other insect, it utters a simple ringing note, which sounds somewhat like *dink*, uttered in a metallic tone; while now and then he pauses to pour forth his piercing song, which is of such volume as to fill the surrounding cañons with its reverberations. In many of its movements it greatly resembles the common Rock Wren, particularly in its manner of bowing and swinging oddly from side to side, when its attention becomes attracted by the presence of an intruder. It was frequently seen to cling to the roof or sides of a cave with the facility of a Creeper, and on one occasion to fly perpendicularly up the face of a cliff for a considerable height.

It seems, however, that in other sections of the country, where it is probably more numerous, this species is not always thus shy and retired in its habits; for Mr. Dresser (see "The Ibis," 1865, p. —) mentions an interesting instance where a pair built a nest in the wall of a dilapidated printing-office in San Antonio, Texas, and were so tame that they became great favorites with the workmen. He also states that at Dr. Heermann's ranche, on the Medina, they often built in cigar-boxes placed for their accommodation.

As stated above, the song of this bird is one of remarkable power; it is also unique in its tone and modulation to such an extent that no other song we ever heard resembles it at all. It consists of a series of clear, sharp, whistling, detached notes, beginning in the highest possible key, and descending the scale with perfect regularity through an octave or more. These notes are occasionally heard echoed and reëchoed against the walls of the cañons, with continued reverberations, such is their power and distinctness.

List of specimens.

345, ♂ *ad.;* near Fort Churchill, December 7, 1867.   5.75—7.50—2.58—2.00—0.83 —0.56—2.25—1.18.   Bill, slate-color, paler, and with a lilaceous tinge toward base of lower mandible; iris, brown; tarsi and toes, black.   [Type of var. *consversus*, Ridgway, *l. c.*]

THRYOMANES BEWICKI.

Bewick's Wren.

γ. spilurus.

Troglodytes spilurus, VIGORS, Zool. Beechey's Voy., 1839, 18, pl. 4, fig. 1.
Thryothorus spilurus. COOPER, Orn. Cal., 1870, 69.
Thryothorus bewicki var. *spilurus*, BAIRD, Review, 1864, 126.—B. B. & R., Hist. N.
   Am. B., I, 1874, 147, pl. IX, fig. 4.—COUES, Key, 1872, 86; Check List, 1873,
   No. 48b.
Thryothorus bewicki. c. spilurus, COUES, B. N.W., 1874, 31.
Thryothorus bewickii, BAIRD, Birds N. Am., 1858, 363 (part).

The "Long-tailed House Wren," or Bewick's Wren, was observed
frequently at Sacramento, where, as in certain portions of the East, it frequented the out-houses in the city, in company with the Barn Swallow and
Black Pewee.   After leaving there, we nowhere identified it with certainty,
although a single individual of what seemed to be this species was noticed at
Glendale, Nevada, in November, 1867.   The specimen in question was seen
among the willows bordering the river, and disappeared before we could
decide whether it was this species or the Wood Wren (*Troglodytes parkmanni*).

TROGLODYTES AËDON.

House Wren; Wood Wren.

β. parkmanni—Parkman's Wren.

Troglodytes parkmanni, AUD., Orn. Biog., V, 1839, 310.—BAIRD, B. N. Am. 1858,
   367; Cat. N. Am. B., 1859, No. 271; Review, 1864, 140.—COOPER, Orn. Cal.,
   71.
Troglodytes aëdon var. *parkmanni*, COUES, Key, 1872, 87; Check List, 1873, No. 49a;
   B. N.W., 1874, 32.—B. B. & R., Hist. N. Am., I, 1874, 153.—HENSHAW, 1875,
   184.

The range of this Wren is apparently co-extensive with the distribution
of the timber, or governed strictly by the presence or absence of trees,
without special regard to their kind.   Its vertical range, like that of the
Robin, Louisiana Tanager, and many other species, was consequently very
considerable, it being equally abundant among the cotton-woods of the river-

valleys and the aspen copses of the higher cañons of the mountains. Indeed it is the only strictly arboreal species of this family which resides in summer in the Middle Province, and there much more rarely seeks the society of man or the protection of his presence than the Rock or Bewick's Wrens. That they are somewhat inclined to do so, however, we saw occasional evidence, particularly in one instance, where a pair had a nest somewhere about the trading-house on the Indian Reservation near Pyramid Lake. This pair had become so familiar and confiding that the constant presence or passing in and out of persons did not alarm them in the least. Among the large cotton-wood trees near by, which extended in scattered groves or clumps for several miles along the river, they were extremely abundant, and their lively, agreeable songs were continually heard. They were equally abundant in the high cañons of the East Humboldt and Wahsatch Mountains, their favorite resort in the latter being the aspen copses of the pine-region, where they and the Robins were the most abundant birds. Very numerous nests of this species were found, their situation being various, although most of them were similar in this respect; the prevailing character being that of a large mass of rubbish filled in behind the loosened bark of the trunk of a tree, usually only a few feet from the ground, the entrance a natural crevice or a woodpecker's hole; it was always warmly lined with feathers, and very frequently possessed the ornamental addition of a cast-off snake-skin. One nest was placed behind a flat mass of a small shrub (*Spiræa cæspitosa*), which grew in moss-like patches against the face of a cliff. Another one, and the only one not concealed in some manner, was built in the low crotch of an aspen, having for its foundation an abandoned Robin's nest. It consisted of a somewhat conical pile of sticks, nearly closed at the top, but with a small opening just large enough to admit the owner. Including its bulky base, the total height of this structure was about fifteen inches.

List of specimens.

170, ♂ ad.; West Humboldt Mountains, September 7, 1867. $5\frac{1}{4}$—$6\frac{3}{4}$—$2\frac{3}{16}$—$1\frac{13}{16}$—$\frac{1}{2}$—$\frac{5}{8}$—$1\frac{5}{8}$—$1\frac{1}{16}$. Upper mandible, horn-black, the tomium lilaceous-white; lower, lilaceous whitish, deepening into purplish-slaty at end; iris, umber; tarsi and toes, brownish-whitish.

360, ♀ *ad.;* Truckee Bottom, December 17. 5—6½—2$\frac{7}{16}$—1$\frac{11}{16}$—$\frac{1}{2}$—$\frac{5}{8}$—2—$\frac{7}{8}$. Bill, black, lilaceous-whitish on basal half of lower mandible and along commissure; interior of mouth, deep naples-yellow; iris, raw-umber; tarsi and toes, livid brownish-white.

839, ♂ *ad.;* East Humboldt Mountains, July 13, 1868. 5—6½—1¾. Bill, black; commissure, with basal half of lower mandible, deep pinkish-lilac; iris, grayish choco-late-brown; tarsi and toes, dilute ashy-sepia.

864, ♂ *juv.;* East Humboldt Mountains, August 7. 5⅛—6¾—(?)—1$\frac{11}{16}$. Upper mandible, dull black; commissure and lower mandible, pale lilaceous; rictus, pale yellow; interior of mouth, intense yellow; tarsi and toes, delicate pale ashy-sepia.

903, ♂ *ad.;* Secret Valley, Nevada, September 7. 5¼—6¾—(?)—1¾. Upper mandi-ble, olivaceous-black; lower mandible and commissure, lilaceous-white, the former more dusky terminally; iris, olivaceous-umber; tarsi and toes, pale lilaceous-sepia.

1260, nest and eggs (6); Parley's Park (Wahsatch Mountains), Utah, June 23, 1869. Built on an old Robin's nest, in crotch of aspen, deep woods.

1261, nest and eggs (7); nest in hollow aspen-snag.

1286, nest and eggs (7); Parley's Park, June 25. Nest in hollow snag, entrance through knot-hole.

1308, nest and eggs (6); Parley's Park, June 27. Nest in deserted woodpecker's hole.

1309, nest and eggs (6); same locality and date. Nest behind loosened bark of dead aspen.

1421, eggs (3); Parley's Park, July 17, 1869. Nest in hollow of tree.

TROGLODYTES HYEMALIS.

Winter Wren.

β. *pacificus*—*Western Winter Wren.*

Troglodytes hyemalis var. *pacificus*, BAIRD, Review, 1864, 145.

Troglodytes parvulus var. *pacificus*, B. B. & R., Hist. N. Am. B., I, 1874, 155, pl. IX, fig. 10.

Anorthura troglodytes var. *hyemalis*, COUES, Key, 1872, 351 (part); Check List, 1873, No. 50 (part); B. N.W., 1874, 33 (part).

Troglodytes hyemalis (part), BAIRD, B. N. Am., 1858, 369; Cat. N. Am. B., 1859, No. 273.—COOPER, Orn. Cal., 73.

The Winter Wren seemed to be quite rare in the Interior, since but one individual, the one obtained, was observed.

List of specimens.

369, ♂ *ad.;* Truckee Bottom, near Pyramid Lake, Nevada, December 25, 1867. 4—6—2—1½—$\frac{7}{16}$—(?)—1$\frac{5}{16}$—$\frac{9}{16}$. Upper mandible, black, tomium dilute brown; lower, dilute brown, dusky along the side; iris, deep burnt-umber; tarsi and toes, deep brown.

TELMATODYTES PALUSTRIS.

Long-billed Marsh Wren.

β. paludicola—Tule Wren.

Cistothorus palustris var. *paludicola*, BAIRD, Review Am. B., 1864, 148.—B. B. &
R., Hist. N. Am. B., I, 1874, 161.—HENSHAW, 1875, 185.

Telmatodytes palustris, COUES, Key, 1872, 87 (part); Check List, 1873, No. 51; B,
N.W., 1874, 35 (part).

Cistothorus (Telmatodytes) palustris (part), BAIRD, B. N. Am., 1858, 364; Cat. N.
Am. B., 1859, No. 268 (part).—COOPER, Orn. Cal., 75.

In all marshy localities where there existed even a limited growth of
tules, the Long-billed Marsh Wren was more or less abundant. It was
consequently found in numerous places, but it abounded most in those
extensive marshes adjoining the lower portions of the Truckee, Humboldt,
and Jordan Rivers, it being so abundant at the latter locality that several
nests were often visible at one time in the thick growth of reeds. The
song of this Wren is very peculiar, being a confused sputtering, scolding
harangue, somewhat similar to, but harsher and less pleasing than, the song
of *Troglodytes aëdon*.

List of specimens.

273, ♂ ad.; Truckee Meadows, Nevada, November 15, 1867. $5\frac{1}{16}$—$6\frac{5}{8}$—$2\frac{3}{16}$—$1\frac{11}{16}$—$\frac{9}{16}$
—$\frac{11}{16}$—$1\frac{3}{14}$—$\frac{15}{16}$. Upper mandible, slaty-black; commissure and lower mandible, lilaceous-white, the latter more dusky terminally; iris, umber; tarsi and toes, delicate
brownish-white, strongly tinged with bluish-lilaceous.

370, ♂ ad.; Truckee Bottom, near Pyramid Lake, December 25. $5\frac{1}{8}$—$6\frac{5}{8}$—$2\frac{3}{16}$—$1\frac{3}{4}$—
$\frac{1}{2}$—$\frac{11}{16}$—2—$\frac{7}{8}$. Same remarks. Tarsi and toes, deep light-brown, with yellowish tinge.

737, nest and five eggs; Truckee Bottom, near Pyramid Lake, May 18, 1868.
Nest among reeds in deep water, near lake-shore.

738, nest. Same remarks as to preceding.

950, ♂ ad.; Deep Creek, Utah, October 5, 1868. $5\frac{3}{8}$—7—(?)—$1\frac{13}{16}$. Bill, black; commissure and basal two-thirds of lower mandible, pure lilaceous; iris, umber; tarsi and
toes, deep sepia, the latter darkest.

951, ♂ ad.; 952, ♀ ad.; $5\frac{3}{8}$—$7\frac{1}{8}$—(?)—$1\frac{13}{16}$. Same remarks.

1010, 1011, 1012, 1013, 1014, 1015, May 21, 1869; 1079, 1080, 1081, 1082, June 2,
1869; nests and eggs; Jordan River (near Salt Lake City), Utah. Nests each attached
to several stalks of upright reeds, or *tules*, standing in the water, near nests of
Xanthocephalus icterocephalus. Maximum number of eggs four, but the number probably sometimes exceeds this.

1159, ♂ juv.; Parley's Park (Wahsatch Mountains), Utah, July 26, 1869. $4\frac{5}{8}$—$6\frac{1}{4}$.

Upper mandible, sepia-black; commissure and lower mandible, pale lilaceous; iris, brown; tarsi, dark sepia-plumbeous; toes, paler, whitish beneath.

1467, ♂ *juv.;* Parley's Park, July 28. $4\frac{5}{8}$—$6\frac{5}{8}$. Same remarks.

1476, ♂ *juv.;* July 29. $5\frac{1}{4}$—7.

1494, ♂ *juv.;* $5\frac{3}{8}$—$6\frac{7}{8}$. 1495, ♂ *juv.;* $5\frac{1}{4}$—$6\frac{7}{8}$. August 7. Same remarks as to 1459.

FAMILY MOTACILLIDÆ—WAGTAILS and TIT-LARKS, or PIPITS.

ANTHUS LUDOVICIANUS.

Tit-lark.

Alauda ludoviciana, GMELIN, Syst. Nat., I, 1788, 793.

Anthus ludovicianus, LICHT., Verz., 1823, 27.—BAIRD, B. N. Am., 1858, 232; Cat. N. Am. B., 1859, No. 165; Review, 1864, 153.—B. B. & R., Hist. N. Am. B., I, 1874, 171, pl. x, fig. 3.—COOPER, Orn. Cal., 78.—COUES, Key, 1872, 90, fig. 34; Check List, 1873, No. 55; B. N.W., 1874, 40.—HENSHAW, 1875, 187.

Perhaps no bird of the Interior is more abundant in winter than the Tit-lark is, at times, in localities of a nature calculated to attract them. At the Truckee Meadows they came in immense flocks in November, and spread over the soggy meadows, where they remained during the moderately cold weather for the greater portion of the winter, occasionally congregating by thousands about the haystacks and corrals. They were equally abundant at Carson City, particularly in the vicinity of the warm springs, where the high temperature of the water kept the meadow soft and comparatively green, even during the coldest weather. In April, just before their departure for the North, we observed them in their more highly-colored plumage.

List of specimens.

193, ♀ *ad.;* West Humboldt Mountains, Nevada, September 17, 1867. (Stream, in garden.) 6—10—$3\frac{3}{16}$—$2\frac{5}{8}$—$\frac{7}{16}$—$\frac{13}{16}$—$2\frac{7}{16}$—1. Upper mandible, dark horn-color, darker terminally; lower, paler, nearly straw-yellow at base; iris, hazel; tarsi and toes, dark horn-color.

270, ♀ *ad.;* Truckee Meadows, November 8. $6\frac{15}{16}$—$10\frac{7}{8}$—$3\frac{9}{16}$—$2\frac{7}{8}$—$\frac{15}{32}$—$\frac{13}{16}$—$2\frac{3}{4}$—$1\frac{3}{16}$. Bill, black; basal half of lower mandible, light-brown; iris, hazel; tarsi and toes, very dark blackish-brown.

274, ♀ *ad.;* Truckee Meadows, November 15. $6\frac{1}{2}$—10—$3\frac{5}{16}$—$2\frac{11}{16}$—$\frac{1}{2}$—$\frac{13}{16}$—$2\frac{1}{2}$—$1\frac{5}{16}$. Upper mandible and tip of lower, nearly black, remaining portion dull wax-yellow, deepest basally—almost lemon-yellow on rictus; iris, deep vandyke; tarsi and toes, uniform blackish, toes *not* darker—dull light-yellowish beneath.

275, ♂ *ad.;* Truckee Meadows, November 15. $6\frac{7}{8}$—$11\frac{1}{16}$—$3\frac{5}{8}$—$2\frac{15}{16}$—$\frac{1}{2}$—$\frac{13}{16}$—$2\frac{7}{8}$—$1\frac{1}{8}$. Toes more blackish than tarsus.

276, ♂ *ad.*; $6\frac{3}{4}$—$10\frac{7}{8}$—$3\frac{9}{16}$—$2\frac{7}{8}$—$\frac{1}{2}$—$\frac{3}{4}$—$2\frac{13}{16}$—$1\frac{1}{8}$. Same remarks.
277, ♂ *ad.*; $6\frac{3}{4}$—$10\frac{3}{4}$—$3\frac{1}{2}$—$2\frac{11}{16}$—$\frac{1}{2}$—$\frac{13}{16}$—$2\frac{7}{8}$—$1\frac{1}{8}$. Same remarks.
278, ♂ *ad.*; 7—$10\frac{3}{4}$—$3\frac{1}{2}$—$2\frac{13}{16}$ - $\frac{1}{2}$—$\frac{13}{16}$—$2\frac{3}{4}$—1. Same remarks.
279, ♂ *ad.*; $6\frac{5}{8}$—$10\frac{1}{2}$—$3\frac{7}{16}$—$2\frac{11}{16}$—$\frac{1}{2}$—$\frac{3}{4}$—$2\frac{9}{16}$—1. Tarsi, dark sienna-brown; toes, more blackish, distinctly pale yellowish beneath.
280, ♂ *ad.*; $6\frac{11}{16}$—$10\frac{7}{8}$—$3\frac{1}{2}$—$2\frac{13}{16}$—$\frac{1}{2}$—$\frac{3}{4}$—$2\frac{3}{4}$—1. Same remarks.
281, ♂ *ad.*; $6\frac{9}{16}$—$10\frac{1}{2}$—$3\frac{1}{2}$—$2\frac{15}{16}$—$\frac{1}{2}$—$\frac{3}{4}$—$2\frac{3}{4}$—$1\frac{1}{4}$. Same remarks.
282, ♂ *ad.*; $6\frac{1}{2}$—$10\frac{3}{8}$—$3\frac{3}{8}$—$2\frac{13}{16}$—$\frac{1}{2}$—$\frac{3}{4}$—$2\frac{5}{8}$—(?). Same remarks.
283, ♂ *ad.*; $6\frac{5}{8}$—$10\frac{3}{4}$—$3\frac{5}{8}$—$2\frac{15}{16}$—$\frac{1}{2}$—$\frac{13}{16}$—$2\frac{3}{4}$—(?). Same remarks.

FAMILY MNIOTILTIDÆ—AMERICAN WARBLERS.

HELMINTHOPHAGA RUFICAPILLA.

Nashville Warbler.

Sylvia ruficapilla, WILS., Am. Orn., III, 1811, 120, pl. 27, fig. 3.

Helminthophaga ruficapilla, BAIRD, B. N. Am., 1858, 256; Cat. N. Am. B., 1859, No. 183; Review, 1864, 175.—B. B. & R., Hist. N. Am. B., I, 1874, 196, pl. XI, figs. 7, 8.[1]—COOPER, Orn. Cal., 82.—COUES, Key, 1872, 94; Check List, 1873, No. 67; B. N.W., 1874, 50.—HENSHAW, 1875, 188.

Although not observed in summer, this bird was more or less common in September in the thickets along the streams in the lower portion of the cañons. It is not as yet definitely known whether this species breeds anywhere within the Western Region, or whether, on the other hand, the individuals which have been obtained at so many localities west of the Rocky Mountains were migrants from the Eastern Region, which, near the northern boundary of the United States, extends so much farther toward the Pacific coast. The same doubt exists in the case of *Lanivireo solitarius*. It is well known, however, that toward our northern border the Rocky Mountains form much less of a barrier to the westward range of eastern species, many of which, following the head-waters of the Yellowstone and other tributaries of the Missouri River, have but a short flight to reach the head-streams of the Columbia, and thus reach the Pacific coast in Oregon and Washington Territory, by passing down the valley of the latter stream.

---

[1] On p. 191 a "var. *gutturalis*" is characterized, supposed to be distinguished by having the yellow of the throat confined strictly within the maxillæ, and not, as in true *ruficapilla*, covering the cheeks; the race being based on No. 901 of this catalogue, = No. 53,354, National Museum catalogue. Should this peculiarity prove constant, the western birds may be distinguished by that name. Figure 8, Hist. N. Am. Birds, quoted above, represents this form.

These same individuals, in the case of non-resident species, during their autumnal migration, probably follow the bases of the mountain ranges directly southward, instead of returning by the devious route by which they reached the western portions of the country. The occasional capture of such species as those named above, and the more accidental occurrence of others, as *Ectopistes migratoria* (see pp. 355, 380, 385, and 596), at localities in the Western Region, may thus be accounted for.

List of specimens.

901, ♂ ad.; East Humboldt Mountains (Secret Valley), Nevada, September 6, 1868. 4⅞—7⅞—2⅛. Upper mandible, plumbeous-black, the tomium slightly paler; lower, plumbeous-white, with lilaceous glow; iris, burnt-umber; tarsi, bluish-plumbeous; toes, stained with yellow. [Type of *Helminthophaga ruficapilla* var. *gutturalis*, Baird, Brewer, and Ridgway, History of North American Birds, Vol. I, 1874, p. 191, pl. XI, fig. 8.]

HELMINTHOPHAGA VIRGINIÆ.

Virginia's Warbler.

Helminthophaga virginiæ, BAIRD, B. N. Am., ed. 1860, p. xi, pl. 79, fig. 1; Cat. N. Am. B., 1859, No. 183a; Review, 1865, 177.—B. B. & R., Hist. N. Am. B., I, 1874, 199, pl. XI, fig. 12.—COOPER, Orn. Cal., 85.—COUES, Key, 1872, 94; Check List, 1873, No. 66; B. N.W., 1874, 51.—HENSHAW, 1875, 189.

This interesting little Warbler was first observed among the cedar and piñon groves on the eastern slope of the Ruby Mountains. It was not met with west of this locality, but eastward it occurred on all those ranges having a similar or equally extensive growth. At the first-named locality it was rather common in July and August, and was found in the same groves with the Black-throated Gray Warbler (*Dendrœca nigrescens*) and the Lead-colored Vireo (*Lanivireo plumbeus*). On the Wahsatch and Uintah Mountains it was more abundant, being particularly plentiful among the scrub-oaks on the foot-hills near Salt Lake City. They lived entirely among the bushes, which there were so dense that the birds were difficult to obtain, even when shot. The usual note of this species is a soft *pit*, very different from the sharp *chip* of *H. celata*, while its song is so exceedingly similar to that of the Summer Yellow-bird (*Dendrœca œstiva*) that we often found it difficult to distinguish them.

List of specimens.

859, *juv.;* East Humboldt Mountains, Nevada, August 5, 1868. 5—7¼—(?)—2. Upper mandible, plumbeous-black, the tomium yellowish-white; lower mandible, dull light-ashy, darker terminally; tarsi and toes, yellowish-plumbeous, the latter pale yellow beneath.

1040, ♂ *ad.;* Salt Lake City, Utah (City Creek Cañon), May 24, 1869. 5—8. Bill, lilaceous-blue, the upper mandible nearly black; iris, brown; tarsi, hepatic-slate; toes, yellowish.

1041, ♀ *ad.* (mate of preceding); 4¾—7¼. Same remarks.

1053, ♀ *ad.;* Salt Lake City, May 26. 5—7¼. Same remarks.

1192, ♂ *ad.;* Salt Lake City, June 21. 4¹⁵⁄₁₆—7⅝. Same remarks.

1188, nest and eggs (4); Salt Lake City, June 19. Nest imbedded in the layer of dead leaves covering the ground under oak-thicket, on side of ravine; female shot.

HELMINTHOPHAGA CELATA.

Orange-crowned Warbler.

α. *celata—Common Orange-crowned Warbler.*

Sylvia celata, SAY, Long's Exped., I, 1823, 169.
Helminthophaga celata (part), BAIRD, B. N. Am., 1858, 257; Cat., 1859, No. 184 (part); Review, 1865, 176.—COOPER, Orn. Cal., 83.—COUES, Key, 1872, 95; Check List, 1873, No. 68 (part); B. N.W., 1874, 52.—B. B. & R., Hist. N. Am. B., I, 1874, 202, pl. XI, fig. 5.—HENSHAW, 1875, 191.

β. *lutescens.—Yellow Orange-crowned Warbler.*

Helminthophaga celata var. *lutescens*, RIDGWAY, Am. Jour. Sci. & Arts, Jan., 1872, 457; Am. Nat., VII, Oct., 1873, p.——.—B. B. & R., Hist. N. Am. B., I, 1874, 204, pl, XI, fig. 4.
Helminthophaga celata. b. *lutescens*, COUES, B. N.W., 1874, 52.
Helminthophaga celata (part), BAIRD, B. N. Am., and Rev.—COUES, Key, and Check List.—COOPER, Orn. Cal., 83.

The Orange-crowned Warbler was most frequently met with during its autumnal migration, at which time it was the most abundant of all the species of the family; it was also not uncommon in summer in the high aspen woods of the loftier mountains. In the fall, the thickets and lower shrubbery along the streams, particularly those of the lower cañons, would fairly swarm with them during the early portion of the mornings, as they busily sought their food, in company with various insectivorous birds, especially the Black-capped Green Warbler (*Myiodioctes pusillus*) and Swainson's Vireo (*Vireosylvia swainsoni*). At such times they uttered frequently their sharp note of *chip*. The brightly-colored specimens representing *H. lutescens* were prevalent in the western depression of the Basin, but were not observed eastward of the upper portion of the Valley of the Humboldt, nor at any locality during the summer; and wherever found, were associated with individuals of the other form, which is the only one found breeding on the mountains. It is therefore inferred that all these individuals were migrants from the northern Pacific Coast region and the Sierra Nevada, while those of *H. celata* proper were from the higher portions of the more eastern mountains, or from farther northward in the Rocky Mountain ranges; full-fledged young birds being numerous in the high aspen woods of the Wahsatch Mountains in July and August.

List of specimens.

a. celata.

921, ♂ *ad.;* "Dearing's Creek," Upper Humboldt Valley, September 11, 1868. 5—$7\frac{5}{8}$—(?)—$2\frac{1}{8}$. Upper mandible, brownish plumbeous-black, the tomium whitish; lower, pale lilaceous-plumbeous, darker terminally; iris, bright sienna; tarsi and toes, plumbeous, with yellow cast.

922, ♀ *ad.;* "Dearing's Creek," Upper Humboldt Valley, September 11, 1868. $4\frac{3}{4}$—$7\frac{1}{8}$—(?)—$1\frac{15}{16}$. Bill rather more lilaceous.

1425, ♂ *juv.;* Parley's Park, Wahsatch Mountains, Utah, July 17, 1869. $4\frac{13}{16}$—$7\frac{5}{8}$. Upper mandible, black; commissure and lower mandible, dark lilaceous, latter paler basally; iris, brown; tarsi, plumbeous; toes, olive.

1505, ♂ *ad.;* Parley's Park, August 12, 1869. 5—$7\frac{1}{2}$. Same remarks.

1516, ♂ *ad.;* Parley's Park, August 16, 1869. $5\frac{3}{16}$—$5\frac{7}{8}$. Upper mandible, black, paler along tomium; lower, lilaceous-blue, whitish basally, blackish terminally; iris, brown; tarsi, dull plumbeous; toes, more greenish.

β. lutescens.

215, ♂ *ad.;* Camp 19, West Humboldt Mountains, Nevada, September 24, 1867. $4\frac{7}{8}$—$7\frac{3}{8}$—$2\frac{3}{8}$—2—$\frac{3}{8}$—$\frac{11}{16}$—$1\frac{13}{16}$—$\frac{13}{16}$. Bill, blackish horn-color, the lower mandible, paler; iris, brown; tarsi and toes, deep horn-color.

907, ♂ *ad.;* "Secret Valley," East Humboldt Mountains, Nevada, September 8, 1868. $4\frac{7}{8}$—$7\frac{5}{16}$—(?)—2. Upper mandible, purplish-black, the tomium deep lilac; lower mandible, bluish-lilac, more pinkish basally, more dusky toward tip; iris, vandyke-brown; tarsi and toes, plumbeous, the latter stained with yellow.

926, ♂ ad.; "Dearing's Creek," Upper Humboldt Valley, Nevada, September 12. 4 15/16—7 3/8—(?)—2. Upper mandible, plumbeous-black, the tomium edged with paler; lower, plumbeous-white, darker terminally; iris, burnt-sienna; tarsi and toes, plumbeous, latter with a yellowish tinge.

DENDRŒCA ÆSTIVA.

Summer Yellow-bird; Golden Warbler.

Motacilla æstiva, GMELIN, Syst. Nat., I, 1788, 996.

Dendrœca æstiva, BAIRD, B. N. Am., 1858, 282; Catal., 1859, No. 203; Review, 1865, 195.—COOPER, Orn. Cal., 87.—COUES, Key, 1872, 97; Check List, 1873, No. 70; B. N.W., 1874, 54.—B. B. & R., Hist. N. Am. B., I, 1874, 222, pl. XIV, fig. 1.—HENSHAW, 1875, 192.

This common and familiar little bird was met with everywhere, except during the winter season; and in all wooded localities, with the exception of the higher forests, which it gave up chiefly to *D. auduboni*, was the most abundant and generally distributed member of the family. At Sacramento it was one of the commonest birds, inhabiting every copse, whether of willow, cotton-wood, or oak; and throughout the Interior it was equally plentiful in every locality producing a growth of willows or other shrubbery, being most multiplied in the river-valleys or lower cañons, and gradually decreasing in numbers toward the summits of the mountains. No difference whatever exists, apparently, between the western and eastern birds of this species.

List of specimens.

11, nest and eggs (3); Sacramento, California, June 8, 1867. Nest on small oak, in grove.

24, 25, 26, 27, nest and eggs; Sacramento, California, June 11, 1867. Nests in a small oak-grove, nearly similarly situated, being generally placed on a high branch near the top of the trees, about fifteen or twenty feet from the ground.

121, ♂ jur.; valley of the Truckee, Nevada, August 6, 1867. 5 5/16—7 13/16—2 9/16—2 3/8 —1/2—5/8—1 3/4—5/8. Upper mandible, leaden-black, the tomium whitish; lower, leaden-bluish; iris, hazel; tarsi and toes, yellowish horn-color, latter yellowish beneath.

158, ♀ ad.; valley of the Humboldt (Camp 17), September 2. 5 3/16—7 1/2—2 7/16—2— 7/16—5—1 3/4—1 3/16. Upper mandible, black, the tomium pale ashy-lilac; lower mandible, pale ashy-lilac; iris, hazel; tarsi and toes, liver-brown, scutellæ margined with ashy-blue.

881, ♀ juv.; East Humboldt Mountains, Nevada, August 29, 1868. 4 7/8—7 1/4—(?)—2. Upper mandible, olive-brown, edged with paler; lower, uniform greenish-white; iris, bister; tarsi and toes, dilute sepia, strongly washed with yellow.

1254, 1255, 1256, nests and eggs; Parley's Park, Utah, June 23, 1869. Nests in willows along stream.

1306, nest and eggs (4); Parley's Park, June 27. Nest in rose-bush near stream.

1415, nest and egg (1); Parley's Park, July 16, 1869. Nest in willows.

DENDRŒCA OCCIDENTALIS.

Western Warbler.

Sylvia occidentalis, TOWNSEND, Journ. Ac. Nat. Sci. Philad., VII, ii, 1837, 190.

Dendrœca occidentalis, BAIRD, B. N. Am., 1858, 268; Catal., 1859, No. 190; Review, 1865, 183.—COOPER, Orn. Cal., 92.—COUES, Key, 1872, 98; Check List, 1873, No. 72.—B. B. & R., Hist. N. Am. B., I, 1874, 266, pl. XII, fig. 5.—HENSHAW, 1875, 201.

On the 29th of August, 1868, a single individual of this strongly-marked species was seen in the lower portion of one of the eastern cañons of the East Humboldt Mountains. It was busily engaged in searching for its insect food, in a thicket along the stream, during which occupation it uttered an occasional note, sounding like a lisped and faint enunciation of *pzeet*.

DENDRŒCA TOWNSENDI.

Townsend's Warbler.

"*Sylvia townsendi*, NUTTALL," TOWNSEND, Journ. Ac. Nat. Sci. Philad., VII, ii, 1837, 191.

Dendrœca townsendi, BAIRD, B. N. Am., 1858, 269; Catal., 1859, 191; Review, 1865, 185.—COOPER, Orn. Cal., 91.—COUES, Key, 1872, 98; Check List, 1873, No. 73.—B. B. & R., Hist. N. Am. B., I, 1874, 265, pl. XII, fig. 7.—HENSHAW, 1875, 200.

This Warbler, like the *D. occidentalis*, was exceedingly rare along our route, only one other specimen besides that obtained having been seen. The one in question was observed on the 8th of September, in an alder-thicket high up one of the eastern cañons of the East Humboldt Mountains. The manners and notes of this species, as observed at this season, seemed much like those of *D. occidentalis*, neither possessing any strikingly distinctive trait, so far as could be observed.

List of specimens.

942, ♂ ad.; Thousand Spring Valley, Nevada, September 24, 1868. (Specimen badly mutilated; no measurements.)

DENDRŒCA NIGRESCENS.

Black-throated Gray Warbler.

Sylvia nigrescens, TOWNSEND, Journ. Ac. Nat. Sci. Philad., VII., ii, 1837, 191.

Dendrœca nigrescens, BAIRD, B. N. Am., 1858. 270; Catal., 1859, No. 192; Review, 1865, 186.—COOPER, Orn. Cal., 90.—COUES, Key, 1872, 98; Check List, 1873, No. 75; B. N.W., 1874, 55.—B. B. & R., Hist. N. Am. B., I, 1874, 258, pl. XII, fig. 8.—HENSHAW, 1875, 188.

The Black-throated Gray Warbler doubtless breeds on all the higher mountains of the Western Region, since Mr. C. E. Aiken has discovered it to be a summer resident on the most eastern ranges in Colorado, while it has long been known as a summer bird of the Pacific Coast district; but the mountains of the Great Basin having sufficient timber-growth—a condition essential to the presence of this species—are very few, and so far between, that we met with it at few localities. On the eastern slope of the Ruby Mountains, it was abundant in July and August, in the piñon and cedar woods, never entering the brushwood in the cañons. A few individuals were also seen in Pack's Cañon, Uintah Mountains, where they inhabited the lower slopes which were covered with a scattered growth of scrub-oaks and mountain-mahogany. At the former locality, several families of full-grown young were observed still following their parents. Their song was not heard, but their ordinary note greatly resembled the sharp *chip* of the eastern Yellow-rump (*D. coronata*).

List of specimens.

840, ♂; East Humboldt Mountains. Nevada, July, 14, 1868. $4\frac{3}{4}$—$7\frac{3}{4}$—(?)—$2\frac{3}{16}$. Bill, deep black; iris, dark sepia; tarsi and toes, sepia-black.

855, ♂; East Humboldt Mountains, August 4, 1868. $5\frac{3}{8}$—$7\frac{1}{8}$—(?)—$2\frac{1}{4}$. Same remarks.

863, ♂; August 7, 1868. $5\frac{1}{8}$—$7\frac{5}{8}$—(?)—$2\frac{1}{8}$. Same remarks.

866, ♀; August 10, 1868. 5—$7\frac{5}{8}$—(?)—2. Bill, black, slightly lilaceous at base of lower mandible.

DENDRŒCA AUDUBONI.

Audubon's Warbler.

Sylvia audubonii, TOWNSEND, Journ. Acad. Nat. Sci. Philad., VII, ii, 1837, 190.

Dendrœca audubonii, BAIRD, B. N. Am., 1858, 273; Catal., 1859, No. 195; Review, 1865, 188.—COOPER, Orn. Cal., 88.—COUES, Key, 1872, 100; Check List, 1873, No. 79; B. N.W., 1874, 58.—B. B. & R., Hist. N. Am. B., I, 1874, 229, pl. XIII, fig. 1.—HENSHAW, 1875, 194.

As is the case with the eastern Yellow-rumped Warbler (*D. coronata*),

28 P R

except in the southern portion of its habitat, Audubon's Warbler, the western representative of that species, is the only one of the family which remains during the winter. Its migrations seem to be mainly, if not entirely, vertical, its summer-home being the pine forests of the mountains, while in winter it dwells among the cotton-woods of the river-valleys, or the brushwood of the lower cañons. In its habits and manners it is an exact counterpart of *D. coronata*, which it also resembles so strikingly in plumage; but its notes are markedly different, the usual one being a feeble *wit*, very unlike the sharp *chip* of the eastern species.

List of specimens.

218, ♂ *ad.;* West Humboldt Mountains, Nevada, September 25, 1867. $5\frac{7}{8}$—9—$3\frac{1}{8}$—$2\frac{13}{16}$—$\frac{13}{32}$—$\frac{11}{16}$—$2\frac{1}{2}$—1. Bill, tarsi, and toes, deep black; iris, hazel.

245, ♂ *ad.;* West Humboldt Mountains, October 8, 1867. $5\frac{7}{8}$—$9\frac{1}{8}$—$3\frac{1}{2}$—$2\frac{5}{8}$—$\frac{3}{8}$—$\frac{1}{2}$—$2\frac{7}{16}$—$1\frac{1}{16}$. Same remarks.

346, ♀ *ad.;* Truckee Valley, Nevada, December 7, 1868. $5\frac{1}{2}$—$8\frac{3}{4}$—$2\frac{7}{8}$—$2\frac{3}{8}$—$\frac{7}{16}$—$\frac{11}{16}$—$2\frac{3}{8}$—$\frac{7}{8}$. Same remarks.

493, ♂ *ad.;* Carson City, Nevada, April 4, 1868. 6—$9\frac{5}{8}$—$3\frac{5}{16}$—$2\frac{3}{4}$. Iris, burnt-umber.

500, ♂ *ad.;* Carson, April 18, 1868. 6—$9\frac{1}{2}$—$3\frac{1}{4}$—$2\frac{5}{8}$. Bill, jet-black; iris, burnt-umber; tarsi and toes, sepia-black.

1257, single egg; Parley's Park, Wahsatch Mountains, Utah, June 23, 1869. Nest near extremity of horizontal branch of pine tree, about ten feet from ground; contained, besides, three young.

GEOTHLYPIS TRICHAS.

Maryland Yellow-throat.

Turdus trichas, LINN., Syst. Nat., I, 1766, 293.

Geothlypis trichas, CABANIS, Mus. Hein., 1850, 16.—BAIRD, B. N. Am., 1858, 241; Catal., 1859, No. 170; Review, 1865, 220.—COOPER, Orn. Cal., 95.—COUES, Key, 1872, 107, fig. 47; Check List, 1873, 97; B. N.W., 1874, 74.—B. B. & R., Hist. N. Am. B., I, 1874, 297, pl. XV, figs. 7, 8.—HENSHAW, 1875, 204.

In all bushy places contiguous to water, this little bird was invariably to be found; but it was confined to the valleys, being replaced among the mountains, even in the lower cañons, by the *G. macgillivrayi.* Clumps of wild-rose briers and the banks of the sloughs seemed to be its favorite resorts, and in such localities near Pyramid Lake it was one of the most abundant species in May, and all day long enlivened the vicinity of one of our camps by its pleasant song of *witch'ity, witch'ity, witch'ity*—often from several rival males at the same time.

List of specimens.

750, eggs (4); mouth of Truckee River, May 19, 1868. Nest in sage-bush, in moist depression.

883, *juv.;* Ruby Valley, Nevada, August 29, 1868. 5¼—6¾—(?)—1¾. Upper mandible, sepia-black, the tomium pale brownish-yellow; lower, dilute lilaceous-sepia; iris, plumbeous-brown; tarsi and toes, dilute pinkish-sepia, the toes strongly washed with yellow.

899, ♀ *juv.;* Secret Valley, Nevada, September 23, 1868. 5⅛—7—(?)—1⅞. Same remarks.

953, ♂ *ad.;* Deep Creek, Utah, October 5, 1868. 5₇⁄₁₆—7—(?)—1⅞. Bill, black; commissure and basal half of lower mandible, dilute brownish-lilac; iris, bister; tarsi and toes, uniform sepia.

1400, nest and eggs; valley of Weber River, June, 1869. [J. C. Olmsted.]

GEOTHLYPIS MACGILLIVRAYI.

McGillivray's Warbler.

Sylvia macgillivrayi, AUDUBON, Orn. Biog., V, 1839, 75, pl. 399, figs. 4, 5.

Geothlypis macgillivrayi, BAIRD, B. N. Am., 1858, 244, pl. 99, fig. 4; Catal., 1859, No. 173; Review, 1865, 227.—COOPER, Orn. Cal., 96.—COUES, Key, 1872, 107; Check List, 1873, No. 99.—B. B. & R., Hist. N. Am. B., I, 1874, 303, pl. xv, figs. 4, 5.—HENSHAW, 1875, 205.

Geothlypis philadelphia var. *macgillivrayi,* ALLEN, Bull. Mus. Comp. Zool., III, July, 1872, 175.—RIDGWAY, Am. Journ. Sci. & Arts, Dec., 1872, 459.

Geothlypis philadelphia. a. *macgillivrayi,* COUES, B. N.W., 1874, 75.

Representing the Maryland Yellow-throat in the mountains, this species was found in all the fertile cañons from the Sierra Nevada to the Uintahs. It inhabited the rank herbage near the streams, or the undergrowth of the thickets and aspen copses. We did not hear the song of this species, but were very familiar with its ordinary note, a strong *chip*, greatly resembling that of the Indigo-bird, or its western representative (*Cyanospiza cyanea* and *C. amœna*), the notes of both old and young being alike.

List of specimens.

175, ♀ *juv.;* West Humboldt Mountains, Nevada, September 9, 1867. 5½—7₇⁄₁₆— 2₇⁄₁₆—2₁⁄₁₆—₇⁄₁₆—¾—2¼—1¼. Upper mandible, brownish-black; commissure and lower mandible, brownish lilaceous-white, the latter darker terminally; iris, hazel; tarsi and toes, brownish-white.

900, ♂ *juv.;* East Humboldt Mountains, Nevada (Camp 23), September 6, 1868. 5½—7½—(?)—2₁⁄₁₆. Iris, grayish-sepia; tarsi and toes, pinkish-white.

906, ♂ *ad.;* East Humboldt Mountains, September 8, 1868. 5₅⁄₁₆—7⅝—(?)—2¼. Upper mandible, brownish-plumbeous, paler toward commissure; lower, paler brownish, lilaceous-white, darker terminally; iris, grayish-sepia; tarsi and toes, sepia-white.

1258, 1259, nests and eggs; Parley's Park, Wahsatch Mountains, Utah, June 23, 1869. Nests about eighteen inches above the ground, in small briers or bushes, in weedy undergrowth near stream. (Parents of both shot.)

1307, nest and eggs (4); Parley's Park, June 27, 1869. Nest in bush, about a foot from ground.

1365, nest and eggs (3); Uintah Mountains, July 3, 1869. Nest among undergrowth of aspen-grove, in bush, a foot from ground.

1380, ♂ juv.; Uintah Mountains, July 7, 1869. 5⅜—7⅛. Bill, black, the commissure and basal two-thirds of lower mandible, deep lilaceous; iris, brown; tarsi, light lilaceous-brown; toes, darker.

1432, ♂ juv.; Parley's Park, July 19, 1869. 5½—7¾. Upper mandible, black, the tomium white; lower, lilaceous-white, the terminal third dusky; iris, brown; tarsi, purplish-brown; toes, dark brown.

ICTERIA VIRENS.

Yellow-breasted Chat.

β. longicauda—Long-tailed Chat.

Icteria longicauda, LAWRENCE, Ann. Lyc. N. H., N. Y., VI, April, 1853, 4.—
    BAIRD, B. N. Am., 1858, 249, pl. 34, fig. 2; Catal., 1859, No. 177; Review,
    1865, 230.—COOPER, Orn. Cal., 98.
Icteria virens var. longicauda, COUES, Key, 1872, 108; Check List, 1873, No. 100a.
    —B. B. & R., Hist. N. Am. Birds, I, 1874, 309.—HENSHAW, 1875, 206.
Icteria virens. b. longicauda, COUES, Birds N.W., 1874, 77.

The distribution of the Yellow-breasted Chat corresponds so nearly with that of the Maryland Yellow-throat, that they were generally to be found in the same thicket; but its vertical range is somewhat greater, it being frequently met with in the lower portion of the cañons. It was equally common in California and the Interior, and appeared to be in all respects the same bird as the eastern race. Its song during the breeding-season, like that of the eastern bird, is conspicuous from its extreme oddity, as well as for its power and variety; and we were often awakened at midnight by its notes, when, but for the yelping of the prowling Coyotes (Canis latrans), the stillness would have been unbroken. It was also observed that they were particularly musical on bright moonlight nights.

List of specimens.

23, nest and eggs (3); Sacramento, California, June 11, 1867. Nest in wild-rose brier, among undergrowth of oak grove.

49, ♂ ad. (parent of No. 48); Sacramento, California, June 17, 1867. $7\frac{7}{8}$—$10\frac{1}{8}$— $3\frac{5}{16}$—$2\frac{3}{4}$—$\frac{5}{8}$—$\frac{5}{16}$—$3\frac{5}{8}$—$1\frac{7}{8}$. Bill, entirely pure black; whole inside of mouth, intense black; iris, hazel; tarsi and toes, pale slate-blue.

165, ♀ ad.; West Humboldt Mountains (Camp 18), September 4, 1867. $7\frac{7}{8}$—$10\frac{1}{8}$— $3\frac{1}{2}$—$2\frac{15}{16}$—$\frac{5}{8}$—1—$3\frac{1}{2}$—$1\frac{1}{16}$. Upper mandible, horn-black, *tomium bluish-white; lower mandible, lilaceous-white,* point of gonys, black; iris, hazel; *tarsi and toes, plumbeous, without any shade of blue.*

168, ♂ ad.; West Humboldt Mountains, September 7, 1867. 8—10—$3\frac{3}{8}$—$2\frac{13}{16}$—$\frac{9}{16}$— $\frac{15}{16}$—$3\frac{5}{16}$—$1\frac{5}{8}$. Upper mandible, horn-black, *tomium bluish-white; lower mandible, pearl-white,* tip of gonys, black; *tarsi and toes, dull plumbeous.*

48, nest and eggs (3); Sacramento, June 17, 1867. Nest about three feet from ground, in thorny bush in dense thicket.

568, ♂ ad.; Truckee Reservation, May 15, 1868. $7\frac{7}{8}$—10—$2\frac{3}{4}$. Bill, and whole interior of mouth, intense black; iris, blackish-brown; tarsi and toes, plumbeous.

MYIODIOCTES PUSILLUS.

Black-capped Yellow Warbler.

α. pusillus.

Muscicapa pusilla, WILSON, Am. Orn., III, 1811, 103, pl. 26, fig. 4.
Myiodioctes pusillus, BONAP., Consp. Av., I, 1850, 315.—BAIRD, B. N. Am., 1858, 293 (part); Catal., 1859, No. 211; Review, 1865, 240 (part).—COOPER, Orn. Cal., 101.—COUES, Key, 1872, 109, fig. 50 (part); Check List, 1873, No. 102; B. N.W., 1874, 79 (part).—B. B. & R., Hist. N. Am. B., I, 1874, 317, pl. XVI, figs. 3, 4.—HENSHAW, 1875, 207.
Myiodioctes pusillus var. *pusillus,* RIDGWAY, Am. Journ. Sci. & Arts, Dec., 1872, 457.

β. pileolata.

Myiodioctes pusillus (part), AUCT.
Motacilla pileolata, PALLAS, Zoog. Rosso-As., I, 1811, 497.
Myiodioctes pusillus var. *pileolata,* RIDGW., Am. Journ. Sci. & Arts, Dec., 1872, 457.—B. B. & R., Hist. N. Am. B., I, 1874, 319.

This sprightly Warbler was not seen at Sacramento, but in the valley of the Truckee, and in many suitable localities to the eastward, it was a rare summer resident, becoming exceedingly numerous in autumn. Its haunts during the breeding-season were much the same as those of the Summer Yellow-bird (*Dendrœca æstiva*), but in September it was most abundant in the shrubbery along the cañon streams.

List of specimens.

a. pusillus.

203, ♂ *ad.;* West Humboldt Mountains, September 20, 1867. $4\frac{13}{16}$—$6\frac{7}{8}$—$2\frac{2}{3}$—$1\frac{15}{16}$—$\frac{3}{8}$ —$1\frac{1}{16}$—$1\frac{15}{16}$—$\frac{31}{32}$. Upper mandible, blackish horn-color edged with pale brownish; lower mandible, pale lilaceous-brown; iris, brown; tarsi and toes, yellowish-brown, the former strongly stained with yellow posteriorly.

880, ♂ *ad.;* East Humboldt Mountains, August 29, 1868. $5\frac{1}{8}$—$6\frac{7}{8}$—(?)—$1\frac{7}{8}$. Upper mandible, deep-black, tomium edged with lilaceous; lower, dilute-lilac, more whitish beneath; iris, sepia; tarsi and toes, dilute brownish-yellow, the tarsi more sulphury, the toes deeper.

887, ♂ *ad.;* East Humboldt Mountains, September 1, 1868. 5—7—(?)—2. Upper mandible, blackish-olivaceous, tomium and lower mandible, dilute reddish lilaceous-brown; iris, sepia; tarsi and toes, pale olivaceous-yellow.

888, ♀ *ad.;* same locality and date. $4\frac{7}{8}$—$6\frac{7}{8}$—$1\frac{7}{8}$. Tarsi, pale purplish-brown; toes, olive-yellow.

1039, ♀ *ad.;* Antelope Island, Great Salt Lake, May 24, 1869. $4\frac{3}{4}$—7. Upper mandible, brownish-black; lower, paler, basal two-thirds, pale wood-brown; iris, brown; tarsi and toes, dilute-brown.

β. pileolata.

120, ♂ *ad.;* valley of the Truckee, Nevada, August 6, 1867. 5—$6\frac{5}{16}$—$2\frac{1}{16}$. Bill, delicate pinkish horn-color, darker on the culmen; iris, hazel; tarsi and toes, dilute horn-color, stained with yellow.

166, ♀ *ad.;* valley of the Lower Humboldt, Nevada, September 5, 1867. $4\frac{3}{4}$—$6\frac{13}{16}$— $2\frac{1}{4}$. Bill, dark horn-color, lower mandible paler, dilute brown basally; iris, dark hazel; tarsi and toes, horn-color, latter yellowish beneath.

176, ♂ *ad.;* West Humboldt Mountains, September 9, 1867. $5\frac{1}{8}$—$6\frac{3}{4}$—$2\frac{5}{16}$. Bill, dark horn-color, paler beneath, the lower mandible inclining to lilaceous; iris, hazel; tarsi and toes, pale livid horn-color.

SETOPHAGA RUTICILLA.

American Redstart.

Muscicapa ruticilla, LINN., Syst. Nat., I, 1766, 326.

Setophaga ruticilla, SWAINS., Zool. Jour., III, 1827, 358.—BAIRD, Birds N. Am., 1858, 297; Catal., 1859, No. 217; Review, 1865, 256.—COUES, Key, 1872, 110; Check List, 1873, No. 104; Birds N.W., 1874, 81.—B. B. & R., Hist. N. Am. Birds, I, 1874, 319, pl. XVI, figs. 1, 5.—HENSHAW, 1875, 209.

This beautiful little bird was common in summer throughout the Wah-satch district, being one of several eastern species which have their westward range limited only by the commencement of the arid and treeless region of the Great Basin. It was abundant in the valleys and the lower portion of the cañons, but it did not extend far up into the mountains. A few were seen, in June, in the orchard of the "Church Ranche," on Antelope Island.

List of specimens.

1104, ♂ ad.; Antelope Island, Great Salt Lake, Utah, June 4, 1869. 5⅜—7⅜. Bill, tarsi, and toes, deep black; iris, brown.

FAMILY HIRUNDINIDÆ—SWALLOWS.

PROGNE SUBIS.

Purple Martin.

Hirundo subis, LINN., Syst. Nat. (10th ed.), 1758, 192.

Progne subis, BAIRD, Review Am. B., 1865, 274.—B. B. & R., Hist. N. Am. B., I, 1874, 329, pl. XVI, figs. 7, 10.—HENSHAW, 1875, 213.

Hirundo purpurea, LINN., Syst. Nat. (12th ed.), 1766, 344.

Progne purpurea, BOIE, Isis, 1826, 971.—BAIRD, B. N. Am., 1858, 314; Catal., 1859, No. 231.—COOPER, Orn. Cal., 113.—COUES, Key, 1872, 114; Check List, 1873, No. 117; B. N.W., 1874, 91.

In the more thickly-populated districts of California, the handsome Purple Martin has become, as it has long since in the Eastern States, semi-domesticated, and almost entirely allured from its original haunts, the forests, by the superior advantages afforded by the surroundings of civilized man; but in the more scantily-settled Interior it was found still retaining its primitive habits. In the cities of San Francisco and Sacramento it was a very abundant species, while eastward of the Sierra Nevada it was rare, except among the aspen woods of the pine-region on certain of the higher mountain ranges. In Carson City it was not common, while in Virginia City but a single individual was seen, the date being June 18, 1868. Among the aspens of the Wahsatch, near Parley's Park, however, it was extremely abundant, and nested in the deserted or captured excavations of the Red-naped Woodpecker (*Sphyrapicus nuchalis*), most of which were bored into the trunks of living trees, these holes being freely shared with the White-bellied Swallows (*Tachycineta bicolor*).

As a rule, the Swallows, although true Oscines, are not considered singers; the present species, however, is at least one notable exception, since it is a warbler of high merit. Often have we reclined on some mossy or fern-covered bank beneath the aspens, and given respectful attention to the performance of a voluble male Purple Martin, as, with glossy violet head thrust from the entrance to his nest, he entertained his mate with liquid warblings, varied by sweet cadences, his throat swelling and vibrating with the volume of his song.

PETROCHELIDON LUNIFRONS.

Cliff Swallow.

Hirundo lunifrons, SAY, Long's Exped., II, 1823, 47.—BAIRD, B. N. Am., 1858, 309; Catal., 1859, No. 226.—COOPER, Orn. Cal., 104.

Petrochelidon lunifrons, SCLATER, Cat. Am. B., 1862, 40.—BAIRD, Review, 1865, 288.—COUES, Key, 1872, 114; Check List, 1873, No. 114; B. N.W., 1874, 88. —B. B. & R., Hist. N. Am. B., I, 1874, 334, pl. XVI, 13.—HENSHAW, 1875, 215.

The first land-bird observed after arriving at San Francisco, was this familiar and widely-diffused species, multitudes of which were observed to swarm about certain old buildings along with smaller numbers of Purple Martins (*Progne subis*). It was also noticed along every portion of our route across the Great Basin, especially in the vicinity of rivers or lakes, or at the settlements, whether large or small. The species may be considered the most abundant one of the family throughout the West, the next in order being the White-bellied and Rough-winged Swallows (*Tachycineta bicolor* and *Stelgidopteryx serripennis*). In localities most remote from settlements it of course built its nest only on the face of overhanging cliffs, but if near a settlement, any large building, as a barn or church, was almost sure to be selected; in either case, vast numbers congregating together and fixing their peculiar gourd-shaped nests side by side or upon each other, the same as in the east. It was not observed to build in any other way, and it is probable that the nesting-habits of this species are less variable than those of its kindred, excepting, perhaps, the common Barn Swallow (*Hirundo horreorum*), which differs chiefly in selecting caves or the interior of dwellings, and in being not gregarious.

List of specimens.

852, ♂ ad.; East Humboldt Mountains, Nevada, July 22, 1868. 6—12¼—(?)—3¾. Bill, deep black; interior of mouth, pinkish-dusky; iris, dark claret-brown; tarsi and toes, dark horn-color.

871, egg (1); East Humboldt Mountains, August 25, 1868. Nest attached to side of a rafter, underneath roof of a shed, at ranche.

HIRUNDO ERYTHROGASTER.

Barn Swallow.

β. *horreorum*.[1]

Hirundo horreorum, BARTON, Frag. Nat. Hist. Penn'a, 1799, 17.—BAIRD, Birds N.
Am., 1858, 308; Catal., 1859, No. 225; Review, 1865, 294.—COOPER, Orn.
Cal., 103.—COUES, Key, 1872, 113, fig. 54; Check List, 1873, No. 111; Birds
N.W., 1874, 85.—B. B. & R., Hist. N. Am. Birds, I, 1874, 339, pl. XVI, fig.
9.—HENSHAW, 1875, 217.

Although inhabiting the same localities as the Cliff Swallow, the present species was observed to be everywhere much less numerous. It was
most common along the shore and on the islands of Pyramid Lake, where
it nested among the tufa domes, each nest being attached to the ceiling of
a cave among the rocks. In few instances were more than a single pair
found in one cave. Several nests were also found in caverns among the limestone cliffs on the eastern side of the Ruby Mountains.

List of specimens.

408, ♂ ad.; valley of the Humboldt, September, 1867.

1451, nest and eggs (3); Parley's Park, Wahsatch Mountains, Utah, July 26, 1869.
Nest in stable, attached to rafter.

TACHYCINETA BICOLOR.

White-bellied Swallow.

Hirundo bicolor, VIEILLOT, Ois. Am. Sept., I, 1807, 61, pl. 31.—BAIRD, Birds N.
Am., 1858, 310; Catal., 1859, No. 227; Review, 1865, 297.—COOPER, Orn.
Cal., 106.—B. B. & R., Hist. N. Am. B., I, 1874, 344, pl. XVI, fig. 8.
Tachycineta bicolor, CABANIS, Mus. Hein., 1850, 48.—COUES, Key, 1872, 113;
Check List, 1873, No. 112; Birds N.W., 1874, 86.—HENSHAW, 1875, 217.

This species and the Purple Martin were the only Swallows which were

---

[1] It is not yet satisfactorily determined whether the North American birds of this
species differ constantly from South American examples to the extent that the two
series may be separated as geographical races. In case they should not prove thus
constantly different, the proper name of the North American bird is *H. erythrogaster*,
Boddaert, while the following synonyms are to be added to the above citations:—

Hirundo erythrogaster, BODD., Tabl. Pl. enl. (724, fig. 1), 1783, 45 (Cayenne).—
SCLATER, Catal. Am. Birds, 1861, 39 (Brazil).

Hirundo rufa, GM., Syst. Nat., I, 1788, 1018 (Pl. enl., 724, fig. 1).—BURM., Ueb.,
III, 148 (Brazil).

Hirundo cyanopyrrha, VIEILL., Nouv. Dict., XVI, 1817, 510.

confined strictly to wooded districts or to settlements, their distribution being much the same, except that, in the case of wooded localities, the former was most abundant in the river-valleys, while the latter occurred oftenest on the mountains. Among the cotton-woods of the Lower Truckee, near Pyramid Lake, in May, the White-bellied Swallow abounded more than elsewhere, and every knot-hole or other cavity among the trees seemed to have been taken possession of by a pair. They were then engaged in building their nests, and throughout the day would come to the door-yard of the Reservation-house to pick up the feathers, or bits of rag or paper, scattered about the ground, after hurriedly seizing which they would fly with the article selected in a direct line to their nests. As they sat on the ground, they were beautiful little birds, and though they squatted some-what awkwardly, on account of the smallness of their feet, they raised their heads so proudly, and glanced so sharply, yet timidly, about them, that they seemed graceful in their motions; while each movement caused the sunlight to glance from their burnished backs of lustrous steel-blue, with which the snowy white of their breasts contrasted so strikingly. Although the object picked up was most often a feather, it occasionally happened that one would take hold of a string, or a long shred of cloth, perhaps a yard or more in length, in which case, so conspicuous an object was certain to be seized upon by others, as the bearer labored to carry it to his nest, thus becoming the subject of quite a struggle, and much twittering.

The White-bellied Swallow was by no means confined to the wooded river-valleys, however, but it was equally abundant among the aspen woods, high up in the Wahsatch Mountains, at an altitude of 8,000 or 9,000 feet; it was also common in the Sacramento Valley, but a few feet above sea-level, among the oak trees of the plain. Neither is it invariably arboreal, for it seems to have become, in certain localities, more "civilized," like its cousin, the Purple Martin, and to have taken advantage of the abode of man in localities where there are no trees to accommodate them. Such was conspicuously the case at Carson City, where they were quite numerous, and built their nests under the eaves, behind the weather-boarding, or about the porches of dwellings or other buildings, and were quite familiar. The specimens in the collection were shot on the wing; and when one was brought down the rest would exhibit great concern, circling about the victim, and uttering a plaintive twitter, as their suffering companion lay fluttering on the ground.

List of specimens.

473, ♀ ad.; Carson City, Nevada, March 30, 1868. 6—13—4¾—4⅛. Bill, deep black; *interior of mouth, fleshy white;* tarsi and toes, dark sepia, the latter pinkish beneath.

474, ♂ ad.; Carson City, Nevada, March 30, 1868. 5¾—13—4¾—4¹⁄₁₆. *Interior of mouth, pale yellow.*

475, ♀ ad.; Carson City, Nevada, March 30, 1868. 6—12⅝—4⅝—3¹⁵⁄₁₆. *Interior of mouth, fleshy white.*

748, eggs; Truckee Bottoms, May 19, 1868. Nest of straw and feathers, in deserted woodpecker's hole, in willow tree.

768, 769, eggs (3—4); Truckee Bottoms, May 29, 1868. Nests with same location, etc., as preceding.

1038, ♂ ad.; Salt Lake City, Utah, May 24, 1869. 6—13. Bill, black; iris, brown; feet, dark purplish-brown.

1416, eggs (3); Parley's Park, Wahsatch Mountains, Utah, July 16, 1869. Eggs in knot-hole in aspen-tree. Nest of feathers.

1484, ♂ juv.; Parley's Park, Wahsatch Mountains, Utah, July 30, 1869. 5¾—12. Bill, black; rictus and interior of mouth, yellow; iris, brown; feet, dark livid sepia.

1485, ♂ juv.; Parley's Park, Wahsatch Mountains, Utah, July 30, 1869. 5⅝—11¾. *Feet, light pink.*

TACHYCINETA THALASSINA.

Violet-green Swallow.

Hirundo thalassina, SWAINSON, Philos. Mag., I, 1827, 365.—BAIRD, Birds N. Am., 1858, 311; Catal., 1859, No. 228; Review, 1865, 299.—COOPER, Orn. Cal.. 107.—B. B. & R., Hist. N. Am. Birds, I, 1874, 347, pl. XVI, fig. 11.
Tachycineta thalassina, CABANIS, Mus. Hein., 1850, 48.—COUES, Key, 1872, 113; Check List, 1873, No. 113; Birds N.W., 1874, 86.—HENSHAW, 1875, 217.

The beautiful Violet-green Swallow was first seen on the main island in Pyramid Lake, during the month of May. They were very abundant, and frequented chiefly the cliffs of calcareous tufa, where they were observed to enter the fissures of the rock to their nests within. In July we saw it again among the limestone walls of the eastern cañons of the Ruby Mountains, where it also nested in the crevices on the face of the cliffs, its associates being the White-throated Swift (*Panyptila saxatilis*), and Cliff Swallow (*Petrochelidon lunifrons*). Their nests were in almost every case out of reach, only two of those that were found being accessible. Both were in horizontal fissures, scarcely large enough to admit the hand; the nest consisting of a flattened mass of sticks and straws, lined with feathers, like those of the Bank Swallows (*Cotyle* and *Stelgidopteryx*); one of them contained five young birds, but the other had apparently been tampered with in some way, since the parent was dead and her three eggs broken. The latter, like those of *T. bicolor* and the two species above mentioned, were pure white, without markings.

Although other observers, whose statements we do not in the least doubt, have described the habits of this bird as arboreal, like those of the White-bellied Swallow (*T. bicolor*) and the Purple Martin, we never found it so in any locality during our trip, it being everywhere a strictly saxicoline species, and an associate of *Panyptila saxatilis*, *Petrochelidon lunifrons*, and *Hirundo horreorum* rather than of the species named, and to be found only where precipitous rocks, affording suitable fissures, occurred. When on the wing the appearance of this lovely Swallow is very striking, and so unlike that of any other that it may be immediately distinguished. No other species resembles it except the *T. bicolor*, which is somewhat similar on account of the pure white lower parts; but a more attentive examination discovers the greater amount of white on the side of the head, and if the bird is viewed from above the plumage is seen to be tricolored—the rump rich intense violet, and the back lustrous green, the two colors being separated by a very conspicuous, broad, and apparently continuous, band of snowy white across the upper part of the rump, caused by the close approximation of the two white flank-patches.

This Swallow appeared to be a very silent species, but a few notes were heard, which called to mind the chirping of young Purple Martins, as heard in rainy weather.

List of specimens.

761, ♂ ad.; island in Pyramid Lake, Nevada, May 23, 1868. 5¼—12¾—(?)—4⅝. Bill, deep black; iris, burnt-umber; tarsi and toes, deep sepia.

847, ♀ ad.; East Humboldt Mountains, Nevada, July 20, 1868. 5¼—11¾—(?)—3⅜. Bill, deep black; interior of mouth, pale naples-yellow; iris, dark sepia; tarsi and toes, pale sepia-purple.

1070, ♀ ad.; Salt Lake City, Utah (City Creek Cañon), May 29, 1869.

COTYLE RIPARIA.

Bank Swallow.

Hirundo riparia, LINN., Syst. Nat., I, 1766, 344.
Cotyle riparia, BOIE, Isis, 1822, 550.—BAIRD, B. N. Am., 1858, 313; Catal., 1859,
No. 229; Review, 1865, 319.—COOPER, Orn. Cal., 110.—COUES, Key, 1872,
114; Check List, 1873, No. 115; B. N.W., 1874, 90.—B. B. & R., Hist. N. Am.
B., I, 1874, 353, pl. XVI, fig. 14.—HENSHAW, 1875, 220.

The distribution of the common Bank Swallow was the same as that of the Rough-winged species, but it was everywhere less abundant. We never found it except when associated with the latter bird, and its habits and appearance seemed so much the same that it required somewhat close observation to distinguish them readily. The pure white lower parts, crossed by a dusky band across the breast, however, served as a good and unfailing mark by which to distinguish the present species, the lower parts of the Rough-winged Swallow being uniform mouse-color, growing gradually paler behind; while the flight of the Bank Swallow is swifter and more graceful, more like that of the species of *Tachycineta*, or true *Hirundo*.

While on the Truckee Reservation, in May, it was daily our custom to visit a small pond, situated in a broad meadow, for the purpose of studying the several species of Swallows which came there in large numbers every evening. Having taken our post of observation a little before sunset, a few individuals of the Rough-winged and White-bellied species were sure to be already there, having but a few rods to come from the ravines and cotton-woods near by. In a short time the Barn Swallows would make their appearance, gliding easily and swiftly over the surface of the water in pursuit of their insect-food. This soon became the most abundant species, excepting the Cliff Swallow, there having arrived in the meantime a very few individuals of the Violet-green and Bank Swallows, the latter being the least numerous of all. In one evening, as we sat on the grassy bank of this pond, we killed specimens of each of these species as they flew by us.

List of specimens.

1410, 1411, 1412, eggs. Valley of Weber River, June, 1869. [J. C. Olmstead.]

STELGIDOPTERYX SERRIPENNIS.

Rough-winged Swallow.

Hirundo serripennis, AUDUBON, Orn. Biog., IV, 1838, 593.

Cotyle serripennis, BONAP., Consp. Av., I, 1850, 342.—BAIRD, B. N. Am., 1858, 313; Catal., 1859, No. 230.—COOPER, Orn. Cal., 110.

Stelgidopteryx serripennis, BAIRD, Review Am. B., 1865, 316.—COUES, Key, 1872, 114; Check List, 1873, No. 116; B. N.W., 1874, 90.—B. B. & R., Hist. N. Am. B., I, 1874, 350, pl. XVI, fig. 12.—HENSHAW, 1875, 219.

Next to the Cliff and White-bellied Swallows, this was the most abundant species of the family. It was found only in the river-valleys, however, or in the lower ravines of the mountains, where, in company with the Bank Swallow, it excavated the earthy banks or took possession of holes dug by the Kingfisher (*Ceryle alcyon*). Its habits in general are quite similar to those of the species with which it so freely associates.

List of specimens.

534, ♀ *ad.*; Carson City, Nevada, April 25, 1868. 5¼—11½—4 1/16—3½. Bill, black; iris, bister; tarsi and toes, dark horn-sepia.

1194, ♀ *ad.*; Salt Lake City, Utah, June 21, 1869. 5—11½. Bill, deep black; iris, brown; feet, black.

1409, eggs; valley of Weber River, June, 1869. [J. C. Olmstead.]

FAMILY AMPELIDÆ—WAX-WINGS or CHATTERERS.

AMPELIS CEDRORUM.

Cedar-bird.

Bombycilla cedrorum, VIEILLOT, Ois. Am. Sept., I, 1807, 88, pl. 57.

Ampelis cedrorum, SCLATER, Proc. Zool. Soc. Lond., 1856, 299.—BAIRD, Birds N. Am., 1858, 318; Catal., 1859, No. 233; Review, 1866, 407.—COOPER, Orn. Cal., 129.—COUES, Key, 1872, 115, pl. 56; Check List, 1873, 119; Birds N.W., 1874, 93.—B. B. & R, Hist. N. Am. Birds, I, 1874, 401, pl. XVIII, fig. 2.— HENSHAW, 1875, 229.

At only one locality did we meet with this elegant bird, and that was in the Upper Humboldt Valley, where it was common in September in the thickets along the streams flowing from the Clover Mountains. It was found in small companies, feeding on the fruit of a species of thorn-apple, or haw (*Cratægus rivularis*), which abounded in the thickets.

List of specimens.

915, ♂ *ad.;* Dearing's Ranch, Upper Humboldt Valley, September 10, 1868. 7 7/16—
11½—(?)—3¼. Bill, tarsi and toes, deep black ; iris, purplish-brown.

916, ♂ *ad.* Same date, locality, and remarks. 7¼—11⅜—(?)—3.

? PHÆNOPEPLA NITENS.

Shining Ptilogonys.

Ptiliogonys nitens, SWAINSON, Anim. Menag., 1838, 285.
Cichlopsis nitens, BAIRD, Birds N. Am., 1858, 320, 923.
Phænopepla nitens, SCLATER, Proc. Zool. Soc. Lond., 1858, 543. —BAIRD, Cat. N.
    Am. Birds, 1859, No. 234; Review, 1866, 416.—COOPER, Orn. Cal., 131.—
    COUES, Key, 1872, 116; Check List, 1873, No. 120.—B. B. & R., Hist. N.
    Am. Birds, I, 1874, 405, pl. XVIII, figs. 3, 4.—HENSHAW, 1875, 229.

On several occasions we heard, among the cedar and piñon woods of the desert ranges in western Nevada, a note so similar to the prolonged, querulous, rattling call of Nuttall's Woodpecker (*Picus nuttalli*), that we entered the fact among our notes as evidence of the occurrence of that species eastward of the Sierra. We could never see the author of these notes, however, until, on the 27th of June, 1868, when exploring the Soda Lakes of the Carson Desert, we heard near by, in a ravine of that remarkable locality, the same familiar call and immediately started in search of the bird which produced it. It was soon discovered, perched upon the summit of a large grease-wood bush, but at our approach immediately took wing, and, notwithstanding every artifice and caution on our part, kept out of gunshot range, although enticing us on by frequent halts, during which it perched upon the topmost branch of the most prominent bushes. At each flight the peculiar rattling call referred to was uttered, so that the bird so long sought was at last before us. We were greatly surprised, however, to find that it was not the species we had supposed, but one we had never seen before.

Several shots were fired at it during the most favorable opportunities, but it escaped unscathed, and we were therefore unable to identify it with certainty. The appearance of the bird was so remarkable that we are able to refer it to only one known North American species—the *Phænopepla nitens,* with the female or young male of which it corresponded in plumage, as well as could be ascertained from the distant view obtained. In its motionless attitude while perched, it called to mind *Oreoscoptes montanus*, which it closely resembled in size, general form, and dull, grayish colors; but when it flew its markings were more varied, *the wings presenting a large white patch, apparently on the primaries.* The manner of its flight was quite similar to that of the Mocking-bird (*Mimus polyglottus*), the wings and tail being widely spread; while the resemblance was still more striking from the white patch on the primaries. These characteristics correspond well with those of the female or young male of *Phænopepla nitens*, so that all circumstances taken into consideration render it extremely probable that this species is a rare summer inhabitant of the desert portions of western Nevada, a supposition strengthened by the fact that it was obtained in the southern portion of the State by Mr. Bischoff, the naturalist of Lieutenant Wheeler's expedition, in 1871.

FAMILY VIREONIDÆ—GREENLETS.

VIREOSYLVIA GILVA.

Warbling Vireo, or Greenlet.

β. swainsoni.

Vireo swainsoni, BAIRD, B. N. Am., 1858, 336 (in text, *sub V. gilvus*).
Vireosylvia swainsoni, BAIRD, Review Am B., 1866, 343.
Vireosylvia gilva var. *swainsoni*, BAIRD, in Coop. B. Cal., I, 1870, 116.—B. B. & R., Hist. N. Am. B., I, 1874, 371.—HENSHAW, 1875, 221.
Vireo gilvus var. *swainsoni*, COUES, Key, 1872, 121, fig. 64; Check List, 1873, No. 125a.
Vireo gilvus. b. *swainsoni*, COUES, B. N.W., 1874, 98.

Few, if any, of the western birds are more extensively distributed or more abundant than this Greenlet, for it abides in all fertile localities. Altitude makes no difference with it, since it is equally common among the willows or cotton-woods of the lowest valleys and the aspens just below the timber-line—the only condition required being, seemingly, the existence of deciduous trees or shrubbery. The food of this bird consists in summer chiefly of worms and other insects, but in the autumn it seems to subsist almost exclusively on the small bluish berries of a species of cornel (*Cornus pubescens*), which grows abundantly along the mountain streams.

The habits and notes of the western birds of this species are in all respects like those of the eastern ones.

List of specimens.

122, ♀ *ad.*; valley of the Truckee (Camp 12), August 6, 1867. $5\frac{3}{8}$—$8\frac{1}{4}$—$2\frac{11}{16}$—$2\frac{1}{4}$—$\frac{7}{16}$—$\frac{5}{8}$—$1\frac{15}{16}$—1. Upper mandible, dark horn-color, commissure and lower mandible, lilaceous-white; iris, deep brown; tarsi and toes, light plumbeous-blue.

153, ♂ *ad.*; valley of the Humboldt (Camp 17), September 7, 1867. $5\frac{5}{16}$—$8\frac{5}{16}$—$2\frac{11}{16}$—$2\frac{1}{4}$—$\frac{3}{8}$—$\frac{5}{8}$—$1\frac{7}{8}$—$\frac{11}{16}$. Bill, black, commissure and basal two-thirds of lower mandible, more lilaceous; iris, hazel; tarsi and toes, plumbeous-blue, almost ultramarine.

177, ♀ *ad.*; West Humboldt Mountains (Camp 18), September 9, 1867. 5—$7\frac{7}{8}$—$2\frac{11}{16}$—$2\frac{1}{4}$—$\frac{3}{8}$—$\frac{5}{8}$—$1\frac{7}{8}$—$1\frac{1}{4}$. Same remarks.

180, ♀ *ad.*; West Humboldt Mountains, September 10, 1867. $5\frac{1}{4}$—8—$2\frac{9}{16}$—$2\frac{1}{4}$—$\frac{7}{16}$—$\frac{9}{16}$—$1\frac{3}{4}$—$\frac{3}{4}$. Upper mandible, slaty horn-color, tomium edged with lilaceous; lower, pearl-whitish basally, then pale blue, the tip as dark as the upper mandible; iris, brown; tarsi and toes, light ashy-ultramarine.

187, ♂ *ad.*; West Humboldt Mountains, September 12, 1867. $5\frac{1}{2}$—$8\frac{3}{8}$—$2\frac{11}{16}$—$2\frac{1}{4}$—$\frac{3}{8}$—$\frac{5}{8}$—2—$1\frac{2}{16}$. Same remarks.

809, nest and eggs (2); Fort Churchill (Carson River), Nevada, June 24, 1868. Nest in cotton-wood copse, about four feet from ground. Female seen on nest.

878, ♀ *ad.*; East Humboldt Mountains, August 27, 1868. $5\frac{7}{16}$—$8\frac{11}{16}$—(?)—$2\frac{5}{16}$. Upper mandible, plumbeous-black with lilaceous edge; lower, plumbeous-blue with lilaceous glow basally, and darker terminally; iris, burnt-umber; tarsi and toes, delicate light ashy-blue.

879, (sex unknown); East Humboldt Mountains, August 27, 1868. $5\frac{3}{8}$—$8\frac{1}{2}$—$2\frac{5}{16}$. Same remarks.

1109, ♂ *ad.*; Antelope Island, Great Salt Lake, June 5, 1869. $5\frac{1}{2}$—$8\frac{15}{16}$. Bill, dull blackish, the basal two-thirds of lower mandible lilaceous-bluish; iris, brown; tarsi and toes, plumbeous-blue.

1251, 1252, 1253, nests and eggs; Parley's Park, Wahsatch Mountains, Utah; June 23, 1869. Nests all about four feet from ground, in aspens of a grove.

1317, nest and eggs; Parley's Park, June 27, 1867. Aspens.

1497, ♂ *ad.*; Parley's Park, August 10, 1869. $5\frac{7}{16}$—$8\frac{11}{16}$. Upper mandible, blackish-brown; commissure and lower mandible, lilaceous; iris, vandyke-brown; tarsi and toes, fine light blue.

1504, ♂ *ad.*; Parley's Park, August 12, 1869. $5\frac{3}{8}$—$8\frac{3}{4}$. Same remarks.

LANIVIREO CASSINI.

Cassin's Vireo.

Vireo cassini, XANTUS, Pr. Ac. Nat. Sci. Philad., 1858, 117.—BAIRD, B. N. Am., 1858, 340, pl. 78, fig. 1; Catal., 1859, No. 251.

Lanivireo solitarius var. *cassini*, B. B. & R., Hist. N. Am. B., I, 1874, 377, pl. XVII, fig. 9.

Vireo solitarius var. (?) *cassini*, HENSHAW, 1875, 223.

"*Vireo solitarius*" (part), COOPER, Orn. Cal., I, 1870, 117.

This rare and little-known species was noticed only in the cañons of the West Humboldt Mountains, where it was not uncommon in September. Those found had probably migrated from the region to the northwestward, or from the Cascade Mountains or the country adjacent, since examples of *Zonotrichia coronata*, *Pipilo oregonus*, and *Melospiza guttata* were obtained at the same place.

List of specimens.

174, *ad.*; west slope of West Humboldt Mountains, Nevada, September 9, 1867. $5\frac{1}{2}$—9—$2\frac{15}{16}$—$2\frac{1}{4}$—$\frac{1}{2}$—$\frac{9}{16}$—$2\frac{1}{16}$—1. Upper mandible black, tomium bluish-lilac; lower mandible pure pale blue, the tip black; iris, hazel; tarsi and toes, fine ashy-ultramarine.

217, ♂ *ad.*; east slope of West Humboldt Mountains, September 25, 1867. $5\frac{1}{8}$—$7\frac{15}{16}$—$2\frac{3}{4}$—$2\frac{3}{16}$—$1\frac{3}{32}$—$\frac{5}{8}$—$2\frac{1}{8}$—$\frac{15}{16}$. Same remarks.

LANIVIREO SOLITARIUS.

Solitary Vireo.

Muscicapa solitaria, WILSON, Am. Orn., II, 1810, 143, pl. 17, fig. 6.
Vireo solitarius, VIEILL., Nouv. Dict. Hist. Nat., XI, 1817.—BAIRD, B. N. Am., 1858, 340; Catal., 1859, No. 250.—COOPER, Orn. Cal., 117 (part).—COUES, Key, 1872, 66, 121; Check List, 1873, 127; B. N.W., 1874, 99.—HENSHAW, 1875, 222.
Vireosylvia solitaria, BAIRD, Review Am. B., 1866, 347.
Lanivireo solitarius, B. B. & R., Hist. N. Am. B., I, 1874, 373, pl. XVII, fig. 8.

This species was met with only during its autumnal migrations, when it seemed to be not uncommon in the month of September among the cañon thickets of the western slope of the Clover Mountains. A single specimen was also shot in a buffalo-berry thicket in Buena Vista Cañon, on the eastern slope of the West Humboldt Mountains, in September of the preceding year. It is still a question whether such individuals of this species were migrants from the higher portions of the mountains or from a more northern region; but that their migration was not vertical is most probable.

List of specimens.

920, ♂ *ad.*; head of Humboldt Valley (Camp 24), September 11, 1868. $5\frac{5}{16}$—9—(?)—$2\frac{3}{4}$. Bill black, basal half of lower mandible, plumbeous-blue; iris, burnt-umber; tarsi and toes, fine ashy-blue.

LANIVIREO PLUMBEUS.

Lead-colored Vireo.

Vireo plumbeus, COUES, Pr. Ac. Nat. Sci. Philad., 1866, 73; Key, 1872, 122, fig. 6.
Vireosylvia plumbea, BAIRD, Review Am. B., 1866, 349.—COOPER, Orn. Cal., 119.
Vireo solitarius var. *plumbeus*, ALLEN, Bull. Mus. Comp. Zool., III, 1872, 176.—
    COUES, Key, 1872, 351; Check List, 1873, No. 127a; B. N.W., 1874, 100.—
    HENSHAW, 1875, 224.
Lanivireo solitarius var. *plumbeus*, B. B. & R., Hist. N. Am. B., I, 1874, 377, pl.
    XVII, fig. 10.

The first locality where we met with this species in traveling eastward,
was the eastern slope of the Ruby Mountains, where several other species
characteristic of the Rocky Mountain district were first encountered, as
Helminthophaga virginiæ and *Selasphorus platycercus*.   It was rather common
in July and August, its usual abode being the cedar and nut-pine groves on
the lower slopes of the mountains, along with *Dendrœca nigrescens* and *Helminthophaga virginiæ*, or in the brushwood of the ravines.   Certain of its
notes so closely resembled those of *Troglodytes parkmanni* that they were
hard to distinguish.

List of specimens.

858, *ad.* (sex unknown); East Humboldt Mountains, Nevada, August 5, 1868.
$5\frac{3}{4}$—$9\frac{1}{2}$—(?)—$2\frac{9}{16}$. Bill, plumbeous-black, basal half of lower mandible, plumbeous-
blue; iris, dark bister; tarsi and toes, fine ashy-ultramarine.

861, ♂ *ad.;* East Humboldt Mountains, August 5, 1868. (Specimen too badly
mutilated for measuring.) Same remarks as to preceding.

VIREO PUSILLUS.

Least Vireo.

Vireo pusillus, COUES, Pr. Ac. Nat. Sci. Philad., 1866, 76.—BAIRD, Review Am.
    B., 1866, 360.—COOPER, Orn. Cal., 124.—COUES, Key, 1872, 124; Check
    List, 1873, No. 132.—B. B. & R., Hist. N. Am. B., I, 1874, 391, pl. XVII, fig.
    14.—HENSHAW, 1875, 226.

This Vireo was the characteristic and most abundant species at Sacramento City, where it inhabited the dense willow copses along with
Empidonax pusillus.   It was not observed anywhere else during our explorations, and it is probable that its northward range in California is limited
to the immediate vicinity of the Sacramento River.   Its notes most resemble

those of *V. belli*, of the eastern prairie districts, but they are somewhat different. A single nest was found, the one in question being attached to a forked twig of a low bush among the undergrowth of a dense willow copse; it was about three feet from the ground, and contained no eggs.

List of specimens.

47, ♂ *ad.;* Sacramento, California, June 17, 1867. $5\frac{1}{4}$—7—$2\frac{3}{16}$—$1\frac{15}{16}$—$\frac{7}{16}$—$\frac{11}{16}$—$2\frac{3}{16}$ —$1\frac{1}{4}$. Upper mandible, dusky; lower, brownish-white; iris, dark hazel; tarsi and toes, fine plumbeous-blue.

55, ♂ *ad.;* Sacramento, June 18, 1867. 5—7—$2\frac{3}{16}$—$1\frac{7}{8}$—$\frac{3}{8}$—$1\frac{1}{16}$—$2\frac{1}{8}$—$1\frac{1}{4}$. Bill, blackish-brown, commissure and lower mandible, pale brownish-lilaceous; iris, dark hazel; tarsi and toes, deep ashy-ultramarine.

FAMILY LANIIDÆ—SHRIKES OR BUTCHER BIRDS.

COLLURIO BOREALIS.

Great Northern Shrike.

Lanius borealis, VIEILLOT, Ois. Am. Sept., I, 1807, 90, pl. 50.

Collyrio borealis, BAIRD, Birds N. Am., 1858, 324; Cat. N. Am. Birds, 1859, No. 236.

Collurio borealis, BAIRD, Review Am. B., 1866, 440.—COOPER, Orn. Cal., 137.— COUES, Key, 1872, 125, fig. 73; Check List, 1873, No. 134; Birds N.W., 1874, 101.—B. B. & R., Hist. N. Am. B., I, 1874, 415, pl. XIX, figs. 1, 2.—HENSHAW, 1875, 233.

During the winter of our residence at Carson City, several examples of this northern bird were seen, but it was at all times less common than the smaller species (*C. excubitoroides*), and seemed to be confined to the sheltered ravines among the foot-hills of the mountains. Those observed were perched on the summits of the willows along a stream, patiently surveying the surrounding fields and thickets, after the manner of other species of the genus.

List of specimens.

412, ♀ *ad.;* Carson City, Nevada, February 21, 1868. $10\frac{1}{4}$—$14\frac{1}{4}$—$4\frac{11}{16}$—$3\frac{11}{16}$. Bill, dull black, lower mandible more ashy, duller basally; iris, umber; tarsi and toes, black.

455, ♀ *ad.;* Carson City, March 25, 1868. $10\frac{1}{4}$—$14\frac{4}{8}$—$14\frac{13}{16}$—$3\frac{7}{8}$. Bill, nearly uniform dull slaty, lower mandible more ashy, paler basally; iris, burnt-umber; tarsi and toes, black.

COLLURIO LUDOVICIANUS.

Southern Shrike.

β. excubitoroides—White-rumped Shrike.

Lanius excubitoroides, SWAINSON, Fauna Bor. Am., II, 1831, 115, pl. 35.
Collyrio excubitoroides, BAIRD, B. N. Am., 1858, 527, pl. 75, fig. 2 ; Cat. N. Am. B., 1859, No. 238.
Collurio excubitoroides, BAIRD, Review Am. B., 1866, 445.—COOPER, Orn. Cal., 133.
Collurio ludovicianus var. *excubitoroides*, COUES, Key, 1872, 125 ; Check List, 1873, No. 135a.—B. B. & R., Hist. N. Am. B., I, 1874, 421, pl. XIX, fig. 3.—HENSHAW, 1875, 233.

Scarcely a locality was visited where this Shrike was not found, in greater or less plenty, its range including both the Sacramento Valley and the country eastward of the Sierra Nevada. At Sacramento it was frequently observed about the outskirts of the city, where it frequented the oak-groves and scattered trees, or the borders of the fields. In the Interior it was most common at those localities where there was a greater or less extent of willow thickets, with meadow-lands and sage-brush adjacent; but it was not rare on the higher mountain ranges, where it inhabited the mahogany and cedar groves in preference to other places. It was most usually observed perching quietly on the summit of a dead weed-stalk or prominent naked branch of a bush or tree, patiently watching for its food, or during its curious undulating flight, so strikingly characteristic of the species of this genus.

List of specimens.

156, ♂ *juv.;* valley of the Humboldt (Camp 17), September 2, 1867. 9—12¼—3$\frac{15}{16}$—3$\frac{5}{16}$—$\frac{11}{16}$—1—2$\frac{7}{16}$. Bill, slaty horn-black, basal portion of lower mandible paler; iris, brown; tarsi and toes, black.

344, *juv.;* cotton-woods of Carson River, Fort Churchill, Nevada, December 6, 1867. 9¼—12⅜—4—3¼—$\frac{11}{16}$—1—4—2⅜. Bill deep black, lower mandible paler basally; iris, brown; tarsi and toes, black.

442, ♂ *ad.;* Carson City, Nevada, March 10, 1868. 9⅛—13—4¼—3⅜. Bill, pure black; iris, bister; tarsi and toes, black.

482, ♂ *ad.;* Carson, April 2, 1868. 9¼—13⅛—4$\frac{3}{16}$—3$\frac{7}{16}$. Same remarks.

524, ♂ *ad.;* Carson, April 24, 1868. 9—13—4¼—3⅜. Same remarks.

849, ♀ *ad.;* East Humboldt Mountains, Nevada, July 21, 1868. (Mahoganies; altitude 9,000 feet.) 9⅛—13—(?)—3⅞. Bill, pure black; interior of mouth, livid fleshy-white; iris, bister; scutellæ of tarsi and toes, pure black, the interspaces dirty white.

889, *juv.;* East Humboldt Mountains, September 4, 1868. 8⅞—12¼—(?)—3$\frac{3}{16}$. Bill, slate-black, pale purplish on base of lower mandible; iris, brown; tarsi and toes, black.

1044, nest and eggs (4); Salt Lake City, Utah, May 24, 1869. Nest in oak-bush, about four feet from ground.

1055, nest and eggs; Salt Lake City, Utah, May 27, 1869. Nest in sage-bush.

1095, nest and egg (1); Antelope Island, Great Salt Lake, June 4, 1869. Nest in sage-bush.

1129, nest and eggs (4); Antelope Island, Great Salt Lake, June 7, 1869. Nest in rose-bush in ravine.

1427, eggs (2); Promontory Point, Utah, June, 1869. [F. A. Clark.]

1521, eggs; Fremont's Island, Great Salt Lake, August 16, 1869. [F. A. Clark.]

Family TANAGRIDÆ—Tanagers.

Pyranga ludoviciana.

Western Tanager; "Louisiana Tanager." [1]

Tanagra ludoviciana, Wilson, Am. Orn., III, 1811, 27, pl. 22, fig. 1.

Pyranga ludoviciana, Audubon, Synop., 1839, 137.—Baird, B. N. Am., 1858, 303; Catal. N. Am. B., 1859, No. 223.—Cooper, Orn. Cal., 145.—Coues, Key, 1872, 112; Check List, 1873, No. 110; B. N. W., 1874, 83.—B. B. & R., Hist. N. Am. B., I, 1874, 437, pl. xx, figs. 3, 4.—Henshaw, 1875, 235.

This beautiful Tanager, one of the most brilliant of western birds, was found to be very generally distributed through the wooded portions of the route traversed, excepting in the valley portions of California, none having been seen from Sacramento eastward until well into the pine forest of the Sierra Nevada. It was first observed on the western portion of that range, at an altitude of about 5,000 feet, its song first attracting attention, from its extreme similarity to that of the Scarlet Tanager (*P. rubra*) of the East. From this point eastward it was met with in every wooded locality, being much more frequently seen on the mountains than along the rivers of the lower valleys. In May, soon after their arrival from the south, these Tanagers were very numerous in the rich valley of the Truckee, near Pyramid Lake, where they were observed to feed chiefly on the buds of the grease-wood bushes (*Obione confertifolia*), in company with the Black-headed Grosbeak and Bullock's Oriole. Very few were seen later in the season, however, nearly all having departed for the mountain woods. During July and August it was a common species on the eastern slope of the Ruby Mountains, where it inhabited the groves

---

[1] Geographically inappropriate.

of cedar, nut-pine, and mountain mahogany; while from June to August
it was an abundant bird in the pine forests of the Wahsatch and Uintah
ranges. In September they were noticed to feed extensively on the fruit
of the *Cratægus rivularis*, in company with the Red-shafted Flicker, Gaird-
ner's Woodpecker, the Cedar-bird, and the Cross-bills (*Loxia americana* and
L. leucoptera).

In its habits this species is almost a perfect counterpart of the eastern
P. rubra, while its song is scarcely distinguishable, being merely of a slightly
finer, or more silvery, tone; but the ordinary note, sounding like *plit'-it*, is
very different from the *chip'-a-rā, ree* of the eastern species. The note of
the young is quite peculiar, being a low whistle, something like the complaining call of the Eastern Blue-bird (*Sialia sialis*), but louder.

List of specimens.

565, ♂ *ad.*; Truckee Reservation, May 15, 1868. 7⅜—11⁹⁄₁₆—3¼. Bill, dilute wax-
yellow, with a greenish cast, except along commissure, darker greenish-brown toward
the culmen, which is dark sepia, with the terminal half sharply, black; iris, grayish-
brown; tarsi and toes, pale plumbeous, the latter whitish beneath.

838, ♀ *ad.*; East Humboldt Mountains, Nevada, July 13, 1868. (Mahogany woods.)
7⅝—11¾—(♀)—3¼. Upper mandible, dark greenish-sepia, the tomium and lower mandible, light greenish-yellow; iris, burnt-umber; tarsi and toes, plumbeous.

1283, nest and eggs (3); Parley's Park, Wahsatch Mountains, Utah, June 25, 1869.
Nest on extreme end of horizontal branch of pine tree in grove.

1376, nest and eggs (3); Uintah Mountains, Utah, July 7, 1869. Nest on mountain-mahogany tree, near end of horizontal branch.

FAMILY FRINGILLIDÆ—FINCHES, SPARROWS, and BUNTINGS.

LOXIA AMERICANA.

Common Crossbill.

Curvirostra americana, WILSON, Am. Orn., IV, 1811, 44, pl. 31, figs. 1, 2.—BAIRD,
B. N. Am., 1858, 426; Catal., 1859, No. 318.—COOPER, Orn. Cal., I, 148.

Loxia americana, BONAP., Comp. & Geog. List, 1838, 38.

Loxia curvirostra var. *americana*, COUES, Key, 1872, 351; Check List, 1873, No.
143; B. N.W., 1874, 109.—B. B. & R., Hist. N. Am. B., I, 1874, 484, pl. XXIII,
figs. 1, 4.—HENSHAW, 1875, 248.

The Common Crossbill may breed on the higher portions of the loftier
ranges in the Interior, but none were seen by us until toward the last of

August, when they became gradually common in the lower cañons of the East Humboldt Mountains. They were usually observed in small flocks among the willows or aspens, and uttered frequently, especially while on the wing, a soft whistling note, somewhat like *chih, chih, chih,* quite unlike the note of any other bird of our acquaintance.

List of specimens.

884, ♂ *ád.;* Willows, foot of East Humboldt Mountains (Camp 21), August 29, 1868. 6—10¼—(?)—2⅜. Bill, uniform horn-sepia; tarsi and toes, grayish sepia; iris, raw-umber.

[This specimen is remarkable for its unusually small bill.]

LOXIA LEUCOPTERA.

White-winged Crossbill.

Loxia leucoptera, GMELIN, Syst. Nat., I, 1788, 844 —B. B. & R., Hist. N. Am. Birds, I, 1874, 488, pl. XXIII, figs. 2, 3.—COUES, Check List, 1873, No. 142; Birds N.W., 1874, 110.

Curvirostra leucoptera, WILSON, Am. Orn., IV, 1811, 48, pl. 31, fig. 3.—BAIRD, Birds N. Am., 1858, 427; Cat. N. Am. B., 1859, No. 319.—COOPER, Orn. Cal., I, 149.—COUES, Key, 1872, 129, fig. 76.

On the 12th of August, a male of what was probably this species, but in very unusually brilliant plumage, was seen among the cedars on the eastern slope of the Ruby Mountains. It is therefore probable that this species breeds sparingly on the higher portion of the loftier ranges.[1] In September it was common in the lower cañons on the eastern slope of the East Humboldt Mountains, where it inhabited the same localities as the more rare *L. americana.* The note of this Crossbill is a plaintive *week,* very different from the hurried *chih, chih* of the other species, or, indeed, the note of any other bird known to us.

---

[1] When first seen, this individual called instantly to mind the adult male of *Pyranga erythromelæna,* of Mexico and Central America, so rich and uniform was the bright carmine-red of the plumage, while the pure white wing-bands contrasted conspicuously with the deep black of the wings and tail. It is scarcely possible, however, that it could have been this southern Tanager, which has not yet been taken near our southern border. It should be considered, however, that a specimen of *Psaltriparus melanotis,* also a Mexican bird, not before detected in the United States, was observed in the same locality at nearly the same time.

CARPODACUS CASSINI.

Cassin's Purple Finch.

Carpodacus cassini, BAIRD, Pr. Ac. Nat. Sci. Philad., 1854, 119 ; B. N. Am., 1858, 414; Catal., 1859, No. 307.—COOPER, Orn. Cal., I, 155.—COUES, Key, 1872, 128; Check List, 1872, No. 146; B. N.W., 1874, 106.—B. B. & R., Hist. N. Am. B., I, 1874, 469, pl. XXI, figs. 4, 5.—HENSHAW, 1875, 240.

Although this Finch was observed to be essentially pinicoline, it was occasionally found among deciduous trees when such occurred in the immediate vicinity of coniferous forests, this being notably the case during the breeding-season. In the pine forests of the Sierra Nevada, near Carson City, these birds were first observed on the 21st of March, at which date large flocks were found among the trees. They continued to increase in abundance until about the middle of April, when they gradually dispersed through the forest, the greater number going higher up the mountains. At the time of their arrival they were in full song, and continued so during the season, and it was noticed that the young males, in the plumage of the females (possibly the latter also), sang almost if not quite as vigorously and sweetly as those in the adult livery. In certain localities on the eastern slope of the Ruby Mountains they were quite abundant on several occasions, the flocks consisting chiefly of young-of-the-year, which, with their parents, had apparently come from the higher coniferous woods near the summits of the range, since no nests were found among the cedar and piñon groves of the lower slopes. In the pine-belt of the Wahsatch and Uintah Mountains they were abundant from May to August, during the whole of which time they were nesting. Most of the nests found were among the aspens and narrow-leafed cotton-woods (*Populus tremuloides* and *P. angustifolia*) of the higher portions of the ravines, where these trees replaced the conifers.

The song of this species is clear and sweet, and is even superior to that of the Eastern Purple Finch (*C. purpureus*), which, however, it greatly resembles. Many passages are loud and clear, and so much like the notes of certain Vireones that we were several times led by them in search of a new Greenlet. Other portions of its song, which was greatly varied, were sweet, soft warblings, and tender, whistling calls.

List of specimens.

446, ♂ *ad.;* Carson City, Nevada, March 21, 1868. 6⅝—11—3¹¹⁄₁₆—3¹⁄₁₆. Bill, uniform horn-color, with delicate lilaceous tinge; iris, burnt-umber; tarsi and toes, dark horn-sepia.

447, ♂ ad.; Carson City, Nevada, March 21, 1868. 6$\frac{4}{16}$—11$\frac{1}{8}$—3$\frac{3}{4}$—3$\frac{1}{8}$. Same remarks. Bill, lilaceous-sepia.

463, ♂ ad.; Carson, March 28, 1868. 6$\frac{11}{16}$—11$\frac{1}{4}$—3$\frac{3}{4}$—3$\frac{1}{2}$. Same remarks.

464, ♂ ad.; Carson, March 28, 1868. 6$\frac{11}{16}$—11$\frac{1}{4}$—3$\frac{1}{16}$—3$\frac{1}{4}$. Same remarks.

465, ♀ ad.; Carson, March 28, 1868. 6$\frac{5}{8}$—11—3$\frac{3}{4}$—3. Same remarks.

466, ♀ ad.; Carson, March 28, 1868. 6$\frac{13}{16}$—11$\frac{1}{2}$—3$\frac{13}{16}$—3$\frac{1}{2}$. Same remarks.

494, ♂ ad.; Carson, April 4, 1868. 6$\frac{3}{4}$—11—3$\frac{5}{8}$—3$\frac{1}{2}$. Same remarks.

865, ♂ ad.; Camp 19, East Humboldt Mountains, August 10, 1868. 7$\frac{1}{8}$—11$\frac{7}{8}$—(?)—3$\frac{3}{16}$. Same remarks.

1182, nest and eggs (5); City Creek Cañon, Utah, June 18, 1869. Nest in box-elder bush, about 7,000 feet altitude.

1239, nest and eggs (4); Parley's Park, Wahsatch Mountains, Utah, June 23, 1869. Nest in top of cotton-wood tree by cañon-stream.

1240, nest and eggs (4); Parley's Park, Wahsatch Mountains, Utah, June 23, 1869. Nest in top of aspen.

1270, ♀ ad.; Parley's Park, June 23, 1869. 6$\frac{3}{8}$—11. Bill, umber-drab, paler and more lilaceous basally and beneath; iris, brown; tarsi and toes, horn-color.

1329, nest and eggs (2); Parley's Park, June 28, 1869. Nest in aspen along stream.

1342, 1343, nests and eggs (3, 1); Parley's Park, June 28, 1869. Nests in aspens near stream.

1347, ♂ ad.; Parley's Park, June 28, 1869. 7—11$\frac{3}{4}$.

1433, ♂ ad.; Parley's Park, July 19, 1869. 6$\frac{1}{2}$—11$\frac{1}{4}$. Bill, pinkish-drab, becoming gradually paler on commissure and on lower mandible, there fading basally into dull whitish; rictus, pale-yellow; iris, brown; tarsi and toes, purplish-sepia.

1434, nest; Parley's Park, July 19, 1869. Nest on horizontal branch of cotton-wood tree.

1517, ♂ juv.; Parley's Park, August 16, 1869. 6$\frac{3}{4}$—11$\frac{3}{4}$.

1518, ♀ juv.; Parley's Park, August 16, 1869. 6$\frac{3}{8}$—10$\frac{3}{4}$.

CARPODACUS FRONTALIS.

House Finch; "Red-head Linnet."

(*Wé-to-wich* of the Paiutes.)

α. frontalis.

Fringilla frontalis, SAY, Long's Exped., II, 1824, 40.

Carpodacus frontalis, GRAY, Gen. Birds, 1844–'49.—BAIRD, Birds N. Am., 1858, 415; Catal., 1859, No. 308.—COOPER, Orn. Cal., I, 156.—COUES, Key, 1872, 129; Check List, 1873, No. 141.—HENSHAW, 1875, 241.

Carpodacus frontalis var. *frontalis*, RIDGW., Am. Journ. Sci. and Arts, Jan., 1873, 40.—B. B. & R., Hist. N. Am. B., I, 1874, 466, pl. XXI, figs. 3, 6.

Carpodacus frontalis. a. *frontalis*, COUES, B. N.W., 1874, 107.

The "Red-head Linnet" was the most familiar and one of the most abundant of the birds found at Sacramento, where it frequented the shade-trees of the streets or the door-yards and gardens in the city in preference to groves in the suburbs or country. In its abundance and semi-domestic habits it thus reminds one somewhat of the European House Sparrow (*Pyrgita domestica*), but, unlike that bird, has endeared itself to its protectors by the possession of a sweet song and brilliant plumage. It is greatly prized as a cage-bird, and justly, too, for while its plumage is equally pretty, its notes excel those of the Canary in sweetness, while at the same time they are fully equal in vivacity and power. All the notes are decidedly Canary-like, the usual utterance being a soft, musical *tweet*. The song itself differs from that of the Canary chiefly in being more tender, less piercing, and interspersed with more varied warblings. The males were observed to be shyer than the females, their wariness being perhaps explained by the fact that several were noticed which had their tails clipped, showing that they had once been in captivity. When their nests were disturbed, however, the males exhibited as much concern as the females, and kept up a lively *chinking* from an adjoining tree.

Few birds are more variable as to the choice of a location for their nests than the present species, since it adapts itself readily to any sort of a place where safety is assured. At Sacramento, they usually built among the small oak trees, generally near the extremity of a horizontal branch, but one nest was placed inside the pendulous, basket-like structure of a "Hanging-bird" (*Icterus bullocki*); in the narrow gorge of the Truckee River, where that stream breaks through the Virginia Mountains, one was found inside the abandoned nest of a Cliff Swallow; along the eastern shore of Pyramid Lake numerous nests were found among the rocks, placed on shelves in the interior of caves, along with those of the Barn Swallow and Say's Pewee, or in crevices on the outside of the tufa-domes, while in the neighboring valley of the Truckee, where there was an abundance of cotton-wood timber, their nests were nearly all built in the low grease-wood bushes. On Antelope Island, in the Great Salt Lake, they preferred the sage-brush, like the Black-throated and Brewer's Sparrows; in City Creek Cañon, near Salt Lake City, one was found in a mountain-mahogany tree, while in Parley's Park another was in a cotton-wood tree along a stream. At all the towns or larger settlements, however, a large proportion of the individuals of this species have abandoned such nesting-places as those described above, and resorted to the buildings, where "odd nooks and crannies" afforded superior attractions.

Although chiefly a bird of the lower valleys, this species was sometimes found in the lower cañons of the mountains, it being common in Buena Vista Cañon, in the West Humboldt range, in September, having apparently nested among the ruined adobe houses of the deserted town. In City Creek Cañon, near Salt Lake City, several nests were found at an altitude of about 1,800 feet above the level of the mesa, or at the lower limit to the breeding-range of *C. cassini*, a single nest of which was found on a tree adjoining one in which was a nest of the present bird. In Parley's Park it was likewise found, but in small numbers, and only on the floor of the park, the *C. cassini* inhabiting the upper portion of the streams.

List of specimens.

2, 3, 4, nests and eggs; nests in oak-grove. Sacramento, California, June 6, 1867.

28, 29, nests and eggs; nests in oak-grove. Sacramento, California, June 11, 1867.

34, $\male$ ad.; Sacramento, June 12, 1867. $5\frac{15}{16}$—$9\frac{9}{16}$—$3\frac{1}{4}$—$2\frac{1}{4}$.

41, nest and eggs (5); nest in oak-grove. Sacramento, California, June 13, 1867.

52, nest and eggs; nest in oak-grove. Sacramento, California, June 18, 1867.

57, nest and eggs; nest in oak-grove. Sacramento, California, June 19, 1867.

73, nest and eggs (4); nest in oak-grove. Sacramento, California, June 20, 1867.

765, nest and eggs (5); nest in niche in rocks. Tufa domes, Pyramid Lake, Nevada, May 25, 1868.

569, $\male$ ad.; Truckee Reservation, May 15, 1868. $6\frac{1}{16}$—$9\frac{7}{8}$—$2\frac{5}{8}$. Upper mandible, brownish horn-color, edged with pale rosy; lower mandible, paler and more pinkish than the upper, with wider rosy edge; iris, dark brown; tarsi and toes, pale brown.

774, nest and eggs (5); nest in grease-wood bush. Truckee Reservation, Nevada, May 31, 1868.

780, 781, nests and eggs (5); nest in grease-wood bush. Truckee Reservation, Nevada, June 2, 1868.

805, nest and eggs (4); nest in grease-wood bush. Truckee Valley, Nevada, June 6, 1868.

806, nest and eggs (5); nest in old one of Cliff-Swallow, on face of a precipice. Truckee Valley, Nevada, June 6, 1868.

1066, nests and eggs (4); near Salt Lake City, May 29, 1869. Nest on mountain-mahogany bush, 1,800 feet above the level of the city!

1076, $\male$ ad.; Salt Lake City, Utah, June 1, 1869. $6\frac{1}{4}$—$9\frac{7}{8}$. Bill, lilaceous-brown, darker above; iris, brown; legs and feet, sepia.

1092, nest; Antelope Island, Great Salt Lake, June 4, 1869. Sage-bush.

1093, ♂ ad.; Antelope Island, Great Salt Lake, June 4, 1869. 6¼—9⅜. Same remarks as to 1076.

1114, nest; Antelope Island, June 5, 1869. Sage-bush.

1131, ♂ ad.; Antelope Island, June 7, 1869.

1140, nest; Antelope Island, June 8, 1869. Sage-bush.

1183, nest and eggs; Salt Lake City, June 18, 1869. Sage-bush, 1,800 feet above camp (altitude above 7,000 feet).

1191, nest and eggs (2); Salt Lake City, June 21, 1869. Mountain-mahogany, 1,800 feet above camp.

1193, ♀ ad.; Salt Lake City, June 21, 1869. 6—10. Bill, purplish-drab, lower mandible, more lilaceous basally beneath; iris, brown; tarsi and toes, deep brown.

1238, nest and eggs (2); Parley's Park, Wahsatch Mountains, Utah, June 23, 1869. Nest in cotton-wood tree along stream.

LEUCOSTICTE LITTORALIS.

Hepburn's Leucosticte.

Leucosticte littoralis, BAIRD, Trans. Chicago Acad. Sci., I, ii, 1869, 318, pl. 28, fig. 1.—COOPER, Orn. Cal., I, 162.

Leucosticte tephrocotis var. *littoralis*, COUES, Key, 1872, 130.—B. B. & R., Hist. N. Am. Birds, I, 1874, 507, pl. XXIII, fig. 6.—RIDGWAY, Bull. Geol. & Geog. Expl. Ter., No. 2, sec. ser., 1875, 74.

Leucosticte tephrocotis. b. *griseinucha*, COUES, Birds N.W., 1874, 111 (part).

A single flock of this species was seen on the 5th of January in the outskirts of Virginia City, Nevada. The flock comprised perhaps fifty individuals, all busily engaged in gleaning from the surface of the snow, flitting restlessly over one another, in the manner of Lapland Longspurs, at the same time uttering a twittering note.

CHRYSOMITRIS TRISTIS.

Common Goldfinch, Lettuce Bird, etc.

Fringilla tristis, LINN., Syst. Nat., I, 1766, 320.

Chrysomitris tristis, BONAP., Comp. & Geog. List, 1838, 33.—BAIRD, B. N. Am., 1858, 421; Catal., 1859, No. 313.—COOPER, Orn. Cal., I, 167.—COUES, Key, 1872, 131, pl. 3, figs. 7, 8, 9, 10; Check List, 1873, No. 149; B. N.W., 1874, 116—B. B. & R., Hist. N. Am. B., II, 1874, 471, pl. XXII, figs. 7, 8.—HENSHAW, 1875, 243.

Few birds were so abundant at Sacramento as this widely-distributed species; but eastward of the Sierra Nevada it was found to be extremely rare at all places along our route. Its great abundance at Sacramento may possibly be explained by the extensive and luxuriant growth of thistles which occupied many waste-places in the suburbs, the seeds of these plants supplying them, in season, with a plentiful supply of food.

List of specimens.

5, 6, 7, nests and eggs; Sacramento City, California, June 6, 1867. Nests in an oak-grove, resting on horizontal branches of the small trees.

54, nest and eggs; Sacramento City, California, June 18, 1867. Nest on horizontal branch of small cotton-wood, in copse.

81, nest and eggs; Sacramento, June 24, 1867.

87, nest and eggs; Sacramento, June 28, 1867.

93, nest and eggs; Sacramento, June 29, 1867. Nest in small cotton-wood, in copse.

778, ♂ ad.; Truckee Reservation, Nevada, May 31, 1868. $5\frac{7}{16}$—$9\frac{1}{4}$—(?)—$2\frac{1}{2}$. Bill, orange-yellow, the point darker; iris, very dark sepia; tarsi and toes, dilute reddish-sepia.

1369, nest and eggs (3); Pack's Cañon, Uintah Mountains, Utah, July 4, 1869. Nest in thorn-apple shrub, by stream.

CHRYSOMITRIS PSALTRIA.

Green-backed Goldfinch; "Arkansas Goldfinch."[1]

Fringilla psaltria, SAY, Long's Exped., II, 1823, 40.

Chrysomitris psaltria, BONAP., Comp. and Geog. List, 1838, 33.—BAIRD, B. N. Am., 1858, 422; Catal., 1859, No. 314.—COOPER, Orn. Cal., I, 168.—COUES, Key, 1872, 132; Check List, 1873, No. 151.—HENSHAW, 1875, 244.

Chrysomitris psaltria var. *psaltria*, RIDGWAY, Am. Jour. Arts and Sci., Dec., 1872, 454.—B. B. & R., Hist. N. Am. B., II, 1874, 474, pl. XXII, figs. 9, 10.

Chrysomitris psaltria. a. *psaltria*, COUES, B. N.W., 1874, 116.

This species we found only among the Wahsatch and Uintah Mountains, where it was not common, and usually found associated in small numbers with the large flocks of *C. pinus*. Attention was first called to it by its extraordinary note, a plaintive, mellow whistle, difficult to describe, but totally unlike that of any other bird we have heard. When the bird takes flight this note is changed to a simple fifing *cheer*, in a fine, high key, and somewhat resembling the anxious note uttered by the male Red-winged Black-bird (*Agelæus phœniceus*) when its nest is disturbed.

[1] Geographically inappropriate.

1189, ♂ ad.; Salt Lake City, Utah (City Creek Cañon), June 19, 1869. 4⅜—8. Bill, purplish-brown, the culmen nearly black, the lower mandible inclining to wax-brown; iris, brown; tarsi and toes, sepia-brown.

1224, nest and egg (1); Parley's Park, Wahsatch Mountains, June 22, 1869. Nest in top of willow-bush along stream.

CHRYSOMITRIS LAWRENCII.

Lawrence's Goldfinch.

Carduelis lawrencii, CASSIN, Pr. Ac. Nat. Sci. Philad., 1850, 105, pl. v.

Chrysomitris lawrencii, BONAP., Comp. Rend., 1853, 913.—BAIRD, B. N. Am., 1858, 424; Catal., 1859, No. 316.—COOPER, Orn. Cal., I, 171.—COUES, Key, 1872, 132; Check List, 1873, No. 150.—B. B. & R., Hist. N. Am. B., II, 1874, 478, pl. XXII, figs. 14, 15.

This beautiful little Goldfinch was observed only among the western foot-hills of the Sierra Nevada, where we had only occasional glimpses at it, just sufficient to identify the species, and passed so rapidly through its range that no opportunity was afforded to study its habits. It was common among the trees by the roadside, and uttered very pleasant and quite peculiar notes.

CHRYSOMITRIS PINUS.

Pine Goldfinch.

Fringilla pinus, WILSON, Am. Orn., II, 1810, 133, pl. 17, fig. 1.

Chrysomitris pinus, BONAP., Comp. & Geog. List, 1838, 33.—BAIRD, B. N. Am., 1858, 425; Catal., 1859, No. 317.—COOPER, Orn. Cal., I, 172.—COUES, Key, 1872, 131, pl. 3, figs. 11, 12; Check List, 1873, No. 148; B. N.W., 1874, 115.—B. B. & R., Hist. N. Am. B., II, 1874, 480, pl. XXII, fig. 16.—HENSHAW, 1875, 246.

The range of the Pine Goldfinch was strikingly similar to that of Cassin's Purple Finch, the two being almost invariably found in the same localities, whether during their migrations or in the nesting-season. In summer it was abundant in all the pine forests, from the Sierra Nevada to the Uintahs, and like the bird above mentioned occurred also among the aspen copses which usually replaced the conifers at the head of the cañons. The species was more or less gregarious, even in midsummer, and although their nests were extremely scattered, the birds themselves were seldom seen except in flocks. They had no song, but uttered frequently a peculiar screeching note, sounding like *sweer*, very unlike that of any other bird, except the *Empidonax obscurus;* and when a flock suddenly took flight, they all joined in a more rattling note.

Besides the nest described below, another was found, in an aspen bush, but it was abandoned by the owners before any eggs were laid.

List of specimens.

892, ♂ *juv.;* East Humboldt Mountains, Nevada, September 5, 1868. 5¼—9. Bill, ashy horn-color; iris, burnt-umber; tarsi and toes, dark purplish-brown.

913, ♂ *ad.;* East Humboldt Mountains, Nevada, September 8, 1868. 5—9. Bill, purplish-plumbeous, paler basally; iris, grayish-sepia; tarsi and toes, sepia.

1241, nest and egg (1); Parley's Park, Wahsatch Mountains, Utah, June 23, 1869. Nest near extremity of horizontal arm of fir-tree, about fifteen feet from ground.

1519, ♂ *juv.;* 4⅞—9. 1520, ♀ *juv.;* 4⅞—8⅞. Parley's Park, August 10, 1868. Bill, purplish-plumbeous, paler basally; iris, sepia; tarsi and toes, plumbeous sepia-black.

PLECTROPHANES LAPPONICUS.

Lapland Longspur.

Fringilla lapponica, LINN., Syst. Nat., I, 1766, 317.

Plectrophanes lapponicus, SELBY, Linn. Trans., XV, 126, pl. 1.—BAIRD, B. N. Am., 1858, 433; Cat. N. Am. B., 1859, No. 326.—COOPER, Orn. Cal., I, 178.— COUES, Key, 1872, 133, fig. 81; Check List, 1873, No. 153; B. N.W., 1874, 120.—B. B. & R., Hist. N. Am. B., I, 1874, 515, pl. XXIV, fig. 7.

During the more severe portion of winter, individuals of this species were frequently detected among the large flocks of Horned Larks (*Eremophila alpestris*) around Carson City. They were recognized by their peculiar and unmistakable notes.

PASSERCULUS SANDVICHENSIS.

Savannah Sparrow.

α. *alaudinus.*

Passerculus alaudinus, BONAP., Comp. Rend., XXXVII, 1853, 918.—BAIRD, B. N. Am., 1858, 446; Cat. N. Am. B., 1859, No. 335.—COOPER, Orn. Cal., I, 1870, 181.

Passerculus savanna var. *alaudinus.* B. B. & R., Hist. N. Am. Birds, I, 1874, pl. XXIV, fig. 11.—HENSHAW, 1875, 254.

Passerculus savanna, COUES, Key, 1872, 135 (part); Check List, 1873, No. 159 (part).

Passerculus savanna. a. *savanna,* COUES, Birds N.W., 1874, 127 (part).

This well-known and widely-distributed Sparrow was an abundant species in every moist meadow and' grassy marsh, not only in the valleys but also in the lower cañons of the mountains. It was found during the greater portion of the year, or from March to November, inclusive. During the breeding-season the male has a weak, lisping song, which may be somewhat nearly expressed by the syllables *witz, witz, wilk'—tzul,* uttered as the bird perches upon a fence-post, or a bush by the brook-side, or as it nestles in the grass upon the ground.

List of specimens.

239, ♂ ad.; Camp 19, West Humboldt Mountains, Nevada, October 7, 1867. $5\frac{7}{8}$—$9\frac{1}{8}$—3—$2\frac{1}{2}$—$\frac{7}{16}$—$\frac{3}{4}$—$2\frac{1}{4}$—$\frac{13}{16}$. Bill, horn-color, darker on culmen, lower mandible paler, with lilaceous glow; iris, hazel; tarsi, straw-color, toes more brownish.

254, ♂ ad.; Camp 19, West Humboldt Mountains, Nevada, October 23, 1867. $5\frac{3}{4}$—$9\frac{9}{16}$—$3\frac{1}{16}$—$2\frac{1}{2}$—$\frac{13}{32}$—$\frac{3}{4}$—$2\frac{1}{4}$—$\frac{7}{8}$. Tarsi, clear pinkish-white, with tinge of straw-yellow, the toes stained with brownish.

471, ♂ ad.; Carson City, Nevada, March 28, 1868. $5\frac{3}{8}$—8—$2\frac{7}{8}$—$2\frac{3}{8}$. Bill, lilac-bluish, the upper mandible nearly black; iris, sepia; tarsi and toes, brownish lilaceous-white.

480, ♂ ad.; Carson, March 30, 1868. $5\frac{11}{16}$—$9\frac{1}{4}$—3—$2\frac{7}{16}$. Same remarks.

553, ♀ ad.; Carson City, Nevada, April 27, 1868. $5\frac{7}{8}$—9—$2\frac{7}{8}$—$2\frac{3}{8}$. Same remarks.

885, ♂ ad.; Ruby Valley, Nevada, August 29, 1868. $5\frac{5}{8}$—(?)—(?)—$2\frac{3}{8}$. Same remarks.

933, ♀ ad.; Camp 25, Humboldt Valley, September 16, 1868. $5\frac{13}{16}$—$8\frac{13}{16}$—(?)—$2\frac{1}{4}$. Upper mandible, purplish-black, paler toward rictus; lower, deep salmon-purple, darker terminally; iris, plumbeous-bister; tarsi, straw-white, toes more brownish.

970, ♂ ad.; Salt Lake City, May 21, 1869. $5\frac{5}{8}$—$9\frac{5}{8}$. Bill, ashy-lilaceous, the upper mandible dusky—nearly black on the culmen.

971, ♂ ad.; same locality and date. $5\frac{5}{8}$—$8\frac{7}{8}$.

972, ♂ ad.; same locality and date. $5\frac{3}{4}$—$9\frac{1}{2}$.

1016, nest and eggs (5); Salt Lake City, May 21, 1869. Nest imbedded in ground, in wet meadow.

1017, nest and eggs (4); same locality, May 22. Nest in tuft of grass, in wet meadow.

1883, nests and eggs (4); same locality, June 3, 1869. Same remarks.

1090, nest and eggs (4); Antelope Island, Great Salt Lake, June 4, 1869. Nest on ground, beneath strip of sage-brush bark, in wet meadow.

1458, ♂ juv.; Parley's Park, Utah, July 26, 1869. $5\frac{3}{8}$—9. Bill, brownish-lilaceous, darker on the culmen; iris, brown; tarsi and toes, pale pink.

1480, ♂ juv.; Parley's Park, July 30, 1869. $5\frac{1}{2}$—$9\frac{1}{4}$.

1481, juv.; Parley's Park, July 30. $5\frac{3}{4}$—$9\frac{3}{8}$.

30 P R

POOECETES GRAMINEUS.

Bay winged Bunting; Grass Bunting; Vesper Sparrow.

β. confinis.

Poocœtes gramineus var. *confinis*, BAIRD, B. N. Am., 1858, 448 (in text, *sub P. gram-
ineus*).—COUES, Key, 1872, 136; Check List, 1872, No. 161a.—B. B. & R.,
Hist. N. Am. B., I, 1874, 545 (*sub P. gramineus*).—HENSHAW, 1875, 256.
Poœcetes gramineus, COOPER, Orn. Cal., I, 1870, 186.

This common species was most frequently met with during the summer
on the open grassy slopes of the higher cañons, where it and the Green-
tailed Bunting were the chief songsters. Its song is sweet and varied,
though simple and brief, and its clear, cheery notes are among our most
pleasant recollections of those elevated regions. In the fall it descends to
the lower valleys, and in September becomes exceedingly abundant among
the rye-grass meadows along the foot-hills of the higher ranges. In winter
it appears to make a complete southward migration, none having been seen
at Carson City until the first of April.

List of specimens.

483, ♀ *ad.*; Carson City, Nevada, April 2, 1868. $6\frac{3}{4}$—$11\frac{1}{8}$—$3\frac{9}{16}$—3. Upper mandible, dull brownish-plumbeous, tomium paler; rictus and whole lower mandible, dilute
brownish-lilaceous; iris, raw-umber; tarsi and toes, dilute brownish, toes darkest.

902, ♂ *ad.*; Secret Valley, Nevada, September 6, 1868. $6\frac{3}{4}$—$10\frac{1}{4}$—(?)—$2\frac{5}{8}$. Upper
mandible, umber-brown, darker at point, paler on rictus; lower, pale, fleshy lilaceous-
brown, the extreme tip dusky; iris, vandyke; tarsi, clear brownish-white; toes, similar but stained with brownish.

1037, ♂ *ad.*; Salt Lake City, Utah, May 24, 1869. $6\frac{5}{8}$—$10\frac{5}{8}$. Bill, brownish-lilaceous, upper half of upper mandible nearly black; iris, brown; tarsi and toes, lilaceous
brownish-white.

1233, nest and eggs (3); Parley's Park, June 23, 1869. Nest on ground, beneath
prostrate sage-bush, by roadside.

1280, nest and eggs (3); Parley's Park, Wahsatch Mountains, June 25, 1869.
Nest in grassy bank of brook.

1398, nest and egg (1); Parley's Park, July, 1869. Nest on ground beneath sage-
bush.

1464, ♂ *juv.*; Parley's Park, July 28, 1869. $6\frac{7}{16}$—$11\frac{1}{2}$. Bill, clear light lilaceous,
darker toward culmen; iris, brown; tarsi and toes, clear pale flesh-color.

COTURNICULUS PASSERINUS.

Yellow-winged Sparrow.

β. perpallidus.

Coturniculus passerinus var. perpallidus, RIDGWAY, Coues' Key, 1872, 137 ; Check
List, 1873, 162a.—B. B. & R., Hist. N. Am. Birds, I, 1874, 556.—HENSHAW,
1875, 257, pl. I, fig. 2 (adult).
Coturniculus passerinus. b. perpallidus, COUES, Birds N.W., 1874, 132.
Coturniculus passerinus, COOPER, Orn. Cal., I, 1870, 189.

Like the Savanna Sparrow, this little Bunting is essentially a bird of
the valley portions. It is also generally distributed, but instead of inhabiting the wet meadows, or the borders of marshes, it frequents only the
dryer grassy places. It was found to be abundant in the fields about Sacramento City, as well as throughout the Interior.

List of specimens.

853, ♂ juv.; Ruby Valley, Nevada, July 22, 1868. 5—7⅞—(?)—1¹⁵⁄₁₆. Bill, pale,
pinkish-lilaceous, the culmen darker; iris, grayish-umber; tarsi and toes, pale rosa-
ceous-pink.

1102, ♂ ad.; Antelope Island, Great Salt Lake, Utah, June 4, 1869. 5½—8¼. Bill,
lilaceous, upper half of upper mandible blackish; iris, brown; tarsi, pale yellowish
brownish-white; toes, darker.

CHONDESTES GRAMMACA.

Lark Sparrow; Skylark Bunting.

Fringilla grammaca, SAY, Long's Exped., I, 1823, 139.
Chondestes grammaca, BONAP., Comp. & Geol. List, 1838, 32.—BAIRD, Birds N.
Am., 1858, 456 ; Cat. N. Am. B., 1859, No. 344.—COOPER, Orn. Cal., I, 193.—
COUES, Key, 1872, 146, fig. 90; Check List, 1873, No. 186; B. N.W., 1874,
159.—B. B. & R., Hist. N. Am. Birds, I, 1874, 562, pl. XXXI, fig. 1.—HEN-
SHAW, 1875, 259.

This handsomely-marked and interesting bird is an exceedingly abundant species in favorable localities throughout the entire extent of the
Western Region. Though essentially a western species, it is not restricted
to that portion of the country which extends from the Rocky Mountains
westward, as is most often the case with the birds peculiar to the western
division of the continent, but it also inhabits nearly every portion of the
Mississippi Valley, where it is no less numerous than in the most favored
portions farther west. Indeed, this species seems to be gradually extending
its range to the eastward, probably in consequence of the general and wide-

spread denudation of the forests, the country thus undergoing a physical change favorable to the habits of the species, having already become a regular summer resident in many sections of the country north of the Ohio. It was not noticed in Ohio, so far as the records show, previous to 1860, when Mr. J. M. Wheaton first observed it in the vicinity of Columbus, near the central portion of the State, and "since which time it has increased in numbers, and at present (1874) is not uncommon." [See Coues' *Birds of the Northwest*, p 234.] Single specimens have already been taken in Massachusetts and Florida, where, in course of time, the species may become established.

The Lark Sparrow is essentially a prairie bird, although it prefers semi-wooded districts to the open prairies. It is equally common in the Sacramento Valley and in southern Illinois, inhabiting in each case places which are neither completely wooded nor entirely destitute of trees, and evincing a marked preference for localities where oak-groves alternate with meadow-lands and cultivated fields; and in its great abundance in the widely-separated districts named above, particularly when taken into consideration with its association in both with such species as *Thryomanes bewicki*, *Dendrœca œstiva*, *Icteria virens*, *Collurio excubitoroides*, *Chrysomitris tristis*, *Coturniculus passerinus*, *Melospiza fasciata*, *Spizella socialis*, *Guiraca cœrulea*, etc., adds to the marked similarity in the general *facies* of the avifaunæ of the two localities, the difference between them consisting in the possession by each of a small percentage of *representative* species and a very few peculiar forms.[1]

The habits of this bird are chiefly terrestrial, since it lives mostly on the ground, where it may often be seen walking[2] gracefully along or hopping in the usual manner of Sparrows; the male ascending to a fence-post the top of a small tree, or other prominent object, during the delivery of his song. Its habits in this respect vary greatly, however, it being quite arboreal in some localities, as was conspicuously the case at Sacramento

---

[1] See pages 328-332.

[2] It may not be generally known that many of the terrestrial Fringillidæ are walkers as well as hoppers. We have often seen both this species and *Melospiza fasciata* walking on the ground with a step as firm and graceful as that of a Meadow Lark or Blackbird.

where it nested almost invariably in the small oak trees at heights varying from 15 to 30 feet from the ground; while, on the other hand, in southern Illinois, where the proportionate area of wood-land is much greater, we never found a nest of this species except on the ground, notwithstanding many nests were found.[1]

The principal characteristic of the Lark Sparrow is the excellence of its song, which far surpasses that of any other member of the family we have ever heard, while in sprightliness and continuity, qualities so often lacking in our finer singers, we do not know its equal in any bird. We have not heard the song of the famed Skylark (*Alauda arvensis*), but from numerous descriptions imagine it to be somewhat similar in character to that of the present bird; and we very seriously doubt whether it is superior, if, indeed, it should prove equal. The Lark Sparrow sings all day long, even during the hottest part of summer, beginning in the early morn before any other bird, and not ceasing until the darkening of the evening shades have quieted the other songsters; often, in fact, have we been awakened at night by its song when all else was quiet. The song of this bird begins with a chant of clear, ringing notes, each uttered with great distinctness; then follows a silvery trill—the very expression of emotion—and then a succession of sprightly, sparkling notes, varied by rising and falling cadences, finally dying away until scarcely audible, but immediately resumed in all its sprightliness and vigor, and continued as before, until the singer seems actually exhausted by his efforts.

At Sacramento this bird is known as the Mexican Lark; it was familiar to all the boys, who in season eagerly searched for its nests in order to obtain the young, which were readily sold in the city for $4.00 per pair.

---

[1] Many other birds exhibit the same variability in the selection of a site for their nests. A notoriously variable species is *Carpodacus frontalis* (see p. 459); and *Zenædura carolinensis* is another case in point, this species, *in the same locality*, nesting indifferently on the ground, on the top of a stump or rock, on a flat fence-rail, in a tree, or on the remnant of an old nest of another species. Mr. E. W. Nelson informs me that he found a nest of *Pipilo erythrophthalmus* in a bush, a foot or two from the ground, on Fox Prairie, Illinois; while at Mt. Carmel, in the same State, we have found a nest of *Agelæus phœniceus* in an elm tree, full 20 feet from the ground, and a nest of *Cyanura cristata* inside of a barn.

List of specimens.

8, nest and eggs (3); Sacramento, California, June 8, 1867. Lower branch of small oak, in grove.

30, nest and eggs (3); Sacramento, California, June 11, 1867. Cotton-wood copse, ten feet from ground.

50, nest and eggs (3); Sacramento, California, June 18, 1867. Twenty feet from ground, in oak-grove.

72, nest and eggs (3); Sacramento, California, June 20, 1867. Twenty feet from ground, in oak-grove.

85, nest and eggs; Sacramento, California, June 28, 1867. Six feet from ground, in cotton-wood copse.

90, nest and eggs; Sacramento, California, June 29, 1867. Six feet from ground, in cotton-wood copse.

783, nest and eggs (4); Truckee Reservation, Nevada, June 3, 1868. On ground beneath sage-bush, on *mesa*.

960, ♂ ad.; Salt Lake City, Utah, May 20, 1869. 7¼—11⅗. Upper mandible, brownish-ash, lower whitish-blue; iris, brown; tarsi and toes, brownish-white.

1020, nest and eggs; Salt Lake City, May 22, 1869.

1045, nest and eggs (5); Salt Lake City, May 25, 1869.

1046, nest and eggs (5); same locality and date.

1047, 1048, nests and eggs; Salt Lake City, May 26, 1869.

1056, nest and eggs; Salt Lake City, May 27, 1869.

1174, nest and eggs (4); Salt Lake City, June 10, 1869.

1175, nest and eggs (4); Salt Lake City, June 17, 1869.

1197, nest and eggs; Salt Lake City, June 21, 1869.

Nests, all on the ground beneath sage-bushes; maximum number of eggs, five.

ZONOTRICHIA LEUCOPHRYS.

White-crowned Sparrow.

Emberiza leucophrys, FORSTER, Phil. Trans., LXII, 1772, 382, 403, 426.

Zonotrichia leucophyrs, BONAP., Comp. & Geog. List, 1838, 32.—BAIRD, B. N. Am.,
    1858, 458, pl. 69, fig. 2; Cat. N. Am. B., 1859, No. 345.—COOPER, Orn. Cal.,
    I, 196.—COUES, Key, 1872, 144; Check List, 1873, No. 183.—B. B. & R., Hist.
    N. Am. B., I, 1874, 566, pl. xxv, figs. 9, 10.—HENSHAW, 1875, 260.

Throughout the Rocky Mountain ranges, westward to the very verge of the desert-region of the Great Basin, this eastern form entirely replaces in summer the more western *Z. intermedia* of the Sierra Nevada. It was a very abundant summer species in the elevated parks of the Wahsatch and Uintah Mountains, where, from May to the latter part of August, not a single individual of *Z. intermedia* was found. At our camp in Parley's Park these birds were our most familiar neighbors, and by reason of their confiding habits and sweet morning carols endeared themselves to the members of the party. One young individual, bred in a nest close to the camp, became so sociable as to visit daily the cook's tent for the crumbs scattered on the ground.

List of specimens.

1068, ♀ *ad.;* Salt Lake City, Utah, May 29. 1869. 6⅞—9¼. Bill, orange-brown, lower mandible paler, tips of both black ; iris, brown ; tarsi and toes, deep brown.

1292, nest and eggs (5); Parley's Park, Wahsatch Mountains, Utah, June 26, 1869. Nest on ground, under Geranium bush.

1430, ♂ *ad.;* 7—9⅞. 1431, ♀ *ad.;* 6⁹⁄₁₆—9⅝. Parley's Park, July 19, 1869. Bill, perfectly uniform, deep purplish, mahogany-brown ; iris, brown ; tarsi, reddish hepatic-brown ; toes, darker.

1463, ♂ *juv.;* Parley's Park, July 28, 1869. 6⅝—10. Bill, mahogany-brown, darker on culmen and tip ; iris, brown ; tarsi and toes, dark purplish-brown.

ZONOTRICHIA INTERMEDIA.

Ridgway's Sparrow.[1]

(*Mooh'-um-pooh* of the Washoes; *You-oo-hoot'-se-pah* of the Paiutes.)

Zonotrichia gambeli, BAIRD, Birds N. Am., 1858, 460 (part); Cat. N. Am. Birds, 1859, No. 346 (part).—COOPER, Orn. Cal., I, 1870, 195 (part).

Zonotrichia leucophrys var. *gambeli,* ALLEN, Bull. Mus. Comp. Zool., III, 1872, 157, 177.—COUES, Key, 1872, 145 (part); Check List, 1873, No. 183a (part).—B. B. & R., Hist. N. Am. Birds, I, 1874, 569, pl. XXV, figs. 11, 12.

Zonotrichia leucophrys var. *intermedia,* RIDGWAY, Coues' Check List, App., 1872, No. 183b.—COUES, Birds N.W., 1874, 156.—HENSHAW, 1875, 261, pl. VII, fig. 2 (adult).

At the Summit Meadows, the most elevated portion of the Donner Lake Pass of the Sierra Nevada, these birds were so extremely abundant on the 9th day of July, that, on the evening we camped there, twenty-seven of their eggs were found after a hurried search of less than twenty minutes' duration. The pleasing songs of the males were heard on every hand, not only during daylight, but at intervals through the night, these songs resembling those of *Z. leucophrys,* although they seemed somewhat more vigorous and distinct. They were exceedingly unsuspicious little birds, the pair usually remaining close by when their nest and eggs were being appropriated, the male even, on several occasions, singing, as he perched on the summit of a neighboring bush, while we were preparing the eggs for preservation.

---

[1] COUES, *Birds of the Northwest,* p. 156.

List of specimens.

95, 96, 97, 98, nest and eggs (4); Summit Meadows, Donner Lake Pass, Sierra Nevada, July 9, 1867. Maximum number of eggs, 5; usual number, 4.

172, ♂; West Humboldt Mountains, Nevada, September 7, 1867. $6\frac{1}{4}$—$9\frac{1}{4}$—$3\frac{1}{4}$—$2\frac{9}{16}$—$\frac{7}{16}$—$1\frac{3}{16}$—$2\frac{3}{4}$—$1\frac{1}{2}$. Bill, wax-yellow, upper mandible more ocher-reddish, point of culmen and gonys, black; iris, umber; tarsi and toes, yellowish horn-color.

183, ♂; West Humboldt Mountains, September 11, 1867. $6\frac{3}{4}$—$9\frac{1}{4}$—3—$2\frac{1}{2}$—$\frac{7}{16}$—$\frac{3}{4}$—$2\frac{13}{16}$—$1\frac{7}{16}$. Same remarks.

197, ♂; West Humboldt Mountains, September 18, 1867. $6\frac{15}{16}$—$10\frac{1}{4}$—$3\frac{1}{4}$—$2\frac{3}{4}$—$\frac{7}{16}$—$1\frac{3}{16}$—3—$1\frac{9}{16}$. Upper mandible, deep, light mahogany-brown, inclining to wax-yellow on rictus; lower mandible, paler than upper, inclining to deep wax-yellow, more citreous basally; extreme point of culmen and gonys, black; iris, umber; tarsi, clear, light reddish horn-color; toes, darker and more opaque-brownish.

200, ♂; West Humboldt Mountains, September 20, 1876. $6\frac{7}{8}$—$9\frac{5}{8}$—$3\frac{1}{4}$—$2\frac{11}{16}$—$\frac{7}{16}$—$\frac{3}{4}$—$2\frac{7}{8}$—$1\frac{7}{8}$. Same remarks.

201, ♂; West Humboldt Mountains, September 20, 1867. $6\frac{5}{8}$—$9\frac{5}{8}$—$3\frac{1}{4}$—$2\frac{9}{16}$—$\frac{7}{16}$—$\frac{25}{32}$—$2\frac{7}{8}$—$1\frac{5}{16}$. Same remarks.

202, ♀; West Humboldt Mountains, September 20, 1867. $6\frac{5}{8}$—$9\frac{11}{16}$—$3\frac{1}{4}$—$2\frac{5}{8}$—$\frac{7}{16}$—$1\frac{3}{16}$—$2\frac{13}{16}$—$1\frac{3}{4}$. Same remarks.

207, ♂; West Humboldt Mountains, September 21, 1867. [Intermediate between *intermedia* and *leucophrys*.] $6\frac{3}{4}$—$9\frac{15}{16}$—$3\frac{1}{4}$—$2\frac{11}{16}$—$\frac{7}{16}$—$\frac{3}{4}$—3—$1\frac{3}{4}$. Same remarks.

209, ♂; West Humboldt Mountains, September 21, 1867. $6\frac{7}{8}$—$9\frac{5}{8}$—$3\frac{1}{4}$—$2\frac{5}{8}$—$\frac{7}{16}$—$\frac{3}{4}$—$2\frac{15}{16}$—$1\frac{1}{2}$. Same remarks.

210, ♂; West Humboldt Mountains, September 21, 1867. $6\frac{15}{16}$—$9\frac{1}{4}$—$3\frac{1}{16}$—$2\frac{9}{16}$—$\frac{7}{16}$—3—$2\frac{7}{8}$—$1\frac{1}{2}$. Same remarks.

211, ♂; West Humboldt Mountains, September 21, 1867. $7\frac{1}{16}$—$9\frac{7}{8}$—$3\frac{3}{16}$—$2\frac{5}{8}$—$\frac{7}{16}$—$1\frac{3}{16}$—3—$1\frac{5}{8}$. Same remarks.

212, ♀; West Humboldt Mountains, September 21, 1867. 7—10—$3\frac{1}{4}$—$2\frac{3}{4}$—$\frac{7}{16}$—$1\frac{3}{16}$—$2\frac{7}{8}$—$1\frac{5}{8}$. Same remarks.

385, ♀; Truckee Reservation, December 26, 1867. $6\frac{5}{8}$—9—3—$2\frac{7}{16}$—$\frac{7}{16}$—$\frac{3}{4}$—$2\frac{7}{8}$—$1\frac{3}{8}$. Same remarks.

930, ♂; head of Humboldt Valley (Camp 25), September 16, 1868. 7—$9\frac{1}{2}$—(?)—$2\frac{5}{8}$. Same remarks.

939, ♂; Camp 25, September 20, 1868. 7—$9\frac{3}{4}$—(?)—$2\frac{9}{16}$. Same remarks.

944, ♀; Deep Creek, Utah, October 5, 1868. $6\frac{1}{2}$—$9\frac{3}{8}$—(?)—$2\frac{7}{16}$. Same remarks.

ZONOTRICHIA CORONATA.

Golden-crowned Sparrow.

Emberiza coronata, PALLAS, Zoog. Rosso-As., II, 1811, 44, pl. [5] fig. 1 (♂ ad.).

Zonotrichia coronata, BAIRD, B. N. Am., 1858, 461; Catal., 1859, No. 347.—COOPER, Orn. Cal., I, 197.—COUES, Key, 1872, 145; Check List, 1873, No. 184; Birds N.W., 1874, 159 (*sub Z. querula*).—B. B. & R., Hist. N. Am. B., I, 1874, 573, pl. XXVI, fig. 1.

The only specimen of this species seen by us was the one obtained, which was shot from a flock of *Z. intermedia*. Its occurrence on the West Humboldt Mountains may be accounted for by the fact that many of the Pacific-coast species have a tendency to straggle eastward during their migrations, among those which reach this range, besides the bird under consideration, being *Melospiza guttata*, *Pipilo oregonus*, *Lanivireo cassini*, *Helminthophaga lutescens*, etc.[1] [See pp. 379, 380.]

List of specimens.

237, ♀ ad.; West Humboldt Mountains, Nevada (Camp 19), October 7, 1867. $7\frac{13}{16}$— $10\frac{1}{2}$—$3\frac{3}{8}$—$2\frac{3}{4}$—$1\frac{5}{12}$—$\frac{7}{8}$—$3\frac{1}{4}$—$1\frac{7}{8}$. Upper mandible, slaty horn-color, darker on culmen, tomium paler; lower mandible, pale lilaceous-brown; iris, olivaceous-hazel; tarsi and toes, clear horn-color.

JUNCO OREGONUS.

Oregon Snow-bird.

(*Tah'-bah-klat'-uk* of the Washoes; *Nebah'-tone* of the Paiutes.)

Fringilla oregona, TOWNSEND, Jour. Ac. Nat. Sci. Phila., VII, 1837, 188.

Junco oregonus, SCLATER, Pr. Zool. Soc. Lond., 1857, 7.—BAIRD, B. N. Am., 1858, 466; Cat. N. Am. B., 1859, No. 347.—COOPER, Orn. Cal., I, 199.—COUES, Key, 1872, 141; Check List, 1873, No. 175; B. N.W., 1874, 142.—B. B. & R., Hist. N. Am. B., I, 1874, 584, pl. XXVI, fig. 2.—HENSHAW, 1875, 267.

Junco hyemalis var. *oregonus*, RIDGWAY, Am. Nat., 1873, 613.

This representative of the Eastern Snow-bird (*J. hyemalis*) is very abundant in winter from the Pacific coast to the Wahsatch Mountains, but in summer has a more restricted distribution, being then confined to the coniferous forest-region of the higher western ranges. At the Summit Meadows, nearly 7,000 feet above the sea, on the Sierra Nevada, it was one of the commonest and most characteristic birds of the locality, but eastward of these mountains none were seen during the summer. In its winter migrations this bird shows the same remarkable movements as *Zonotrichia intermedia*, *Turdus guttatus*, etc., for while its summer habitat seems strictly limited on the eastward to the Sierra Nevada, it becomes generally dispersed in winter over the entire area of the Western Region, being a more or

---

[1] According to Mr. E. W. Nelson, an adult male of *Z. coronata* was captured by Dr. Hoy, at Racine, Wisconsin, during the spring migration.

less regular visitant during that season as far east as Kansas. We did not, however, meet with it farther eastward than the East Humboldt Mountains.

In all respects this species appears to be a perfect counterpart of the eastern *J. hyemalis*, being equally familiar in its habits during winter, while its notes are apparently precisely similar.

List of specimens.

224, ♀ *ad.;* West Humboldt Mountains, Nevada, October 3, 1867. 6—9—3—2½—$\frac{3}{8}$—$\frac{3}{4}$—2$\frac{3}{16}$—1$\frac{3}{4}$. Bill, delicate lilaceous-white, the point dusky; iris, burnt-sienna; tarsi, clear horn-white; toes, deep sepia.

378, ♀ *ad.;* Truckee Reservation, Nevada, December 24, 1867. 6$\frac{3}{4}$—9¼—3½—2½—$\frac{7}{16}$—$\frac{3}{4}$—2$\frac{3}{4}$—1¼. Same remarks.

384, ♂ *ad.;* Truckee Reservation, December 26, 1867. 6¼—9¼—3¼—2$\frac{2}{3}$—$\frac{7}{16}$—1$\frac{1}{16}$—2$\frac{3}{4}$—1$\frac{3}{4}$. Iris, purplish-claret; tarsi, dilute reddish-umber; toes, darker leaden-umber.

484, ♂ *ad.;* Carson City, Nevada, April 3, 1868. 6$\frac{3}{8}$—9$\frac{3}{4}$—3¼—2$\frac{2}{3}$. Iris, dark purplish-carmine.

485, ♂ *ad.;* Carson City, Nevada, April 3, 1868. 6½—9$\frac{7}{8}$—3¼—2$\frac{11}{16}$. Same remarks.

938, ♂ *ad.;* Trout Creek, Upper Humboldt Valley, Sept. 19, 1868. 6$\frac{3}{4}$—9$\frac{3}{5}$—2$\frac{5}{8}$. Upper mandible, light sepia-brown, the tip black; lower mandible, pinkish-white; iris, madder-brown; tarsi, dilute sepia; toes, deeper sepia.

JUNCO CANICEPS.

Gray-headed Snow-bird.

Struthus caniceps, WOODHOUSE, Pr. Ac. Nat. Sci. Philad., 1852, 202.
Junco caniceps, BAIRD, B. N. Am., 1858, 468, pl. 72, fig. 1; Cat. N. Am. B., 1859,
   No. 353.—COOPER, Orn. Cal., I, 1870, 201.—B. B. & R., Hist. N. Am. B., I,
   1874, 587, pl. XXVI, fig. 3.
Junco cinereus var. *caniceps*, COUES, Key, 1872, 141; Check List, 1873, No. 176;
   B. N.W., 1874, 143.—HENSHAW, 1875, 269.
Junco hyemalis var. *caniceps*, RIDGWAY, Am. Nat., 1873, 613.

The Gray-headed Snow-bird was met with only in the pine forests of the Wahsatch and Uintah Mountains, where it was rather common from May to August, inclusive. Its habits and notes closely resemble those of *J. hyemalis* and *J. oregonus*, but its song, a simple monotonous trill, is somewhat louder and more steady.

AMPHISPIZA BILINEATA.

Black-throated Sparrow.

(*Wut'-tu-ze-ze* of the Paiutes.)

Emberiza bilineata, CASSIN, Pr. Ac. Nat. Sci. Philad., 1850, 104, pl. 3.
Poospiza bilineata, SCLATER, Proc. Zool. Soc. Lond., 1857, 7.—BAIRD, B. N. Am.,
   1858, 470; Cat. N. Am. B., 1859, No. 355.—COOPER, Orn. Cal., I, 203.—
   COUES, Key, 1872, 140; Check List, 1873, No. 172.—B. B. & R., Hist. N. Am.
   B., I, 1874, 590, pl. XXVI, fig. 8.—HENSHAW, 1875, 274.
Amphispiza bilineata, COUES, B. N.W., 1874, 234.[1]

This interesting little bird was found throughout the sage-brush country, the most desert-tracts of which are its favorite abode. It was equally common in the western depression and in the Salt Lake Valley, as well as in intermediate localities. Unlike the *A. nevadensis*, which frequents chiefly the more thrifty growth of artemisia in the damper valleys, this species prefers the arid mesas, where the growth is scant and stunted; and we found it nowhere else so abundant as on the Carson Desert, near the Soda Lakes, where much of the surface consisted of loose, shifting sand. It also differs markedly from that species in being migratory, being merely a summer sojourner, and one of the latest to arrive, few, if any, making their appearance in the Truckee Valley before the first of May, the advance individuals being noted on the 13th of that month, in 1868.

Like *A. nevadensis*, this species is remarkable for its peculiar song, which in pensive tone and sad expression harmonizes so perfectly with its desolate surroundings. It is from this song that the Indian name, *Wut-tu-ze-ze*, is derived, for the notes are very nearly expressed by the syllables *wut'*, *wut'*, *zeeeeè*, repeated once or twice, the first two notes quick and distinct, the last one a prolonged, silvery trill. Frequently a singer reverses, at each alternate repetition of the song, the accent of the first and last portions, thus producing a very peculiar effect.

List of specimens.

106, ♂ *juv.*; valley of the Truckee, July 25, 1867. 5½—8½—2½—2$\frac{3}{16}$—$\frac{7}{16}$—$\frac{11}{16}$—2$\frac{7}{16}$
—1¾. Upper mandible, plumbeous-black; lower, pale blue, lilaceous basally, the tip, dusky; iris, umber; tarsi and toes, dark plumbeous-sepia.

---

[1] "*Amphispiza*, COUES, n. g. (type *Emberiza bilineata*, Cass.)."

123, *juv.;* Truckee Valley, August 6, 1867. $5\frac{5}{8}$—$8\frac{1}{8}$—$2\frac{5}{8}$—$2\frac{1}{4}$—$\frac{3}{8}$—$\frac{5}{8}$—$2\frac{3}{8}$—$1\frac{1}{2}$. Same remarks.

167, *juv.;* West Humboldt Mountains, September 4, 1867. $5\frac{5}{8}$—$8\frac{1}{4}$—$2\frac{5}{8}$—$2\frac{3}{16}$—$\frac{3}{8}$—$\frac{5}{8}$—$2\frac{1}{2}$—$1\frac{1}{2}$. Same remarks.

961, ♂ *ad.;* Salt Lake City, Utah, May 20, 1869. $5\frac{3}{4}$—$8\frac{1}{2}$. Upper mandible and tip of lower, deep black, rest of lower plumbeous-blue; iris, brown; tarsi and toes, purplish-plumbeous.

1113, nest and eggs (3); Antelope Island, Great Salt Lake, June 5, 1869. Nest in sage-bush.

1126, 1127, nests and eggs (3, 1); Antelope Island, June 7, 1869. Nests in sage-bushes, one foot from ground.

1136, nest; Antelope Island, June 8, 1869. Sage-bush, one foot above ground.

1195, 1196, nests and eggs (3); Salt Lake City, June 21, 1869. Nests in sage-bushes, about one foot from ground.

1402, 1403, nests; valley of the Weber River, July, 1869. [J. C. Olmstead.]

AMPHISPIZA NEVADENSIS.

Artemisia Sparrow.

(*Tok'-et-se-whah'* of the Paiutes.)

"*Poospiza bellii*," BAIRD, B. N. Am., 1858, 470 (part); Cat. N. Am. B., 1859, No. 356.—COOPER, Orn. Cal., I, 1870, 204 (part).—COUES, Key, 1872, 141 (part); Check List, 1873, No. 173. [Not *P. bellii*, Cass.]

Poospiza bellii var. *nevadensis*, RIDGWAY, Bull. Essex Inst., V, Nov., 1873, 191.—COUES, Check List, 1873, App., p. 127.—B. B. & R., Hist. N. Am. B., I, 1874, 594, pl. XXVI, fig. 9.—HENSHAW, 1875, 275, pl. XI (adult).

Amphispiza bellii, COUES, B. N.W., 1874, 234 (part).

The distribution of this species seems to be strictly governed by that of the sage-brush plants, since it is present in nearly all districts where these are found, while it is apparently wanting in localities of any other description. It is most partial to the moister valleys, where the growth is most thrifty, and in such places is generally the most abundant bird. It was observed to be most numerous in the valleys of the western depression, few being seen in the Salt Lake Valley, where the *A. bilineata* was so abundant; but it does occur there, as well as much farther eastward—at least to the valleys of Green River and its tributary streams. In the neighborhood of Carson City it was by far the most abundant bird of the open wastes, and its abundance did not abate with the approach of winter. In walking through the sage-brush one was almost certain to see these birds at every few steps. They were exceedingly unsuspicious, and very reluctant to take flight, if not pursued too persistently; merely keeping a few feet in advance, running swiftly on the ground, their tails elevated at an angle of about 45°, but unexpanded, and keeping thus in front for several rods; when too nearly approached, merely dodging in and out among the low bushes, or concealing themselves momentarily behind a scraggly shrub. Should they be startled, even, they merely fly up, with a chipping twitter, and after a short meandering flight for a few rods, again alight and run out of sight.

They began singing toward the last of February, and by the beginning of April the first eggs were laid. During a walk through the sage-brush, on the ninth of the latter month, several nests were found, the female in nearly every instance betraying the position of the nest by remaining on it until we had approached quite near. Often, by carefully watching the ground a rod or two ahead, did we detect one of these birds steal slyly out from beneath a scraggly, usually nearly prostrate, bush, and, with tail elevated, run rapidly and silently away and soon disappear in the shrubbery. On such an occasion, a careful examination of the spot was almost certain to reveal an artfully-concealed nest, either imbedded in the ground, or, as was more rarely the case, resting among the lower branches of the bush.

The song of this bird, although not brilliant in execution nor by any means loud, is nevertheless of such a character as to attract attention. It has a melancholy pensiveness, remarkably in accord with the dreary monotony of the surroundings, yet as a sort of compensation, is possessed of delicacy of expression and peculiar pathos—just as the fine lights and shadows on the sunlit mountains, combined with a certain vagueness in the dreamy distance, subdue the harsher features of the desert landscape. This song, when first heard was mistaken for that of a lark (*Sturnella neglecta*) half a mile or so away; but we soon found that the bird was scarcely two rods distant. The early spring is when they sing most beautifully, the usual note during other seasons being a faint twitter or chirp, generally uttered as one chases another through the sage-brush.

List of specimens.

151, ♂ *ad.;* valley of the Humboldt (Oreana), August 31, 1867. $6\frac{9}{16}$—10—$3\frac{1}{4}$—$2\frac{3}{4}$—$\frac{5}{8}$—$\frac{3}{4}$—$2\frac{15}{16}$—$1\frac{9}{16}$. Upper mandible, plumbeous-black, tomium paler; lower, pure pale, bluish-lilaceous basally, the tip plumbeous; iris, bister; tarsi and toes, bluish-sepia.

157, ♂ *ad.;* Camp 17, September 2, 1867. $6\frac{3}{4}$—10—$3\frac{1}{2}$—$2\frac{7}{8}$—$\frac{7}{16}$—$\frac{11}{16}$—$3\frac{1}{3}$—$1\frac{1}{2}$. Tarsi and toes, purplish-black.

182, ♂ *ad.;* Wright's Cañon, West Humboldt Mountains, September 11, 1867. $6\frac{5}{8}$—$8\frac{1}{2}$—$3\frac{1}{4}$—$2\frac{11}{16}$—$\frac{13}{32}$—$\frac{3}{4}$—3—$1\frac{1}{4}$. Upper mandible, plumbeous-black, edged with whitish; lower, pale blue, the tip of the gonys dusky; iris, hazel; tarsi and toes, liver-brown with a plumbeous cast.

379, ♀ *ad.;* Truckee Reservation, December 26, 1867. (Sage-brush of the mesa.) 7—$9\frac{1}{2}$—$3\frac{3}{16}$—$2\frac{9}{16}$—$\frac{7}{16}$—$\frac{3}{4}$—3—$1\frac{7}{16}$. Upper mandible, plumbeous-slate; lower mandible and commissure, pure, fine, light plumbeous-blue, the tip dusky; iris, reddish-vandyke; tarsi, deep sepia-brown; toes, more blackish.

380, ♂ *ad.;* same locality, date, etc. $6\frac{3}{4}$—$9\frac{1}{4}$—$3\frac{3}{8}$—$2\frac{3}{4}$—$\frac{7}{16}$—$\frac{3}{4}$—$3\frac{1}{8}$—$1\frac{1}{2}$. Same remarks.

522, nest and eggs (2); Carson City, Nevada, April 27, 1868.

535, nest and eggs (3); Carson City, Nevada, April 27, 1868.

537, nest and eggs (3); same locality and date. (Nests on the ground, underneath sage-bushes.)

SPIZELLA MONTICOLA.

Canada Sparrow; Tree Sparrow.

Fringilla monticola, GMELIN, Syst. Nat., I, 1788, 912.

Spizella monticola, BAIRD, Birds N. Am., 1858, 427; Cat. N. Am. Birds, 1859, No. 357.—COOPER, Orn. Cal., I, 206.—COUES, Key, 1872, 142; Check List, 1873, No. 177; Birds N.W., 1874, 146.—B. B. & R., Hist. N. Am. Birds, II, 1874, 3, pl. XXVII, fig. 5.—HENSHAW, 1875, 277.

During the winter this well-known Sparrow was common and very generally distributed through the valleys of the western depression of the Great Basin. As in the East, it associated with Snow-birds and White-crowned Sparrows, although in this case its companions were different species (*Junco oregonus* and *Zonotrichia intermedia,* instead of *J. hyemalis* and *Z. leucophrys*).

List of specimens.

301, ♂ *ad.;* Truckee Meadows, Nevada, November 19, 1867. $6\frac{3}{4}$—$9\frac{7}{8}$—$3\frac{1}{4}$—$2\frac{11}{16}$—$\frac{3}{4}$—$\frac{3}{4}$—3—$1\frac{3}{8}$. Upper mandible, deep black, base of the culmen, yellow; lower mandible, citreous wax-yellow on basal two-thirds, then lilaceous-white, the tip black; iris, brown; tarsi, deep reddish sienna-brown; toes, blackish-brown.

SPIZELLA SOCIALIS.

Chipping Sparrow.

β. arizonæ.

(*So'-ho-quoy'-e-tse* of the Shoshones.)

Spizella socialis, BAIRD, Birds N. Am., 1858, 473 (part); Cat. N. Am. Birds, 1859, No. 359 (part).—COOPER, Orn. Cal., I, 1870, 207.

Spizella socialis var. *arizonæ,* COUES, Key, 1872, 143; Check List, 1873, No. 178a. —B. B. & R., Hist. N. Am. Birds, II, 1874, 11.—HENSHAW, 1875, 277.

Spizella socialis. a. *arizonæ,* COUES, Birds N.W., 1874, 148.

The common Chipping Sparrow was found to be very generally distributed, although it was a commoner species in the valley portions than on the mountains. It was a strictly arboreal bird, however, and thus inhabited different localities from *S. breweri,* even when both were found in the same neighborhood. In the environs of Sacramento City it was particularly numerous; and although the door-yards, gardens, and orchards were alike inhabited by it, the groves of small oak-trees in the inclosed fields were its favorite abode, where it nested in company with *Chondestes grammaca, Chrysomitris tristis,* and other equally abundant species.

In the Interior it was found in all wooded districts, but, contrary to the rule elsewhere, was less abundant among the cotton-woods of the river-valleys than in the groves of cedars and mahoganies on the lower slopes of the mountains, of which it was eminently characteristic. Nowhere did we find it in greater abundance than among these woods on the eastern slope of the Ruby Mountains, for there it was the most numerous of all the birds in July and August, associating in large flocks during the latter month, evidently preparing for their departure southward, which commenced in September. We have never observed the eastern form of this species to be gregarious to this extent, but no differences could be detected in its habits during the breeding-season, nor in any of its notes.

List of specimens.

848, ♀ ad.; East Humboldt Mountains, July 20, 1868. 5½—8¼—(?)—2 3/16. Bill, dark sepia-slate, darker terminally, lower mandible more lilaceous; iris, vandyke; tarsi and toes, pinkish sepia-white.

860, nest and eggs (4); Ruby Mountains (east slope), altitude about 8,000 feet, August 5, 1868. Nest in mountain-mahogany tree, six feet from ground.

1187, nest and eggs (4); Salt Lake City (City Creek Cañon), Utah, June 19, 1869. Nest in scrub-oak, six feet from ground.

SPIZELLA BREWERI.

Brewer's Sparrow.

Spizella breweri, CASSIN, Pr. Ac. Nat. Sci. Phila., VIII, 1856, 40.—BAIRD, B. N.
    Am., 1858, 475; Cat. N. Am. B., 1859, No. 361.—COOPER, Orn. Cal., I, 1870,
    209.

Spizella pallida var. *breweri*, COUES, Key, 1872, 143; Check List, 1873, No. 180*a*;
    B. N.W., 1874, 151.—B. B. & R., Hist. N. Am. B., II, 1874, 13, pl. XXVII, fig.
    4.—HENSHAW, 1875, 279.

A counterpart of the eastern Field Sparrow (*S. pusilla*), in its predilection for fields, or any open bushy localities, this species was found in every
place adapted to its habits. It was first observed at Sacramento, where it
was quite common, inhabiting the bushy fields along with *Chondestes grammaca, Coturniculus perpallidus*, and *Sturnella neglecta*. In the sage-brush
country, eastward of the Sierra Nevada, it was still more numerous than
in the Sacramento Valley; and throughout the entire extent of the Great
Basin was everywhere one of the commonest birds of the open wastes, and
an almost constant associate of *Oreoscoptes montanus* and the two species
of *Amphispiza*.

The resemblance of this species to *S. pusilla* extends no further than to
a similarity of general habits, however, for its nest and eggs are extremely
different, being more like those of *S. socialis*, while its song is remarkable
for vivacity and variety, in this respect fully equaling that of the best
Canaries, though it is considerably inferior to the latter in power. It is
interspersed throughout with a variety of trills or water-notes, and plaintive
chants which resemble somewhat the well-known notes of the Field Sparrow

List of specimens.

105, $\female$ *ad.*; valley of the Truckee, Nevada, July 24, 1867. $5\frac{3}{8}$—$7\frac{9}{16}$—$2\frac{7}{16}$—2—$\frac{5}{16}$—
$\frac{5}{8}$—$2\frac{1}{2}$—$1\frac{1}{2}$. Bill, pale lilaceous-brown, darker along the culmen; iris, hazel; tarsi
and toes, pale brownish flesh-color.

785, nest and eggs (3); Truckee Reservation, June 3, 1868. Nest in sage-bush,
about three feet from ground.

810. nest and eggs (2); "Old River" (near sink of Carson), Nevada, June 27, 1868.
Nest in sage-bush, about four feet from ground.

834, nest and eggs (3); Austin, Nevada, July 4, 1868. Sage-bush.

874, *ad.*; Ruby Valley, Nevada, August 28, 1868. $5\frac{7}{16}$—8—(?)—$2\frac{1}{2}$. Upper mandible, black, approaching to ashy-lilac on the tomium; lower mandible, lilaceous-ashy;
iris, ashy-umber; tarsi and toes, grayish horn-color.

1049, 1050, nests and eggs; Salt Lake City, Utah, May 26, 1869. Nests in sage-bushes. about three feet from ground.

1059, 1060, nests and eggs (3); Salt Lake City, May 27, 1869.

1067, nest and eggs (2); Salt Lake City, May 29, 1869.

1077, 1078, nests and eggs (4); Salt Lake City, June 1, 1869.

1091, 1097, 1098, 1099, nests and eggs; Antelope Island, Great Salt Lake, June 4, 1869.

1115 (3), 1116, 1117, 1118, nests and eggs; Antelope Island, Great Salt Lake, June 5, 1869.

1119 (3), 1120 (3), 1121 (3), 1122, nests and eggs; Antelope Island, Great Salt Lake, June 7. 1869.

1128, nest and egg (1): Antelope Island, June 7, 1869. Nest in sage-bush.

1132, ♀ ad.; Antelope Island, June 5, 1869.

1137 (3), 1138 (3), 1139, nests and eggs; Antelope Island, June 8, 1869.

1152, nest and eggs: Antelope Island, June 9, 1869.

1156, nest and eggs (4); southern shore. Great Salt Lake, June 11, 1869.

All nests in sage-bushes, about three feet from ground.

1157, nest and eggs (3); Rabbit Island, Great Salt Lake, June 11, 1868. Nest in grease-wood bush.

1164 (4), 1165 (3), 1166 (3), nests and eggs; Salt Lake City, June 14, 1869.

1171, 1172, 1173, nests and eggs; Salt Lake City, June 16, 1869.

1176 (4), 1177 (2), nests and eggs; Salt Lake City, June 17, 1869.

1198, nest and eggs (4); Salt Lake City, June 21, 1869.

1236, nest and eggs (2); Salt Lake City, June 23, 1869.

1318, nest and eggs (2); Parley's Park, June 27, 1869. Nest in sage-bush.

1354, nest and eggs; Parley's Park, June 27, 1869. In sage-bush.

1396 (2), 1397 (1), nests and eggs; Parley's Park, July, 1869. Nests in sage-bushes.

1406 and 1407, nests; Cash Valley, July, 1869. [J. C. Olmstead.]

1466, ♀ *juv.;* Parley's Park, Wahsatch Mountains, Utah, July 28, 1869. 5⅝—7⅝. Bill, yellowish-lilac, upper half of upper mandible dark plumbeous; iris, brown; tarsi and toes, light brown.

1482, ♀ *ad.;* Parley's Park, July 30, 1869. 5⅝—7¾.

MELOSPIZA FASCIATA.

Song Sparrow.

β. *heermanni.*

(*See'-hoot'-se-pah* of the Paiutes.)

Melospiza heermanni. BAIRD, B. N. Am., 1858, 478; Ib., ed. 1860, 478, pl. 70, fig. 1; Cat. N. Am. B., 1859, No. 364.—COOPER, Orn. Cal., I, 1870, 212.

Melospiza melodia var. *heermanni,* COUES, Key, 1872, 139; Check List, 1873, No. 169d.—B. B. & R., Hist. N. Am. B., II, 1874, 24, pl. XXVII, fig. 9.—HENSHAW, 1875, 282.

Melospiza melodia. a. heermanni. COUES. B. N.W., 1874. 139.

γ. *fallax.*

Zonotrichia fallax, BAIRD, Pr. Ac. Nat. Sci. Phila., 1854, 119.

Melospiza fallax, BAIRD, B. N. Am., 1858, 481; ed. 1860, 481, pl. 27, fig. 2; Cat. N. Am. B., 1859, No. 367.—COOPER, Orn. Cal., I, 215.

Melospiza melodia var. *fallax,* COUES, Key, 1872, 139; Check List, 1873, No. 169a.—B. B. & R., Hist. N. Am. B., II, 1874, 22, pl. XXVII, fig. 10.—HEN- SHAW, 1875, 281.

Melospiza melodia. a. *fallax,* COUES, B. N.W., 1874, 139.

δ. *guttata.*

Fringilla (Passerella) guttata, NUTTALL, Man., I, 2d ed., 1840, 581.

Melospiza melodia var. *guttata,* COUES, Key, 1872, 139; Check List, 1873, No. 169b.—B. B. & R., Hist. N. Am. B., II, 1874, 27, pl. XXVII, fig. 12.

Melospiza melodia. f. *guttata,* COUES, B. N.W., 1874, 139.

"*Melospiza rufina,*" BAIRD, B. N. Am., 1858, 480; Cat. N. Am. B., 1859, No. 366. [Not *Emberiza rufina,* BRANDT, 1836, = *Melospiza rufina.*]

Speaking of its different races collectively, the Song Sparrow is a widely-distributed bird. The race known as *M. heermanni* was very common in the thickets at Sacramento, and also throughout western Nevada, its eastern limit being, apparently, the West Humboldt Mountains, where the *M. fallax* began to replace it; the latter being the only form found thence to the Wahsatch and Uintah Mountains of Utah. The more northern *M. guttata* was encountered only in the range above mentioned, where a very few individuals were found in the month of October, in the sheltered cañons of the eastern slope. Since *Zonotrichia coronata* was met with in the same locality, it is likely that, as in the case of the latter species, they were not residents, but migrants from the northwestward. Whatever the race, however, the habits, and, so far as we could judge, the notes also, were nearly the same, the geographical modifications in these respects being by no means in proportion to those of form and plumage.

The Song Sparrow was found to be most partial to the dense thickets along streams or in the vicinity of other bodies of water, and was consequently most frequently seen in the lower valleys; indeed, we have no recollection of having observed it at a greater elevation than the meadow-like parks of the Wahsatch Mountains, where the var. *fallax* was abundant among the willows bordering the streams, along with *Passerella schistacea.*

According to our notes it was there confined to the floor of the park, or did not ascend to any great distance up the cañons along the streams. At Sacramento, as well in the river-valleys of western Nevada, it was common among the *tules* or rushes fringing the sloughs and ponds near the larger bodies of water. The species was stationary in all portions of its range, or at least did not perform more than a partial vertical migration, although the fact that individuals of the var. *guttata* were met with in the West Humboldt Mountains would seem to indicate that while the species, collectively, may be found in one locality throughout the year, *individuals* perform more or less of a latitudinal migration.

List of specimens.

β. heermanni.

150 ♀ *ad.;* Humboldt River (Oreana), August 31, 1867. $7—9\frac{1}{4}—3—2\frac{1}{2}—\frac{1}{2}—\frac{7}{8}—3—(2\frac{5}{8})$. Bill, dull liver-brown, the upper mandible darker, nearly black on the culmen; iris, hazel; tarsi and toes, dark liver-brown.

216, ♂ *ad.;* Camp 19, West Humboldt Mountains, Nevada, September 24, 1867. $6\frac{5}{8}—8\frac{11}{16}—2\frac{3}{4}—2\frac{1}{4}—\frac{7}{16}—\frac{13}{16}—2\frac{3}{4}—1\frac{1}{2}$. Bill, blackish hepatic-olive, paler and more slaty on lower mandible; iris, hazel; tarsi and toes, deep purplish horn-color.

236, ♂ *ad.;* Camp 19, October 7, 1867. $6\frac{7}{8}—9—2\frac{7}{8}—2\frac{7}{16}—\frac{7}{16}—\frac{13}{16}—3—1\frac{7}{8}$. Upper mandible, slaty horn-black, lower paler brownish-slaty; iris, hazel; tarsi and toes, pale horn-color.

368, ♂ *ad.;* Truckee Reservation, Nevada, December 25, 1867. $7—9\frac{1}{8}—2\frac{7}{8}—2\frac{7}{16}—\frac{7}{16}—\frac{13}{16}—3\frac{1}{8}—1\frac{1}{2}$. Upper mandible horn-black, paler along tomium; lower, brownish-slaty.

381, ♀ *ad.;* Truckee Reservation, December 26, 1867. $6\frac{1}{4}—8\frac{3}{8}—2\frac{5}{8}—2\frac{1}{8}—\frac{7}{16}—\frac{13}{16}—2\frac{5}{8}—1\frac{3}{8}$. Upper mandible hepatic-black, paler along tomium; lower, lilaceous-brown, with yellowish tinge basally beneath.

382, ♀ *ad.;* Truckee Reservation, December 26, 1867. $6\frac{3}{8}—8\frac{1}{2}—2\frac{3}{4}—2\frac{3}{16}—\frac{7}{16}—\frac{3}{4}—2\frac{7}{8}—1\frac{3}{8}$. Same remarks.

383, ♂ *ad.;* Truckee Reservation, December 26, 1867. $6\frac{3}{4}—8\frac{7}{8}—2\frac{15}{16}—2\frac{3}{8}—\frac{7}{16}—\frac{13}{16}—3—1\frac{1}{2}$. Same remarks.

470, ♂ *ad.;* Carson City, Nevada, March 28, 1868. $6\frac{5}{8}—8\frac{11}{16}—2\frac{7}{8}—2\frac{1}{4}$. Upper mandible, plumbeous-black, tomium paler; lower, dull plumbeous, with lilaceous glow basally and beneath; iris, bister; tarsi,, whitish-brown; toes, deeper brown.

479, ♂ *ad.;* Carson, March 30, 1868. $6\frac{3}{8}—8\frac{5}{8}—2\frac{12}{16}—2\frac{5}{16}$. Same remarks.

γ. fallax.

890, *juv.;* Camp 22, Ruby Valley, Nevada, September 4, 1868. $6\frac{1}{8}—8\frac{1}{2}—(?)—2\frac{1}{4}$. Bill, lilaceous ashy-brown, darkest terminally, lower mandible more lilaceous; rictus, pale yellow; iris, very dark sepia; tarsi and toes, dilute lilaceous-sepia, latter pale yellow beneath.

931, ♀ *ad.;* Camp 25, Humboldt Valley, September 16, 1868. $6\frac{1}{4}$—$8\frac{9}{16}$—(?)—$2\frac{3}{16}$. Same remarks as to No. 470.

945, ♀ *ad.;* Camp 35, Deep Creek, Utah, October 5, 1868. $6\frac{5}{8}$—$8\frac{3}{4}$—(?)—$2\frac{1}{4}$. Same remarks.

946, ♀ *ad.;* Camp 35, Deep Creek, Utah, October 5, 1868. $6\frac{1}{4}$—8—(?)—$2\frac{1}{4}$. Same remarks.

947, ♀ *ad.;* Camp 35, Deep Creek, Utah, October 5, 1868. $6\frac{1}{2}$—$8\frac{7}{8}$—(?)—$2\frac{1}{4}$. Same remarks.

948, ♀ *ad.;* Camp 35, Deep Creek, Utah, October 5. $6\frac{5}{8}$—$8\frac{1}{2}$—(?)—$2\frac{3}{16}$. Same remarks.

1228, nest and eggs; Parley's Park, Wahsatch Mountains, Utah, June 23, 1869. Nest among bushes in willow-thicket along stream, about one foot from ground.

1232, nest and eggs (2); Parley's Park, June 23, 1869. Situated like preceding.

1275, nest and eggs (5); Parley's Park, June 24, 1869. Nest in thorn-apple bush along stream, six feet from ground.

1314, nest and eggs (3); Parley's Park, June 27, 1869. Nest in willows by stream.

1327, 1328; nests and eggs (4); Parley's Park, June 28, 1869. Nests in willows.

1363, 1364; nests and eggs (4); Pack's Cañon, Uintah Mountains, July 4, 1869. Nests in willows by stream, about three feet from ground.

1388, 1389; nests; Provo River, Utah, July 10, 1869. Willows.

1391, nest and eggs (3); Provo River, July 11, 1869. Nest in willows by stream.

1405, nest; Bear River Valley, July, 1869. (Collected by Mr. J. C. Olmstead.)

1419, nest and eggs; Parley's Park, July 16, 1869.

1457, ♂ *juv.;* July 26, 1869. $6\frac{5}{8}$—$9\frac{1}{8}$. Bill, dark hepatic-plumbeous, lower mandible with pinkish flush, the upper almost black on the culmen; iris, brown; tarsi and toes, deep purplish-brown.

1461, nest; Parley's Park, July 26, 1869. Willows by stream.

1465, ♂ *juv.;* Parley's Park, July 28, 1869. $6\frac{7}{8}$—$8\frac{7}{8}$. Same remarks as to No. 1457.

1475, ♀ *juv.;* July 29, 1869. $6\frac{1}{8}$—$8\frac{1}{2}$. Same remarks.

1506, ♂ *juv.;* August 13, 1869. $6\frac{1}{2}$—9. Same remarks.

δ. guttata.

223, ♀ *ad.;* Camp 19, October 3, 1867. $6\frac{5}{8}$—$8\frac{1}{2}$—$2\frac{11}{16}$—$2\frac{1}{4}$—$\frac{9}{16}$—$\frac{3}{4}$—$2\frac{7}{8}$—$1\frac{1}{4}$. Upper mandible horn-black, paler along tomium; lower, horn-blue, darker terminally.

MELOSPIZA LINCOLNI.

Lincoln's Sparrow.

Fringilla lincolnii, AUDUBON, Orn. Biog., II, 1834, 539, pl. 193.

Melospiza linconii, BAIRD, Birds N. Am., 1858, 483; Catal. N. Am. Birds, 1859, No. 368.—COOPER, Orn. Cal., I, 216.—COUES, Key, 1872, 138; Check List, No. 167; Birds N.W., 1874, 135.—B. B. & R., Hist. N. Am. Birds, II, 1874, 31, pl. XXVII, fig. 13.—HENSHAW, 1875, 283.

During the summer we found this species only in the elevated parks of the higher mountain ranges; but during its migrations it was very plentiful in the lower valleys. In Parley's Park it was a rather common summer resident, inhabiting the open slopes or level pieces of ground covered by low shrubs, weeds, and grass, in company with *Zonotrichia leucophrys* and *Pooecetes confinis*. We did not hear its song, but its ordinary note was a rather strong *chuck*, much like that of *Passerella schistacea*. In the autumn it was common among the willows along Deep Creek, in northwestern Utah, and in April was quite abundant in the bushy fields at the base of the Sierra Nevada, near Carson City, particularly in places near springs or close by the streams.

List of specimens.

563, ♀ ad.; Carson City, Nevada, April 29, 1868. $5\frac{7}{16}$—$7\frac{7}{8}$—$2\frac{2}{8}$—2. Upper mandible, blackish, tomium and lower mandible, dull brownish-ashy; rictus, pale yellow; iris, bister; tarsi and toes, dilute horn-color.

932, ♂ ad.; Upper Humboldt Valley, September 16, 1868. $5\frac{7}{8}$—$8\frac{1}{8}$—$2\frac{3}{16}$—$1\frac{7}{8}$—$3\frac{1}{8}$—$2\frac{3}{16}$. Upper mandible, plumbeous-black, the tomium pale yellowish-olive; lower mandible, pale grayish-olive, more yellowish basally; rictus, light yellow; iris, hazel; tarsi, pale brown, toes darker.

949, ♂ ad.; Deep Creek, Utah, October 5, 1868. $5\frac{7}{8}$—$7\frac{7}{8}$—(?)—$2\frac{1}{4}$. Upper mandible, dull plumbeous-black, tomium and lower mandible, light dull cinereous, more yellowish-lilaceous basally beneath; rictus, pale yellow; iris, sepia-drab; tarsi and toes, pale horn-color.

1276, nest and eggs (4); Parley's Park, Wahsatch Mountains, Utah, June 24, 1869. Nest on ground, beneath prostrate sage-bush, near stream.

PASSERELLA MEGARHYNCHA.

Thick-billed Sparrow.

Passerella megarhyncha, BAIRD, Birds N. Am., 1858, 925, pl. LXIX, fig. 4; Cat. N. Am. Birds, 1859, No. 376a.—COOPER, Orn. Cal., I, 1870, 222.

Passerella townsendi var. *megarhyncha*, B. B. & R., Hist. N. Am. Birds, II, 1874, 57, pl. XXVIII, fig. 10.

Passerella townsendi var. *schistacea*, COUES, Birds N.W., 1874, 162 (part).

This very interesting bird was met with only in the ravines of the Sierra Nevada, near Carson City and Washoe. Unlike *P. schistacea*, it was strictly a migrant, being entirely absent during the winter, and not arriving from the south until about the 20th of April. It was found mostly in damp or swampy places in the lower portion of the mountains, and was particularly numerous where the alders grew abundantly along the streams. In such places they were singing loudly on every hand, and their songs, when first heard, seemed so similar to those of the Large-billed Water Thrush (*Seiurus ludovicianus*), of the east, that they were mistaken for the notes of that bird, until the singers were seen and the species identified. The song possessed but little resemblance to that of the *P. schistacea*, being so far superior as to be comparable only to that of the bird above mentioned, its chief qualities being great volume and liquidness.

List of specimens.

530, ♂ *ad.;* Carson City, Nevada, April 25, 1868. $7\frac{3}{4}$—$10\frac{5}{16}$—$3\frac{1}{2}$—$2\frac{13}{16}$. General hue of bill, milky lilaceous-white, palest and purest on lower mandible, which has a delicate rosy tint basally beneath; culmen, pale plumbeous-sepia; iris, bister; tarsi and toes, deep, rather dilute sepia-brown.

531, ♀ *ad.;* Carson City, Nevada, April 25, 1868. 7—$9\frac{3}{4}$—$3\frac{1}{8}$—$2\frac{9}{16}$. Same remarks.

PASSERELLA SCHISTACEA.

Slate-colored Sparrow.

Passerella schistacea, BAIRD, B. N. Am., 1858, 490, pl. LXIX, fig. 3; Cat. N. Am. B., 1859, No. 376.—COOPER, Orn. Cal., I, 1870, 223 (figs. of head and feet).

Passerella iliaca var. *schistacea*, ALLEN, Bull. Mus. Comp. Zool., III, 1872, 168.— COUES, Key, 1872, 147.

Passerella townsendi var. *schistacea*, COUES, Key, 1872, 352; Check List, 1873, No. 189a; B. N.W., 1874, 162.—B. B. & R., Hist. N. Am. B., II, 1874, 56, pl. XXVIII, fig. 9.—HENSHAW, 1875, 293.

This species was first met with at Carson City, Nevada, during its northward migration, which began late in February or early in March, some few individuals having doubtless remained during the winter in the shelter of the dense willow-thickets along the river. The following September it was observed in similar localities in the Upper Humboldt Valley; we may therefore judge that it is found, in proper season, and in suitable localities, throughout the country between the Sierra Nevada and the Wahsatch. During the summer months it was one of the commonest birds in Parley's Park, where it was a constant associate of *Melospiza fallax* in the willow-thickets. It is quite a counterpart of that species in manners and notes, while the nests and eggs are similar to such a degree that it often required the sacrifice of the parent, and always a very close observation for the positive identification of the species. The ordinary note is a sharp chuck; but the song is scarcely distinguishable from that of *Melospiza fallax*.

List of specimens.

433, ♂ ad.; Carson City, Nevada, March 9, 1868. 7⅝—10¼—3$\frac{7}{16}$—2¾. Upper mandible, olivaceous-sepia, darkest basally, tomium ashy-lilac; rictus and basal two-thirds of lower mandible, bright maize-yellow, deepest beneath; terminal portion, brownish-lilaceous, the point dusky; iris, precisely the color of pectoral spots; tarsi and toes, dilute-sepia.

919, ♂ ad.; head of Humboldt Valley (Camp 24), September 11, 1868. 7⅜—10½ —(?)—2$\frac{13}{16}$. Upper mandible, sepia-plumbeous, darker along culmen, more lilaceous along tomium; lower paler, point dusky, the basal half deep maize-yellow; iris, burnt-sienna; tarsi and toes, very deep sepia.

1223, nest and eggs (4); Parley's Park, June 22, 1869. Nest in a bunch of willow sprouts about two feet from the ground, bank of stream.

1225, 1226, 1227, 1229, and 1230, nests and eggs; Parley's Park, June 23, 1869. 1289, nest and eggs; Parley's Park, June 25, 1869. Nests among bushes or willow-stubs in thickets along streams, from one to six feet above the ground.

1460, nest; Parley's Park, July 26, 1869. Nest among willows.

CALAMOSPIZA BICOLOR.

Lark Bunting.

Fringilla bicolor, TOWNSEND, Jour. Acad. Nat. Sci. Philad., VII, 1837, 189.

Calamospiza bicolor, BONAP., Comp. & Geog. List, 1838, 30.—BAIRD, B. N. Am., 1858, 492; Cat. N. Am. B., 1859, No. 377.—COOPER, Orn. Cal., I, 225.—COUES, Key, 1872, 147; Check List, 1873, No. 190; B. N.W., 1874, 163.—B. B. & R., Hist. N. Am. B., II, 1874, 61, pl. XXIX, figs. 2, 3.—HENSHAW, 1875, 294.

But a single specimen of this species was observed by us, and this was doubtless a straggler from the Great Plains on the eastern side of the Rocky Mountains. The individual in question was on the ground when shot, its appearance and manners being quite similar to those of *Chondestes grammaca*. On the plains just east of the town of Cheyenne, we noticed in August, from the car-windows, numerous large flocks of this species, startled by the approach of the train, the flocks rising from the grass on either side, and wheeling about in their flight in the irregular manner of Horned Larks (*Eremophila*).

List of specimens.

1477, ♂ juv.; Parley's Park, July 30, 1869. 7¼—11½. Bill, ashy-white; upper half of upper mandible, pale ash, gonys with pinkish glow; iris, brown; tarsi and toes, purplish-brown.

HEDYMELES MELANOCEPHALUS.

Black-headed Grosbeak.

(*Look'-em* of the Washoes; *Uni-gu'-eet* of the Paiutes.)

Guiraca melanocephala, SWAINSON, Philos. Mag., I, 1827, 438.—BAIRD, Birds N.
Am., 1858, 498; Cat. N. Am. Birds, 1859, No. 381.—COOPER, Orn. Cal., I,
1870, 228.

Hedymeles melanocephalus, CABANIS, Mus. Hein., I, 1851, 153.—B. B. & R, Hist.
N. Am. Birds, II, 1874, 73, pl. xxx, figs. 1, 2.—HENSHAW, 1875, 296.

Goniaphea (*Hedymeles*) *melanocephala*, GRAY, Hand List, I, 1869, No. 7547.

Goniaphea melanocephala, COUES, Key, 1872, 149; Check List, 1873, No. 194; Birds
N.W., 1874, 167.

This fine bird was quite abundant in the fertile valleys and lower
cañons along the entire route, from Sacramento to the Wahsatch and
Uintahs. Its range was exactly that of *Cyanospiza amœna*, and it was
observed that in the Interior both these species reached their upper
limit about where the summer range of *Pyranga ludoviciana* commenced,
viz, about the middle portion of the cañons. It was abundant both at
Sacramento and in the valley of the Truckee, in western Nevada, but was
nearly restricted in the former locality to the willow thickets, while in the
latter it preferred the shrubbery of buffalo-berry and other bushes. At
the latter locality it was observed to feed, in May, upon the buds of the
grease-wood (*Obione confertifolia*), in company with *Pyranga ludoviciana*,
Icterus bullocki, and several other birds. It was also found in the shrubbery along the lower portion of the mountain-streams, but was there less
numerous than in the river-valleys, while at an altitude of about 7,000
feet it appeared to be entirely absent. It was consequently rare in Parley's Park, where, however, a few pairs were nesting in the thickets
along the streams. It was very frequently observed that the male of this
species assists in incubation, being, in fact, more often seen on the nest
than his mate.

This species appears to be a perfect counterpart of the eastern Rose-
breasted Grosbeak (*H. ludovicianus*), its notes especially, in all their variations, being quite the same.

List of specimens.

21, nest and eggs (3); Sacramento, California, June 11, 1867. Nest in willow, about ten feet from ground. *Male on nest when found.*

22, ♀ *ad.* (parent of eggs No. 21); Sacramento, California, June 11, 1867. $8\frac{1}{2}$—13—$4\frac{1}{4}$—$3\frac{1}{2}$—$\frac{3}{4}$—$\frac{7}{8}$—$3\frac{1}{4}$—2. Upper mandible, slate-color, lower bluish-white, with tinge of lilaceous beneath; iris, dark hazel; tarsi and toes, pure light ashy-blue.

32, ♂ *ad.;* Sacramento, June 12, 1867. 8—$12\frac{1}{4}$—$4\frac{1}{8}$—$3\frac{5}{16}$—$\frac{3}{4}$—$\frac{7}{8}$—$3\frac{1}{4}$—$1\frac{3}{8}$. Same remarks.

173, ♂ *juv.;* West Humboldt Mountains, September 7, 1867. $8\frac{3}{8}$—$12\frac{3}{4}$—$4\frac{3}{16}$—$3\frac{7}{16}$—$\frac{3}{4}$—$\frac{7}{8}$—$3\frac{1}{4}$—$1\frac{3}{8}$. Same remarks.

564, ♂ *ad.;* Truckee Reservation, May 15, 1868. $8\frac{11}{16}$—$13\frac{1}{8}$—(?)—$3\frac{1}{2}$. Same remarks.

804, nest and eggs (3); Truckee River, June 6, 1868. Nest in buffalo-berry thicket.

964, ♂ *ad.;* Salt Lake City, Utah, May 20, 1869.

1036, ♂ *ad.;* Salt Lake City, Utah, May 24, 1869. $8\frac{1}{2}$—$12\frac{7}{8}$. Upper mandible, slate-color, lower bluish-white; iris, brown; tarsi and toes, plumbeous.

1062, ♂ *ad.;* Salt Lake City, May 27, 1869. $8\frac{1}{2}$—$12\frac{5}{8}$.

1300, nest and eggs (3); Parley's Park, Wahsatch Mountains, Utah, June 27, 1869. Nest in willows along stream. *Male on nest.*

1324, nest; Parley's Park, June 28, 1869. Nest in a willow copse.

1399, eggs; Cash Valley, Utah, July, 1869. [J. C. Olmstead.]

1474, ♀ *juv.;* Parley's Park, July 29, 1869. $8\frac{1}{8}$—$12\frac{3}{8}$. Bill, dull lead-color, darker on culmen, lighter and more pinkish toward gonys; iris, brown; tarsi and toes, ashy-blue.

GUIRACA CŒRULEA.

Blue Grosbeak.

Loxia cœrulea, LINN., Syst. Nat., I, 1766, 306.

Guiraca cœrulea, SWAINS., Philos. Mag., I, 1827, 438.—BAIRD, Birds N. Am., 1858, 499; Cat. N. Am. Birds, 1859, No. 382.—COOPER, Orn. Cal., I, 1870, 230.—B. B. & R., Hist. N. Am. Birds, II, 1874, 77, pl. XXIX, figs. 4, 5.—HENSHAW, 1875, 298.

Goniaphea cœrulea, SCLATER, Proc. Zool. Soc. Lond., 1856, 301.—COUES, Key, 1872, 149, fig. 93; Check List, 1873, No. 195; Birds N.W., 1874, 169.

The Blue Grosbeak was met with only at Sacramento, where it was a very common bird in the bushy fields in the outskirts of the city. The distribution of this species is quite remarkable, it being more or less common on both coasts northward as far, at least, as the parallel of 40°, but of exceedingly rare occurrence in the Interior, except along the southern border. This fact seems equally true of the eastern half of the continent as of the western, for there are few local lists pertaining to the Mississippi Valley which include it, while on the Atlantic coast it is more or less common, locally, north to New Jersey, having even been taken in the eastern portion of Maine! Its distribution seems, therefore, not to be governed strictly by climatic conditions, but the facts adduced rather seem to indicate a somewhat littoral range for the species.

At Sacramento this species was found in the same localities with *Cyanospiza amœna*, it being as characteristic of the edges of the copses of young cotton-woods as was *Hedymeles melanocephalus* of the willow thickets.

List of specimens.

18, 19, nests and eggs (3); Sacramento, California, June 11, 1867.

20, ♀ ad. (parent of No. 18); Sacramento, California, June 11, 1867.   7—10¾—3½—2¹⁵₁₆—⅝—1¹₁₆—2⅞—1½.   Upper mandible, dark bluish horn-color, lower light, somewhat lilaceous, ashy-white; iris, hazel; tarsi and toes, horn-color.

44, ♂ ad.; Sacramento, June 17, 1867. 7½—11¼—3⅝—3¼—⅝—⅝—3—1½. Upper mandible blackish-slate, lower light plumbeous-blue; iris, hazel; tarsi and toes, plumbeous-brown.

51, nest and eggs (3); Sacramento, California, June 18, 1867.

82, nest and eggs (3); Sacramento, California, June 24, 1867.

91, nest and eggs (3); Sacramento, California, June 29, 1867.

Nests, all similarly situated, being placed about six feet from ground, in small cotton-woods, in edge of copse.

CYANOSPIZA AMŒNA.

Lazuli Bunting.

Emberiza amœna, SAY, Long's Exped., II, 1823, 47.

Cyanospiza amœna, BAIRD, B. N. Am., 1858, 504; Cat. N. Am. B., 1859, No. 386.—COOPER, Orn. Cal., I, 1870, 233.—COUES, Key, 1872, 149; Check List, 1873, No. 198; B. N.W., 1874, 170.—B. B. & R., Hist. N. Am. B., II, 1874, 84, pl. XXX, figs. 11, 12.—HENSHAW, 1875, 300.

This pretty little Bunting was a very common species in all the fertile valleys, as well as in the lower cañons of the mountains, its range being co-extensive with that of *Hedymeles melanocephalus*. Like its eastern congener, *C. cyanea*, of which it is a perfect counterpart in habits, manners, and notes, it frequents bushy places only ; but it avoids the sage-brush tracts, and resorts to the more thrifty shrubbery in the vicinity of the streams.

List of specimens.

9, nest and egg (1); Sacramento, California, June 8, 1867. Nest on extremity of drooping branch of small oak, in grove, about four feet from ground.

38, nest and eggs; Sacramento, June 12, 1867. Nest in bush.

92, nest and eggs; Sacramento, June 29, 1867. Nest in bush.

99, nest and eggs (2); Hunter's Station, Nevada, July 1, 1867. Nest in bush, along stream.

835, nest and eggs (3); Austin, Nevada, July 4, 1868. Nest in wild-rose brier, along stream in cañon.

850, ♀ ad.; East Humboldt Mountains, July 21, 1868. 5⅝—8¾—(?)—2⅜. Upper mandible, black, tomium pale bluish; lower, pale blue, point blackish; iris, dark vandyke; tarsi and toes, dull sepia.

962, ♂ ad.; Salt Lake City, May 20, 1869. 5¼—9¼. Bill, generally deep black, lower mandible plumbeous, strip of black on gonys; iris, dark brown; tarsi and toes, deep black.

1063, ♂ ad.; Salt Lake City, Utah, May 27, 1869. 5⅝—9¼. Upper mandible, black; lower, bluish-white, a streak of black on the gonys (a constant feature in adult males); iris, brown; tarsi and toes, sepia-black.

1237, nest and eggs (3); Parley's Park, Utah, June 23, 1869. Nest in wild-rose brier, by stream.

1303, nest and eggs (4); Parley's Park, Utah, June 27, 1869. Nest in bush near stream.

1357, nest and eggs (4); Parley's Park, July 2, 1869. Nest among rose-bushes, by stream.

1418, nest and eggs; Parley's Park, July 16, 1869.

PIPILO MACULATUS.

Western Towhee.

β. megalonyx—Long-clawed Ground Robin.

Pipilo megalonyx, BAIRD, B. N. Am., 1858, 515, pl. LXXIII; Cat. N. Am. B., 1859, No. 394.—COOPER, Orn. Cal., I, 1870, 242.

Pipilo maculatus var. *megalonyx*, COUES, Key, 1872, 152; Check List, 1873, No. 205b.—B. B. & R., Hist. N. Am. B., II, 1874, 113, pl. XXXI, fig. 12.—HENSHAW, 1875, 303.

γ. oregonus—Oregon Ground Robin.

Pipilo oregonus, BELL, Ann. Lyc. N. H., New York, V, 1852, 6.—BAIRD, B. N. Am., 1858, 513; Cat. N. Am. B., 1859, No. 302.—COOPER, Orn. Cal., I, 241.

Pipilo maculatus var. *oregonus*, COUES, Key, 1872, 152; Check List, 1873, No. 205. B. B. & R., Hist. N. Am. B., II, 1874, 116, pl. XXI, fig. 9.

Of the western species of this genus, which resemble in their general markings the *P. erythrophthalmus* of the East, three definable forms have been recognized, these representing separate geographical areas, and thus corresponding to what are termed geographical, or climatic, races.[1] These

---

[1] Typical *maculatus*, representing a fourth race, inhabits the table-lands of Mexico; additional forms are, *P. carmani*, Baird, of Socorro Island, and *P. consobrinus*, Ridgway, of Guadalupe.

forms are sufficiently easy to recognize in typical or extreme specimens, but such constitute so small a proportion of the number usually embraced in collections, that if called upon to define these supposed races by trenchant characters, it is very doubtful whether we could succeed to our own satisfaction, while the concurrence of others could scarcely be expected. This is especially the case with regard to the *oregonus* and *megalonyx* types, both of which came under our observation in the field. Judging from the specimens alone, of these two forms, we should not think of recognizing two races in the series before us, for it is absolutely impossible to distinguish certain specimens obtained in western Nevada from others taken in Utah. But since the notes of the birds of the two localities were so extremely dissimilar as to really astonish us upon the discovery of the fact, we cannot ignore this difference between the birds of the two districts; this, therefore, is our reason for arranging their synonymy as above.

In their manners and general appearance these western Ground Robins call at once to mind the eastern Towhee (*P. erythrophthalmus*), for they have the same colors (with merely minor differences, not distinguishable at a distance), the same flirting flight, while they are inseparably attached to the most bushy localities. But in direct contrast to the familiar eastern species, we found the western Towhee to be everywhere one of the very shyest birds of the country. The notes, too, are most remarkably different, since none of them are in the least attractive, but, on the contrary, simple and rude almost in the extreme.

The Oregon Ground Robin was found from Sacramento to the West Humboldt Mountains, it being equally common on both sides of the Sierra Nevada. Within the Great Basin, its range was strictly confined to the valleys and connecting cañons of the western depression, while it was abundant in proportion to the proximity of a locality to the Sierra. In summer it was generally distributed—that is, included the lower cañons of the mountains in its range, as well as the river-valleys; but in winter, it appeared to make a more or less extensive vertical migration, nearly, if not quite, forsaking the mountain localities. At Sacramento, it frequented the thickets around the border of fields in the outskirts of the city, in the same places as those inhabited by the Yellow-breasted Chat and Song Sparrow

(*Icteria longicauda* and *Melospiza heermanni*); and in the lower fertile valleys
of the Interior, as those of the Truckee and Carson rivers, it chose similar
localities along the river-banks. It was extremely rare in the fertile
mountain cañons, excepting their lower portions, being far from common in
the vicinity of our camps in the West Humboldt range. It was nowhere
else so numerous as along the eastern base of the Sierra Nevada, near Carson
City, where it was the most abundant bird among the scattered scraggy
shrubs of dwarf-plum (*Prunus demissa?*) mixed with currant bushes, which
grew plentifully in the old fields just below the commencement of the pine
timber. There it was found chiefly during the spring, summer, and autumn,
none having been observed during the coldest part of the winter, at which
time they had sought shelter in the dense willow thickets in the river-valleys.
About the middle of February, however, they began returning to their summer haunts at the foot of the mountains, and were observed, at first sparingly,
in the locality described above, as well as in the dense chaparral of laurel
(*Ceanothus velutinus*) and manzanita (*Arctostaphylus glauca*) on the sides of the
ravines. Up to about the 9th of March they were nearly silent, their only
note being a very common-place *teish*, uttered usually in an impertinent tone.
At about the above date, however, the males commenced to sing, or rather to
utter their rude trill, during the delivery of which the performer occupied a
conspicuous position, as the summit of a tall bush or the top of a high rock,
where he sat for an hour at a time, as he performed his part in the morning chorus, the black and white of his markings contrasting boldly, and his
form clearly defined against the blue sky. The quality of the performance,
however, it seemed to us, by no means justified such ostentation, for it
amounted to no more than a rude trill, so simple as not to deserve the name
of song, notwithstanding the frequency of its repetition and the earnestness
of the performer. None of the few notes uttered by this bird bear the
remotest resemblance to those of the eastern species (*P. erythrophthalmus*),
although the spring-call described above may be compared to the final trill
of the very creditable performance of the latter bird. At all times this
bird was excessively shy—another striking contrast to its eastern relative—
and was thus extremely difficult to procure, seldom allowing one to approach
within gunshot; if too closely followed, flitting in its peculiar manner, for

short distances at a time, over the bushes, flirting the expanded white-tipped tail at each heavy beat of the wings.

Eastward of the West Humboldt Mountains, few Ground Robins were observed until we arrived at Salt Lake City; indeed, none were seen except at our camp near Austin, in the Toyabe Mountains, and in the eastern cañons of the Ruby range, at both of which places they were so extremely rare that we could not determine the race.[1] At Salt Lake City, however, we found the species again very abundant, even more so than at Carson City, and also inhabiting the chaparral on the foot-hills, which in this case consisted of scrub-oaks instead of manzanita, laurel, and wild-plum bushes. It was noticed immediately, however, that while to all appearance they were the same birds as those found near Carson City, they uttered totally different notes, which we found to agree perfectly with Dr. Coues' description in his "Prodrome," a fact which impressed us at once, for we had previously striven in vain to detect in the notes of the birds of this species at Carson the *remotest* resemblance to any uttered by the Cat-bird or the "Dickcissel" (*Euspiza*)[2]; and since in their characters the specimens agreed perfectly with the diagnosis of *megalonyx*, we had considered the description of the notes above referred to as erroneous, and were thus glad to find so satisfactory a relief from our dilemma. Instead of the rude, rather suppressed *teish* with which we had been familiar, a sharp *mew* was heard, scarcely distinguishable from the notes of the Cat-bird, found in the same locality; and the song was a very decided improvement on that of the western individuals, for, instead of a short, simple trill, apparently "strained out" after considerable effort, these trills were multiplied and connected by other notes, so that a passable song resulted. There was still no approach to the notes of *P. erythrophthalmus*, however, excepting a very slight one in the song; but the habits of the birds were much less shy, though they were far from being so confidingly familiar as the very tame eastern species.

---

[1] Judging from the circumstance that accessions from the Rocky Mountain fauna were first encountered at these two localities, it seems most probable that the Ground Robins met with were also the Rocky Mountain form—*P. megalonyx.*

[2] "Ordinary call-note almost exactly like that of *Mimus carolinensis*; the song a rather harsh and monotonous repetition of four or six syllables, something like that of *Euspiza americana.*"—Pr. Ac. Nat. Sci., 1866, p. 89.

List of specimens.

β. *megalonyx.*

956, nest and eggs (2); Salt Lake City, May 20, 1869. Nest on ground, among scrub-oaks on hill-side.

957, nest and eggs (3); Salt Lake City, May 20, 1869. Same remarks.

958, ♂ *ad.;* Salt Lake City, Utah, May 20, 1869. $8\frac{1}{2}$—$10\frac{7}{8}$. Bill, pure black; iris, red-lead color; tarsi and toes, slaty-sepia.

1023, ♂ *ad.;* Salt Lake City, May 24, 1869. $8\frac{13}{16}$—11. Bill, pure black; iris, intense scarlet; tarsi, purplish-sepia, toes darker.

1034, ♂ *ad.;* Salt Lake City, May 24, 1869. $8\frac{3}{4}$—$11\frac{1}{2}$. Same remarks.

1035, ♂ *ad.;* Salt Lake City, May 24, 1869. $8\frac{1}{2}$—11. Same remarks.

1043, nest and eggs (4); Salt Lake City, May 24, 1869. Nest on ground, beneath sage-bush.

1069, ♀ *ad.;* Salt Lake City, May 29, 1869. $8\frac{5}{8}$—11. Same remarks.

1096, nest and eggs (4); Antelope Island, Great Salt Lake, June 4, 1869. Side of ravine. Nest on ground, beneath sage-bush.

1185, nest and eggs (3); Salt Lake City, June 18, 1869. Nest on ground, among scrub-oaks.

1186, nest and eggs (3); Salt Lake City, June 18, 1869. Nest on ground, beneath uprooted oak in thicket.

γ. *oregonus.*

35, nest and eggs (3); Sacramento City, California, June 12, 1867. Nest on ground, beneath fallen dead thistle, in thick cotton-wood copse.

199, ♂ *ad.;* West Humboldt Mountains, Nevada, September 20, 1867. $8\frac{5}{8}$—$10\frac{3}{4}$—$3\frac{9}{16}$—3—$\frac{17}{32}$—$\frac{7}{8}$—4—$2\frac{3}{4}$. Bill, blackish-slate, commissure and lower mandible inclining to ashy; iris, *deep brownish vermilion-red;* tarsi and toes, dark horn-color.

222, ♀ *ad.;* West Humboldt Mountains, October 3, 1867. $8\frac{5}{8}$—$10\frac{5}{8}$—$3\frac{1}{2}$—$2\frac{7}{8}$—$\frac{1}{2}$—1—$4\frac{1}{2}$—$2\frac{1}{2}$. Bill, black, lower mandible inclining to dusky slate, paler basally; *iris, light hazel-red;* tarsi and toes, deep purplish horn-color.

227, ♂ *ad.;* West Humboldt Mountains, October 4, 1867. $8\frac{5}{8}$—$11\frac{1}{8}$—$3\frac{3}{4}$—$3\frac{1}{16}$—$\frac{9}{16}$—1—$4\frac{3}{16}$—$1\frac{3}{4}$. Bill, slate-black, ashy on lower mandible; iris, *light brownish-yellow;* tarsi and toes, light horn-color.

235, ♂ *ad.;* West Humboldt Mountains, October 7, 1867. $8\frac{5}{8}$—$10\frac{3}{16}$—$3\frac{1}{2}$—$2\frac{7}{8}$—$\frac{9}{16}$—$1\frac{5}{16}$—4—$2\frac{1}{2}$. *Iris, deep rufous.*

434, ♀ *ad.;* Carson City, Nevada, March 9, 1868. $8\frac{1}{2}$—$10\frac{1}{2}$—$3\frac{1}{4}$—$2\frac{3}{4}$. Bill, slate-black; iris, *intense orange-chrome;* tarsi and toes, dilute purplish-sepia, the toes with a violaceous cast.

476, ♂ *ad.;* Carson City, March 30, 1868. $8\frac{5}{8}$—$11\frac{5}{8}$—$3\frac{5}{8}$—3. Bill, perfectly uniform, slaty black; *iris, rich scarlet.*

495, ♂ *ad.;* Carson City, April 4, 1868. $8\frac{5}{8}$—11—$3\frac{5}{8}$—3. Same remarks.

[In the western species, the iris when intense red—indicating high maturity—is never of the carmine shade often seen in *erythrophthalmus,* but inclines more to scarlet or orange-red.]

PIPILO CHLORURUS.

Green-tailed Bunting.

(*Pooe-tse'-tse* of the Washoes.)

"*Fringilla chlorura*, TOWNSEND," AUDUBON, Orn. Biog., V, 1839, 336.

Pipilo chlorurus, BAIRD, Birds N. Am., 1858, 519; Cat. N. Am. Birds, 1859, No.
　　398.—COOPER, Orn. Cal., I, 248.—COUES, Key, 1872, 153; Check List, 1873,
　　No. 208; Birds N.W., 1874, 176.—B. B. & R., Hist. N. Am. Birds, II, 1874,
　　131, pl. XXXI, fig. 4.—HENSHAW, 1875, 307.

This very interesting species was met with on all the higher ranges,
from the Sierra Nevada to the Uintahs, particularly in the elevated parks
and cañons, where it was one of the most characteristic birds.　We never
observed it at a lower altitude than the beginning of the cañons, or, as
happened rarely, in ravines of the foot-hills, while, in the river-valleys, it
appeared to be entirely wanting.　It is apparently migratory, as none were
observed between the months of September and April, and in its passage
to and from the south appears to follow the mountain ranges without
performing sufficient vertical migration to reach the lower valleys.　In
the cañons of the lofty Toyabe Mountains, near Austin, this species was
exceedingly abundant in the early part of July; it was also very common
in the higher cañons and elevated garden-like slopes of the Ruby range,
while in similar places near the station of Evanston, on the high Uintahs,
numbers were heard singing on every hand during our brief stay there, in
the month of May.　Like its congeners, this species is a bird of the chaparral, living chiefly in the brushwood of the cañons and ravines; but it is
also found among the rank herbage of those flowery slopes so characteristic
of the higher portions of that mountainous region.

In the position of its nest there was a rather unusual uniformity of
habit manifested, especially by the birds of one locality; thus, those found
at Austin were all placed in the thickest part of low bushes of the
Symphoricarpus montanus, at a height of eighteen inches to two feet above
the ground; the same was usually the case in Parley's Park, although
sometimes other shrubs, as wild-currant bushes, were selected.　The
maximum number of eggs found in a nest was four.

The song of this bird is possessed of great strength and clearness, as well as considerable variety, approaching most nearly that of the Bay-winged Bunting (*Pooecetes gramineus*) in style, tone, and modulation. It is louder, however, and more continued, though in the latter respect it is far inferior to that of *Chondestes grammaca*. The ordinary note is remarkably sweet, sounding like a laughing pronunciation of the syllables *keek, keek'*, very much in the tone of the *tweet* of a Canary-bird; this note is uttered on the approach of anyone, when the bird hops familiarly about the stranger, without manifesting any symptoms of uneasiness at his presence, but rather expressing pleasure in its notes.

List of specimens.

169, ♀ *ad.;* Camp 18, West Humboldt Mountains, Nevada, September 7, 1867. $7\frac{11}{16}$—10—$3\frac{3}{16}$—$2\frac{5}{8}$—$\frac{9}{16}$—$1\frac{3}{16}$—$3\frac{1}{4}$—$1\frac{1}{2}$. Upper mandible, slate-black, tomium bluish-white; lower, bluish-white, almost milk-white at the base; *iris, purplish-rufous;* tarsi, and toes, bluish horn-color.

532, ♂ *ad.;* Carson City, Nevada, April 25, 1868. $7\frac{13}{16}$—$10\frac{1}{4}$—$3\frac{7}{16}$—$2\frac{3}{4}$. Upper mandible, black, tomium plumbeous-blue; lower, pure pale plumbeous-blue, tip black: *iris, deep purplish-ferruginous* (very similar to color of crown); tarsi, dilute whitish-sepia; toes, deeper sepia.

817 (4), 818 (3), nests and eggs; Austin, Nevada, July 2, 1868.

822 (4), 823 (4), 824 (2), 825 (2), 826 (2), nests and eggs; Austin, Nevada, July 3, 1868.

929, ♂ *ad.;* Camp 25, Humboldt Valley, September 16, 1868. $7\frac{1}{2}$—10—(?)—$2\frac{5}{8}$. Same remarks.

959, ♀ *ad.;* Salt Lake City, May 20, 1869. $7\frac{1}{2}$—$9\frac{3}{4}$. Upper mandible and gonys, black, lower pale blue; iris, raw-sienna; tarsi, lilaceous-sepia, toes darker, more plumbeous-sepia.

1052, ♂ *ad.;* Salt Lake City, Utah, May 26, 1869. $7\frac{5}{8}$—10. Upper mandible, plumbeous-black, lower plumbeous-blue; *iris, cinnamon;* tarsi, pale brown; toes, darker.

1234, 1235, nests and eggs (3); Parley's Park, Wahsatch Mountains, Utah, June 23, 1869. Thick low bush, by stream.

1274, nest and eggs (3); Parley's Park, Wahsatch Mountains, Utah, June 24, 1869. Thick low bush, by stream.

1295, nest and eggs (3); Parley's Park, Wahsatch Mountains, Utah, June 25, 1869. Nest on ground, beneath bush.

1313, nest and eggs (3); Parley's Park, Wahsatch Mountains, Utah, June 27, 1869. Nest on ground, beneath bush.

1320 (4), 1321 (2), nests and eggs; Parley's Park, Wahsatch Mountains, Utah, June 27, 1869. Bushes by stream.

1325 (4), 1326 (2), nests and eggs; Parley's Park, Wahsatch Mountains, Utah, June 28, 1869. Bushes by stream.

1478, ♂ *juv.;* Parley's Park, July 30, 1869.　7¾—10½.　General hue of bill, livid slate, pinkish along the tomium and base beneath; *iris, ashy-umber;* tarsi and toes, deep horn.

1479, ♀ *juv.;* Parley's Park, July 30, 1869.　7½—9¾.　Same remarks.

PIPILO CRISSALIS.

Brown Bunting.

Fringilla crissalis, VIGORS, Zool. Beechey's Voyage, 1839, 19.

Pipilo fuscus var. *crissalis,* COUES, Key, 1872, 153; Check List, 1873, No. 206b. B. B. & R., Hist. N. Am. Birds, II, 1874, 122, pl. XXXI, fig. 8.

Pipilo fuscus, BAIRD, Birds N. Am., 1858, 517 [not of SWAINSON, Philos. Mag., I, 1827]; Cat. N. Am. Birds, 1859, No. 396.—COOPER, Orn. Cal., I, 1870, 245.

This large Bunting was noticed only during our ascent of the western slope of the Sierra Nevada, the species being easily recognized by its large size and uniform tawny color.　It was first encountered in the ravines of the lowest foot-hills, and was continually observed among the thickets and chaparral by the roadside until the pine-forest grew dense and closed in to the roadside, after which none were seen.　It appeared to be a very silent species, since no notes were heard.

FAMILY ALAUDIDÆ—LARKS.

EREMOPHILA ALPESTRIS.

Horned Lark; Shore Lark.

α. *alpestris.*

Alauda alpestris, FORSTER, Philos. Trans., LXII, 1772, 398.

Eremophila alpestris, BOIE, Isis, 1828, 322.—COUES, Key, 1872, 89, fig. 32; Check List, 1873, No. 53.—HENSHAW, 1875, 309.

Eremophila alpestris var. *alpestris,* B. B. & R., Hist. N. Am. B., II, 143, pl. XXXII, figs. 1, 2.

Eremophila alpestris. a. *alpestris,* COUES, B. N.W., 1874, 37.

Alauda cornuta, WILSON, Am. Orn., I, 1808, 87 (in text).

Eremophila cornuta, BOIE, Isis, 1828, 322.—BAIRD, B. N. Am., 1858, 403; Cat. N. Am. B., 1859, No. 302.

β. *leucolæma.*

? *Otocorys occidentalis,* McCALL, Pr. Philad. Acad. Nat. Sci., V, 1851, 218 (*juv.?*). —BAIRD, Stansbury's Salt Lake, 1852, 318.

Eremophila alpestris var. *leucolæma,* COUES, B. N.W., 1874, 38.—HENSHAW, 1875, 309.

γ. chrysolæma.

Alauda chrysolæma, WAGLER, Isis, 1831, 350.

Eremophila cornuta var. *chrysolæma*, BAIRD, B. N. Am., 1858, 403.

Eremophila alpestris var. *chrysolæma*, COUES, Key, 1872, 89; Check List, 1873, No. 53a.—B. B. & R., Hist. N. Am. B., II, 1874, 144.—HENSHAW, 1875, 310.

Eremophila alpestris. c. chrysolæma, COUES, B. N.W., 1874, 38.

Eremophila cornuta, COOPER, Orn. Cal., I, 1870, 251 (part).

Few birds are more widely distributed than this one; and if the sage-brush deserves the title of "everlasting," from its abundance and uniform distribution, it would be as proper to designate this species as "omnipresent," so far as the more open portions of the western country are concerned. No locality is too barren for it, but, on the contrary, it seems to fancy best the most dry and desert tracts, where it is often the only bird to be seen over miles of country, except an occasional Dove (*Zenædura carolinensis*), or a solitary Raven, seen at wide intervals. Neither does altitude appear to affect its distribution, except so far as the character of the ground is modified, since we saw them in July and August on the very summit of the Ruby Mountains, at an altitude of about 11,000 feet, the ground being pebbly, with a stunted and scattered growth of bushes. The small, deep-colored race known as *chrysolæma* was the usual form found in summer, but in winter most of these seemed to have migrated southward, their place being taken by flocks from the north, composed of migratory individuals of the races called *alpestris* and *leucolæma*, of which the former predominated.

List of specimens.

a. alpestris and β. leucolæma.[1]

148, ♂ ad.; valley of the Humboldt (Camp 17), August 21, 1867. 7¼—12⅝—4½—3½—7/16—¾—2⅞—11/16. Bill, plumbeous-black, basal half of lower mandible pearl-white; iris, umber; tarsi and toes, purplish-cinereous.

232, ♂ ad.; West Humboldt Mountains (Camp 19), October 4, 1867. 7 1/16—12½—4¼—3⅝—½—¾—2 15/16—15/16. Tarsi and toes, plumbeous-black.

---

[1] We include the specimens of these two races together for the reason that they are not distinguished in our note-books, while the specimens themselves are not accessible at the present time. All the examples referable to these two races were collected in autumn or winter, during their migrations southward. Throughout the winter they were found in large flocks, frequenting all open places, and in severe weather daily venturing into the streets and door-yards of the towns. During the winter-season the present, or northern-bred, birds nearly replace the summer-resident, var. *chrysolæma*, though sometimes individuals of the latter may be shot from a large flock.

302, ♀ ad.; Truckee Meadows, November 19, 1867. $7\frac{1}{16}$—13—$4\frac{3}{8}$—$3\frac{1}{2}$—$\frac{1}{2}$—$1\frac{1}{1}$—?—$\frac{7}{8}$. Tarsi and toes, livid-black.

395, ♂ ad.; Washoe Valley, January 3, 1868. $7\frac{1}{4}$—13—$4\frac{5}{16}$—$3\frac{1}{2}$. Bill, plumbeous-black, basal two-thirds of lower mandible abruptly, bluish-white; iris, umber; tarsi and toes, deep black.

397, ♂ ad.; Washoe Valley, January 3, 1868. $7\frac{1}{2}$—$13\frac{3}{8}$—$4\frac{3}{8}$—$3\frac{3}{4}$. Same remarks.

417, ♂ ad.; Washoe Valley, January 3, 1868. $7\frac{5}{16}$—$13\frac{1}{8}$—$4\frac{1}{3}$—$3\frac{1}{2}$. Same remarks.

γ. chrysolœma.

394, ♂ ad.; Washoe Valley, Nevada, January 3, 1868. 7—$13\frac{1}{4}$—$6\frac{3}{4}$—$3\frac{5}{8}$—?—$\frac{13}{14}$ —$2\frac{3}{4}$—$\frac{7}{8}$. Bill, *plumbeous-white*, culmen and terminal third slaty; iris, umber; tarsi, *reddish-sepia*, toes, more blackish, yellow beneath (much as in *Anthus ludovicianus*).

396, ♀ ad.; Washoe Valley, Nevada, January 3, 1868. $6\frac{1}{2}$—$11\frac{5}{8}$—$3\frac{5}{16}$—$3\frac{1}{4}$. Same remarks.

398, ♂ ad.; Washoe Valley, Nevada, January 3, 1868. 7—$12\frac{1}{2}$—$4\frac{1}{4}$—$3\frac{3}{4}$. Same remarks.

784, nest and eggs (4); Truckee Reservation, June 3, 1868. Nest imbedded in hard gravelly ground, beneath small scraggy sage-bush, on *mesa* between river and mountains.

819, nest and eggs (3); Fort Churchill, Nevada, June 24, 1868. Nest on ground, underneath sage-bush.

1032, ♂ ad.; Salt Lake City, Utah, May 22, 1869. 7—$12\frac{7}{8}$. Bill, black, basal two-thirds of lower mandible bluish-white; iris, brown; tarsi and toes, sepia-black.

1094, ♂ ad.; Antelope Island, Great Salt Lake, June 4, 1869. $7\frac{1}{4}$—$13\frac{1}{4}$. Bill, pure blue-black, basal two-thirds of lower mandible fine pale blue; iris, brown; tarsi and toes, dark sepia.

Family ICTERIDÆ — Hang-nests, American Orioles, or American Starlings.

DOLICHONYX ORYZIVORUS.

Bob-o-link.

β. albinuchus.

Dolichonyx oryzivorus var. *albinucha*, Ridgway, Bull. Essex Inst., V, Nov., 1873, 192.—Coues, Check List, 1873, App., p. 129.

Dolichonyx oryzivorus, Cooper, Orn. Cal., I, 1870, 255 (part).—Henshaw, 1875, 311.

The Bob-o-link seems to be spreading over all districts of the " Far West" wherever the cultivation of the cereals has extended. We found it common in August in the wheat-fields at the Overland Ranche in Ruby Valley, and we were informed at Salt Lake City that it was a common species on the meadows of that section of the country in May, and again in the latter part of summer, when the grain ripened. We did not meet with it in summer, however, and doubt whether it breeds anywhere in the Interior south of the 40th parallel.[1]

List of specimens.

873, ♀ *ad.;* Ruby Valley, Nevada (Camp 21), August 28, 1868.

MOLOTHRUS ATER.

Cow Blackbird.

α. ater.

Molothrus ater, GRAY, Hand List, II, 1870, 36, No. 6507 [cites BODD., Pl. Enl., 1783, 606, fig. 1].—BAIRD, Orn. Simpson's Exped., 1876, 379.

Fringilla pecoris, GMELIN, Syst. Nat., I, 1788, 910.

Molothrus pecoris, SWAINS. & RICH., Fauna Bor. Am., II, 1831, 277.—BAIRD, B. N. Am., 1858, 524; Cat. N. Am. B., 1859, No. 400.—COOPER, Orn. Cal., I, 257.—COUES, Key, 1872, 155; Check List, 1873, No. 211.—B. B. & R., Hist. N. Am. B., II, 1874, 154, pl. XXXII, figs. 6, 7.—HENSHAW, 1875, 312.

Molothrus pecoris. a. pecoris, COUES, B. N.W., 1874, 180.

We found this species to be so rare in the country traversed by the expedition that the list of specimens given below comprises every individual seen during the whole time.

List of specimens.

146, ♂ *juv.;* Camp 17, valley of the Humboldt, August 31, 1867. $8—13\frac{7}{8}—4\frac{1}{2}—3\frac{3}{4}—\frac{11}{16}—1—2\frac{3}{4}—1\frac{1}{8}$. Bill, slate-black, paler and more lilaceous on lower mandible; iris, hazel; tarsi and toes, black.

147, ♀ *juv.;* Camp 17, valley of the Humboldt, August 31, 1867. $7\frac{5}{16}—12\frac{7}{16}—4\frac{1}{16}—3\frac{3}{8}—\frac{5}{8}—\frac{7}{8}—2\frac{5}{8}—1\frac{1}{4}$. Same remarks.

782, ♂ *ad.;* Truckee Reservation, June 2, 1868. $8\frac{1}{2}$—14—(?)—$3\frac{3}{4}$. Bill, tarsi, and toes, deep black; iris, burnt-umber.

1231, egg; Parley's Park, Wahsatch Mountains, Utah, June 23, 1869. Deposited in nest of *Passerella schistacea*.

1401, egg; Bear River Valley, Utah, June, 1869. Deposited in nest of *Geothlypis trichas*. (Collected by Mr. J. C. Olmstead.)

---

[1] According to Mr. Henshaw (*l. c.*), the Bobolink apparently breeds at Provo, Utah, parent birds having been noticed feeding their young, July 25th.

XANTHOCEPHALUS ICTEROCEPHALUS.

Yellow-headed Blackbird.

(*Se-zooh'* of the Washoes.)

Icterus icterocephalus, BONAP., Am. Orn., I, 1835, 27, pl. 3.
Xanthocephalus icterocephalus, BAIRD, B. N. Am., 1858, 531 ; Cat. N. Am. B., 1859,
   No. 404.—COOPER, Orn. Cal., I, 267.—COUES, Key, 1872, 156, fig. 98 ; Check
   List, 1873, No. 213 ; B. N.W., 1874, 188.—B. B. & R., Hist. N. Am. B. II, 1874,
   167, pl. XXXII, fig. 9 ; pl. XXXIII, fig. 9.—HENSHAW, 1875, 315.

In order to be assured of the presence of this large and conspicuous
species, it was only necessary to find an extensive marsh with a sufficient
extent of tall rushes, or, as termed in western parlance, *tules*.   It was most
abundant in the vicinity of Sacramento City and along the southeastern
margin of the Great Salt Lake, near the mouth of the Jordan River; but it
was also plentiful at all intermediate points where suitable localities existed.
These birds generally frequent the same marshes as the Red-wings (*Agelæus*),
but usually the two congregate in colonies in separate portions of a marsh.
In general habits there is much resemblance to the Red-wings, especially
in their fondness for marshy localities ; but in many respects there is a
closer approach to the Cow-bird (*Molothrus*), notably in their very terrestrial nature ; for they may be very often observed walking over the green-
sward of the damp meadows with a firm, stately, and graceful gait, in the
manner of the species alluded to above.   The eggs, also, are more like those
of *Molothrus* than those of *Agelæus*.

The notes of the Yellow-headed Blackbird are among the harshest and
rudest we have heard in any species.   Their general character is that characteristic of most "Blackbirds" of this family, the ordinary note being a
deep *chuck*, similar to that of *Quiscalus purpureus* or *Q. æneus*, but louder ;
while the song of the male is a discordant squawk, apparently "strained
out" by great effort, in a squeaking, rasping sort of way, like the similar
performance of *Molothrus* or *Quiscalus*, but differing in that many of the
notes compare, in loudness and grating tone, with those of the Guinea Hen
(*Numida meleagris*).   The singer, however, evidently thinks his performance pleasing, and it probably is to his mate, for he makes a great parade

of himself, spreading his tail widely, drooping his wings, and swelling out his body at each effort.

The species was partially migratory in the Interior, only a few examples being seen during the winter at Carson City, these being mostly solitary individuals mixed in with flocks of *Scolecophagus cyanocephalus*, although occasionally small troops visited the corrals for the purpose of gleaning the half-digested grain from the manure. Their gregarious nature was manifest at all times, however, even in summer, for they nested in large communities, apart from the other marsh-birds, although always found in close proximity to them.

List of specimens.

39, nest and eggs (3); Sacramento, California, June 12, 1867. Nest in tule-slough.

140, ♂ ad.; Camp 17, valley of the Humboldt, Nevada, August 30, 1867. 11—17¼—5¹³⁄₁₆—4⅞—⅞—1³⁄₁₆—4³⁄₁₆—1¹³⁄₁₆. Bill, tarsi, and toes, deep black; iris, hazel.

523, ♂ ad.; Carson City, Nevada, April 24, 1868. 10⅝—17—5¹¹⁄₁₆—4⅝. Remarks as above.

965, ♂ ad.; Salt Lake City, Utah, May 21, 1869. 11—18¼. Bill, tarsi, and toes, deep black; iris, brown.

966, ♂ ad.; Salt Lake City, Utah, May 21, 1869. 11¼—18¼. Remarks as above.

973—1004, thirty-two nests with eggs; Salt Lake City, Utah, May 21, 1869. Nests among the *tules*. in a slough, near Warm Spring Lake; maximum number of eggs, four.

1021, ♂ ad.; Salt Lake City, May 22, 1869. 11¼—18¼. Bill, tarsi, and toes, black; iris, brown.

1022, ♀ ad.; Salt Lake City, May 22, 1869. 9—14⅜. Bill, dusky horn color, darker above; iris, brown; tarsi and toes, black.

AGELÆUS PHŒNICEUS.

Red-shouldered Blackbird.

α. *phœniceus—Red-and-buff-shouldered Blackbird.*

(*Se-zoo'-te-mo-lah'-gehk* of the Washoes; *Pah-cool'-up-at'-su-que* of the Paiutes.)

Oriolus phœniceus, LINN., Syst. Nat., I, 1766, 161.
Agelæus phœniceus, VIEILL., Analyse, 1816.—BAIRD, Birds N. Am., 1858, 526; Cat. N. Am. Birds, 1859, No. 401.—COOPER, Orn. Cal., I, 1870, 261.—COUES, Key, 1872, 156, pl. 4; Check List, 1873, No. 212.—B. B. & R., Hist. N. Am. Birds, II, 1874, 159, pl. XXXIII, figs. 1, 2, 3.—HENSHAW, 1875, 313.
Agelæus phœniceus. a. phœniceus, COUES, Birds N.W., 1874, 186.

β. *gubernator—Red-and-black-shouldered Blackbird.*

Psarocolius gubernator, WAGLER, Isis, 1832, 281.

Agelæus gubernator, BONAP., Comp. and Geog. List, 1838, 30.—BAIRD, Birds N. Am., 1858, 529; Cat. N. Am. Birds, 1859, No. 402.—COOPER, Orn. Cal., I, 1870, 263.

Agelæus phœniceus var. *gubernator*, COUES, Key, 1872, 156; Check List, No. 212a. —B. B. & R., Hist. N. Am. Birds, II, 1874, 163, pl. XXXIII, figs. 4, 8.

Agelæus phœniceus. c. gubernator, COUES, Birds N.W., 1874, 186

The Red-winged Blackbird was found in all marshy places, being especially numerous in the vicinity of the great lakes of the Interior and along the larger rivers. The form distinguished as *gubernator* was exceedingly abundant among the tules near Sacramento, where it was associated with *A. tricolor* and *Xanthocephalus icterocephalus;* but east of the Sierra Nevada it was found only in the western depression, and was there very rare compared with the commoner form, *A. phœniceus.*

List of specimens.

a. phœniceus.

141, ♂; Camp 17, valley of the Humboldt, Nevada, August 30, 1867. $9\frac{1}{4}$—$14\frac{5}{8}$ —$(4\frac{2}{3})$—$(3\frac{7}{8})$—$1\frac{3}{16}$—1—$3\frac{3}{4}$—$1\frac{1}{2}$. Bill, dark hepatic-brown, stripe of black on side of lower mandible and on the culmen; iris, hazel; tarsi and toes, black.

142, ♂; Camp 17, valley of the Humboldt, Nevada, August 30, 1867. 9—$14\frac{5}{8}$— $4\frac{13}{16}$—$4\frac{1}{16}$—$\frac{7}{8}$—1—$3\frac{1}{4}$—(?). Same remarks.

154, ♂; Camp 17, September 2, 1867. $9\frac{1}{4}$—$14\frac{3}{4}$—$1\frac{3}{4}$—$3\frac{1}{16}$—$1\frac{5}{16}$—1—$3\frac{3}{4}$—$1\frac{1}{4}$. Same remarks.

238, ♂; Camp 19, West Humboldt Mountains, Nevada, October 7, 1867. $9\frac{3}{8}$—$15\frac{5}{8}$ —$5\frac{1}{16}$—$4\frac{1}{4}$—$\frac{7}{8}$—1—$3\frac{3}{4}$—$1\frac{1}{2}$. Bill, tarsi, and toes, black; iris, hazel.

265, ♂; Camp 26, Truckee Meadows, Nevada, November 8, 1867. Willows. $9\frac{1}{2}$ —$15\frac{1}{4}$—$4\frac{3}{4}$—$4\frac{7}{16}$—$\frac{7}{8}$—1—$3\frac{1}{2}$—$1\frac{3}{8}$. Bill, dull blackish, slightly brownish on tomium and gonys; iris, hazel; tarsi and toes, black.

266, ♂; Camp 26, Truckee Meadows, Nevada, November 8, 1867. $9\frac{1}{2}$—$15\frac{3}{8}$—$4\frac{15}{16}$ —4—$\frac{7}{8}$—1—$3\frac{1}{2}$—$1\frac{1}{4}$. Same remarks.

267, ♂; Camp 26, Truckee Meadows, Nevada, November 8, 1867. 9—$14\frac{1}{4}$—$4\frac{11}{16}$— $3\frac{13}{16}$—$1\frac{5}{16}$—$1\frac{5}{16}$—$3\frac{1}{2}$—$1\frac{1}{4}$. Bill, uniform brownish-black, lower mandible rather paler.

268, ♂; Camp 26, November 8, 1867. Willows. $9\frac{3}{8}$—15—$4\frac{7}{8}$—4—$\frac{7}{8}$—1—$3\frac{3}{8}$—$1\frac{1}{2}$. Bill, uniform dull black.

293, ♂; Camp 26, November 18, 1867. $9\frac{1}{4}$—$15\frac{1}{8}$—$5\frac{1}{8}$—$4\frac{1}{4}$—$1\frac{3}{16}$—$1\frac{1}{16}$—$3\frac{7}{8}$—$1\frac{3}{8}$. Bill, uniform slate-black; iris, vandyke-brown; tarsi and toes, black.

294, ♂; Camp 26, November 18, 1867. $9\frac{1}{4}$—$15\frac{1}{4}$—$5\frac{1}{8}$—$4\frac{1}{4}$—$\frac{7}{8}$—$1\frac{1}{16}$—$3\frac{3}{4}$—$1\frac{1}{4}$. Bill, slaty-black, inclining to brownish-cinereous on basal portion of lower mandible.

295, ♂; Camp 26, November 18, 1867. 9—$14\frac{3}{8}$—$4\frac{5}{8}$—$3\frac{5}{8}$—$\frac{23}{32}$—$1\frac{1}{16}$—$3\frac{1}{2}$—$1\frac{3}{8}$. Same remarks.

296, ♂; Camp 26, November 18, 1867. $9\frac{1}{2}$—$15\frac{3}{4}$—$5\frac{1}{4}$—$4\frac{3}{16}$—$\frac{29}{32}$—$1\frac{1}{32}$—$3\frac{7}{8}$—$1\frac{1}{2}$. Same remarks. (Prepared by Mr. Parker.)

297, ♀; Camp 26, November 18, 1867. $8\frac{1}{8}$—13—$4\frac{1}{4}$—$3\frac{7}{16}$—$\frac{13}{16}$—$\frac{15}{16}$—$3\frac{1}{2}$—$1\frac{1}{8}$. Upper mandible, dull black, lower dull cinereous; iris, hazel; tarsi and toes, dull black.

298, ♀; Camp 26, November 18, 1867. $7\frac{5}{8}$—$12\frac{1}{4}$—$4\frac{1}{8}$—$3\frac{5}{16}$—$\frac{3}{4}$—$\frac{7}{8}$—$3\frac{3}{8}$—$1\frac{1}{4}$. Upper mandible, brownish slaty-black, tomium paler, lower brownish cinereous; iris, vandyke-brown; tarsi and toes, black.

299, ♀; Camp 26, November 18, 1867. $7\frac{3}{8}$—$12\frac{3}{8}$—$4\frac{1}{4}$—$3\frac{1}{4}$—$\frac{13}{16}$—$\frac{15}{16}$—3—$1\frac{1}{4}$. Same remarks.

403, ♀; Camp 26, November 19, 1867. $7\frac{7}{8}$—$12\frac{1}{2}$—$4\frac{1}{4}$—$3\frac{7}{16}$—$\frac{13}{16}$—$\frac{15}{16}$—$3\frac{3}{16}$—$1\frac{1}{4}$. Upper mandible, horn-black, tomium paler; lower pale horn-color, the point dusky; iris, hazel; tarsi and toes, brownish-black.

566, ♂ *ad.;* Truckee Reservation, May 15, 1868. $9\frac{1}{4}$—$15\frac{1}{4}$—(?)—4. Bill, tarsi, and toes, deep black; iris, sepia.

772 (3), 773 (3); nests and eggs. Truckee Reservation, May 31, 1868. Nests in small bushes, in overflowed meadow.

967, ♂ *ad.;* Salt Lake City, Utah, May 21, 1869. 10—$16\frac{1}{4}$. Bill, tarsi, and toes, black; iris, brown.

968, ♂ *ad.;* Salt Lake City, Utah, May 21, 1869. 10—16. Same remarks.

1005, 1006, 1007, 1008, 1009; nests and eggs. Salt Lake City, May 21, 1869. Tule-meadows; maximum number of eggs, four.

1023, ♂ *ad.;* Salt Lake City, May 22, 1869. $9\frac{7}{8}$—19. Remarks as above.

1024, ♂ *ad.;* Salt Lake City, May 22, 1869. $9\frac{1}{2}$—$15\frac{1}{4}$. Remarks as above.

1025, ♂ *ad.;* Salt Lake City, May 22, 1869. $9\frac{5}{8}$—$15\frac{7}{8}$. Remarks as above.

1089, nest and eggs (4); Antelope Island, Great Salt Lake, June 4, 1869. Grassy marsh, lake-shore.

1142 (4), 1143 (4), 1144, 1145, 1146, 1147, 1148, 1149, 1150, 1151, nests and eggs; Antelope Island, Great Salt Lake, June 9, 1869. *Nests in sage-brush,* in alkaline pond, near lake-shore.

β. gubernator.

432, ♂ *ad.;* Carson City, Nevada, March 9, 1868. $9\frac{3}{8}$—$15\frac{5}{8}$—$5\frac{1}{8}$—$4\frac{1}{4}$. Bill, tarsi, and toes, deep black; iris, hazel.

788, nest and eggs (4); Truckee Reservation, June 3, 1868. Nest in small bush, in wet meadow.

AGELÆUS TRICOLOR.

Red-and-white-shouldered Blackbird.

Icterus tricolor, NUTTALL, Man. Orn., I, 2d ed., 1840, 186.

Agelæus tricolor, BONAP., Comp. & Geog. List, 1838, 30.—BAIRD, B. N. Am., 1858, 530; Cat. N. Am. B., 1859, No. 403.—B. B. & R., Hist. N. Am. B., II, 1874, 165, pl. XXXIII, figs. 5, 6, 7.—COOPER, Orn. Cal., I, 1870, 265.

Agelæus phœniceus var. *tricolor*, COUES, Key, 1872, 156; Check List, 1873, No. 212b.

Agelæus phœniceus. d. *tricolor*, COUES, Birds N.W., 1874, 186.

This very distinct species was seen only in the neighborhood of Sacramento City, where it was excessively abundant, along with the *A. guberna-tor* and *Xanthocephalus icterocephalus*, among the tules near the river. The individuals of this species were easily distinguished by their different appearance, while their notes were strikingly dissimilar.

STURNELLA NEGLECTA.

Western Meadow-Lark.

(*Se-zoo'-te-ya'-lehk* of the Washoes; *Pah'-at-se'-tone* of the Paiutes.)

Sturnella neglecta, AUDUBON, B. Am., VII, 1843, 339, pl. 487.—BAIRD, Birds N. Am., 1858, 537; Catal., 1859, No. 407.—COOPER, Orn. Cal., I, 1870, 270.

Sturnella magna var. *neglecta*, COUES, Key, 1872, 157; Check List, 1873, No. 214a.— B. B. & R., Hist. N. Am. B., II, 1874, 176, pl. XXXIV, fig. 1.—HENSHAW, 1875, 317.

Sturnella magna. b. *neglecta*, COUES, B. N.W., 1874, 190.

The Western Meadow Lark is a generally-distributed species, since it occurs wherever there are grassy tracts, as well as in the sage-brush of the more fertile districts; it is much less common in the mountains, however, than in the lower valleys, and we do not remember meeting with it higher up than an altitude of 7,000 feet. So far as general habits are concerned, it is a counterpart of the eastern species (*S. magna*), but its notes are most strikingly different, while it exhibits some very noticeable peculiarities of manners. It is a much more familiar bird than its eastern relative, and we observed that the manner of its flight differed in an important respect, the bird flitting along with a comparatively steady, though trembling, flutter, instead of propelling itself by occasional spasmodic beatings of the wings, then extending them horizontally during the intervals between these beats, as is the well-known manner of flight of the eastern species.

All observers, we believe, from the earliest explorers to those of the present time, agree as to the wide difference in the notes of the Western Meadow Lark from those of the eastern bird; and this we consider to be a sufficient evidence of specific diversity, notwithstanding the close similarity of general appearance—especially if taken in connection with the other differences alluded to, and the equally important fact, attested by many writers, that in the region where the habitats of the two forms adjoin they are found together, each preserving with perfect distinctness its peculiarities of habits and voice, there not being that gradual transition from one to the other, in proceeding eastward or westward, which would exist in case the differences were merely the impress of geographical causes.

We know of no two congeneric species, of any family of birds, more radically distinct in all their utterances than the eastern and western Meadow Larks, two years of almost daily association with the latter, and a much longer familiarity with the former, having thoroughly convinced us of this fact; indeed, as has been the experience of every naturalist whose remarks on the subject we have read or heard, we never even so much as suspected, upon hearing the song of the Western Lark for the first time, that the author of the clear, loud, ringing notes were those of a bird at all related to the Eastern Lark, whose song, though equally sweet, is far more subdued— half-timid—and altogether less powerful and varied. As to strength of voice, no eastern bird can be compared to this, while its notes possess a metallic resonance equalled only by those of the Wood Thrush. The modulation of the song of the Western Lark we noted on several occasions, and found it to be most frequently nearly as expressed by the following syllables: *Tung'-tung'-tung'ah, tillah'-tillah', tung'*—the first three notes deliberate, full, and resonant, the next two finer and in a higher key, the final one like the first in accent and tone. Sometimes this song is varied by a metallic trill, which renders it still more pleasing. The ordinary note is a deep-toned *tuck*, much like the *chuck* of the Blackbirds (*Quiscalus*), but considerably louder and more metallic; another note is a prolonged rolling chatter, somewhat similar to that of the Baltimore Oriole (*Icterus baltimore*), but correspondingly louder, while the anxious call-note is a liquid *tyur*, which in its tone and expression calls to mind the spring-call (not the warble) of the Eastern Blue-bird (*Sialia sialis*), or the exceedingly similar complaining note of the Orchard Oriole (*Icterus spurius*). In fact, all the notes of the Western Lark clearly indicate its position in the family *Icteridæ*, which is conspicuously not the case in the eastern bird.[1]

---

[1] The song itself is more like that of the Common Troupial (*Icterus vulgaris*) than any other we have ever heard, but it is, if anything, more powerful; the tone and accent are, however, exceedingly similar.

List of specimens.

149, ♂ *juv.;* Camp 17, valley of the Humboldt, Nevada, August 31, 1867. (Grassy river-bottom.) $9\frac{3}{4}$—$14\frac{1}{4}$—$4\frac{1}{2}$—$3\frac{3}{4}$—$1\frac{3}{16}$—$1\frac{5}{16}$—$2\frac{5}{8}$—$\frac{3}{4}$. Upper mandible, light pinkish-sepia; lower brownish lilaceous-white, tip darker; iris, hazel; tarsi and toes, delicate lilaceous-white, faintly tinged with brown.

155, ♂ *juv.;* Camp 17, September 2, 1867. (Grassy river-bottom.) $9\frac{1}{8}$—$14\frac{3}{4}$—$4\frac{5}{8}$—$3\frac{11}{16}$—$1\frac{3}{16}$—$1\frac{5}{16}$—$2\frac{1}{4}$—$\frac{3}{4}$. Upper mandible, clear light sepia, deepening into horn-color at end ; lower brownish lilaceous-whitish, darker terminally.

247, ♂ *juv.;* Camp 19, West Humboldt Mountains, Nevada, October 11, 1867. (Fields.) $10\frac{3}{8}$—15—5—$4\frac{1}{8}$—$1\frac{3}{8}$—$1\frac{5}{16}$—$3\frac{1}{4}$—1. Upper mandible, deep horn-color, blackish terminally; tomium and lower mandible, paler *lilaceous* horn-color, darker terminally; iris, hazel; tarsi, delicate brownish-whitish; toes, slightly darker.

362, ♀ *juv.;* Truckee Reservation, Nevada, December 18, 1867. 9—$14\frac{1}{4}$—$4\frac{1}{2}$—$3\frac{1}{4}$—$1\frac{3}{16}$—$1\frac{1}{4}$—$2\frac{3}{4}$—$\frac{7}{8}$. Bill, generally, delicate lilaceous-white; upper mandible with a dilute brownish tinge, the culmen light sepia; iris, umber; tarsi and toes, delicate lilaceous-white.

415, ♂ *ad.;* Carson City, Nevada, March 5, 1868. $9\frac{3}{4}$—$16\frac{1}{2}$—$5\frac{1}{4}$—$4\frac{1}{16}$. Upper mandible, *black ;* basal portion of culmen, (between frontal feathers,) broad stripe on basal three-fourths of upper tomium, with basal two-thirds of lower mandible *pure pale blue ;* tip of lower mandible, black; iris, umber; tarsi and toes, delicate, uniform, pale ashy-lilaceous.

459, ♂ *ad.;* Carson, City, Nevada, March 26, 1868. $10\frac{1}{4}$—17—$5\frac{1}{4}$—$4\frac{1}{4}$. Same remarks.

460, ♂ *ad.;* Carson City, Nevada, March 26, 1868. 10—16—5—4. Same remarks.

505, nest and eggs (5); Carson City, Nevada, April 21, 1868. Nest imbedded in ground beneath sage-bush; nest precisely like that of *S. magna.*

787, nest and eggs (4); Truckee Reservation, June 3, 1868. Nest imbedded in the ground, beneath a low bush, on the grassy bank of the river.

ICTERUS BULLOCKI.

Bullock's Oriole.

(*Yset'-ke* of the Washoes.)

Xanthornus bullockii, SWAINSON, Synop. Mex. Birds, Philos. Mag., I, 1827, 436.
Icterus bullockii, BONAP., Comp. & Geog. List, 1838, 29.—BAIRD, B. N. Am., 1858, 549; Catal., 1859, No. 416.—COOPER, Orn. Cal., I, 273.—COUES, Key, 1872, 158, fig. 100; Check List, 1873, No. 217; B. N.W., 1874, 195.—B. B. & R., Hist. N. Am. B., II, 1874, 199, pl. XXXIV, figs. 3, 7.—HENSHAW, 1875, 320.

Except in the higher pine forests, this beautiful Oriole is common in all wooded localities of the western country. It abounded at Sacramento to such an extent that several nests were often found in one tree, a large cotton-wood by our camp containing five, some of which, however, were unoccupied. In May we found numbers of them in the rich valley of the Truckee, near Pyramid Lake, and observed that they were then subsisting chiefly on the tender buds of the grease-wood (*Obione confertifolia*), in company with *Hedymeles melanocephalus, Pyranga ludoviciana,* and some other species.

The nest of Bullock's Oriole is very similar in its structure and composition to that of the Baltimore (*I. baltimore*), but it is less frequently pendulous, and seldom, if ever, so gracefully suspended. Its usual position is between upright twigs, near the top of the tree, thus resembling more that of the Orchard Oriole (*I. spurius*), which, however, is very different in its composition.

List of specimens.

1, nest and eggs (2); Sacramento, California, June 6, 1867. Nest in top of large isolated cotton-wood.

220, nest; Camp 19, West Humboldt Mountains, October 1, 1867. In aspen-thicket. (Collected by Mr. J. D. Hague.)

567, ♂ ad.; Truckee Reservation, May 15, 1868. $8\frac{1}{5}$—$12\frac{3}{4}$—(?)—$3\frac{7}{16}$. Upper mandible, black, the tomium bluish-white; lower, pale blue, slightly dusky toward end of gonys; iris, hazel; tarsi and toes, pale brownish-blue.

808, nest; Truckee Reservation, May, 1868. Nest on drooping branch of willow.

1057 (2), 1058 (5), nests and eggs; Salt Lake City, Utah, May 27, 1869. Nests in mountain-mahogany bush, 1,500 feet above camp.

1061, ♂ ad. (parent of No. 1057). 8—$12\frac{3}{4}$. Upper mandible black, tomium and lower mandible fine light blue; iris, brown; tarsi and toes, deep blue, with a faint yellowish stain.

1065, nest and eggs (4); Salt Lake City, May 29, 1869. Nest in maple-sapling, in wooded ravine. (City Creek Cañon.)

1106, nest and eggs (2); Antelope Island, Great Salt Lake, June 5, 1869. Nest in apple-tree, in orchard.

1130, nest and eggs; Antelope Island, June 7, 1869. Willow-copse.

1178, 1179, nests and eggs; Salt Lake City, June 18, 1869. Mountain-mahogany trees, 1,800 feet above camp.

1346, ♂ ad.; Parley's Park, Wahsatch Mountains, Utah, June 28, 1869. $8\frac{1}{4}$—12. Bill black, commissure and lower mandible fine light blue; iris, brown; tarsi and toes, horn-blue.

1387, nest; Provo River, Utah, July 10, 1869. Thorn-apple bush.

1390, nest; Provo River, Utah, July 11, 1869. Thorn-apple bush.

SCOLECOPHAGUS CYANOCEPHALUS.

Brewer's Blackbird.

Psarocolius cyanocephalus, WAGLER, Isis, 1829, 758.
Scolecophagus cyanocephalus, CABANIS, Mus. Hein., I, 1851, 195.—BAIRD, B. N.
    Am., 1858, 552; Cat. N. Am. B., 1859, No. 418.—COOPER, Orn. Cal., I, 278.—
    COUES, Key, 1872, 160; Check List, 1873, No. 322; B. N.W., 1874, 199.—B.
    B. & R., Hist. N. Am. B., II, 1874, 206, pl. XXXV, fig. 3.—HENSHAW, 1875, 321.

Seldom seen there during summer, this Blackbird becomes one of the most abundant species in the lower valleys during the winter season, when immense flocks frequent the settlements and resort daily to the corrals for their food, which at this time consists largely of the grain gleaned from the fresh dung, or found scattered where the stock has been fed. They also visit the slaughter-houses for their share of the offal, of which, however, the Magpies deprive them of the greater portion. In the severer weather small companies even came to the door-yards in Carson City, to feed upon the crumbs and scraps of meat thrown from the tables. During the breeding-season they were observed to have retired to the mountains, where they frequented the trees in the lower cañons, or on the lower slopes, the groves of cedars and nut-pines being a favorite resort. On the 3d of June, 1867, we discovered the breeding-ground of a large colony of this species in a grove of the above-named trees, among the mountains fronting the southern end of Pyramid Lake. More than a hundred pairs had congregated there, and almost every tree contained one or more nests, while as many as three containing eggs or young were sometimes found on a single tree. Each nest was saddled upon a horizontal branch, usually near the top of the tree, or at a height of twelve or fifteen feet from the ground, and was well concealed in a thick tuft of foliage, the position being quite the same in every instance; most of them contained young birds, and when these were disturbed the parents flew very near, exhibiting much concern, and uttering a soft *chuck* as they hovered about us; the maximum number of eggs or young found in a nest was six, the usual number being four or five. In Parley's Park, among the Wahsatch Mountains, they were also abundant during the breeding-season, and although many nests were found, they were more scattered, on account, we suppose, of the surrounding country being more generally wooded—their gregariousness in the instance mentioned above being most likely due to the fact that trees were exceedingly scarce in that portion of the country, and, so far as the mountains were concerned, limited to occasional isolated groves. Along toward the latter part of July and during the month of August, they became exceedingly abundant in Parley's Park, a large proportion of the flocks being composed of young birds; and so numerous were they that an average of ten or a dozen would be brought down by a single shot. They thus contributed very essentially to the subsistence of our tame hawks—four fine examples of *Buteo swainsoni*, reared that season from the nest, and allowed perfect liberty about the camp. A wounded bird, winged in one of these massacres, exhibited great spirit and determination when confronted by one of the hawks mentioned above, for he no sooner saw the latter than he became suddenly possessed of the most infuriate passion, even while yet held in the hand, and, with feathers raised, and silvery eyes flashing, sprang upon the hawk and fastened to the back of his head with bill and claws. The poor hawk was greatly terrified, and with outspread wings hopped frantically over the ground, at the same time uttering such plaintive whistlings that the scene excited shouts of laughter and applause from the spectators. The hawk was finally released from its tormentor, and would never afterward touch a living bird. During a great flight of grasshoppers which devastated the grain-fields of Parley's Park and surrounding districts, these Blackbirds were almost constantly employed in catching these insects, and during their stay appeared to eat nothing else. When engaged in their pursuit it was observed that they often flew from the perch and caught them in the air, in true flycatcher style, this performance being so far from exceptional that it was not uncommon to see several individuals perform the exploit at one time.

List of specimens.

189, ♂ ad.; Camp 19, West Humboldt Mountains, Nevada, September 17, 1867. (Sheep corral.) $9\frac{1}{16}$—$16\frac{1}{4}$—$5\frac{7}{16}$—$4\frac{7}{16}$—$\frac{3}{4}$—$1\frac{1}{8}$—$4\frac{1}{8}$—$1\frac{1}{2}$. Bill, tarsi, and toes, deep black; iris, *whitish sulphur-yellow.*

190, ♂ ad.; Camp 19, West Humboldt Mountains, Nevada, September 17, 1867. 10—16—$5\frac{3}{8}$—$4\frac{3}{8}$—$1\frac{3}{16}$—$1\frac{1}{8}$—4—$1\frac{11}{16}$. Same remarks.

191, ♂ ad.; Camp 19, West Humboldt Mountains, Nevada, September 17, 1867. $9\frac{3}{4}$—$15\frac{3}{4}$—$5\frac{5}{16}$—$4\frac{3}{8}$—$1\frac{3}{16}$—$1\frac{1}{8}$—$3\frac{15}{16}$—$1\frac{5}{8}$. Same remarks.

195, ♂ *ad.;* Camp 19, September 19, 1867. (Sheep corral.) 10—$15\frac{3}{4}$—$5\frac{3}{8}$—$4\frac{7}{16}$—$\frac{3}{4}$—$1\frac{1}{8}$—$4\frac{1}{4}$—$1\frac{5}{8}$. Same remarks.

196, ♀ *ad.;* Camp 19, September 19, 1867. $9\frac{3}{4}$—$14\frac{15}{16}$—$4\frac{13}{16}$—4—$\frac{3}{4}$—$1\frac{1}{8}$—$3\frac{13}{16}$—$1\frac{1}{8}$. Bill, tarsi, and toes, black; iris, *light reddish-hazel.*

198, ♂ *ad.;* Camp 19, September 20, 1867. (Sheep corral.) 10—16—$5\frac{5}{16}$—$4\frac{5}{16}$—$\frac{13}{16}$—$1\frac{1}{8}$—$4\frac{1}{4}$—$1\frac{11}{16}$. Bill, tarsi, and toes, deep black; iris, *whitish sulphur-yellow.*

205, ♀ *ad.;* Camp 19, September 21, 1867. $9\frac{1}{2}$—$14\frac{15}{16}$—5—$4\frac{1}{8}$—$\frac{3}{4}$—$1\frac{1}{16}$—$3\frac{7}{8}$—$1\frac{5}{8}$. Bill, tarsi, and toes, black; iris, *light brownish-hazel.*

206, ♀ *ad.;* Camp 19, September 21, 1867. $9\frac{1}{2}$—$14\frac{3}{4}$—$4\frac{15}{16}$—$4\frac{1}{16}$—$\frac{3}{4}$—$1\frac{1}{16}$—$3\frac{3}{4}$—$1\frac{1}{2}$. Iris, deep (not light) hazel.

789 (4), 790 (6), 791 (4), 792, 793, 794, 795, 796, 797, 798, nests and eggs; near Truckee Reservation, June 3, 1868.

1277, nest and eggs (3); Parley's Park (Wahsatch Mountains), Utah, June 24, 1869. Nest in bush by stream.

1278 (4), 1279 (2), nests and eggs; Parley's Park (Wahsatch Mountains), Utah, June 24, 1869. Nests in cotton-woods, along stream; supported against the trunk by small twigs.

1424, ♂ *ad.;* Parley's Park, June 17, 1869. $10\frac{1}{4}$—$19\frac{1}{4}$. Bill, tarsi, and toes, black; iris, white.

1462, ♂ *juv.;* Parley's Park, July 28, 1869. 10—$16\frac{1}{2}$. Bill, legs, and feet, black; iris, grayish yellowish-white.

FAMILY CORVIDÆ—CROWS and JAYS.

CORVUS CORAX.

Raven.

β. carnivorus—American Raven.

(*Kah'-gehk* of the Washoes; *Ah'-dah* of the Paiutes; *Hih* of the Shoshones.)

Corvus carnivorus, BARTRAM, Travels, Fla., 1793, 290.—BAIRD, Birds N. Am., 1858, 560; Cat. N. Am. Birds, 1859, No. 423.—COOPER, Orn. Cal., I, 1870, 282.

Corvus corax var. *carnivorus*, B. B. & R., Hist. N. Am. Birds, II, 1874, 234, pl. XXXVII, fig. 6.—HENSHAW, 1875, 324.

Corvus corax (var.?), COUES, Key, 1872, 162.

Corvus corax, COUES, Check List, 1873, No. 226; Birds N.W., 1874, 204.

Corvus cacalotl, WAGLER, Isis, 1831, 527.—BAIRD, Birds N. Am., 1858, 563; Cat. N. Am. Birds, 1859, No. 424.

This large bird is one of the most characteristic species of the Great Basin, over which it appears to be universally distributed, no desert-tract being so extensive or sterile that a solitary Raven may not be seen any day, although in such regions it is most usually observed winging its way silently, or with an occasional hoarse croak, from the mountains on one side the desert to the range opposite. It is also plentiful in the most fertile sections. We did not see it in the Sacramento Valley, where the Common Crow (*C. americanus*) was so abundant—the two species being, in fact, nowhere found together in equal abundance; but it became numerous immediately after we had crossed the Sierra Nevada, while the Crow disappeared almost entirely. In those portions where the Raven was the predominant species, as in western Nevada, we found that it went by the popular name of "Crow," while the more rare *C. americanus* was distinguished as the "*Tom* Crow!" At the Truckee Meadows the Ravens were very abundant in November, but were so shy as to be with difficulty approached within gunshot. At the latter locality we once observed an assembly of them annoying a Rough-legged Hawk (*Archibuteo sancti-johannis*) which had alighted on a fence-post; but the hawk did not appear to mind them much, and did not fly until we approached, when he took to flight, and was followed by the Ravens until almost out of sight. At Carson City they were very numerous in winter at the slaughter-house, just outside the town, where they congregated with the Magpies to feed upon the offal; they were then very tame and easily killed. The true home, however, of the Ravens appeared to be in the desert mountains, where their eyries were often seen among the high volcanic rocks, out of reach of an ordinary climber. In the appearance, manners, and voice of the Raven there is such a general resemblance to the Common Crow that after long familiarity with the latter the peculiarities of the former are forgotten. This, probably, accounts for the inappropriateness, or incorrectness, of the western nomenclature of these two birds, for when the two are seen together, which not often happens, the "Tom Crow" appears dwarfed in size, or not as large as a crow should be. The notes, also, are quite similar in their character (far more so than those of the Fish Crow, *C. ossifragus*, and the common species), but they are considerably hoarser and less vehement. The most conspicuous difference is in their manner of flight, the Crow flapping its wings continually, and seldom if ever sailing with outstretched, motionless pinions, while the Raven almost constantly soars in the buoyant and well-sustained manner of certain *Raptores*, a flapping flight being the very rare exception.

33 P R

List of specimens.

271, ♀ *ad ;* Camp 26, November 11, 1867.   25—50½—17—13⅜—3—2½—9½—5¼. Bill, tarsi, and toes, deep black; *interior of mouth, deep slaty violaceous-black;* iris, deep vandyke.

284, ♂ *ad.;* Camp 26, November 15, 1867.   26—51—17—13⅓—3—2⅜—10¼—5¾. Same remarks. Interior of mouth with some flesh-color beneath the tongue and far back.

285, ♀ *ad.;* Camp 26, November 15, 1867.   25—50—17—14—3—2¼—10—6. Same remarks. Interior of mouth with cloudings of livid flesh-color posteriorly.

CORVUS AMERICANUS.

Common Crow.

(*Kah'-gehk Nah'-ming* of the Washoes; *Queh' Ah'-dah* of the Paiutes.)

Corvus americanus, AUDUBON, Orn. Biog., II, 1834, 317.—BAIRD, B. N. Am., 1858, 566; Cat. N. Am. Birds, 1859, No. 426.—COUES, Key, 1872, 162; Check List, 1873, No. 228.—B. B. & R., Hist. N. Am. B., II, 1874, 243, pl. XXXVII, fig. 5.— HENSHAW, 1875, 327.

Corvus americanus. a. *americanus,* COUES, B. N.W., 1874, 206.

Corvus caurinus, COOPER, Orn. Cal., I, 1870, 285 (part, if not entirely).

In crossing the plains from Sacramento City to the Sierra Nevada, we found the Common Crow exceedingly numerous at a certain place along our route, where a considerable stream crossed the plains; they flew about over the ground and up into the trees with the same noisy cawing as in the east, and appeared to be in all respects the same bird. In the country to the eastward of the Sierra Nevada, however, the Crow was so extremely rare as to be met with on but two occasions, when the number of individuals was limited to a very few. The first examples were seen at the stage-station near the Humboldt marshes, in November. Three individuals only were found there, and these walked unconcernedly about the door-yard with the familiarity of tame pigeons, merely hopping to one side when approached too closely. So much confidence displayed by this usually wary bird was in such contrast with the extreme shyness and caution it exhibits in more thickly-populated portions of the country, that we concluded they were domesticated specimens, and found out our mistake only after questioning the station-keeper as to the history of his "pets," when we received permission to shoot one for our collection. Later in the same month a very few—perhaps less than half a dozen individuals—were found at the Truckee Meadows, where they frequented the willows along the river. These also were very tame, but except in this regard seemed to be exactly like the Crow of the Eastern States, the notes being quite identical.[1]

List of specimens.

256, ♂ ad.; Humboldt Meadows (Camp 22), October 31, 1867. 19—(?)—12¼—10—(?)—2—7—4½. Bill, tarsi, and toes, deep black; iris, hazel.

263, ♂ ad.; Camp 26, Truckee Meadows, November 8, 1867. Willows, along river. 19¼—37—12½—10½—2—2—7¼—4¾. Bill, tarsi, and toes, deep black; iris, deep vandyke; *interior of mouth (except corneous portions), deep flesh-color.*

PICICORVUS COLUMBIANUS.

Clarke's Nutcracker.

(*Pah'-bup* of the Washoes; *Toh'-o-kötz* of the Shoshones.)

Corvus columbianus, WILSON, Am. Orn., III, 1811, 29, pl. xx, fig. 2.
Picicorvus columbianus, BONAP., Consp. Av., I, 1850, 384.—BAIRD, B. N. Am., 1858, 573, 925; Cat. N. Am. B., 1859, No. 430.—COOPER, Orn. Cal., I, 289.—COUES, Key, 1872, 162, fig. 104; Check List, 1873, No. 230; B. N.W., 1874, 207.—B. B. & R., Hist. N. Am. B., II, 255, pl. xxxviii, fig. 4.—HENSHAW, 1875, 328.

The dense forest of lofty pinés and kindred trees on the Sierra Nevada was where this remarkable bird most abounded, but it was also found to the eastward wherever extensive coniferous woods occurred, it being common on the Wahsatch and Uintah ranges, and rare on the intermediate Ruby Mountains; but it was never seen except among the pines, which seem necessary to its existence. The habits and manners of this bird deviate so widely from those of the family to which it belongs that no one would suspect its true relationship; it acts like a Woodpecker, screams like a Woodpecker, and looks so much like one that the best ornithologists âre apt to be misled, by the first glimpse of it, into believing it an undescribed species

---

[1] Mr. E. W. Nelson informs me that in November he noticed the Crows exhibiting the same familiarity at Sacramento City, where they were seen about the door-yards and corrals of houses in the suburbs.

of the Woodpecker family; this was our own impression, corrected only by the obtaining of specimens. Prince Maximilian described a white-tailed Woodpecker ("*Picus leucurus*") seen by him in the Rocky Mountains, which was undoubtedly this bird; and Mr. J. A. Allen, an accurate observer, was more recently led into the same error.[1]

In the pine woods near Carson City these birds were very abundant, and, with the Jays (*Cyanura frontalis*), made the forest resound with their harsh, discordant cries. Their notes were often to be heard when the bird could not be seen, and were generally the first indication of its presence. The usual utterence, a guttural *chur-r-r-r-r-r-r-r*, repeated several times, and generally as two or more alighted in the same tree, possessed a peculiar snarling character; occasionally, however, an individual would take up a rather musical piping strain, which being immediately answered by all the others in the neighborhood, made the woods echo with their cries. As before stated, all the actions of this bird call to mind the traits of the Woodpecker tribe; it is a conspicuous object as it floats in gentle undulations above the tops of the tall pine trees, when it resembles in its motions the Ring-necked Woodpecker (*Melanerpes torquatus*); it is also often seen to swoop to the ground to pick up a fallen pine-seed, return to the tree and hammer it vigorously against a branch; and should two or more alight in close proximity a general snarling *chur-r-r-r* ensues, reminding one of the quarrelsome Red-headed Woodpecker (*Melanerpes erythrocephalus*).

We were unable to find the eggs of this bird, but a nest was discovered on the Ruby Mountains, in August, 1868, after the young had flown. This nest was in a hole—apparently the deserted excavation of the Red-shafted Flicker—in a tall pine stump, about twenty feet from the ground; the nest itself was a very elaborate and symmetrical one, composed of pine needles and fine roots, with larger sticks outside, resembling in its general character that made by other species of the family. Attention was first attracted to this nest by observing a pair of these birds enter the cavity in question. It is not known whether it is the constant habit of this species to thus build inside of holes in trees, but on the Sierra Nevada they were

---

[1] See *American Naturalist*, Vol. VI, p. 350, and Bull. Mus. Comp. Zoology, Vol. III, No. 6, June, 1872, p. 150.

often seen to go into hollows about the trees, as if going to and from their nests.[1]

List of specimens.

308, ♀ *ad.;* Pea-Vine Mountain, near Sierra Nevada, November 20, 1867. Pine woods. $12\frac{1}{2}$—$21\frac{3}{8}$—$7\frac{5}{8}$—$6\frac{1}{4}$—$1\frac{11}{16}$—$1\frac{1}{4}$—$4\frac{3}{4}$—$2\frac{3}{4}$. Bill, tarsi, and toes, deep black; iris, bright hazel.

309, ♀ *ad.;* Pea-Vine Mountain, near Sierra Nevada, November 20, 1867. Pine woods. $12\frac{3}{8}$—$21\frac{5}{8}$—$7\frac{5}{8}$—$6\frac{1}{8}$—$1\frac{5}{8}$—$1\frac{3}{16}$—$4\frac{1}{2}$—3. Same remarks.

310, ♀ *ad.;* Pea-Vine Mountain, near Sierra Nevada, November 20, 1867. Pine woods. $12\frac{3}{8}$—$21\frac{5}{8}$—$7\frac{5}{8}$—$6\frac{1}{4}$—$1\frac{5}{8}$—$1\frac{1}{4}$—$4\frac{1}{4}$—$2\frac{1}{2}$. Same remarks.

320, ♂ *ad.;* pine woods, shore of Lake Tahoe. (Mr. H. G. Parker.) 13—(?)—8—$6\frac{3}{4}$—$1\frac{3}{4}$—$1\frac{5}{16}$—$4\frac{3}{4}$—$2\frac{3}{4}$.

443, ♂ *ad.;* Carson, March 21, 1868. Pines. $12\frac{3}{4}$—$22\frac{3}{4}$—8—$6\frac{1}{2}$. Bill, tarsi, and toes, black; iris, blackish-sepia.

444, ♀ *ad.;* Carson, March 21, 1868. Pines. $12\frac{3}{8}$—$22\frac{1}{2}$—$7\frac{3}{4}$—$6\frac{3}{8}$. Same remarks.

854, ♀ *ad.;* Camp 19, East Humboldt Mountains, August 4, 1868. $12\frac{5}{8}$—22—(?)—6. Same remarks.

868, ♂ *ad.;* Camp 19, August 12, 1868. $12\frac{1}{8}$—22—(?)—$6\frac{3}{16}$. Same remarks.

1447, ♂ *ad.;* Parley's Park, Wahsatch Mountains, Utah, July 23, 1869. $12\frac{3}{4}$—$23\frac{1}{4}$. Bill, tarsi, and toes, black; iris, umber.

GYMNOKITTA CYANOCEPHALA.

Blue Nutcracker; Maximilian's "Jay."

Gymnorhinus cyanocephalus, MAXIMILIAN, Reise Nord-Am., 1841, 21.

Gymnokitta cyanocephala, BONAP., Consp. Av., I, 1850, 382.—BAIRD, Birds N. Am., 1858, 574; Cat. N. Am. Birds, 1859, No. 431.—COOPER, Orn. Cal., I, 292.—COUES, Key, 1872, 163; Check List, 1873, No. 231; Birds N.W., 1874, 209.—B. B. & R., Hist. N. Am. Birds, II, 1874, 260, pl. XXXVIII, fig. 2.—HENSHAW, 1875, 331.

This extraordinary bird was found to inhabit exclusively the nut-pine and cedar woods on the mountain ranges of the Interior, of which it was the most characteristic species. It was eminently gregarious, even breeding in colonies, and in winter congregating in immense flocks, which sometimes consisted of thousands of individuals, all uttering their querulous notes as they swept to and fro over the hills, in their restless migrations. Its blue color is about the only feature in this bird which would lead one at first sight to suspect its relationship with the Jays, all its habits being so utterly

[1] According to Captain Charles Bendire, U. S. A., this is by no means the usual position of the nest. [See *Bulletin of the Nuttall Ornithological Club*, Vol. I, No. 2, July, 1876, pp. 44, 45.]

different from those of the more familiar species of this family. It is as essentially migratory as the Passenger Pigeon (*Ectopistes migratoria*) of the east, its appearance in and departure from a locality being equally sudden. We have often visited a nut-pine woods and found it one day full of noisy, roving troops, and the next as gloomy and silent as if a bird had never made its appearance there. In fall and winter, the large flocks, as they sweep back and forth over the scantily-wooded foot-hills, are sure to attract the attention of a stranger to the country, not merely from their appearance, but the more so from the fact that their peculiar piping notes of *pe'-pe'-wè, pe'-pe'-wè, pe'-pe'-wè* are often the only sound which breaks the solitude of these desolate regions, and would thus catch the ear of the most unobservant person.

In its manners, Maximilian's Jay resembles Clarke's Nutcracker (*Picicorvus*) more than any other bird, the chief difference being its migratory nature, the latter being of very sedentary habits. Most of its movements are quite similar, its attitude being much the same as it sits upon the summit of a small cedar, quietly reconnoitering, while it also frequently alights upon the ground to pick up a fallen pine-seed or cedar-berry. Its flight, however, is strikingly different, being almost exactly like that of the Robin (*Turdus migratorius*)—a gliding flight, with the wings rather inclined downward and the head raised—but is perhaps rather swifter. The various notes have all a striking character; the usual one resembles somewhat the tremulous, querulous wailing of the little Screech Owl (*Scops asio*), but is louder, less guttural, and more plaintive, while another is something like the soft love-note of the Magpie (*Pica hudsonica*); besides, there is the peculiar piping whistle of *pe'-wee, pe'*, described above, and usually uttered during the migration of a flock.

The breeding-season of this bird is remarkably early; for on the 21st of April, before we had thought of looking for their nests, full-grown young were flying about in a cedar and piñon grove near Carson City. In this grove we found the abandoned nests, perhaps a hundred or more in number, and also one containing young nearly ready to fly; but we were too late for the eggs. These nests were all saddled upon the horizontal branches, at a height of eight or ten feet from the ground, and, except that they were more bulky, resembled in their construction those of the eastern Blue Jay (*Cyanura cristata*). The single nest which was not deserted contained four fledgelings, which, when taken out for examination and placed in our hat, scrambled out, at the same time squalling vociferously. In color they resembled the old birds, but were of a duller and more uniform blue.

List of specimens.

502, ♂ *ad.;* Carson City, Nevada, April 20, 1868. Cedars. $11\frac{3}{4}$—$18\frac{3}{8}$—$6\frac{1}{8}$—5. Bill, tarsi, and toes, deep black; iris, deep sepia; interspaces of scutellæ and under surface of toes, ashy-whitish.

503, ♀ *ad.;* Carson City, Nevada, April 20, 1868. Cedars. $10\frac{5}{8}$—18—$5\frac{13}{16}$—$4\frac{5}{8}$. Same remarks.

507, ♂ *ad.;* Carson City, Nevada, April 21, 1868. Cedars. $11\frac{3}{4}$—19—$6\frac{5}{8}$—$5\frac{13}{16}$. Same remarks.

PICA NUTTALLI.

Yellow-billed Magpie.

Pica nuttalli, AUDUBON, Orn. Biog., IV, 1838, 450, pl. 362.—BAIRD, Birds N. Am., 1858, 578; Cat. N. Am. Birds, 1859, No. 433.—COOPER, Orn. Cal., I, 295.

Pica melanoleuca var. *nuttalli*, COUES, Key, 1872, 164; Check List, 1873, No. 233a; Birds N.W., 1874, 212.

Pica caudata var. *nuttalli*, B. B. & R., Hist. N. Am. Birds, II, 1874, 270, pl. XXXVIII, fig. 2.

The Yellow-billed Magpie was observed only in the Sacramento Valley, where it was very abundant among the scattered oaks. It was found in the outskirts of Sacramento City as soon as the first large oaks were met with, moving about in small scattered flocks, and incessantly chattering, whether while on the wing or when perched among the branches; it appeared to be both more noisy and more gregarious than the Black-billed Magpie, which, however, it greatly resembled in other respects. Many nests were found, but they were all in the tops of the tallest oaks, and could not be reached; this was one of the most conspicuous differences in its habits from *P. hudsonica*, which was found to invariably build its nest in bushes, or, at most, only in the smallest trees, as alders and cedars, even where large trees were abundant; the dense thickets of willow and buffalo-berry bushes being preferred to any others.

List of specimens.

64, ♂ *juv.;* Sacramento, California, June 20, 1867. Oaks. $14\frac{5}{8}$—22—$7\frac{1}{8}$—$5\frac{7}{8}$—1—$1\frac{9}{16}$—$6\frac{5}{8}$—$5\frac{1}{8}$.

65, ♂ *juv.;* oaks. $16\frac{5}{8}$—$23\frac{3}{4}$—$7\frac{3}{4}$—$6\frac{5}{8}$—$1\frac{1}{4}$—$1\frac{13}{16}$—$8\frac{1}{2}$—$6\frac{1}{2}$.

66, ♂ *juv.;* Sacramento, California, June 20, 1867. Oaks. $15\frac{1}{4}$—23—$7\frac{3}{4}$—$6\frac{1}{8}$—$1\frac{1}{8}$—$1\frac{3}{4}$—7—$5\frac{1}{2}$.

67, ♂ *juv.;* oaks. $16\frac{3}{4}$—$23\frac{1}{4}$—$7\frac{5}{8}$—$6\frac{1}{4}$—$1\frac{1}{8}$—$1\frac{5}{8}$—8—$6\frac{1}{4}$.

68, ♀ *juv.;* oaks. $15\frac{3}{4}$—$22\frac{3}{8}$—$7\frac{1}{2}$—$6\frac{3}{16}$—$1\frac{1}{16}$—$1\frac{5}{8}$—8—6.

69, ♀ *juv.;* oaks. 16—$23\frac{3}{8}$—$7\frac{5}{8}$—$6\frac{3}{8}$—$1\frac{1}{16}$—$1\frac{5}{8}$—$7\frac{5}{8}$—$6\frac{1}{8}$.

70, ♀ *juv.;* oaks. $16\frac{3}{4}$—$23\frac{1}{2}$—$7\frac{3}{4}$—$6\frac{3}{8}$—$1\frac{1}{4}$—$1\frac{3}{4}$—8—$6\frac{1}{4}$.

78, *juv.;* oaks. $16\frac{1}{2}$—$23\frac{3}{4}$—$7\frac{1}{2}$—$6\frac{1}{2}$—$1\frac{1}{4}$—$1\frac{5}{8}$—$8\frac{1}{4}$—$6\frac{1}{2}$.

79, *juv.;* oaks. 14—$22\frac{1}{4}$—$7\frac{1}{8}$—6—$1\frac{1}{16}$—$1\frac{11}{16}$—$6\frac{1}{8}$—$4\frac{1}{2}$.

80, *juv.;* oaks. $16\frac{3}{16}$—$22\frac{3}{8}$—$7\frac{1}{8}$—$6\frac{1}{8}$—$1\frac{3}{16}$—$1\frac{9}{16}$—$8\frac{1}{4}$—$6\frac{3}{4}$.

314, ♂ *ad.;* American River, Sacramento Co., Cal., November, 1867. (H. G. Parker.) 19—(?)—8—$6\frac{1}{2}$—$1\frac{7}{16}$—$1\frac{13}{16}$—$10\frac{1}{2}$—$8\frac{3}{4}$.

[All the specimens obtained, with the exception of the last, were immature and in molting condition; thus the measurements given are of little importance. In all, the bill and bare orbital-region is pure unshaded yellow, varying little, if any, with the specimen, being of a deep lemon-, or nearly chrome-yellow, the face more citreous. The skin over the whole body also, as well as the underside of the claws (possibly only in young birds), is yellow. We did not notice, in examining this species, the leaden-blue outer ring to the iris, afterward found to be a constant feature in *P. hudsonica.*]

PICA RUSTICA.

Black-billed Magpie.

β. hudsonica—American Magpie.

(*Tah'-tut* of the Washoes; *Que'-tou-gih, gih* of the Paiutes.)

Corvus hudsonicus, SABINE, App. Franklin's Journey, 1823, 25, 261.

Pica hudsonica, BONAP., Comp. & Geog. List, 1838, 27.—BAIRD, B. N. Am, 1858, 576; Cat. N. Am. B., 1859, No. 432.—COOPER, Orn. Cal., I, 296.

Pica melanoleuca var. *hudsonica*, COUES, Key, 1872, 164, fig. 106; Check List, 1873, No. 233a; B. N.W., 1874, 211.—HENSHAW, 1875, 334.

Pica caudata var. *hudsonica*, ALLEN, Bull. Mus. Comp. Zool., III, 1872, 178.—B. B. & R., Hist. N. Am. B., II, 1874, 266, pl. XXXVIII, fig. 1.

Pica rustica var. *hudsonica*, BAIRD, Orn. Simpson's Exped., 1876, 380.

The Black-billed Magpie is one of the most characteristic birds of the Interior, but its abundance varies greatly, in fact, almost unaccountably, with the locality; it is also one of the most conspicuous birds of that region, being eminently distinguished by the elegance of its form and the striking contrasts of its plumage. In western Nevada, from the Sierras eastward to the West Humboldt Mountains, it was one of the most abundant species, but on the opposite side of the Great Basin its entire absence from many favorable localities was noted as the most striking peculiarity of the fauna. It was most abundant in the rich valleys of the Truckee and Carson Rivers, and along the eastern base of the Sierra Nevada; and, although less common, it was very far from rare in the lower cañons of the West Humboldt Mountains. It was resident wherever observed, and at all times was rather familiar than otherwise, though when much persecuted in one locality it soon learned, by the natural shrewdness characteristic of the family, to look out for itself. During the winter the Magpies resorted daily, in company with the Ravens, to the slaughter-houses to feed upon the offal.

The Black-billed Magpie is more or less gregarious at all seasons, and when moving about usually goes in small troops, or loose flocks, which chatter in their peculiar manner as they fly. The usual note is a distinct chatter, unlike the note of any other bird of our acquaintance, but during the breeding-season a softer, more musical note is frequently uttered, sounding somewhat like *kay'e-ehk-kay'*. We did not detect any difference between the notes of this and the Yellow-billed species, although slight differences may exis'

List of specimens.

101, ♂ *juv.;* Camp 10, Truckee Meadows, Nevada, July 6, 1867. Willows. 16—$24\frac{1}{4}$—$8\frac{3}{8}$—7—$1\frac{1}{4}$—$1\frac{1}{2}$—$8\frac{3}{8}$—$6\frac{1}{2}$. Bill, slaty-black, fading into ashy on bare orbital region; iris, very dark brown, with pearl-blue outer ring; tarsi and toes, black, the latter ashy beneath.

143, ♂ *ad.;* Camp 17, valley of the Humboldt, August 31, 1867. $19\frac{3}{8}$—$23\frac{5}{8}$—$7\frac{11}{16}$—$6\frac{3}{4}$—$1\frac{5}{16}$—$1\frac{1}{2}$—$10\frac{3}{8}$—$8\frac{3}{4}$. Same remarks.

178, ♂ *ad.;* Camp 18, West Humboldt Mountains, September 10, 1867. $18\frac{1}{2}$—23—$7\frac{3}{4}$—$6\frac{1}{2}$—$1\frac{5}{16}$—$1\frac{9}{16}$—$10\frac{3}{16}$—$8\frac{7}{16}$. Same remarks.

194, ♀ *ad.;* Camp 19, West Humboldt Mountains, September 19, 1867. 20—24—$8\frac{1}{4}$—7—$1\frac{5}{16}$—$1\frac{1}{2}$—$11\frac{1}{8}$—$9\frac{5}{8}$. Same remarks. Bill, pure black.

204, ♀ *ad.;* Camp 19, September 21, 1867. 20—$24\frac{1}{2}$—$8\frac{5}{16}$—7—$1\frac{1}{2}$—$1\frac{5}{8}$—$11\frac{1}{4}$—$9\frac{3}{4}$. Same remarks.

246, ♂ *ad.;* Camp 19, October 11, 1867. $17\frac{3}{8}$—$21\frac{1}{4}$—$7\frac{1}{2}$—$6\frac{1}{4}$—$1\frac{3}{8}$—$1\frac{1}{2}$—$9\frac{1}{2}$—8. Same remarks.

249, $\male$ *ad.;* Camp 19, October 12, 1867. $19\frac{1}{4}$—$24\frac{1}{8}$—8—7—$1\frac{5}{16}$—$1\frac{1}{2}$—$11\frac{3}{8}$—$9\frac{1}{4}$. Same remarks.

289, $\female$ *ad.;* Camp 26, Truckee Meadows, November 18, 1867. $20\frac{1}{2}$—$24\frac{1}{4}$—$8\frac{3}{4}$—$6\frac{1}{16}$—$1\frac{1}{2}$—$1\frac{11}{16}$—$11\frac{3}{8}$—$9\frac{3}{8}$. Same remarks.

290, $\female$; Camp 26, Truckee Meadows, November 18, 1867. $19\frac{3}{4}$—$24\frac{1}{4}$—$8\frac{3}{8}$—7—(?)—(?)—11—$9\frac{1}{2}$. Same remarks.

306, $\male$ *ad.;* Camp 26, November 20, 1867. (Slaughter-house.) $20\frac{1}{4}$—25—$8\frac{3}{8}$—$6\frac{7}{8}$—$1\frac{7}{16}$—$1\frac{13}{16}$—$11\frac{1}{4}$—$9\frac{1}{4}$. Same remarks.

307, $\male$ *ad.;* Camp 26, November 20, 1867. (Slaughter-house.) $17\frac{3}{8}$—$22\frac{7}{8}$—$7\frac{3}{4}$—$6\frac{3}{8}$—$1\frac{5}{16}$—$1\frac{11}{16}$—$9\frac{7}{8}$—8. Same remarks.

338, $\female$ *ad.;* Carson City, Nevada, November 25, 1867. (Slaughter-house.) $18\frac{1}{2}$—23—$7\frac{7}{8}$—$6\frac{1}{2}$—$1\frac{3}{8}$—$1\frac{5}{8}$—$10\frac{1}{8}$—$8\frac{1}{16}$. Same remarks.

392, $\male$ *ad.;* Washoe Valley, Nevada, January 3, 1868. (Willow-copse.) 20—$24\frac{1}{4}$—$8\frac{1}{8}$—$6\frac{3}{4}$. Same remarks.

401, $\male$ *ad.;* Truckee Bottoms, December 19, 1867. $21\frac{3}{4}$—25—$8\frac{1}{2}$—7—$1\frac{3}{8}$—$1\frac{3}{4}$—13—$11\frac{1}{8}$. Same remarks.

407, *ad.;* Truckee Bottoms, December, 1867.

501, eggs (8) ; Carson City, Nevada, April 20, 1868. Nest in cedar.

506, eggs (2) ; Carson City, Nevada, April 21, 1868. Willows.

509 (6), 510 (6), eggs; Carson City, Nevada, April 22, 1868. Willows.

511, egg (1) ; Carson City, Nevada, April 23, 1868. (In nest from which No. 506 were taken.)

512, egg (1) ; Carson City, Nevada, April 23, 1868. Willows.

513, eggs (4) ; Carson City, Nevada, April 23, 1868. Willows.

514 (8), 515 (8), eggs; Carson City, Nevada, April 23, 1868. Buffalo-berry.

526, eggs (3) ; Carson City, Nevada, April 25, 1868. Alder swamp.

538, eggs (9) ; Carson City, Nevada, April 27, 1868. Willows.

539, eggs (9) ; Carson City, Nevada, April 27, 1868. Buffalo-berry.

540, eggs (9) ; Carson City, Nevada, April 27, 1868. Willows.

541, eggs, (7) ; Carson City, Nevada, April 27, 1868. Willows.

542, eggs (8) ; Carson City, Nevada, April 27, 1868. Willows.

543, eggs (7) ; Carson City, Nevada, April 27, 1868. Buffalo-berry.

544, eggs (6) ; Carson City, Nevada, April 27, 1868. Nut-pine.

545, 546, eggs (6) ; Carson City, Nevada, April 27, 1868. Willows.

547, eggs (6) ; Carson City, Nevada, April 27, 1868. Buffalo-berry bushes.

548 (4), 549 (4), eggs; Carson City, Nevada, April 27, 1868. Willows.

550 (3), 551 (2), eggs; Carson City, Nevada, April 27, 1868. Willows.

552, eggs (2) ; Carson City, Nevada, April 27, 1868. Willows.

556 (8), 557 (8), eggs; Carson City, Nevada, April 29, 1868. Alder-bushes.

767, eggs (6) ; Truckee Bottom, May 29, 1868. Nest in willows on river-bank.

[The nest is in every instance " domed," the *real* nest being inclosed in an immense thorny covering, by which it is generally far exceeded in bulk. In the *side* of this covering is a winding passage leading into the nest. The purpose of this canopy is possibly to conceal the very long tail of the bird, which, if exposed, would endanger its safety.]

CYANURA STELLERI.

Steller's Jay.

β. frontalis—Blue-fronted Jay.

(*"Mountain Jay" of Californians.*)

Cyanura stelleri, BAIRD, B. N. Am., 1858, 581 (part).—COOPER, Orn. Cal., I, 1870, 298 (part).

Cyanura stelleri var. *frontalis*, RIDGWAY, Am. Jour. Sci. and Arts, V, Jan., 1873, 43.—B. B. & R., Hist. N. Am. B., II, 1874, 279, pl. XXXIX, fig. 2.

Cyanurus stelleri. b. *frontalis*, COUES, Check List, 1873, No. 235a; B. N.W., 1874, 215.

We found this Jay only among the pines on the Sierra Nevada, since it did not. like the Nutcracker (*Picicorvus*), occur on the higher ranges of the Great Basin, though it was represented on the eastern side by the *C. macrolopha*—neither the latter nor the subject of these remarks occurring at any point intermediate between the Sierra and the Wahsatch, along the line of our route. Except when driven to the lower ravines and foot-hills by the unusual continuance of cold weather or by violent snow-storms upon the mountains, it was not observed to descend to below the coniferous woods, though it was common in the lower edge of this forest-belt. It was almost always found in the same localities as Clarke's Nutcracker, it being usual to see both species in one tree; its voice seemed also exceedingly like that of the bird just mentioned, being a series of rough and grating, squawking or screeching notes, very different indeed from those of its eastern congener, *C. cristata*, whose utterances are far more varied and flexible, and even musical in comparison; but like the eastern species it frequently imitated other birds, particularly the Hawks, some of which it mimicked, on occasion, quite successfully. The usual note of the Blue-fronted Jay is a hoarse monosyllabic squawk, very deep-toned, and grating; but a monotonous chatter is often heard, consisting of a rapid repetition of hollow-toned notes, somewhat like *kuk, kuk, kuk, kuk, kuk, kuk*, the style of utterance being comparable to the "scythe-whetting" call of the Flickers (*Colaptes*), but much more sonorous and less musical. On one occasion we fired at an individual of this species in the top of a tall pine tree, and merely disabling one wing, its fall was broken by the resistance of the uninjured wing and outspread tail, the bird alighting easily upon one of the lower branches of an adjoining tree, when it began to ascend by hopping from one limb to another, at the same time uttering a very perfect imitation of the squealing note of the Red-tailed Hawk (*Buteo borealis*), apparently for the purpose of preventing pursuit.

On the 24th of February, 1868, during a protracted period of extreme cold weather, with deep snows on the mountains, we observed a pair of these Jays in a shade-tree on one of the back streets of Carson City; but they appeared ill at ease so near the habitations of man, skulking about, as if afraid of being seen in town, and evidently anxious to return to their native woods.

List of specimens.

321, ♂ ? *ad.*; El Dorado County, California. Presented by Mr. H. G. Parker. $12\frac{1}{2}$—(?)—$5\frac{5}{8}$—$4\frac{11}{16}$—$1\frac{1}{4}$—$1\frac{1}{2}$—$5\frac{3}{8}$—$4\frac{3}{8}$.

322, ♂ ? *ad.*; El Dorado County, California. Presented by Mr. H. G. Parker. $12\frac{7}{8}$—(?)—6—$4\frac{7}{8}$—$1\frac{1}{4}$—$1\frac{1}{2}$—$5\frac{3}{8}$—$3\frac{1}{4}$.

328, ♂ *ad.*; Carson City, Nevada, November 27, 1867.　$12\frac{1}{2}$—$17\frac{7}{8}$—6—$4\frac{7}{8}$—$1\frac{1}{8}$—$1\frac{1}{2}$—$5\frac{5}{8}$—$3\frac{1}{2}$.　Bill, tarsi, and toes, deep black; iris, vandyke-brown.

329, ♀ *ad.* (mate of preceding); Carson City, Nevada, November 27, 1867.　12—17—$5\frac{3}{4}$—$4\frac{5}{8}$—$1\frac{1}{8}$—$1\frac{1}{2}$—$5\frac{1}{4}$—4.

330, ♀ *ad.*; Carson City, Nevada, November 27, 1867.　12—$17\frac{1}{2}$—$5\frac{5}{8}$—$4\frac{9}{16}$—1—$1\frac{9}{16}$—5—3.

445, ♂ *ad.*; Carson City, March 21, 1868.　$12\frac{3}{8}$—18—6—5.　Bill, tarsi, and toes, black; iris, bister.

477, ♂ *ad.*; Carson City, March 30, 1868.　12—$17\frac{1}{2}$—6—$4\frac{7}{8}$.

497, ♂ *ad.*; Carson City, April 18, 1868.　13—$18\frac{3}{8}$—$6\frac{1}{4}$—$5\frac{1}{4}$.　Bill, tarsi, and toes, deep black; iris, bister. [Type of var. *frontalis*, Ridgw., l. c.]

498, ♀ *ad.* (mate of preceding); Carson City, April 18, 1868.　$11\frac{3}{4}$—$17\frac{1}{4}$—$5\frac{11}{16}$—$4\frac{3}{4}$. [Type of var. *frontalis*, RIDGW., l. c.]

CYANURA MACROLOPHA.

Long-crested Jay.

Cyanocitta macrolopha, BAIRD, Pr. Ac. Nat. Sci. Philad., 1854, 118.

Cyanura macrolophus, BAIRD, Birds N. Am., 1858, 582; Cat. N. Am. Birds, 1859, No. 436.—COOPER, Orn. Cal., I, 1870, 300.

Cyanura stelleri var. *macrolopha*, ALLEN, Bull. Mus. Zool., III, 1872, 178.—COUES, Key, 1872, 165, fig. 107; Check List, 1873, No. 235a.—B. B. & R., Hist. N. Am. Birds, II, 1874, 281, pl. XXIX, fig. 3.—HENSHAW, 1875, 335.

Cyanura coronata var. *macrolopha*, RIDGW., Am. Journ. Sci. and Arts, V, Jan., 1873, 43.

This more eastern representative of Steller's Jay was first met with among the pines of the Wahsatch Mountains, which formed, apparently, the western limit of its range. It was there by no means common, but became more so as we proceeded eastward into the Uintahs, where it was comparatively plentiful. In its habits and manners it seemed a perfect counterpart of *C. frontalis*, but its notes appeared to be less sonorous than those of that form.

List of specimens.

1284, nest and eggs (6); Parley's Park, June 25, 1869. Nest in small fir-tree, in edge of woods, saddled on horizontal branch, about 15 feet from ground. Nest abandoned, and several of the eggs broken.

1373, ♂ *ad.*; Pack's Cañon, Uintah Mountains, July 5, 1869. 13¾—19. Bill, black; iris, brown; legs and feet, black.

1374, nest (of preceding, contained three fully-fledged young). Nest on mountain-mahogany tree, on side of ravine of a secluded cañon in the pine-region, situated in a sort of triple fork, near extremity of horizontal branch.

1375, ♂ *ad.*; Pack's Cañon, July 6, 1869. 13½—19¼. Same remarks.

1445, 1446, *juv.*; Parley's Park, Wahsatch Mountains, Utah, July 23, 1869.

CYANOCITTA CALIFORNICA.

California Valley Jay.

(*Yo-shoo'-ah* of the Washoes.)

Garrulus californicus, VIGORS, Zool. Beechey's Voy., 1839, 21, pl. v.

Cyanocitta californica, STRICKL., Ann. Mag. XV, 1845, 342.—BAIRD, Birds N. Am., 1858, 584; Cat. N. Am. Birds, 1859, No. 437.—COOPER, Orn. Cal., I, 1870, 302.—B. B. & R., Hist. N. Am. Birds, II, 1874, 288, pl. XL, fig. 1.

Aphelocoma floridana var. *californica*, COUES, Key, 1872, 166; Check List, 1873, No. 236b.

Aphelocoma floridana. c. californica, COUES, Birds N.W., 1874, 219.

The common "Valley Jay" of California was observed in abundance only among the western foot-hills of the Sierra Nevada, where it was seen both in the brushwood of the ravines and among the scattered pines. It was also noticed among the oaks of the plains, where, however, it was less plentiful. On the eastern slope it appeared to be quite common, at least on the foot-hills near Carson City, where, in 1868, it made its first appearance toward the last of April.

This species may be instantly distinguished at a distance from the *C. woodhousii* by the conspicuous contrast between the pale gray of the back and the blue of the wings and tail, as well as by the pure white lower parts; the colors of *C. woodhousii* being much more uniform, appearing almost entirely dull grayish-blue, brighter on the wings and tail. The notes, however, appear to be much the same in the two species.

List of specimens.

553, ♂ *ad.;* Carson City, Nevada, April 29, 1868. Sage-brush, below pines. 12¼ —16—5¼—4¼. Bill, tarsi, and toes, deep black; iris, bister.

559, ♂ *ad.;* Carson City, Nevada, April 29, 1868. 12⅛—16—5¼—4¼. Same remarks.

560, ♀ *ad.;* Carson City, Nevada, April 29, 1868. 11½—15¾—5¼—4¼. Same remarks.

CYANOCITTA WOODHOUSII.

Woodhouse's Jay.

(*We'-ahk* of the Paiutes.)

Cyanocitta woodhousii, BAIRD, B. N. Am., 1858, 585, pl. 59; Cat. N. Am. B., 1859, No. 438.—COOPER, Orn. Cal., I, 1870, 304.

Aphelocoma floridana var. *woodhousii,* ALLEN, Bull. Mus. Comp. Zool., III, 1872, 179.—COUES, Key, 1872, 166; Check List, 1873, No. 236a; B. N.W., 1874, 219.

Cyanocitta californica var. *woodhousii,* B. B. & R., Hist. N. Am. B., II, 1874, 291, pl. XL, fig. 3.

Cyanocitta floridana var. *woodhousii,* HENSHAW, 1875, 337.

This very interesting bird we found to be the most generally-distributed species of the family, since it occurred on nearly every range where there was water in the main cañons, or extensive woods of nut-pine and cedar on the slopes; it was said to occasionally visit the wooded valleys of the Truckee and Carson Rivers, but we never saw it at either place, although it was found to be more or less common in the similar valley of the Weber, in Utah. At our camp on the western slope of the West Humboldt Mountains, it was very abundant in September, and one of the most familiar birds of the neighborhood. It was very unsuspicious where not molested, and anything unusual in the occupation of any one about the camp was sure to excite its curiosity. On one occasion, while the writer was at work skinning birds in the shade of the bushes overhanging the stream, one often came and perched upon a branch near by, quietly watching every movement with all the inquisitive curiosity of a Cat-bird (*Galeoscoptes carolinensis*). On the opposite side of the same range, in Buena Vista Cañon, it was also common, and was there several times observed in the gardens and door-yards of the town. It was also rather common on the eastern slope of the Ruby range, in the extensive piñon and cedar woods, while at "City of Rocks," in the southern portion of Idaho, the most northern point reached during our trip, it was very numerous in October, among the woods of the same description. On the western foot-hills of the Wahsatch it was more or less plentiful, according to the locality, among the scrub-oaks, while many were seen in the valley of the Weber. It did not occur in Parley's Park, however, the altitude of that place being probably too great.

In its manners this Jay and its congeners differ strikingly from the species of the genus *Cyanura*, or the Crested Jays, their movements calling to mind the Mocking-bird (*Mimus polyglottus*) and the Cat-bird (*Galeoscoptes carolinensis*), their manner of flight being exactly the same, while they exhibit a similar predilection for thickets and scrubby brushwood. The notes of the present species greatly resemble those of *C. californica*, and are harsh and piercing to an extreme degree. That most frequently uttered is a shrill screech, sounding like *we'-ahk, we'-ahk*, whence the name bestowed upon it by the Paiute Indians.

List of specimens.

162, ♂ *ad.;* Camp 18, West Humboldt Mountains, September 4, 1867. Brushwood, along brook. $11\frac{7}{8}$—$15\frac{3}{8}$—5—$4\frac{3}{8}$—$1\frac{1}{16}$—$1\frac{7}{16}$—$5\frac{5}{8}$—4. Bill, tarsi, and toes, deep black; iris, chestnut-bazel.

186, ♂ *ad.;* Camp 18, West Humboldt Mountains, September 12, 1867. Junipers. 12—$15\frac{7}{16}$—5—$4\frac{3}{16}$—$1\frac{1}{16}$—$1\frac{5}{16}$—5—$\frac{3}{16}$—$3\frac{11}{16}$. Same remarks.

188, ♀ *ad.;* Camp 18, West Humboldt Mountains, September 13, 1867. Brushwood, along brook. $12\frac{1}{2}$—$15\frac{3}{4}$—$5\frac{1}{4}$—$4\frac{3}{8}$—$1\frac{1}{8}$—$1\frac{5}{16}$—$5\frac{5}{8}$—$4\frac{9}{16}$. Same remarks.

242, ♂ *ad.;* Camp 19, West Humboldt Mountains, October 8, 1867. Sage brush. $12\frac{5}{16}$—$15\frac{3}{16}$—$5\frac{1}{4}$—$4\frac{7}{16}$—$1\frac{1}{8}$—$1\frac{5}{16}$—6—4. Same remarks.

1190, *jur.;* Salt Lake City, Utah, June 19, 1869. $11\frac{1}{4}$—15. Bill and feet, black; iris, brown.

Family TYRANNIDÆ—Tyrant Flycatchers.

Tyrannus verticalis.

Western Kingbird; "Arkansas Flycatcher."

Tyrannus verticalis, SAY, Long's Exped., II, 1823, 60.—BAIRD, Birds N. Am., 1858, 173; Cat. N. Am. Birds, 1859, No. 126.—COOPER, Orn. Cal., I, 1870, 312.—COUES, Key, 1872, 170, figs. 110a, 112; Check List, 1873, No. 244; Birds N.W., 1874, 236.—B. B. & R., Hist. N. Am. Birds, II, 1874, 324, pl. XLIII, fig. 2.—HENSHAW, 1875, 342.

Generally distributed throughout all fertile districts of the west, this species was extremely abundant in favorable localities, this being especially the case at Sacramento, where perhaps no other species equaled it in numbers. In its habits, this Kingbird is remarkably similar to the eastern species, *T. carolinensis*, and their nest and eggs cannot be distinguished; but it is of an even more vivacious and quarrelsome disposition, continually indulging in aërial combats, sometimes to such an extent that half a dozen or more may be seen pitching into each other promiscuously, but apparently more from playful than pugnacious motives. They are also of a very sympathetic disposition, for when a nest is disturbed, the owners soon bring around them, by their cries, all the others in the neighborhood; but no sooner do they assemble than they begin their playful contests, and fill the air with their twitterings. Their notes are all weaker and less rattling than those of the eastern species, partaking more of the character of a tremulous, though rather shrill, twitter.

We know of no other bird so easily tamed, or which so thoroughly *enjoys* the society and protection of human beings, when once domesticated, as this species, as the following account of three individuals possessed by us in the field, at various times, may show:—

The first of these pets, familiarly known to the party as "Chippy," was obtained about the middle of July from the Indians, who had just taken him, along with three others, all fully fledged, from the nest. He was carried to camp, and fed with grasshoppers and flies until able to catch them for himself, which he learned to do in about a week after he acquired the power of flight. The little fellow had a most voracious appetite, and during the day continually followed us about, teasing for grasshoppers, until he had eaten enough, after which he quieted down for five minutes or so, when he began to clamor for more—thus appearing to be always hungry. Had one person the office of keeping him supplied with food he would consequently have been extremely troublesome; but, fortunately, all became interested in him, and he thus received favors and caresses from all hands. When gorged with food, he usually remained perched upon the shoulder of the one who carried him, but sometimes he would fly off to his favorite perch, a rope running from the rear of a tent to a stake in the ground; or, if it happened to be midday and the sun particularly oppressive, would take shelter underneath a hoisted umbrella, hung beneath the fly of a tent for the purpose of shading a thermometer, perching upon one of the ribs of the apparatus. Chippy was the earliest riser in camp, and at daybreak his merry twitter aroused his human companions, of whom his favorite one, the writer, he would often awake by alighting in his face, for he would invariably select him from the dozen or more persons who lay on the ground wrapped in their blankets. At all times he was greatly averse to being left alone, and when night approached would nestle more closely against one's neck, twittering contentedly until asleep, and if removed exhibiting the greatest disappointment, while he was often so persistent in keeping his place that repeated removals were necessary to induce him to remain upon the roost provided for him, inside the tent.

His almost insatiable appetite was the subject of comment by us all, and speculations were indulged in as to the probable number of grasshoppers he consumed in a day. It was finally agreed that this should be settled by experiment, so each person was instructed to keep count of the number he himself fed him during the day. At evening notes were compared, and it was found that he had been fed one hundred and twenty grasshoppers since morning!

From the very first he was so completely tame that he did not exhibit under any circumstances the slightest trace of timidity; he always disliked to be handled, however, but this was evidently on account of his plumage, merely, for he would immediately come to any one who called him, or alight upon a hand held out as an invitation. He soon learned his own name, and knew it so well that when he had strayed some distance from camp (as he often did when led away by the temptations of companions

34 P R

of his kind, who often visited the vicinity of our camp for the purpose), it was only necessary to call him, and if within hearing he was sure to leave his comrades with impolite abruptness and fly in haste to camp, twittering gladly as he came. The writer was once leaving the camp for a trip into the mountains, and had scarcely reached the mouth of the cañon, several hundred yards distant, when Chippy's familiar voice was heard, and on looking back he was discovered following, as fast as his wings could carry him, twittering with all his might, as if calling out for us to wait for him. He soon overtook us, and, alighting upon our shoulder, accompanied us on our way, every now and then flying off after a butterfly or other insect that had caught his eye, capturing which he would return and beat his prey against the hard brim of our straw hat until in a condition to be swallowed; or often these little detours were for the purpose of sporting awhile with others of his species encountered by the way, returning in a little while, followed by them to within a few yards, when they would alight on a branch, apparently wondering at the perfect understanding existing between us. After ascending the cañon to where the path became too much obstructed by rocks and brushwood to proceed farther, except on foot, we dismounted and unsaddled; Chippy seemed disposed to rest, so he was placed in the shade of the saddle, as it lay upon the ground, and we proceeded on our way. The little fellow soon missed us, however, and it was not long before he found us out, by the report of our gun—a sound with which he had long been familiar, and which he had not learned to fear, the barrel of our gun often being his perch when he accompanied us on our trips, even the report, though of course startling him, not frightening him from our shoulder. On several occasions did the report of our gun prove the means of directing him to us when he had strayed beyond his usual bounds, such a circumstance once occurring half a mile from camp, after he had been missing all the morning. His natural fondness for the society of the birds of his species living in the neighborhood did not have the effect of in the least alienating his affections, but came, nevertheless, near costing him his life, the circumstances being as follows: He used daily to bring his playmates to the camp, where, after sporting about with them for a half hour or so, they would all leave together and be absent, sometimes the whole afternoon, Chip often not returning until near evening; we began to fear that in consequence of this some harm might befall him while out of our sight, or that some day he might fail to return at all; so, as the best means of preventing such a misfortune, we determined to frighten the wild birds away when they should next make their appearance, and thus keep Chip out of temptation. A favorable opportunity presented one afternoon when three were sporting together at a considerable height near our camp; and having just observed Chippy on his accustomed perch, brought out our gun and fired at them. Fortunately none were hit, for one of them, which proved to be our pet, separated from the rest and flew in terror to the camp, screaming with all his might. We hastened back, fearing he had been injured, and found him perched upon a rope, terribly frightened, but not at all hurt. His disregard for firearms was now at an end, and when we approached him with gun in hand he beat a precipitate retreat, and continued to do so at every attempt, his feathers pressed close to his body and his neck stretched—the very picture of fear. The moment the weapon was laid aside, however, his confidence was restored, and he was then as easily approached as before.

We carried Chippy with us, as we moved from camp to camp, for nearly two months after. Everywhere he excited curiosity and wonder, even among the Indians, while the members of our party grew daily more attached to him. One morning, however, in the latter part of September, we missed his familiar awakening twitter, and when we arose from our blankets he could not be found. Search was made throughout the day, but without success, and a large hawk having been seen early in the morning hovering about the place, seemed to explain the cause of his disappearance. He was never afterward seen.

It was suggested by members of the party that instead of exhibiting the docility and intelligence characteristic of the species, this bird was perhaps an exceptional individual, and that another could not be found which would afford a parallel case. The following summer, however, another young one was taken from the nest, and being reared under exactly the same circumstances developed the same traits to such perfection that he would have absolutely passed for the same bird. As happened with

Chippy No. 1, the new pet after a while attracted others of his species to our camp, and these soon became so familiar that they would perch upon the tents, even during our presence. One individual happened to alight upon the fly of the mess-tent while we were at lunch, and being near the edge of the canvas, and his shadow showing his exact position from beneath, he was easily caught. This proved to be a full-grown bird, although evidently one of the year, and being placed in a cage and sumptuously fed for a day or two, was released in Chip's presence, and would not depart. He had become almost as tame as his companion, and remained with us until both were killed by our domesticated hawks, some fine specimens of *Buteo swainsoni*, which were allowed the liberty of the camp.

List of specimens.

15, nest and eggs (3); Sacramento, California, June 11, 1867. Nest in large cotton-wood tree.

16, nest and eggs (3); Sacramento, June 11, 1867. Nest in small willow, in copse.

17, ♀ *ad.* (parent of No. 15). $8\frac{1}{2}$—$14\frac{7}{8}$—$4\frac{7}{8}$—$4\frac{1}{16}$—$\frac{3}{4}$—$\frac{3}{4}$—$3\frac{5}{8}$—$1\frac{3}{4}$. Bill, tarsi, and toes, deep black; iris, hazel.

37, nest and eggs; Sacramento, June 12, 1867. Nest in small cotton-wood, in copse.

45, nest and eggs (3); Sacramento, June 17, 1867. Nest on horizontal branch of large cotton-wood.

46, ♂ *ad.* (parent of preceding.) $9\frac{1}{8}$—$16\frac{1}{8}$—$5\frac{1}{4}$—$4\frac{3}{8}$—$\frac{3}{4}$—$\frac{11}{16}$—4—$1\frac{3}{4}$. Bill, tarsi, and toes, deep black; iris, hazel.

71, nest and eggs (4); Sacramento, June 20, 1867. Nest in top of small oak, in grove.

1180, nest and eggs (4); Salt Lake City, Utah, June 18, 1869. Nest on small mountain-mahogany bush, overhanging cliff.

1181, nests and eggs; same date and remarks.

1408, nest; Bear River Valley, July, 1869. [J. C. Olmstead.]

TYRANNUS CAROLINENSIS.

Kingbird.

Lanius tyrannus var. *γ carolinensis*, GMEL., Syst. Nat., I, 1788, 302.

Tyrannus carolinensis, TEMMINCK, Tabl. Méth. —, 24.—BAIRD, B. N. Am., 1858, 171; Cat. N. Am. B., 1859, No. 124.—COOPER, Orn. Cal., I, 1870, 311.—COUES, Key, 1872, 169, pl. II, figs. 1, 2, 110b, 111; Check List, 1873, No. 242; Birds N.W., 1874, 235.—B. B. & R., Hist. N. Am. B., II, 1874, 316, pl. XLIII, fig. 4.—HENSHAW, 1875, 341.

In the rich valley of the Truckee River, in western Nevada, two or more pairs of this familiar eastern bird had their abode among the large cotton-wood trees near our camp; in fact, this species seemed to be no more rare in that locality than the *T. verticalis*, which, however, was itself far from common. On the eastern border of the Great Basin it was more abundant, being quite as numerous in the Salt Lake Valley as the *T. verticalis*, both frequently nesting in the same grove.

List of specimens.

1496, ♀ *jur.*; Parley's Park, Wahsatch Mountains, Utah, August 10, 1869. 8½—14½. Bill, tarsi, and toes, black; iris, dark brown.

MYIARCHUS CINERASCENS.

Ash-throated Flycatcher.

Tyrannula cinerascens, LAWRENCE, Ann. Lyc. N. H. New York, V, 1851, 109.

Myiarchus cinerascens, SCLATER, Ibis, 1859, 121.—COUES, Key, 1872, 171; Check List, 1873, No. 248; B. N.W., 1874, 239.

Myiarchus crinitus var. *cinerascens*, B. B. & R., Hist. N. Am. B., II, 1874, 337, pl. XLIII, fig. 6.—HENSHAW, 1875, 345.

Myiarchus mexicanus, BAIRD, Birds N. Am., 1858, 179 (not of KAUP); Catal., 1859, No. 131.—COOPER, Orn. Cal., I, 1870, 316.

This species was apparently not abundant anywhere, being probably more so in the Sacramento Valley than in any locality eastward of the Sierra Nevada. It was not noticed in the vicinity of Sacramento City, in June, but among the oaks of the plains toward the foot-hills of the Sierras it was common early in July. A few were observed among the cotton-woods of the lower Truckee in July and August, and it was also a not infrequent summer-resident in the cañons of the Ruby Mountains, where it was most often observed perched upon a gnarled cedar or mountain-mahogony overhanging the top of a rocky gorge or high cliff. It was very rare in Parley's Park.

Resembling its eastern relative, the Great Crested Flycatcher (*M. crinitus*), in its general habits, its notes, however, are weaker, and do not possess in so great a degree the strikingly wild character so marked in the vehement whistlings of that species.

List of specimens.

104, ♂ *ad.*; Truckee Reservation (Camp 12), Nevada, July 24, 1867. 8½—13—4—3¼—⅞—⅞—3⅝—1¹⁵⁄₁₆. Bill, deep black; iris, hazel; tarsi and toes, black.

SAYORNIS NIGRICANS.

Black Pewee.

Tyrannula nigricans, SWAINSON, Synop. Mex. Birds, Philos. Mag., I, 1827, 367.
Sayornis nigricans, BONAP., Comp. Rend., XXVIII, 1854, 87.—BAIRD, B. N. Am., 1858, 183; Cat. N. Am. B., 1859, No. 134.—COOPER, Orn. Cal., I, 1870, 319.—COUES, Key, 1872, 172; Check List, 1873, No. 251.—B. B. & R., Hist. N. Am. B., II, 1874, 340, pl. XLV, fig. 1.—HENSHAW, 1875, 347.

The Black Pewee was found only at Sacramento, where it was rather common about the out-buildings of habitations near the river. In its sociable disposition, its movements, and its ordinary note of *chip*, it reminded us exactly of the eastern *S. fuscus;* we did not, however, hear it utter a note similar to that from which the latter receives its common name, but judging from the extreme similarity of the other notes, so far as heard, consider it likely that the one to which we refer is also uttered.

SAYORNIS SAYUS.

Say's Pewee.

(*To-que'-oh* of the Paiutes.)

Muscicapa saya, BONAP., Am. Orn., I, 1825, 20, pl. II, fig. 3.
Sayornis sayus, BAIRD, B. N. Am., 1858, 185; Cat. N. Am. Birds, 1859, No. 136. COOPER, Orn. Cal., I, 1870, 320.—COUES, Key, 1872, 172; Check List, 1873, No. 250; B. N.W., 1874, 240.—B. B. & R., Hist. N. Am. B., II, 1874, 347, pl. XLV, fig. 3.—HENSHAW, 1875, 349.

Throughout the country eastward of the Sierra Nevada, this interesting bird was found in all suitable places, though it was not abundant anywhere, since it was seldom that more than one pair inhabited a restricted locality. Its favorite haunts were the rocky shores of the lakes and rivers, or the walls of the lower cañons in the mountains, where it built its bulky but soft and downy nest among the recesses of the rocks, or, as was more often the case, upon a narrow shelf of rock projecting from the ceiling or dome of a cave. In those wild localities it was found to be rather shy in its disposition; but wherever man had fixed his abode upon the dreary waste this species was attracted to his vicinity, thus assuming the semi-domesticated habits of *S. fuscus* and *S. nigricans*, which it represents in this intermediate region. It was even noticed at several stage-stations in the midst of the Humboldt and Carson Deserts, where no water occurred except in the artificial wells. About the larger settlements it was found to be more numerous, and at Unionville, in the West Humboldt Mountains, had, with *Sialia arctica* and *Salpinctes obsoletus*, taken possession of the abandoned adobe houses in the upper portion of the town. At this place we observed a nest which was attached to the under side of the eave of a large stone building, being apparently built upon the base of a deserted nest of the Cliff Swallow (*Petrochelidon lunifrons*).

While this species agrees with its more western and eastern representatives (*S. nigricans* and *S. fuscus*) in nesting-habits, the character of its nest and eggs, its fondness for rocky localities in the vicinity of water, and in the readiness with which it becomes attached to the vicinity of dwellings, it differs from both in notes, the usual utterance being a fine plaintive *peer, peer*, much like a certain wailing note of *Contopus virens*, another common note being a prolonged querulous twitter.

List of specimens.

181, ♀ *ad.;* West Humboldt Mountains (Camp 18), Nevada, September 11, 1867. S$\frac{1}{16}$—12$\frac{7}{8}$—4$\frac{1}{4}$—3$\frac{9}{16}$—$\frac{5}{8}$—$\frac{3}{4}$—3$\frac{1}{2}$—1$\frac{5}{8}$. Bill, tarsi, and toes, deep black; iris, hazel.

456, ♂ *ad.;* Carson City, Nevada, March 25, 1868. 7$\frac{3}{4}$—12$\frac{5}{8}$—4$\frac{5}{16}$—3$\frac{1}{2}$. Bill, deep black; iris, bister; tarsi and toes, plumbeous-black.

457, ♀ *ad.;* Carson City, Nevada, March 25, 1868. 7$\frac{11}{16}$—12$\frac{3}{8}$—4$\frac{1}{16}$—3$\frac{5}{16}$. Same remarks.

762, nest and eggs (2); island in Pyramid Lake, Nevada, May 23, 1868. Nest attached to shelf on roof of cave, on rocky shore.

764, nest and eggs (4); east shore of Pyramid Lake, May 25, 1868. Nest on shelf in cave, among the tufa domes.

CONTOPUS BOREALIS.

Olive-sided Flycatcher.

Tyrannus borealis, SWAINSON, Fauna Bor. Am., II, 1831, 141, pl. XXXV.
Contopus borealis, BAIRD, B. N. Am., 1858, 188; Cat. N. Am. B., 1859, No. 137.—
COOPER, Orn. Cal., I, 1870, 323.—COUES, Key, 1872, 173; Check List, 1873,
No. 253; B. N.W., 1874, 243.—B. B. & R., Hist. N. Am. B., II, 1874, 353, pl.
XLIV, fig. 1.—HENSHAW, 1875, 350.

This interesting bird was a rather common summer-resident in the higher portion of the pine-belt of the Wahsatch, and we have every reason to believe that it is also found in similar localities on the Sierra Nevada. Near the summits of the pine-clad hills in the vicinity of our camp in Parley's Park it was by no means rare in certain parts of the woods, its favorite resort being those portions of the forest where many of the trees had been deadened by fire, the most characteristic associate species being *Chrysomitris pinus, Carpodacus cassini,* and *Junco caniceps.* It was extremely shy, and could be approached only with the greatest difficulty. Attention was usually attracted to it by its mellow whistling notes, which bore a faint resemblance to certain utterances of the Cardinal Grosbeak (*Cardinalis virginianus*), the bird being generally perched upon the summit of a tall dead pine. One of the specimens obtained was secured only by a tedious and difficult climb to the top of a very tall fir-tree, which fortunately began branching near the ground, the bird having lodged among the topmost branches. The first individual of the species that we saw was perched quite a distance off, upon a dead mahogany tree on the side of one of the lower cañons of the East Humboldt Mountains. Being the first example we had ever seen, its appearance struck us as quite peculiar, as it sat quietly in an upright attitude, but it was at last decided to be a Shrike (*Collurio*); upon returning down the cañon an hour or more afterward, however, it was noticed occupying the same position, but presently it flew from the perch and snapped an insect in the air, when it returned to the branch and beat it against the limb in true flycatcher style.

List of specimens.

875, ♂ ad.; East Humboldt Mountains (Camp 21), Nevada, August 29, 1868. 7½—13—(?)—3½. Upper mandible, black, lower dilute brown, more yellowish basally; iris, deep sepia; whole interior of mouth, rich orange-yellow; tarsi and toes, sepia-black.

1273, ♂ ad.; Parley's Park, Wahsatch Mountains, Utah, June 23, 1869. 7⅞—13¼. Bill, black, lower mandible pale wax-brown, more yellowish basally, the tip black; iris, brown; feet, deep black; interior of mouth, deep yellow.

1423, ♂ ad.; Parley's Park, July 17, 1869. 7⅞—13 5/16. Upper mandible, black, lower wood-brown, more yellowish basally; interior of mouth, rich Indian-yellow; iris, brown; tarsi and toes, deep black.

CONTOPUS RICHARDSONI.[1]

Richardson's Pewee.

Tyrannula richardsonii, SWAINSON, Fauna Bor. Am., II, 1831, 146, pl. XLVI, lower
   figure.
Contopus richardsonii, BAIRD, B. N. Am., 1858, 189; Cat. N. Am. B., 1859, No.
   138.—COOPER, Orn. Cal., I, 1870, 325.
Contopus virens var. *richardsonii*, ALLEN, Bull. Mus. Comp. Zool., III, 1872, 179.—
   COUES, Key, 1872, 174; Check List, 1873, No. 255a.—B. B. & R., Hist. N.
   Am. B., II, 1874, 360, pl. XLIV, fig. 4.—HENSHAW, 1875, 353.
Contopus (virens var. ?) *richardsonii*, COUES, Birds N.W., 1874, 247.

Richardson's Pewee was met with in every wooded locality, and was
no less common at an altitude of 8,000 feet, in the Wahsatch Mountains,
than at Sacramento, but little above the sea-level. In all respects except
its notes and the character of its nest, this species is a counterpart of the
eastern Wood Pewee (*C. virens*); its appearance and manners being quite
the same. It seems, however, to be more crepuscular than the eastern
species, for while it remains quiet most of the day, no sooner does the sun
set than it begins to utter its weird, lisping notes, which increase in loudness and frequency as the evening shades deepen. At Sacramento we frequently heard these notes about our camp at all times of the night. This
common note of Richardson's Pewee is a harsh, abrupt lisping utterance,
more resembling the ordinary rasping note of the Night-Hawk (*Chordeiles
popetue*) than any other we can compare it with, though it is of course
weaker, or in strength proportioned to the size of the bird. Being most
frequently heard during the close of day, when most other animals become
silent and Nature presents its most gloomy aspect, the voice of this bird
sounds lonely, or even weird.

The nest of this species, as is well known, differs very remarkably from
that of *C. virens*, being almost invariably placed in the crotch between
nearly upright forks, like that of certain *Empidonaces*, as *E. minimus* and
E. obscurus, instead of being saddled upon a horizontal branch, while its
structure is very different, the materials being chiefly plant-fibers and

---

[1] With almost absolute similarity to *C. virens*, its eastern representative, in all
appreciable details of form, size, and color, this bird presents such radical differences
in notes, accompanied by certain peculiarities of habits, that we feel bound to consider
it a distinct species.

stems of fine grasses, instead of beautiful lichens and mosses, matted together with spiders' webs, and with but a slight admixture of other substances. All its habits, however, especially its deportment, are exactly those of *C. virens*, while the eggs of the two species are scarcely, if at all, distinguishable.

At Sacramento we observed in this bird a remarkable display of attachment to its favorite haunts, especially to the place where the nest is built. The nest and eggs of a pair had been taken and the female killed as she flew from the nest; several days afterward, upon revisiting the locality, and happening to look up at the site of the former nest, we were surprised to see a new one already completed in the very same spot, the male having found another mate. When we climbed to the nest the male exhibited more than usual anxiety, and upon returning the following day it was found to be abandoned, and the only egg it contained broken.

List of specimens.

12, nest and eggs (2); Sacramento, June 10, 1867. Nest at extremity of broken dead branch near top of small oak, in grove.

13, ♀ *ad.* (parent of No. 12); Sacramento, California, June 10, 1867. $6\frac{3}{16}$—$10\frac{1}{3}$—$3\frac{1}{4}$—3—$\frac{9}{16}$—$\frac{7}{16}$—$2\frac{5}{8}$—$1\frac{1}{2}$. Bill, deep black above, light-brownish beneath, more yellow basally, the point nearly black; whole interior of mouth, deep orange-yellow; iris, dark brown; tarsi and toes, black.

42, nest and eggs (2); Sacramento, June 15, 1867. Nest saddled on rather large branch of oak, in grove, about 15 feet from ground.

43, ♀ *ad.* (parent of No. 42); Sacramento, June 15, 1867. $6\frac{1}{4}$—10—$3\frac{5}{16}$—$2\frac{11}{16}$—$\frac{9}{16}$—$\frac{7}{16}$—$2\frac{1}{2}$—$1\frac{1}{4}$. Bill, black, basal half of lower mandible dilute brown.

86, nest and eggs; Sacramento, June 16, 1867. Situated like No. 12.

88, nest and eggs; Sacramento, June 24, 1867. Same situation.

89, nest; Sacramento, June 24, 1867.

898, ♂ *juv.*; East Humboldt Mountains (Camp 23, Secret Valley), September 6, 1868. $6\frac{1}{8}$—$10\frac{7}{8}$—(?)—$2\frac{5}{16}$. Upper mandible, black, lower clear pale yellow, the tip black; iris, sepia; tarsi and toes, black.

1250, nest and eggs; Parley's Park, Utah, June 23, 1869. Nest in aspen, 20 feet from ground.

1282, nest and eggs (3); Parley's Park, June 25, 1869. Nest in crotch of dead aspen, along stream.

1304, nest and eggs (2); Parley's Park, June 27, 1869. Nest in crotch of dead aspen.

1315, nest and eggs (2); Parley's Park, June 27, 1869. Nest in dead aspen.

1503, ♀ *ad.*; Parley's Park, August 12, 1869. $6\frac{7}{16}$—$10\frac{3}{16}$. Upper mandible, black, lower scarcely paler; interior of mouth, rich yellow; iris, brown; legs and feet, black.

EMPIDONAX PUSILLUS.[1]

Little Flycatcher; Traill's Flycatcher.

(*Pish'-e-wah'-e-tse* of the Shoshones.)

? *Platyrhynchus pusillus*, SWAINSON, Synop. Mex. Birds, Philos. Mag., I, 1827, 366.

Empidonax pusillus, CABANIS, Journ. für Orn., 1855, 480.—BAIRD, Birds N. Am.,
1858, 194; Cat. N. Am. Birds, 1859, No. 141.—B. B. & R., Hist. N. Am. B.,
II, 1874, 366, pl. XLIV, fig. 9.

Empidonax traillii var. *pusillus*, COUES, Key, 1872, 175; Check List, 1873, No.
257a.—HENSHAW, 1875, 356.

Empidonax traillii. b. *pusillus*, COUES, Birds N.W., 1874, 252.

Empidonax traillii, COOPER, Orn. Cal., I, 1870, 327.

This is the most abundant and generally distributed of the *Empidonaces*,
being, so far as known, the only one of the genus occurring across the
entire breadth of the continent.[2] It prefers the lower portions of the
country, however, its favorite haunts being the willows of the river-valleys,
and we did not find it higher up among the mountains than an altitude of
about 7,000 feet, where it was confined to the willow thickets bordering
the streams flowing across the parks. In the environs of Sacramento City
it was, next to *Tyrannus verticalis*, the commonest of the Flycatchers, and
was as characteristic of the willow copses as *Contopus richardsoni* was
of the oak groves. In its manners, this species is more lively than its
mountain relatives, *E. obscurus* and *E. hammondi*, especially after sunset,
when they chase one another among the bushes, twittering as they fly,
frequently perching on a high twig and with swelled throats uttering their
not unmusical note of *twip'utawah'*, which is translated by the people
of Parley's Park as "*pretty dear*," by which name it was there familiar to
every one.

---

[1] We are unable to appreciate differences between western and eastern ("*traillii*")
specimens of this species sufficient to constitute the latter a recognizable variety. It
is only those specimens from the dryer and more scantily wooded localities of the West
which are paler and grayer colored than the average of eastern examples, and even
then the difference is not comparable to that existing between *E. flaviventris* and *E.
difficilis*.

[2] As stated above, we consider *pusillus* and "*traillii*" to be in every respect
identical, while we hold *flaviventris* and *difficilis* to be specifically distinct.

List of specimens.

33, nest and eggs (4); Sacramento, California, June 12, 1867. Nest about 2 feet from ground, in small bush in cotton-wood copse.

36, ♀ ad. (parent of above); Sacramento, June 12, 1867. $6\frac{3}{8}$—$8\frac{5}{8}$—(?).

83. nest and eggs; Sacramento, California, June 24, 1867. Nest about 4 feet from ground, in small bush in willow copse.

84, ♀ ad. (parent of eggs No. 83); Sacramento, June 24, 1867. $5\frac{5}{8}$—$8\frac{1}{8}$—$2\frac{9}{16}$— $2\frac{1}{8}$—$\frac{9}{16}$—$\frac{9}{16}$—$2\frac{1}{8}$—$1\frac{1}{4}$. Upper mandible, black, lower dilute brownish-yellow, more whitish basally; iris, hazel; tarsi and toes, deep hazel.

94, nest and eggs; Sacramento, June 29, 1867. Nest situated like No. 83.

876, ♀ ad. (parent of 877); Ruby Valley, Nevada (Camp 21), August 29, 1868. $5\frac{7}{8}$—$8\frac{5}{8}$—(?)—$2\frac{1}{4}$. Upper mandible, black, lower very dilute lilaceous-brown, more yellowish basally; whole interior of mouth, rich orange-yellow; tarsi and toes, deep black.

877, juv.; Ruby Valley, Nevada (Camp 21), August 29, 1878. $5\frac{1}{2}$—$8\frac{1}{4}$—(?)—$2\frac{1}{8}$. Upper mandible, plumbeous-black, lower pale lilaceous, more yellowish basally; whole interior of mouth, rich orange-yellow; iris, purplish-bister; tarsi and toes, pale plumbeous.

1100, ♂ ad.; Antelope Island, Great Salt Lake, Utah, June 4, 1869. $6\frac{1}{4}$—$9\frac{1}{4}$. Upper mandible, black, lower dilute brown; iris, brown; tarsi and toes, deep black.

1101, ♀ ad. (mate of preceding); Antelope Island, Great Salt Lake, Utah, June 4, 1869. 6—$8\frac{5}{8}$. Same remarks.[1]

1242, 1243, 1244, 1245, 1246, 1247; nests and eggs. Parley's Park, Wahsatch Mountains, Utah, June 23, 1869. Nests among willows along stream, generally about 5 or 6 feet from ground.

1288, nest and eggs (2); Parley's Park, June 25, 1869. Nest in wild-rose brier, among undergrowth of thicket, along stream.

1305, nest and eggs (4); Parley's Park, June 27, 1869. Nest in wild-rose brier.

1316, nest and egg (1); Parley's Park, June 27, 1869. Nest in rose-bush.

1330, nest and eggs (4); Parley's Park, June 28, 1869. Same remarks.

1331, nest and eggs (3); Parley's Park, June 28, 1869. Nest in rose-bush, undergrowth of willow-copse.

1358, nest; Parley's Park, July 2, 1869. Nest in rose-bush, by stream.

1420, nest and eggs (3); Parley's Park, July 17, 1869. Nest in willows, along stream.

1469, ♂ ad., $5\frac{7}{8}$—$9\frac{1}{4}$; 1470, ♀ ad., $5\frac{11}{16}$—$8\frac{5}{8}$; 1471, ♀ ad., $5\frac{5}{8}$—$8\frac{5}{8}$; 1472, ♀ ad., $5\frac{11}{16}$—$8\frac{5}{8}$. Parley's Park, July 29, 1869. Upper mandible, deep black, lower light purplish wood-brown; interior of mouth, deep yellow; iris, deep reddish-brown; tarsi and toes, deep black.

1473, ♀ ad.; Parley's Park, July 29, 1869. $5\frac{3}{4}$—$8\frac{1}{2}$. Lower mandible, brownish-white.

1493, ♂ juv.; Parley's Park, August 7, 1869. 6—9.

---

[1] These specimens represent the absolutely typical "traillii" style.

EMPIDONAX OBSCURUS.

Wright's Flycatcher.

(*Yet'-to-gish* of the Paiutes; *Pish'-e-wah'-e-te-tse* of the Shoshones.)

? *Tyrannula obscura*, SWAINSON, Synop. Mex. Birds, Philos. Mag., I, 1827, 367.
Empidonax obscurus, BAIRD, Birds N. Am., 1858, 200; Cat. N. Am. B., 1859, No.
    146.—COOPER, Orn. Cal., I, 1870, 329.—COUES, Key, 1872, 176; Check List,
    1873, No. 261; Birds N.W., 1874, 258.—B. B. & R., Hist. N. Am. B., II, 1874,
    381, pl. XLIV, fig. 6.—HENSHAW, 1875, 360.
Empidonax wrightii, BAIRD, Birds N. Am., 1858, 200 (in text). [Name proposed in
    case SWAINSON'S *T. obscura* should prove a different species.]

This *Empidonax* is as characteristic of the mountains as *E. pusillus* is
of the lower valleys. It inhabits both the aspen groves and copses of the
higher cañons and the mahogany woods of the middle slopes, in which
places it is sometimes one of the most numerous of the smaller birds. It
is probably not entirely restricted to these elevated regions during the
breeding-season, however, since it was common in May among the willow
thickets in the lower Truckee Valley, while the first individual of the season was observed in a cedar and piñon woods on the low hills near Carson
City, on the 21st of April. In September we found it in the lower cañons
of the West Humboldt Mountains, where, as in other ranges, the summer
fauna assimilated that of the river-valleys rather than that of the higher
cañons. It was equally common on both sides of the Great Basin, the
only districts where it was entirely absent being those where the ranges
were destitute of water and vegetation. It was more abundant in the aspen
copses of the high cañons of the lofty Toyabe range, near Austin, than
anywhere else, but it was quite plentiful in similar localities on the Wahsatch and Uintah Mountains.

The habits and manners of this species much resemble those of others
of the genus, while in the location and structure of its nest, and the color
of its eggs, it resembles very closely *E. hammondi* and *E. minimus*. The
notes, however, are decidedly distinctive, and but little like those of its
congeners. The ordinary utterance is an exceedingly liquid *whit*, but when
the nest is disturbed, as well as on some other occasions, a plaintive *sweer*
is uttered, which much resembles the call-note of *Chrysomitris pinus*, but is

rather less loud. We always found this little bird to be exceedingly confiding and unsuspicious; so much so, indeed, that when collecting its eggs on the Toyabe Mountains, an attempt to catch the parent bird with the hand, as it sat upon the nest, proved successful in nearly every instance. One specimen was, on this occasion, frightened from off its eggs by our stumbling against the sapling containing the nest before the latter was discovered, and alighted in another bush some distance off; it was fired at but apparently missed, for it flew and disappeared; we were therefore considerably astonished, upon returning to secure the nest, to find the bird again upon her eggs, where she remained without making the least attempt to escape, and suffered herself to be caught, when it was found that several of her quill and tail-feathers had been carried away, and one toe cut off, by the shot we had fired.

List of specimens.

203, ♂ ad.; eastern slope West Humboldt Mountains, September 21, 1867. $5\frac{11}{16}$—$8\frac{1}{8}$—$2\frac{5}{8}$—$2\frac{1}{4}$—$\frac{7}{16}$—$\frac{5}{8}$—$2\frac{5}{16}$—$1\frac{1}{4}$. Upper mandible, uniform deep black, lower mandible dilute chrome-yellow; iris, hazel; tarsi and toes, deep black.

508, ♂ ad.; Carson City, Nevada, April 21, 1868. $6\frac{5}{16}$—$9\frac{5}{8}$—3—$2\frac{1}{4}$. Upper mandible, black, lower dilute brownish-white, dusky toward end; whole interior of mouth, intense yellow; iris, deep sepia; tarsi and toes, deep black.

827, nest and eggs (4); 828, nest and eggs (3); 829, nest and eggs (2); 830, nest and eggs (4); 831, nest and egg (1). Austin, Nevada, July 3, 1868. No. 827 in mountain-mahogany bush, on extreme summit of hill, about 2,000 feet above camp, or at an altitude of 9,000 feet; the others all in aspen thickets, and within reach of the hand.

832, ♀ ad. (parent of No. 828, *caught on nest, by hand!*); Austin, Nevada, July 3, 1868. $5\frac{5}{8}$—$8\frac{7}{16}$—$2\frac{5}{8}$—$2\frac{3}{16}$. Upper mandible, sepia-black, lower dilute sepia-brown, yellowish basally; iris, dark sepia; tarsi and toes, deep black.

833, ♀ ad. (parent of No. 827, *caught on nest, by hand!*); Austin, Nevada, July 3, 1868. $6\frac{1}{4}$—$8\frac{3}{4}$—$2\frac{3}{4}$—$2\frac{5}{16}$. Same remarks.

867, ♀ juv.; Camp 19, East Humboldt Mountains, August 10, 1868. $5\frac{3}{4}$—$8\frac{1}{2}$—(?)—$2\frac{1}{4}$. Upper mandible, black, lower, with terminal half, light yellowish, basally more pinkish; interior of mouth, lemon-yellow; iris, dark sepia; tarsi and toes, deep black.

895, ♂ ad.; Camp 23, East Humboldt Mountains, September 6, 1868. $5\frac{13}{16}$—$8\frac{3}{4}$—(?)—$2\frac{5}{16}$. Upper mandible, black, lower dilute brown, paler and more yellowish basally; interior of mouth, orange-yellow; iris, umber; tarsi and toes, deep black.

896, ♀ ad.; Camp 23, East Humboldt Mountains, September 6, 1868. $5\frac{11}{16}$—9—(?)—$2\frac{9}{16}$. Same remarks.

897, ♂ ad.; Camp 23, East Humboldt Mountains, September 6, 1868. 6—9—(?)—$2\frac{3}{4}$. Same remarks.

911, ♀ *ad.;* Camp 23, East Humboldt Mountains, September 8, 1868. $6\frac{1}{8}$—$8\frac{7}{8}$—(?)—$2\frac{5}{16}$. Upper mandible deep black, terminal third of lower deep mahogany-brown, basal portion, with rictus, pale chrome-yellow; interior of mouth, rich Indian yellow; iris, umber; tarsi and toes, deep black.

911a, ♀ *ad.;* East Humboldt Mountains, September 8, 1868. $5\frac{3}{4}$—$8\frac{1}{2}$—(?)—$2\frac{1}{4}$. Same remarks.

912, ♀ *ad.;* Camp 23, East Humboldt Mountains, September 8, 1868. $5\frac{7}{8}$—$8\frac{5}{8}$—(?)—$2\frac{5}{16}$. Same remarks.

934, ♂ *juv.;* Camp 25, Humboldt Valley, September 16, 1868. $5\frac{7}{8}$—$8\frac{3}{4}$—(?)—$2\frac{1}{4}$. Bill, black, basal two-thirds of lower mandible, lilaceous-white; iris, very dark sepia; tarsi and toes, plumbeous-black. (This specimen is remarkable for its pure and very light ashy colors.)

940, ♀ *ad.;* Secret Valley, Nevada, September 6, 1867.

1248, 1249, nests and eggs; Parley's Park, Wahsatch Mountains, Utah Territory, June 23, 1869. Nests in aspen-copse.

1281, nest and eggs (4); Parley's Park, June 25, 1869. Nest in crotch of dead aspen, along stream.

1334, nest and eggs; Parley's Park, June 28, 1869. Nest in aspens.

1336 (4), 1337 (3), nests and eggs; Parley's Park, June 28, 1869. Nests in aspens.

1353, nest and eggs (4); Parley's Park, June 28, 1869. Nest in service-berry bush.

1515, ♀ *juv.;* Parley's Park, August 16, 1869. 6—9. Lower mandible, pale pinkish.

EMPIDONAX HAMMONDI.

Hammond's Flycatcher.

Tyrannula hammondii, XANTUS, Pr. Ac. Nat. Sci. Philad., 1858, 117.

Empidonax hammondii, BAIRD, B. N. Am., 1858, 119, pl. 76, fig. 1; Cat. N. Am. B., 1859, No. 145.—COOPER, Orn. Cal., I, 1870, 330.—COUES, Key, 1872, 176; Check List, 1873, No. 260; B. N.W., 1874, 257.—B. B. & R., Hist. N. Am. B., II, 1874, 383, pl. XLIV, fig. 7.—HENSHAW, 1875, 362.

This delicate little Flycatcher was not met with anywhere as a summer resident, but during its autumnal migration was found to be very common on the East Humboldt Mountains. It inhabited exclusively the aspen-groves and copses of tall alders and willows in the higher cañons, and seemed to keep in the darkest and most secluded places. The only note heard was a soft *pit*.

List of specimens.

893, ♂ *ad.;* East Humboldt Mountains, Nevada (Camp 22), September 5, 1868. $5\frac{1}{2}$—$8\frac{1}{8}$—$2\frac{9}{16}$—$2\frac{3}{16}$—$\frac{3}{8}$—$\frac{9}{16}$—$2\frac{1}{4}$—(?). Upper mandible, deep black, lower dilute brown, the edge, with rictus, orange-yellow; iris, dark bister; tarsi and toes, black.

894, ♂ *ad.;* East Humboldt Mountains (Camp 23), September 6, 1868. $5\frac{1}{2}$—$8\frac{5}{8}$—(?)—$2\frac{5}{16}$. Same remarks.

908, ♀ ad.; East Humboldt Mountains (Camp 23), September 8, 1868. 5¼—8¼—
2¾₁₆. Lower mandible, rich brown.

909, ♂ ad.; East Humboldt Mountains (Camp 23), September 8, 1868. 5½—8²₁₆—
(?)—2⁵₁₆. Lower mandible, with rictus, wood-brown.

910, ♂ ad.; East Humboldt Mountains (Camp 23), September 8, 1868. 5¾—8⅞—
(?)—2⁷₁₆. Same remarks.

EMPIDONAX DIFFICILIS.[1]

Western Yellow-bellied Flycatcher.

Empidonax difficilis, BAIRD, B. N. Am., 1858, 198 (in text); ed. 1860, pl. 76, fig. 2;
    Cat. N. Am. B., 1859, No. 144a.
Empidonax flaviventris var. *difficilis*, ALLEN, Bull. Mus. Comp. Zool., III, 1872, 179.
    —COUES, Key, 1872, 176 (in text).—B. B. & R., Hist. N. Am. B., II, 1874, 380.
    —HENSHAW, 1875, 362.
Empidonax flaviventris. b. *difficilis*, COUES, B. N.W., 1874, 256.
Empidonax flaviventris, COOPER, Orn. Cal., I, 1870, 328.

This species was the rarest of the *Empidonaces* met with by us, a few
only being seen in the pine forests high up on the Wahsatch Mountains,
and a still smaller number on the eastern slope of the Sierra Nevada. At
the former place a few pairs were found in July and August, and when
observed were usually perched upon a dead twig, sitting in a nearly vertical position, the tail constantly jerked to one side. The only note heard
was a distinct *chip*, much like that of the Yellow-rump Warbler (*Dendrœca
coronata*).

List of specimens.

1490, ♂ ad.; Parle's Park, Wahsatch Mountains, Utah, August 5, 1869. 6—9¼.
Upper mandible, black, lower lilaceous-white; iris, deep reddish-hazel; tarsi and toes,
purplish-black.

1491, ♀ ad.; Parley's Park, Wahsatch Mountains, Utah, August 5, 1869. 5⅞—8⅝.
Same remarks.

---

[1] It is with little hesitation that we consider this bird as distinct specifically from
E. flaviventris. Not only are there very conspicuous and constant differences in proportions and colors (especially the former), but numerous observers have noticed
remarkable and important peculiarities in the nesting-habits, the present species
almost invariably building its nest in cavities, either of stumps, trees, or rocks, or on
beams inside of buildings, a habit not yet noticed in *E. flaviventris*, nor, indeed, in any
other species of the genus. [See Cooper, Proc. Cal. Acad. Sciences, December 6, 1875,
who, however, is mistaken in supposing that "the differences in the two races seem
to be wholly in shades of color and size, and not in proportions, as formerly supposed."]

FAMILY ALCEDINIDÆ—KINGFISHERS.

CERYLE ALCYON.

Belted Kingfisher.

(*Tat'um-pahl'te* of the Washoes; *Tsan'ak-nuk'ket-ah* of the Paiutes; *Pang'we-chin'ah-moo* of the Shoshones.)

Alcedo alcyon, LINN., Syst. Nat., I, 1766, 180.
Ceryle alcyon, BOIE. Isis, 1828, 316.—BAIRD, B. N. Am., 1858, 158; Cat. N. Am.
   B., 1859, 117.—COOPER, Orn. Cal., I, 1870, 337.—COUES, Key, 1872, 188;
   Check List, 1873, No. 286; B. N.W., 1874, 273.—B. B. & R., Hist. N. Am. B.,
   II, 1874, 392. pl. XLV, fig. 6.—HENSHAW, 1875, 366.

The common Kingfisher was found in the vicinity of all streams and lakes containing fish. In the lower valleys it was resident, but in the mountains was found only in summer.

List of specimens.

292, ♂ ad.; Truckee Meadows, Nevada, November 18, 1867.—14—23¾—6⅝—5⅜—2½—⅜—4—1⅝. Bill, black, more slaty basally, where clouded with pale ashy; iris, dark vivid vandyke-brown; tarsi and toes, livid brownish-black, more bluish on the knees and adjoining part of the tibiæ.

1452, ♀ ad.; Parley's Park, Utah, July 26, 1869. 12⅝—22½ Bill, black, the rictus and basal portion of lower mandible pale ashy; iris, rich dark brown; tarsi and toes, dark plumbeous-sepia in front, purplish salmon-pink behind and beneath.

1492, ♀ ad.; Parley's Park, August 7, 1869. 14¾—22¾. Same remarks as to the preceding.

FAMILY PICIDÆ—WOODPECKERS.

PICUS HARRISI.

Harris's Woodpecker.

(*Kahsoo'te* of the Washoes; *Wahpe'-pannah* of the Paiutes.)

Picus harrisii, AUDUBON, Orn. Biog., V, 1839, 191, pl. 417.—BAIRD, Birds N. Am.,
   1858, 87; Cat. N. Am. Birds, 1859, No. 75.—COOPER, Orn. Cal., I, 375.
Picus villosus var. *harrisii*, ALLEN, Bull. Mus. Comp. Zool., III, 1872, 180.—COUES,
   Key, 1872, 194; Check List, 1873, No. 298a.—B. B. & R., Hist. N. Am.
   Birds, II, 1874, 507.—HENSHAW, 1875, 386.

This perfect counterpart of the Hairy Woodpecker of the East (*P. villosus*) was met with throughout the year in all wooded localities, from the

35 P R

Sierra Nevada eastward. It was equally common in the forests of Coniferæ and among the broad-leafed or deciduous trees. The notes and habits are in all respects identical with those of its eastern representative.

List of specimens.

364, ♀ *ad.;* Truckee Reservation, December 19, 1867. $9\frac{5}{16}$—15—5—$4\frac{3}{16}$—$1\frac{1}{8}$—$1\frac{1}{16}$—$3\frac{1}{4}$—$1\frac{3}{4}$. Bill, slaty horn-color; iris, burnt-sienna; tarsi and toes, plumbeous-green.

372, ♂ *ad.;* Truckee Reservation, December 21, 1867. $9\frac{3}{4}$—$16\frac{3}{4}$—$5\frac{3}{16}$—$4\frac{7}{8}$. Bill, greenish-slate, darker terminally; naked orbital region, similar, but paler; iris, reddish-brown; tarsi and toes, dark slaty-green.

373, ♂ *ad.;* same locality and date. $9\frac{5}{8}$—$16\frac{3}{4}$—$5\frac{5}{16}$—$4\frac{3}{4}$. Same remarks.

438, ♂ *ad.;* Carson City, March 10, 1868. $9\frac{1}{4}$—$15\frac{1}{2}$—$5\frac{1}{4}$—$4\frac{1}{4}$. *Extent of tongue beyond end of bill,* $2\frac{1}{4}$ *inches;* its corneous tip, pale plumbeous.

1435, ♂ *juv.;* Parley's Park, July 21, 1869. 10—17. Bill, dark slate; iris, burnt-sienna; tarsi and toes, cinereous.

1512, ♀ *ad.;* Parley's Park, August 16, 1869. $9\frac{7}{8}$—17.

NOTE.—The two latter specimens, besides being larger than those from western Nevada, are also more spotted with white on the wings, thereby showing an approach to *P. villosus.*

PICUS GAIRDNERI.

Gairdner's Woodpecker.

Picus gairdneri, AUDUBON, Orn. Biog., V, 1839, 317.—BAIRD, Birds N. Am., 1858, 91; ed. 1860, pl. 85, figs. 2, 3; Cat. N. Am. Birds, 1859, No. 76.—COOPER, Orn. Cal., I, 1870, 377.

Picus pubescens var. *gairdneri,* COUES, Key, 1872, 194; Check List, 1873, No. 299a. —B. B. & R., Hist. N. Am. Birds, II, 1874, 512.—HENSHAW, 1875, 388.

Picus pubescens. b. *gairdneri,* COUES, Birds N.W., 1874, 282.

We found this bird to be unaccountably rare in all portions of the country, even where its larger cousin, *P. harrisi,* abounded; indeed, it was seen at only two localities along the entire route, a very few being found in September among the thickets by one of the streams flowing from the lofty Clover Mountains into the Upper Humboldt. At Parley's Park two families of young were met with, on separate occasions, in July and August, but we did not succeed in obtaining specimens. At the former locality they were feeding on the fruit of *Cratægus rivularis,* in company with many other species of birds. In all respects, both as to habits and voice, this bird seems to be a perfect counterpart of the Downy Woodpecker (*P. pubescens*) of the East.

List of specimens.

925, ♂ *ad.;* Upper Humboldt Valley (Camp 25, Deering's Creek), Nevada, September 12, 1868. 7—12¼—(?)—3⁷₁₆. Bill, pure slate; iris, burnt-umber; tarsi and toes, ochraceous olive-green.

935, ♂ *ad.;* Upper Humboldt Valley (Camp 25, Deering's Creek), Nevada, September 17, 1868. 6⁷⁄₈—12¼—(?)—3½.

PICUS NUTTALLI.

Nuttall's Woodpecker.

Picus nuttalli, GAMBEL, Pr. Ac. Nat. Sci. Philad., I, 1843, 259.—BAIRD, Birds N. Am., 1858, 93; Cat. N. Am. Birds, 1859, 78.—COOPER, Orn. Cal., I, 1870, 378.—B. B. & R., Hist. N. Am. Birds, II, 1874, 521, pl. L, figs. 3, 6.
Picus scalaris var. *nuttalli,* COUES, Key, 1872, 193; Check List, 1873, No. 297a.

Among the scattered oaks of the Sacramento plains we found this Woodpecker to be very common, but met with it nowhere else. It was particularly abundant where the oaks attained a large size, and formed more extensive groves, nearer the foot-hills of the Sierra Nevada. Its manners were very much those of the Downy Woodpeckers (*P. pubescens* and *P. gairdneri*), but the notes were entirely different, the usual one consisting of a very prolonged rattling call, quite unlike that of any other bird with which we are acquainted.[1]

PICUS ALBOLARVATUS.

White-headed Woodpecker.

Leuconerpes albolarvatus, CASSIN, Pr. Ac. Nat. Sci. Philad., 1850, 166.
Picus albolarvatus, BAIRD, Birds N. Am., 1858, 96; Cat. N. Am. B., 1859, No. 81. —COOPER, Orn. Cal., I, 1870, 382.—COUES, Key, 1872, 192; Check List, 1873, No. 295.—B. B. & R., Hist. N. Am. B., II, 1874, 526, pl. L, figs. 7, 8.

In the dense forests of lofty and massive coniferæ which cover the slopes of the Sierra Nevada, this Woodpecker was found all the year round. It was first met with in July, on the western slope, at an elevation of about 5,000 feet; it was the most abundant Woodpecker of the locality, and was almost constantly seen sporting about the tops of the tall dead pines, usually

---

[1] In several localities in western Nevada we heard, on different occasions, similar notes, but they turned out to be those of one of the Passeres, and a species which we are not able to identify, unless it may be *Phœnopepla nitens.* (See page 447.)

out of gunshot range. On the eastern slope, it was common near Carson City throughout the winter, keeping entirely among the pines, though sometimes coming down to the lower edge of the woods.

The appearance of the White-headed Woodpecker is very striking, on account of the bold contrast between the white head and neck and the uniform black of the rest of the plumage—the white patch on the primaries showing conspicuously only when the bird is flying. In its habits it resembles the larger "Sapsuckers" (*P. villosus* and *P. harrisi*), except that it is more lively in its disposition, in which respect it approaches quite nearly to the playful Melanerpeæ. Its notes, however, are quite distinctive, for although they bear some resemblance to the clear, sharp *diph* of the species above mentioned, the call forms a connected series of these notes, each ending in a rather suppressed twitter.

List of specimens.

435, ♂ *ad.;* Carson City, March 10, 1868. $9\frac{7}{16}$—$15\frac{3}{4}$—$5\frac{3}{16}$—$4\frac{1}{4}$. Bill, uniform slate-black; iris, dull carmine; tarsi and toes, olivaceous-slate. *Tongue protrudes $\frac{3}{4}$ of an inch beyond the end of the bill;* its corneous tip white. [See under *P. harrisi*, p. 546.[1]]

436, ♀ *ad.* (mate of No. 435). $9\frac{7}{16}$—$15\frac{7}{8}$—$5\frac{1}{4}$—$4\frac{3}{4}$. Same remarks.

527, ♂ *ad.;* Carson City, April 25, 1868. $9\frac{3}{8}$—$16\frac{1}{4}$—$5\frac{3}{16}$—$4\frac{3}{4}$.

528, ♂ *ad.;* Carson City, April 25, 1868. $9\frac{1}{4}$—$15\frac{3}{4}$—$5\frac{1}{16}$—$4\frac{3}{16}$.

529, ♀ *ad.* (mate of No. 528). $8\frac{13}{16}$—$15\frac{1}{2}$—5—$4\frac{3}{16}$.

PICOIDES ARCTICUS.

Black-backed Three-toed Woodpecker.

Picus (Apternus) arcticus, SWAINSON, Fauna Bor. Am., II, 1831, 313, pl. 57.

Picoides arcticus, GRAY, Genera of Birds, II, 184-, 434, pl. 108, fig. 7.—BAIRD, B. N. Am., 1858, 98; Cat. N. Am. B., 1859, No. 82.—COOPER, Orn. Cal., I, 1870, 384.—COUES, Key, 1872, 194; Check List, 1873, 300; B. N.W., 1874, 284.—B. B. & R., Hist. N. Am. B., II, 1874, 530, pl. L, fig. 1.

The only specimen of this species seen was the one obtained. It was engaged in hammering on the trunk of a dead pine tree, near the foot of the mountains.

List of specimens.

409, ♀ *ad.;* pines of the Sierra Nevada, near Carson City, February 19, 1868. $9\frac{1}{2}$—$15\frac{1}{2}$—$5\frac{3}{16}$—$4\frac{1}{2}$. Bill, slate-color; iris, burnt-sienna; tarsi and toes, dull slate.

---

[1] Professor Baird has proposed for this species the generic or subgeneric term *Xenopicus* (Birds N. Am., 1858, p. 83), which, in view of certain marked structural differences from typical *Picus*, it may in future be deemed advisable to adopt.

SPHYRAPICUS RUBER.

Red-breasted Woodpecker.

Picus ruber, GMELIN, Syst. Nat., I, 1788, 429.

Sphyrapicus ruber, BAIRD, Birds N. Am., 1858, 104; Cat. N. Am. Birds, 1859, No.
87.—COOPER, Orn. Cal., I, 1870, 392.—COUES, Key, 1872, 195; Check List,
1873, No. 303.

Sphyrapicus varius var. *ruber*, RIDGW., Am. Journ. Sci. & Arts, V, Jan., 1873, 40.
—B. B. & R., Hist. N. Am. Birds, II, 1874, 544, pl. LI, fig. 6.

Sphyrapicus varius. c. ruber, COUES, Birds N.W., 1874, 286.

The Red-breasted Woodpecker was observed only on the Sierra
Nevada, chiefly on the western side of that range; we are not even certain
of its occurrence on the eastern slope, but it is our impression that we saw
it once among the pines near Carson City, but the occasion was not such
as to afford a satisfactory opportunity to identify the individual in question.[1]

SPHYRAPICUS NUCHALIS.

Red-naped Woodpecker.

(*Qŭ'um-ah'-utz* of the Shoshones.)

Sphyrapicus varius var. *nuchalis*, BAIRD, Birds N. Am., 1858, 103 (in text).—B. B.
& R., Hist. N. Am. Birds, II, 1874, 542, pl. LI, figs. 3, 4.—COOPER, Orn. Cal.,
I, 399.—COUES, Key, 1872, 195; Check List, 1873, No. 302a.—HENSHAW,
1875, 392.

Sphyrapicus nuchalis, BAIRD, Birds N. Am., 1858, 921; ed. 1860, pl. XXXV; Cat.
N. Am. B., 1859, No. 86.

Sphyrapicus varius. b. nuchalis, COUES, Birds N.W., 1874, 286.

Throughout the country between the Sierra Nevada and the Rocky
Mountains, the Red-naped Woodpecker is a common species in suitable
localities. Its favorite summer-haunts are the groves of large aspens near
the head of the upper cañons, high up in the mountains, and for this reason
we found it more abundant in the Wahsatch and Uintah region than
elsewhere; indeed, but a single individual was observed on the Sierra
Nevada, and this one was obtained on the eastern slope of the range, near

---

[1] It has recently been obtained by Mr. Henshaw on the eastern slope, near Lake
Tahoe.

Carson City. It was very rare throughout western Nevada, but became abundant as we approached the higher mountains in the eastern portion of the State. Among the aspen groves in Parley's Park, as well as in similar places throughout that portion of the country, it was by far the most abundant of the Woodpeckers; and it seemed to be as strictly confined to the aspens as *S. thyroideus* was to the pines. Its nest was almost invariably in a living tree, into the soft wood of which it bored with the greatest ease, the excavation being at nearly all heights between eight and thirty feet from the ground, and almost invariably in the trunk of the tree. Both parents incubate and feed the young.

In its general manners, this species is quite a counterpart of the eastern Red-throated Woodpecker (*S. varius*), but its notes are quite appreciably different, the whining utterance so characteristic of all the species of the genus being less plaintive, while we heard other notes which we never knew the eastern bird to utter.

List of specimens.

490, ♀ *ad.;* Carson City, Nevada, April 4, 1868. Pines. 8¾—15½—5¼—4⅜. Bill, black; iris, dark bister; tarsi and toes, olive-cinereous.

936, ♀ *juv.;* Upper Humboldt Valley (Camp 25), September 18, 1868. 8⅜—15⅝—(?)—4¼. Bill, dark sepia-slate; iris, dark bister; tarsi and toes, olive-plumbeous.

938, ♂ *ad.;* Thousand Spring Valley (Camp 27), September 23, 1868. 8⅝—15½—(?)—4⅜. Bill, pure slaty-drab; iris, dark bister; tarsi and toes, greenish olive-cinereous.

1355, ♂ *ad.;* Parley Park, Wahsatch Mountains, Utah, July 1, 1869. 8⅝—15¾. Bill, deep black; iris, brown; feet, greenish-ashy.

1356, ♀ *ad.;* Parley's Park, Wahsatch Mountains, Utah, July 1, 1869. 8⅝—16. Same remarks. [*Stomachs of both specimens filled with ants.*]

1422, ♂ *ad.;* Parley's Park, July 17, 1869. 8¾—15¾. Bill, purplish-black; iris, brown; tarsi and toes, slaty-olive.

1429, ♀ *ad.;* Parley's Park, July 19, 1869. 8¼—15¼. Bill, black; iris, brown; tarsi and toes, olivaceous-blue.

1436, ♂ *ad.;* Parley's Park, July 21, 1869. 8¾—15¾. Bill, black; iris, umber; tarsi and toes, dull light blue.

1438, ♂ *ad.;* Parley's Park, July 22, 1869. 8—15⅝. Bill, black; iris, brown; legs and feet, olivaceous-blue.

1439, ♀ *ad.;* Parley's Park, July 22, 1869. 8½—15¼. Same remarks.

1440, ♀ *ad.;* Parley's Park, July 22, 1869. 8—14⅝. Same remarks.

1448, ♂ *ad.;* Parley's Park, July 23, 1869. 8¼—15. Bill, dark purplish-brown.

SPHYRAPICUS THYROIDEUS

Brown-headed Woodpecker: Williamson's Woodpecker.

Picus thyroideus, CASSIN, Pr. Ac. Nat. Sci. Philad., 1851, 349.

Sphyrapicus thyroideus. BAIRD, Birds N. Am., 1858, 106; Catal., 1859, No. 89.—
COOPER, Orn. Cal., I, 1870, 394.—COUES, Key, 1872, 195; Check List, 1873,
No. 304; Birds N.W., 1874, 288.—B. B. & R., Hist. N. Am. Birds, II, 1874,
547, pl. LVI, fig. 6 (" ♂ = ♀ with red streak on throat!).—HENSHAW, Am.
Nat., 1874, 242 [Identity of *thyroideus* and "*williamsoni*" demonstrated];
Wheeler's Rep., 1875, 394.

Picus williamsoni, NEWBERRY, Pacific R. R. Rep., VI, 1857, 89, pl. XXXIV, fig. 1
(young ♂, or adult ♂ with red of throat destroyed by action of alcohol; *formerly supposed to be* ♀!).

Sphyrapicus williamsoni, BAIRD, Birds N. Am., 1858, 105; Cat. N. Am. Birds, 1859,
No. 88.—COOPER, Orn. Cal., I, 1870, 393.—COUES, Key, 1872, 195; Check
List, 1873, No. 305.—B. B. & R., Hist. N. Am. Birds, II, 1874, 545, pl. LI,
fig. 5.

The discovery of the astonishing fact that the Brown-headed Woodpecker (*S. thyroideus*, Cass.) and Williamson's Woodpecker (*S. williamsoni*,
Newb.) are female and male of the same species, is due to the field-observations of Mr. H. W. Henshaw, the accomplished ornithologist of Lieutenant
Wheeler's expedition; the fact being first announced in 1874, in an article
in the *American Naturalist* (Vol. VIII, p. 242). A suspicion that the two
might eventually prove to be different plumages of one species several
times arose in our mind during the course of our field-work, the chief
occasion for which was the very suggestive circumstance that both were
invariably found in the same woods, and had identical manners and notes,
while they also agreed strictly in all the details of form and proportions,
as well as in the bright gamboge-yellow color of the belly. Our theory
that *thyroideus* was perhaps the *young*, and *williamsoni* the *adult*, proved
erroneous, however; and it never occurred to us that the differences might
be sexual, an oversight caused chiefly by the circumstance of our having
seen in collections many specimens of *thyroideus* with a red streak on the
throat and marked as males, while the type specimen of *williamsoni* had a
white streak on the throat and was said to be a female. We were thus
entirely misled by the erroneous identification of the sex in these speci-

mens. We gave the matter up, however, only after shooting a very young specimen of what was undoubtedly *williamsoni*, and another of *thyroideus*, both of which very closely resembled the adults of the same forms. a circumstance which at once convinced us that the differences could not depend on age; so we finally concluded that the two must be distinct. Now, however, that Mr. Henshaw has so satisfactorily explained the case, we have no hesitation in indorsing his opinion.

We found this species both on the Sierra Nevada and in the Wahsatch, and it is probable that its range extends throughout the entire Western Region. It is confined to the coniferous forests, however, so that its distribution is governed greatly by local conditions. It appears to be constantly pinicoline, since it was a winter resident among the pines near Carson City, while it was found in summer among those of the Wahsatch, in Parley's Park. Excepting the circumstance of its being so strictly confined to the coniferous forests, it resembles the other species of the genus in habits and manners, while the notes appear to be only very slightly different; the latter are finer and less plaintive, however, than in *nuchalis* or *varius*, and uttered in more detached syllables. The female of this species presents when flying a very close resemblance to the species of *Centurus*, the plumage being similarly barred with black and white, while a distinct white area is presented on the lower portion of the rump. The first male killed (No. 331) had the bill thickly coated with the resinous juices of the pine trees among which it had been feeding.

List of specimens.

331, ♂ ad.; pines of the Sierra Nevada, near Carson City, November 27, 1867. $9\frac{3}{4}$—19—$5\frac{1}{2}$—$4\frac{1}{4}$—1—$\frac{5}{8}$—$3\frac{1}{4}$—$1\frac{3}{4}$. Bill, deep purplish sepia-slate; iris, chestnut; tarsi and toes, ashy-olive.

332, ♀ ad.; Carson City, Nevada, November 27, 1867. $9\frac{1}{4}$—$16\frac{3}{4}$—$5\frac{5}{8}$—$4\frac{3}{4}$—$\frac{15}{16}$—$1\frac{1}{16}$—$3\frac{3}{4}$—$1\frac{3}{4}$. Bill, deep brownish-slate; iris, reddish-vandyke; tarsi and toes, ashy-olive.

437, ♀ ad.; Carson, March 10, 1868. $9\frac{1}{4}$—$16\frac{1}{2}$—$5\frac{5}{8}$—$4\frac{3}{4}$. Bill, dusky purplish-slate; iris, umber; tarsi and toes, light ashy-green. (*Tongue protrudes $\frac{3}{4}$ of an inch beyond bill; its corneous tip color of bill.*)

1486, ♂ juv.; Parley's Park, August 5, 1869. $9\frac{1}{2}$—$15\frac{1}{4}$. Bill, black; iris, dark brown; tarsi and toes, greenish-ashy.

1513, ♀ juv.; Parley's Park, Wahsatch Mountains, Utah, August 16, 1869.

MELANERPES FORMICIVORUS.

California Woodpecker.

Picus formicivorus, SWAINSON, Synop. Birds Mex., Philos. Mag., I, 1827, 439.
Melanerpes formicivorus, BONAP., Consp., I, 1850, 115.—BAIRD, B. N. Am., 1858,
   114; Cat. N. Am. B., 1859, No. 95.—COOPER, Orn. Cal., I, 1870, 403.—COUES,
   Key, 1872, 197; Check List, 1873, No. 310.—B. B. & R., Hist. N. Am. B., II,
   1874, 566, pl. LIII, figs. 1, 2.—HENSHAW, 1875, 399.

This handsome Woodpecker was observed only among the oaks in the
Sacramento Valley, where it sported among the trees along with Yellow-
billed Magpies and Valley Jays (*Cyanocitta californica*).   We had no opportunity to observe its habits closely.

MELANERPES TORQUATUS.

Lewis's Woodpecker.

Picus torquatus, WILSON, Am. Orn., III, 1811, 31, pl. 30, fig. 3.
Melanerpes torquatus, BONAP., Consp., I, 1850, 115.—BAIRD, B. N. Am., 1858, 115;
   Cat. N. Am. B., 1859, No. 96.—COOPER, Orn. Cal., I, 1870, 406.—B. B. & R.,
   Hist. N. Am. B., II, 1874, 561, pl. LIV, fig. 5.—HENSHAW, 1875, 397.
Asyndesmus torquatus, COUES, Pr. Ac. Nat. Sci. Phila., 1866, 56; Key, 1872, 197;
   Check List, 1873, No. 311; B. N.W., 1874, 291.

This very remarkable Woodpecker was found along the entire route,
from Sacramento eastward, but only in certain widely-separated localities.
It prefers the scattered trees of plains, or the mere edge of the denser
forests, and was consequently found most abundantly among the oaks of
the Sacramento Valley and the scattered pines along the eastern base
of the Sierra Nevada.   None were seen among the cotton-woods of the
Truckee or Carson Rivers, while only a few were noticed among the very
large aspens in the lower cañons of the East Humboldt Mountains, as well
as in similar groves along the streams of the Upper Humboldt Valley.
None were observed in the Wahsatch or Uintah Mountains, nor in the Salt
Lake Valley.   We cannot account for this apparent irregularity of its distribution, which is somewhat parallel to the case of *Pica hudsonica* in the
same region.

   In its general habits and manners this beautiful species resembles quite
closely the eastern Red-headed Woodpecker (*M. erythrocephalus*), being

quite as lively and of an equally playful disposition. Some of its actions, however, are very curious, the most remarkable of them being a certain elevated flight, performed in a peculiar floating manner, its progress apparently laborious, as if struggling against the wind, or uncertain, like a bird which had lost its course and become confused. At such a time it presents the appearance of a Crow high in the air, while the manner of its flight is strikingly similar to that of Clarke's Nutcracker (*Picicorvus columbianus*—see page 516). After performing these evolutions to its satisfaction, it descends in gradually contracting circles, often to the tree from which it started.

When a nest of this species in an oak tree was disturbed, the parents were observed to alight upon a large horizontal branch, and now and then cautiously look over at the intruder, at the same time uttering a faint rattling or twittering note. When frolicking among the trees the notes of this species are a faint shrill scream and a rattling twitter, somewhat like the notes of *M. erythrocephalus*, but much weaker.

List of specimens.

76, ♂ *ad.;* Sacramento City, California, June 22, 1867. $10\frac{3}{4}$—$20\frac{3}{4}$—$6\frac{5}{8}$—$5\frac{1}{2}$—$1\frac{1}{4}$—$\frac{3}{4}$—$3\frac{1}{2}$—$1\frac{3}{4}$. Bill, deep purplish-slate; iris, deep hazel; tarsi and toes, pale ashy-blue.

77, ♀ *ad.* (mate of No. 76); same locality and date. $10\frac{13}{16}$—$20\frac{5}{8}$—$6\frac{9}{16}$—$5\frac{1}{2}$—$1\frac{3}{16}$—$\frac{3}{4}$—$3\frac{3}{4}$—$1\frac{1}{2}$. Same remarks.

561, ♂ *ad.;* Carson City, Nevada, April 29, 1868. $11\frac{5}{8}$—$21\frac{3}{4}$—7—$5\frac{7}{8}$. Bill, black; iris, hazel; tarsi and toes, olivaceous-blue.

924, ♂ *ad.;* Upper Humboldt Valley (Camp 24), September 12, 1868. $11\frac{3}{8}$—$21\frac{1}{2}$—(?)—$5\frac{13}{16}$. Bill, slate-black, deeper terminally; iris, burnt-sienna; tarsi and toes, rather dark ashy.

MELANERPES ERYTHROCEPHALUS.

Red-headed Woodpecker.

Picus erythrocephalus, LINN., Syst. Nat., I, 1766, 174.

Melanerpes erythrocephalus, SWAINSON, Fauna Bor. Am., II, 1831, 316.—BAIRD, Birds N. Am., 1858, 113; Cat. N. Am. Birds, 1859, No. 94.—COOPER, Orn. Cal., I, 1870, 402.—COUES, Key, 1872, 196; Check List, 1873, No. 309; Birds N.W., 1874, 290.—B. B. & R., Hist. N. Am. Birds, II, 1874, 564, pl. LIV, fig. 4.—HENSHAW, 1875, 398.

A single individual of this common eastern species was seen near Salt Lake City in June, 1869, the one in question being observed among the willows along the stream flowing from Parley's Park. Eastward of the Rocky Mountains, as far west as Laramie, it was abundant about the telegraph-poles along the railroad.

COLAPTES MEXICANUS.

Red-shafted Flicker.

(*Tetsum'* of the Washoes; *Ah'soo-pannah* of the Paiutes; *Gooe-nee'-utz* of the Shoshones.)

Colaptes mexicanus, SWAINSON, Synop. Mex. Birds, Philos. Mag., I, 1827, 440. BAIRD, Birds N. Am., 1858, 120; Cat. N. Am. Birds, 1859, No. 98.—COOPER, Orn. Cal., I, 1870, 408.—COUES, Key, 1872, 198; Check List, 1873, No. 314; Birds N.W., 1874, 294.—B. B. & R., Hist. N. Am. Birds, II, 1874, 578, pl. LV, figs. 3, 4.—HENSHAW, 1875, 400.

Being the most abundant and generally distributed of the Woodpeckers, this species was found in all wooded localities; and though it appeared to be rather partial to the deciduous trees of the lower valleys, it was far from rare among the pines of the mountains, excepting in the denser portions of the forest. As to its general appearance, habits, and notes, it is a perfect counterpart of the eastern Yellow-shafted Flicker (*C. auratus*), its notes especially being absolutely undistinguishable; indeed so great is the similarity between the two species that the western bird is almost universally known as the "Yellow Hammer" by the people of that country, notwithstanding there is not a yellow feather in its plumage. It appeared to be far more shy than the eastern species, however, and we always found it difficult to secure, except when a heavy growth favored a near approach. This wildness may be partly accounted for by the eagerness with which these handsome birds are sought by the Indians, who highly prize the tail and quill-feathers as ornaments for their head-dresses.

List of specimens.

103, ♂ juv.; Truckee Reservation (Camp 12), Nevada, July 24, 1867. 13—20⅝— 6⅛—5¼—1⅜—⅞—4¼—3⅛. Bill, brownish-black; iris, chestnut; tarsi and toes, pale livid blue.

126, ♂ *juv.;* Camp 12, August 1, 1867. $13\frac{1}{4}$—$20\frac{1}{2}$—$6\frac{7}{16}$—$5\frac{3}{8}$—$1\frac{9}{16}$—$\frac{7}{8}$—$4\frac{1}{2}$—$3\frac{3}{16}$. Same remarks.

241, ♂ *ad.;* West Humboldt Mountains (Camp 19), October 8, 1867. 13—21—$6\frac{1}{2}$—$5\frac{5}{16}$—$1\frac{1}{2}$—$\frac{15}{16}$—$4\frac{1}{2}$—$2\frac{1}{4}$. Bill, slate-black, deeper terminally; iris, deep chestnut; naked eyelids, tarsi and toes, fine pale lilaceous-blue.

357, ♂ *ad.;* Truckee Reservation, December 18, 1867. $13\frac{1}{2}$—21—$6\frac{3}{4}$—$5\frac{5}{8}$—$1\frac{11}{16}$—1—5—$2\frac{1}{4}$. Iris, deep cherry-red.

363, ♂ *ad.;* Truckee Reservation, December 19, 1867. 14—$21\frac{1}{2}$—7—$5\frac{3}{4}$—$1\frac{5}{8}$—1—5—$2\frac{1}{4}$. Same remarks.

374, ♂ *ad.;* Truckee Reservation, December 21, 1867. $13\frac{3}{8}$—$21\frac{1}{4}$—$6\frac{7}{8}$—$5\frac{3}{4}$. Same remarks.

391, ♂ *ad.;* Washoe Valley, January 3, 1868. $13\frac{1}{4}$—21—$6\frac{13}{16}$—$5\frac{5}{8}$. Same remarks.

393, ♀ *ad.;* Washoe Valley, January 4, 1868. $12\frac{3}{4}$—$20\frac{1}{2}$—$6\frac{5}{8}$—$5\frac{7}{16}$.

461, ♂ *ad.;* Carson City, March 28, 1868. $13\frac{1}{2}$—22—$6\frac{15}{16}$—$5\frac{3}{4}$.

462, ♂ *ad.;* same locality and date. $13\frac{1}{2}$—22—$6\frac{7}{8}$—$5\frac{3}{4}$.

481, ♀ *ad.;* same locality, March 30, 1868. $13\frac{3}{8}$—$21\frac{1}{4}$—$6\frac{7}{8}$—$5\frac{11}{16}$.

736, eggs (5); Truckee Reservation, May 17, 1868. Excavation in a small willow, on bank of the river.

1345, ♂ *juv.;* Parley's Park, Utah, June 28, 1869.

1428, ♂ *juv.;* Parley's Park, Utah, July 19, 1869. $12\frac{1}{2}$—$20\frac{1}{4}$. Bill, slate-black; iris, bister; tarsi and toes, light ashy-blue.

COLAPTES HYBRIDUS.[1]

"Hybrid" Flicker.

Colaptes ayresii, AUDUBON, Birds Am., VII, 1843, 348, pl. 494.

Colaptes hybridus, BAIRD, Birds N. Am., 1858, 122; Cat. N. Am. Birds, 1859, No. 98a.—B. B. & R., Hist. N. Am. Birds, II, 1874, 582, pl. LIV, fig. 3.

List of specimens.

400, ♂; Washoe Valley, January 4, 1868. 13—$20\frac{3}{4}$—$6\frac{3}{4}$—$5\frac{5}{8}$.

[General appearance of typical *mexicanus*, having ashy throat and scarlet "moustaches," but occiput with a distinct scarlet crescent, and the red of the remiges and rectrices inclining decidedly to orange.]

[1] Whether the puzzling specimens included under this name are really hybrids, or whether they are remnants of a generalized form from which two "incipient species" have become differentiated, must long remain an open question. The latter view, however, seems the more rational; and it is altogether probable that this "hybrid" series is gradually losing its neutral character, through the nearer approach, generation by generation, of its members to the characters of one or the other of the two specialized forms. [For a full and very sensible discussion of this subject, see Coues's *Birds of the Northwest*, pp. 293, 294.]

COLAPTES AURATUS?

Yellow-shafted Flicker.

Cuculus auratus, LINN., Syst. Nat., I (ed. 10), 1758, 112.
Colaptes auratus, SWAINS., Zool. Journ., III, 1827, 353.—BAIRD, Birds N. Am.,
1858, 118; Catal. N. Am. B., 1859, No. 97.—COUES, Key, 1872, 197; Check
List, 1873, No. 312; Birds N.W., 1874, 292.

Early in October, 1867, we saw near Unionville, in the West Humboldt Mountains, a Flicker which had bright gamboge-yellow shafts to the quills and tail-feathers. It flew from the brushwood of a ravine close by, and was followed over the hills, from rock to rock, through the sage-brush and across fields, and from one ravine to another, for nearly an hour, until it finally disappeared. It was so extremely shy that we found it impossible to get within fair gunshot range, but several shots were risked at it, one of which brought several feathers, which on examination were found to be pure, bright gamboge-yellow, without the faintest trace of orange. On the 22d of November following, a similar individual was seen among the willows along the Truckee River, at the Glendale Meadows; but being on the opposite side of the stream, it could not be obtained. Whether these birds were the typical eastern *C. auratus* or *C. chrysoides*[1] of the southern portion of the Middle Province, we cannot, of course, be sure; but geographical considerations render the former more probable. It is almost certain they were not specimens of *C. hybridus*, since the latter is seldom, if ever, without more or less of an orange tinge to the wings and tail.[2]

---

[1] *Geopicus chrysoides*, MALHERBE, Rev. et Mag. Zool., IV, 1852, 553.
Colaptes chrysoides, BAIRD, Birds N. Am., 1858, 125; Cat. N. Am. Birds, 1859, No. 99.—COOPER, Orn. Cal., I, 1870, 410.—COUES, Key, 1872, 198; Check List, 1873, No. 313.—B., B. & R., Hist. N. Am. Birds, II, 1874, 583, pl. LIV, figs. 1, 2.

[2] In the "Ornithology of California," page 412, Dr. J. G. Cooper mentions two specimens from Oakland, near San Francisco, " which are evidently of the form *hybridus*, Baird," one of which " differs from the *auratus* only in having the head grayish like *mexicanus* and the *black* of the cheek-feathers tipped with *red*."

Family CUCULIDÆ—Cuckoos.

COCCYZUS AMERICANUS.

Yellow-billed Cuckoo.

Cuculus americanus, LINN., Syst. Nat., I, 1766, 170.

Coccyzus americanus, BONAP., Obs. Wils. Orn., 1825, No. 47.—COUES, Key, 1872, 190, fig. 126; Check List, 1873, No. 291; B. N.W., 1874, 275.

Coccygus americanus, BAIRD, B. N. Am., 1858, 76; Cat. N. Am. B., 1859, No. 69.— COOPER, Orn. Cal., I, 1870, 371.—B. B. & R., Hist. N. Am. B., II, 1874, 477, pl. XLVIII, fig. 4 ("3" err.).—HENSHAW, 1875, 386.

The Yellow-billed Cuckoo was so often seen or heard during our sojourn in the West, that we cannot regard it as a particularly rare bird in certain portions of that country. At Sacramento City its well-known notes were heard on more than one occasion in June, among the oak groves in the outskirts of the city, while across the Sierra Nevada several individuals were seen in July in the wooded valley of the lower Truckee.

Family TROCHILIDÆ—Humming-birds.

CALYPTE ANNÆ.

Anna's Hummer.

Ornismya anna, LESSON, Oiseaux Mouches, 1830, pl. CXXIV.

Athis anna, BAIRD, B. N. Am., 1858, 137; Cat. N. Am. B., 1859, No. 105.

Calypte annæ, GOULD, Introd. Trochilidæ, 1861, 88.—B. B. & R., Hist. N. Am. B., 1874, 454, pl. XLVII, fig. 7.—HENSHAW, 1875, 375.

Selasphorus anna, COUES, Key, 1872, 185; Check List, 1873, No. 279.

Calypte anna, COOPER, Orn. Cal.. I, 1870, 358.

This beautiful Hummer was found only at Sacramento City, where it was rare, or at least far less common than the *Trochilus alexandri*. We did not see enough of it to detect anything distinctive in its habits.

List of specimens.

10, nest and eggs (2); Sacramento City, California, June 9, 1867. Nest at extremity of a small dead twig, underneath lower branches of small oak, in grove.

TROCHILUS ALEXANDRI.

Black-chinned Hummer.

(*Soong-ooh'-eh* of the Paiutes.)

Trochilus alexandri, BOURCIER & MULSANT, Ann. de la Soc. d'Agric. de Lyons, IX, 1846, 330.—BAIRD, B. N. Am., 1858, 133; ed. 1860, pl. 44, fig. 3; Cat. N. Am. B., 1859, No. 102.—COOPER, Orn. Cal., I, 1870, 353.—COUES, Key, 1872, 184; Check List, 1873, 276.—B. B. & R., Hist. N. Am. B., II, 1874, 450, pl. XLVII, fig. 1.—HENSHAW, 1875, 373.

This was the only Hummer which was encountered along every portion of our route, in the proper localities, it being equally common at Sacramento City and among the mountains of Utah, as well as at favorable intermediate points.   Since we found it in the Wahsatch, where it was associated with *Selasphorus platycercus*, among the flowery meadows of the higher slopes, it will be seen that its vertical range during the breeding-season extends through fully 9,000 feet of altitude.   At Sacramento it nested in the oak groves in the outskirts of the city, where it was apparently more numerous than *Calypte annæ;* while in the Interior it was equally common in the river-valleys and on the higher slopes of the mountains.   In its habits it appeared to be a perfect counterpart of the eastern Ruby-throat (*T. colubris*).

List of specimens.

776, nest and eggs (2); Truckee Reservation, June 1, 1868.   Nest attached to dead twig of grease-wood bush, on river-bank.

777, ♂ ad. (parent of the preceding). $3\frac{13}{16}$—$4\frac{3}{8}$—(?)—$1\frac{5}{8}$.   Bill, black; iris, deep sepia; tarsi and toes, black.

1285, nest and eggs (2); Parley's Park, June 25, 1869.   Nest on branch of scrub-oak, in a grove.

1352, ♀ ad.; Parley's Park, Utah, June 28, 1869. $3\frac{7}{8}$—$4\frac{3}{4}$.   Bill, black; iris, very dark brown; tarsi and toes, purplish-black.

1483, ♂ juv.; Parley's Park, July 30, 1869. $3\frac{7}{8}$—$4\frac{3}{8}$.   Same remarks.

SELASPHORUS RUFUS.

Rufous Hummer.

(*Soong-ooh'-eh* of the Paiutes.)

Trochilus rufus, GMELIN, Syst. Nat., I, 1788, 497.

Selasphorus rufus, SWAINSON, Fauna Bor. Am., II, 1831, 324.—BAIRD, B. N. Am., 1858, 134; Cat. N. Am. B., 1859, No. 103.—COOPER, Orn. Cal., I, 355.—COUES, Key, 1872, 185; Check List, 1873, No. 277.—B. B. & R., Hist. N. Am. B., II, 1874, 452, pl. XLVII, fig. 4.—HENSHAW, 1875, 375.

Among the sun-flowers (*Helianthus giganteus ?*), which covered acres of ground, in the rich valley of the lower Truckee, this was the only species of Humming-bird found in August, at which time great numbers were seen sporting in all their elegance and beauty among these flowers; they displayed the greatest activity and grace of motion, and were ever restless and moving, now chasing each other, then hovering in front of a golden flower for a few moments, then off like a flash. Upon revisiting the same locality in May and June of the following season, not one of this species was to be found, its place being apparently entirely taken by the Black-chinned species (*Trochilus alexandri*). We next saw the Rufous-backed Hummer in the fertile cañons of the West Humboldt Mountains, where it was more or less common in October. Eastward of the latter locality, the species was seen only in Secret Valley, near the northern extremity of the East Humboldt range, where it was much more rare than *S. platycercus*, this point being the most eastern to which it is known to extend, so far as we are at present aware. It was not found during the breeding-season anywhere along our route.

List of specimens.

124, ♂ juv.; Truckee Reservation, Nevada, August 6, 1867. $3\frac{11}{16}$—$4\frac{1}{4}$—$1\frac{3}{4}$—$1\frac{1}{2}$— $\frac{11}{16}$—$\frac{1}{16}$—1—$\frac{3}{8}$. Bill and feet, black; iris, dark brown.

905, ♂ juv.; East Humboldt Mountains (Camp 23), September 8, 1868. $3\frac{3}{8}$—$4\frac{7}{16}$ —$1\frac{7}{16}$.

SELASPHORUS PLATYCERCUS.

Broad-tailed Hummer.

(*Pe'-esh-a-tse* and *Toowith'-e-kim'-booah* of the Shoshones.)

Trochilus platycercus, SWAINSON, Synop. Mex. Birds, Philos. Mag., I, 1827, 441.
Selasphorus platycercus, BONAP., Consp., I, 1850. 82.—BAIRD, B. N. Am., 1858, 135, 922; Cat. N. Am. B., 1859, No. 104. —COOPER, Orn. Cal., I, 357.—COUES, Key, 1872, 185; Check List, 1873, No. 278; Birds N.W., 1874, 271.—B. B & R., Hist. N. Am. B., II, 1874, 462, pl. XLVII, fig. 5 —HENSHAW, 1875, 377.

In traveling eastward across the Great Basin, we first encountered the Broad-tailed Hummer on the Ruby Mountains, where it was very abundant in July and August, on the flower-covered slopes of the upper cañons on the eastern side of the range, in company with *Stellula calliope*; in September we found it associated with the latter species and *Selasphorus rufus* in the northern continuation of the same range (the East Humboldt Mountains), while on the Wahsatch and Uintahs it was found still more abundantly throughout the summer in company with *Trochilus alexandri*. The distribution of Humming-birds being governed by the presence or absence of tracts where a profusion of flowers flourish, this species is consequently mainly confined to the higher slopes of the mountains; but whenever a portion of the lower valleys is made to bloom by irrigation, this Hummer soon finds it out and at once appears. Under such circumstances its vertical range is very great, amounting, in one instance which came under our observation, to fully 6,000 feet; for one morning we killed a specimen near the ranche in Ruby Valley, and later during the same day, when we had ascended to the summit of one of the highest peaks, which towered to nearly 12,000 feet, a single individual buzzed past us.

The flight of this Humming-bird is unusually rapid, and that of the male is accompanied by a curious screeching buzz, while it is followed through an undulating course. Long before the author of this curious sound was detected its source was a mystery to us. This shrill screeching note is heard only when the bird is passing rapidly through the air, for when hovering among the flowers its flight is accompanied by only the usual muffled hum common to all the species of the family. During the nesting-season the male is of an exceedingly quarrelsome disposition, and intrepid, probably beyond any other bird, the Flycatchers not excepted. All birds that approach the vicinity of his nest, whether they be his own species or of the size of hawks, are immediately assaulted with great force and pertinacity by this seemingly insignificant little creature, the vigor of whose attacks, accompanied as they are by the shrill piercing noise we have mentioned, invariably puts to flight any bird assaulted. We have thus seen the Western Kingbird (*Tyrannus verticalis*), the Black-headed Grosbeak (*Hedymeles melanocephalus*), and the Sharp-shinned Hawk (*Nisus fuscus*) beat a hasty retreat before the persevering assaults of this Humming-bird. When thus teasing an intruder the little champion ascends almost perpendicularly to a considerable height, and then descends with the quickness of a flash at the object he would annoy, which is probably more frightened by the accompanying noise than by the mere attack itself. As we chanced, while hunting

36 P R

on the mountains, to pass through the haunts of this Hummer, it frequently happened that one of the little creatures, prompted apparently by curiosity, would approach close to us and remain poised in one spot, its wings vibrating so rapidly as to appear as a mere haze around the body; now and then it would shift from one side to another, its little black eyes sparkling as it eyed us intently. So close would it finally approach that to strike it with the hat or a stick seemed to be quite an easy matter, but upon the slightest motion on our part the little thing would vanish so quickly that its direction could scarcely be traced.

On the mountains we found many nests of this Humming-bird, every one of them being discovered by frightening the female from off her eggs or young. They were variously situated, most of them being in the scrub-oaks on the slopes of the hills; many were in willows or other bushes bordering the streams, and not a few on drooping twigs of cotton-wood trees, along the water-courses. One of those which we secured (No. 1377) affords good evidence of the possession by this bird of a high degree of instinct, if not an approach to reason. This nest was built upon a dead twig of a small cotton-wood; the bark of this twig gradually loosened, and after the eggs were laid slipped around (perhaps by the parent bird alighting upon one edge of the nest), so that the nest was turned round to the under side of the limb and the eggs thrown out. Instead of abandoning this nest, however, the sharp little owners built an addition to it, making another complete nest on the upper side, which was now secured in position by the superior weight of the more bulky pendant one.[1]

List of specimens.

963, ♂ ad.; Salt Lake City, May 20, 1869, (City Creek Cañon). 4—4⅞. Bill and feet black; iris, dark sepia.

1042, ♂ ad.; Salt Lake City, May 24, 1869. 4—5. Same remarks.

1054, ♂ ad.; Salt Lake City, May 26, 1869. 4—4¹³⁄₁₆. Same remarks.

1064, ♂ ad.; Salt Lake City, May 29, 1869. 4—4¹⁵⁄₁₆. Same remarks.

1272, ♀ ad.; Parley's Park, June 23, 1869. 4⅛—5³⁄₁₆. (Caught in a tent during a hard shower.)

1311, ♂ ad.; Parley's Park, June 28, 1869. 4.

---

[1] In Gould's *Introduction to the Trochilidæ* (page 20), it is stated that certain South American Humming-Birds adjust the equilibrium of their nests by weighting the lighter side with a small stone or bit of hard earth!

1312. ♂ ad.; Parley's Park, June 28, 1869. 4.

1319, nest and eggs (2); Parley's Park, June 26, 1869. Nest on drooping branch of a cotton-wood tree, by a stream.

1332, nest and eggs (2); Parley's Park, June 28, 1869. Nest on bush, along stream.

1333, nest; Parley's Park, June 28, 1869. Nest on drooping branch of a cotton-wood tree, by stream.

1348, ♂ ad.; Parley's Park, June 28, 1869.

1349, ♂ ad.; Parley's Park, June 28, 1869.

1350, ♂ ad.; Parley's Park, June 28, 1869.

1351, ♂ ad.; Parley's Park, June 28, 1869.

1366, nest and eggs (2); Uintah Mountains (Pack's Cañon), July 3, 1869. Nest in a sage-bush.

1377, nest; Pack's Cañon, July 7, 1869. Nest on dead twig of a small cotton-wood.

1437, ♂ ad.; Parley's Park, July 21, 1869.

1441, nest and eggs (2); Parley's Park, July 23, 1869. Nest among willows, along stream.

1442, nest and eggs (2); same date and remarks.

1449, ♀ ad.; Parley's Park, July 23, 1869.

STELLULA CALLIOPE.

Calliope Hummer.

Trochilus calliope, GOULD, Proc. Zool. Soc. Lond., 1847, 11.

Stellula calliope, GOULD, Introd. Trochilidæ, 1861, 90.—COOPER, Orn. Cal., I, 1870, 363.—COUES, Key, 1872; Check List, 1873, No. 282.—B. B. & R., Hist. N. Am. Birds, II, 1874, 445, pl. XLVII, fig. 9.—HENSHAW, 1875, 372.

On the flowery slopes of the Ruby and East Humboldt Mountains, at an altitude of 7,500–10,000 feet, this little Hummer was abundant in August and September, in company with *Selasphorus platycercus;* the habits and appearance of the two species being so much alike that we never knew which was before us until the specimen was secured. The range of the species is doubtless almost universal throughout the Basin, like that of *Trochilus alexandri* and *Selasphorus rufus.*

List of specimens.

869, ♀ ad.; East Humboldt Mountains (Camp 19), August 12, 1868. $3\frac{2}{16}$—$4\frac{1}{4}$—(?)—$1\frac{3}{4}$. Bill and feet, black; iris, very dark brown.

882, ♂ juv.; East Humboldt Mountains (Camp 21), August 29, 1868. $3\frac{15}{16}$—$4\frac{13}{16}$—(?)—$1\frac{5}{8}$. Same remarks.

904, ♀ ad.; Secret Valley (Camp 22), September 7, 1868. $3\frac{1}{2}$—(?)—(?)—$1\frac{9}{16}$. Same remarks.

FAMILY CYPSELIDÆ—SWIFTS.

PANYPTILA SAXATILIS.

White-throated Swift.

Acanthylis saxatilis, WOODHOUSE, Sitgreaves' Rep., 1853, 64.

Panyptila saxatilis, COUES, Key, 1872, 182; Check List, 1873, No. 269; Birds
 N.W., 1874, 265.—HENSHAW, 1875, 370.

Cypselus melanoleucus, BAIRD, Pr. Ac. Nat. Sci. Philad., 1854, 118.

Panyptila melanoleuca, BAIRD, Birds N. Am., 1858, 141; Cat. N. Am. Birds, 1859,
 No. 107.—COOPER, Orn. Cal., I, 1870, 347.—B. B. & R., Hist. N. Am. Birds,
 II, 1874, 424, pl. XLV, fig. 5.

We first noticed this singular bird in the early part of July, 1868, on
the Toyabe Mountains, near Austin. A single individual only was observed
at that place, the one in question passing rapidly by, as if bound for some
distant locality; the direction of its course was southward, where the peaks
of the range are more lofty and precipitous, so it is probable that in favorable portions of these mountains the species may have occurred in abundance. Upon arriving at the Ruby Mountains, a little later in the same
month, we found it extremely numerous about the high limestone cliffs
which formed the walls of the cañons leading back from our camp. At
this place they literally swarmed, and were associated with smaller numbers
of *Petrochelidon lunifrons* and *Tachycineta thalassina*, both of which nested
among the same rocks. It was afterward seen in City Creek Cañon, near
Salt Lake City, but it was not abundant there.

The appearance of this bird calls to mind at first sight the Chimney
Swifts (*Chætura pelagica* and *C. rauxi*) on a large scale, or *Nephœcetes*, but
it has more conspicuous colors, and more active and varied manners; the
deeply-forked tail, and the abrupt contrast between the black and white
areas of its plumage distinguishing it at a glance from all other North
American Swifts. It was our frequent amusement to clamber half-way up
a cliff, or to where farther progress was impossible, and, hidden among the
rocks, watch the movements of these extraordinarily active birds. Every
few moments a pair would rush by with such velocity as to be scarcely
seen, one chasing the other, and both uttering a sharp rattling twitter.
Another pair would collide high up in the air, and, fastening upon each

other with their strong claws, come whirling to the ground, just before reaching which they would loosen their clutches and separate, or after again ascending resume the struggle. Others hovered around overhead, and without seeming aware of our presence, entered, now and then, the small horizontal fissures in the overhanging cliff to their nests, which were utterly inaccessible.

Specimens of this bird were extremely difficult to procure from the fact that most of those shot fell among the rocks where they could not be reached, while when away from the cliffs they flew at too great a height to be reached with shot.

The notes of this Swift are strong and rattling, sometimes rather shrill, certain ones resembling very much the chatter of young Baltimore Orioles (*Icterus baltimore*) as uttered while being fed by their parents.

List of specimens.

836, ♂ *ad.;* Camp 19, East Humboldt Mountains, July 13, 1868. $6\frac{11}{16}$—$13\frac{3}{4}$—(?)— $4\frac{7}{8}$. Bill, deep black; iris, dark bister; tarsi and toes, pale livid-pinkish; naked eyelids, sepia-brown.

837, ♀ *ad.;* same locality and date. $6\frac{1}{2}$—14—(?)—$4\frac{15}{16}$.

846, ♂ *ad.;* same locality, July 20, 1868. 7—$14\frac{1}{8}$—(?)—5. Interior of mouth, livid flesh-color.

NEPHŒCETES NIGER.

Black Swift.

β. borealis.

Cypselus borealis, KENNERLY, Pr. Ac. Nat. Sci. Philad., 1857, 202.
Nephœcetes niger var. *borealis,* COUES, Key, 1872, 183; Check List, 1873, No. 270.
Nephœcetes niger. b. *borealis,* COUES, Birds N.W., 1874, 269.
Nephœcetes niger, BAIRD, Birds N. Am., 1858, 142; Cat. N. Am. Birds, 1859, No. 108, [not *Hirundo nigra,* GMEL.,1788, = *Nephœcetes* [1]].—COOPER, Orn. Cal., I, 1870, 349.—B. B. & R., Hist. N. Am. B., 429, pl. XLV, fig. 4.

The occurrence of this Swift in the valley of the Truckee was made known to us only through the discovery of the remains of an individual which had been devoured by a hawk or owl, the sternum, wings, tail, and feet having been left upon a log in a cotton-wood grove. On the 23d of

---

[1] The West Indian form.

June, following, we found it abundant in a very similar portion of the valley of Carson River; they were observed early in the morning, hovering over the cotton-wood groves in a large swarm, after the manner of Night-Hawks (*Chordeiles*), but in their flight resembling the Chimney Swifts (*Chætura*), as they also did in their uniform dusky color, the chief apparent difference being their much larger size. They were evidently breeding in the locality, but whether their nests were in the hollow cotton-wood trees of the extensive groves along the river, or in crevices on the face of a high cliff which fronted the river near by, we were unable to determine on account of the shortness of our stay. They were perfectly silent during the whole time they were observed.

List of specimens.

807, wings, tail, feet, and sternum; Truckee Reservation, May 31, 1868. (Found on a log in the woods, where left by a hawk or owl.)

? CHÆTURA VAUXI.

Oregon Swift.

Cypselus vauxii, TOWNSEND, Journ. Acad. Nat. Sci. Philad., VIII, 1839, 148.
Chætura vauxii, DEKAY, Zool. New York, II, 1844, 36.—BAIRD, Birds N. Am., 1858, 145; ed. 1860, pl. 18; Cat. N. Am. Birds, 1859, No. 110.—COOPER, Orn. Cal., I, 1870, 351.—COUES, Key, 1872, 183; Check List, 1873, No. 272; Birds N.W., 1874, 268.
Chætura (pelagica var.?) *vauxi*, B. B. & R., Hist. N. Am. Birds, II, 1874, 435, pl. XLV, fig. 8.

During our sojourn at the Truckee Reservation, near Pyramid Lake, in May and June, 1868, we saw, nearly every evening, but never until after sundown, quite a number of small Swifts which must have been this species; but they always flew at so great a height that we found it impossible to obtain a specimen in order to determine the species. In appearance, manner of flight, and, apparently, in size also, they resembled the eastern Chimney Swift (*C. pelagica*), but they differed in their entirely crepuscular habits, and the fact that they were perfectly silent—the latter in particular being a very marked difference from the eastern species.

FAMILY CAPRIMULGIDÆ—GOATSUCKERS.

ANTROSTOMUS NUTTALLI.

Poor-will.

.(*Koo-ta-guck'* of the Paiutes; *Toet-sa-guck'* of the Shoshones.)

Caprimulgus nuttalli, AUDUBON, Orn. Biog., V, 1839, 335.
Antrostomus nuttalli, CASSIN, Journ. Ac. Nat. Sci. Philad., II, 1852, 123.—BAIRD,
　　Birds N. Am., 1858, 149; Cat. N. Am. Birds, 1859, No. 113.—COOPER, Orn.
　　Cal., I, 1870, 341.—COUES, Key, 1872, 181; Check List, 1873, No. 266; Birds
　　N.W., 1874, 261.—B. B. & R., Hist. N. Am. B., II, 1874, 417, pl. XLVI, fig. 3.
　　—HENSHAW, 1875, 369.

Unlike its eastern representative, the well-known Whip-poor-will (*A.
vociferus*), this western species is an inhabitant of open places exclusively,
the sage-brush country being, so far as we observed, its only habitat. It
appeared to be most abundant on the *mesas* and about the foot-hills of the
mountains, but it was often observed or heard in the lower valleys, as well
as in the mountain-parks, below an altitude of 8,000 feet. This bird was
seen only when startled from the ground by our too near approach, when
it would fly up suddenly and flutter off in a manner similar to that of
certain Owls, the flight being also noiseless. Often while returning late
from the mountains, and while following the road or trail homeward across
the *mesa*, we have beheld one of these birds start up in front of us, as
noiselessly as a shadow, again settling down a few rods ahead; we have
followed one thus for a hundred yards or more before it would diverge
from our course.

The call of this bird is somewhat like that of the Whip-poor-will,
but is far less distinctly uttered, as well as weaker, sounding more like
poor-will, the last syllable only being distinctly enunciated. This call we
have heard at all hours of the day, but they sing most vigorously as night
approaches. Both sexes incubate.

List of specimens.

799, ♂ ad.; Truckee Reservation, Nevada, June 3, 1868. $8\frac{3}{16}$—$17\frac{1}{2}$—(?)—5. Bill,
black; iris, raw-umber; tarsi and toes, dusky sepia.

843, eggs 2; East Humboldt Mountains, July 20, 1868. Deposited on bare
ground, beneath sage-bush, on hill-side. Male killed while flying from eggs.

844, ♂ ad. (parent of preceding); East Humboldt Mountains, July 20, 1868. 8¼—17¾—(?)—4⅜. Bill, deep black; interior of the mouth, flesh-color; iris (very narrow), umber; eyelids, ochraceous-brown; tarsi, pale ashy-lilaceous, the toes darker.

937, ♂ ad.; Upper Humboldt Valley, September 19, 1868. 8⅜—17⅞—(?)—5. Same remarks.

1379, ♂ ad.; Uintah Mountains, Utah, July 7, 1869. 8¼—17¾. Bill, black; iris (narrowly), brown; eyelids, dull ochraceous; tarsi and toes, dull dusky purplish.

CHORDEILES POPETUE.

Night-Hawk.

β. henryi.

(*Kow'a-look* of the Washoes; *Wy'-e-up-ah'-oh* of the Shoshones.)

Chordeiles henryi, CASSIN, Illust. Birds Cal., Texas. &c., 1855, 239.—BAIRD, Birds N. Am., 1858, 153, 922; Cat. N. Am. Birds, 1859, No. 115.

Chordeiles popetue var. henryi, ALLEN, Bull. Mus. Comp. Zool., III, 1872, 179.— B. B. & R., Hist. N. Am. Birds, II, 1874, 404, pl. XLVI, fig. 4.—HENSHAW, 1875, 367.

Chordeiles virginianus var. henryi, COUES, Key, 1872, 181; Check List, 1873, No. 267a.

Chordeiles virginianus. b. henryi, COUES, Birds N.W., 1874, 264.

Chordeiles popetue, COOPER, Orn. Cal., I, 1870, 343.

The Night-Hawk was a common summer inhabitant of the country traversed. It was most numerous during the months of August and September, when just before dark they congregated in immense numbers and overspread in scattered flocks those localities where insect-life most abounded. In July, their well-known booming sound was often heard. During the greater portion of the day they remained inactive, and were then frequently surprised during their *siesta*, as they perched on a horizontal limb, a board of a fence, or a stick lying on the ground, their position being, according to our experience, invariably lengthwise with the perch.[1] While thus resting they often evince a strong attachment to the perch they occupy, returning

---

[1] This disposition to sit lengthwise with the perch may be considered by some a constant habit of the Caprimulgidæ; we should be inclined to so regard it ourselves, were it not for the fact that the first specimen of *Antrostomus vociferus* we ever killed was shot while asleep on a small branch of a hickory tree, its position being at right-angles with the direction of the twig, in the manner usual among the true "perchers" (Passeres, etc.).

to it repeatedly when frightened away; No. 118 of the specimens enumerated below being killed after it had been frightened off a stick lying on the ground in a corral three times by unsuccessful shots at it. In all its habits, as well as in the notes, there appears to be no difference whatever between the western and eastern birds of this species.

List of specimens.

118, ♂ ad.; Truckee Valley, Nevada, August 4, 1867. 9½—23¾—7$\frac{13}{16}$—6$\frac{9}{16}$—1—$\frac{5}{16}$—4¼—2¼. Bill, black; iris, dark hazel; tarsi and toes, dusky purplish.

842, 1 egg; East Humboldt Mountains, Nevada, July 17, 1868. Egg on the bare ground, beneath a sage-bush.

856, ♂ ad.; East Humboldt Mountains, Nevada, August 4, 1868. 9¾—23½—(?)—6⅞. Same remarks.

857, ♂ ad.; same locality and date. 10—23½—(?)—6. Same remarks.

1344, ♂ ad.; Parley's Park, Utah, June 28, 1869.

1383, 1 egg; Uintah Mountains (head of Du Chesne River), Utah, July 8, 1869.

1426, 1 egg; Parley's Park, July 17, 1869.

1443, 2 eggs; Parley's Park, July 23, 1869.

1450, ♂ ad.; Parley's Park, July 24, 1869. 9⅛—23¼.

1507, ♀ ad.; Parley's Park, August 13, 1869. 9⅛—22½.

1514, ♀ ad.; Parley Park, August 26, 1869. 9½—23¼.

FAMILY STRIGIDÆ—OWLS.

STRIX FLAMMEA.

Barn Owl.

β. pratincola.

Strix pratincola, BONAPARTE, Comp. & Geog. List, 1838, 7.—CASSIN, in Baird's Birds N. Am., 1858, 47.—BAIRD, Cat. N. Am. Birds, 1859, No. 47.—COOPER, Orn., Cal., I, 415.

Strix pratincola var. *pratincola,* RIDGWAY, B. B. & R., Hist. N. Am. Birds, III, 1874, 13.

Strix americana, AUDUBON, Synopsis, 1839, 25.

Strix flammea americana, SCHLEG., Mus. Pays-Bas, 1862, Striges, 4.

Strix flammea var. *americana,* COUES, Key, 1872, 201, fig. 134; Check List, 1873, No. 316; Birds N.W., 1874, 298.

The Barn Owl was seen only in the vicinity of Sacramento, the single one observed being frightened from a hollow tree.

List of specimens.

422 ♂ *ad.*; "San Francisco, California, February 11, 1868. $14\frac{3}{4}$—$42\frac{1}{2}$—(?)—$11\frac{1}{4}$. Bill, bluish-yellow, growing white at the point; eyes, blue-black." (Presented by Mr. H. G. Parker.)

OTUS WILSONIANUS.

Long-eared Owl.

Otus wilsonianus, LESSON, Traité Orn., I, 1831, 110.—CASSIN, in Baird's B. N. Am., 1858, 53.—BAIRD, Cat. N. Am. Birds, 1859, No. 51.—COOPER, I, 1870, 426.

Otus vulgaris var. *wilsonianus*, ALLEN, Bull. Mus. Comp. Zool., III, 1872, 180.—COUES, Key, 1872, 204; Check List, 1873, No. 320; Birds N.W., 1874, 304.—B. B. & R., Hist. N. Am. Birds, III, 1874, 18.—HENSHAW, 1875, 403.

Seldom, if ever, did we enter a willow-copse of any extent, during our explorations in the West, without starting one or more specimens of this Owl from the depths of the thicket. This was the case both near Sacramento and in the Interior, and in summer as well as in winter. In these thickets they find many deserted nests of the Magpie, and selecting the most dilapidated of these, deposit their eggs on a scant additional lining. This practice is so general, so far as the birds of the Interior are concerned, that we never found the eggs or young of this species except as described above. On the 27th of May we found a nest containing four downy young among the willows along the bank of the Truckee River.

List of specimens.

56, ♂ *ad.*; Sacramento, California, June 18, 1867. $14\frac{1}{2}$—$39\frac{1}{2}$—$12\frac{1}{4}$—$10\frac{3}{4}$—$\frac{13}{16}$—$1\frac{3}{4}$—$6\frac{1}{2}$—4. Bill, black; iris, bright lemon-yellow; toes, beneath, pale yellowish-ashy, their scutellæ more yellowish.

74, ♂ *juv.*; Sacramento, June 22, 1867.—$11\frac{3}{4}$—$30\frac{1}{4}$—$8\frac{3}{4}$—$6\frac{1}{8}$—$\frac{11}{16}$—$1\frac{5}{8}$—$4\frac{1}{2}$—3. Bill, brownish-blue; iris, bright yellow; exposed scutellæ of the toes, pale brownish-blue; soles, ashy-whitish.

389, ♀ *ad.*; Washoe Valley, Nevada, January 3, 1868. $14\frac{1}{4}$—39—$11\frac{5}{8}$—$10\frac{1}{2}$. Bill, deep black; iris, rich gamboge-yellow; toes pale ashy naples-yellow beneath, the scutellæ light yellowish-brown; claws, deep black.

390, ♂ *ad.* (mate of preceding). 14—36—$11\frac{1}{4}$—$9\frac{1}{2}$. Same remarks.

424, "♀ *ad.*; San Francisco, California, January 31, 1868. $14\frac{3}{8}$—$39\frac{1}{4}$—(?)—$10\frac{1}{2}$. Eyes, bright yellow." (Presented by Mr. H. G. Parker.)

536, eggs (2); Carson City, Nevada, April 27, 1868. Eggs deposited in a deserted nest of the Magpie (*Pica hudsonica*), in a willow-thicket along the Carson River. Parent shot.

BRACHYOTUS PALUSTRIS.

Short-eared Owl.

β. cassini.

Strix brachyotus, FORSTER, Phil. Trans., LXII, 1772, 384.

Otus brachyotus, BOIE, Isis, 1822, 549.

Otus (Brachyotus) brachyotus, B. B. & R., Hist. N. Am. B., III, 1874, 22.—HENSHAW, 1875, 404.

Brachyotus palustris, BONAP., Comp. List., 1838, 7.—COUES, Key, 1872, 204; Check List, 1873, No. 321; B. N.W., 1874, 306.

Brachyotus cassinii, BREWER, Pr. Boston Soc. N. H., 1856, —.—CASSIN, in Baird's B. N. Am., 1858, 54.—BAIRD, Cat. N. Am. B., 1859, No. 52.—COOPER Orn. Cal., I, 428.

This Owl we did not meet with anywhere, the only specimen in the collection having been presented by Mr. H. G. Parker. It is said, however, to be an abundant species in certain portions of California.

List of specimens.

425, "♀ *ad.;* San Francisco, California, February 17, 1868. 16⅛—43¼—(?)—11. Eyes, bright yellow."

SCOPS ASIO.

Mottled Owl; Little Red Owl.

α. asio.

Strix asio, LINN., Syst. Nat., I, 1766, 132.

Scops asio, BONAP., Comp. and Geog. List, 1838, 6.—CASSIN, in Baird's Birds N. Am., 1858, 51.—BAIRD, Cat. N. Am. Birds, 1859, No. 49.—COOPER, Orn. Cal., I, 1870, 420.—COUES, Key, 1872, 202, fig. 136; Check List, 1873, No. 318.—B. B. & R., Hist. N. Am. Birds, III, 1874, 49.

Scops asio. a. asio, COUES, Birds N.W., 1874, 303.

Scops asio var. *maccalli*, HENSHAW, Orn. Wheeler's Exp., 1875, 405. (Not *S. maccalli*, CASS.)

This common little Owl we observed only in the vicinity of Sacramento City; not a single individual was seen in the Interior, nor did we hear of its occurrence there. It was not met with in the red plumage, which appears to be rare—perhaps unknown—on the Pacific coast.

List of specimens.

61, ♀ *jur.;* Sacramento, California, June 20, 1867. 8¾—22¾—6¼—5—$\frac{9}{16}$—1½—3⅛—2. Bill, pale ashy pea-green; iris, lemon-yellow; toes, pale grayish.

62, ♂ *jur.;* same locality and date. 8⅝—21⅝—6—4$\frac{13}{16}$—$\frac{9}{16}$—1⅜—3—2⅛. Same remarks.

75, ♂ ad.; Sacramento, June 22, 1867. 9—22—7—5⅜—⅝—1⅜—3⅜—2¼. Bill, light brownish-blue; iris, lemon-yellow; toes, very pale ashy.

NYCTALE ACADICA.

Saw-whet Owl.

Strix acadica, GMELIN, Syst. Nat., I, 1788, 296. (*Adult.*)

Nyctale acadica, BONAP., Comp. and Geog. List, 1838, 7.—CASSIN, in Baird's Birds N. Am., 1858, 58.—BAIRD, Cat. N. Am. Birds, 1859, No. 57.—COOPER, Orn. Cal., I, 436.—COUES, Key, 1872, 205; Check List, 1873, No. 328; Birds N.W., 1874, 315.—B. B. & R., Hist. N. Am. Birds, III, 1874, 43.

Strix albifrons, SHAW, Nat. Misc., V, 1794, pl. 171. (*Young.*)

Nyctale albifrons, CASSIN, Illustr. Birds Cal., Tex., &c., 1854, 187; in Baird's Birds N. Am., 1858, 57.—BAIRD, Cat. N. Am. Birds, 1859, No. 56.—COOPER, Orn. Cal., I, 435.

But a single individual of this pretty little Owl was met with; this one was captured alive by Mr. O. L. Palmer, of our party, who found it asleep and placed his hat over it. It was perched on the edge of an old Robin's nest, in a dense willow thicket near the camp.

List of specimens.

941, ♀ ad.; Thousand Spring Valley (Camp 27), September 24, 1868. 8—20—(?) —4¾. Bill, deep black; iris, clear bright gamboge-yellow; toes, pale naples-yellow; claws, deep black.

BUBO VIRGINIANUS.

Great Horned Owl.

β. subarcticus.

(*Temooh-mooh'* of the Washoes; *Moo-hoo'* of the Paiutes.)

Bubo subarcticus, HOY, Pr. Ac. Nat. Sci. Philad., VI, 1852, 211.

Bubo virginianus var. *arcticus*, CASSIN, Illustr. Birds Cal., Tex., &c., 1854, 178. [Not *Strix (Bubo) arcticus*, SWAINS., 1831, = albinescent arctic form.]— COUES, Key, 1872, 202; Check List, 1873, No. 317.—B. B. & R., Hist. N. Am. B., III, 1874, 60, 64.—HENSHAW, 1875, 407.

Bubo virginianus var. *pacificus*, CASSIN, Illustr. Birds Cal., Tex., &c., 1854, 178; in Baird's B. N. Am, 1858, 49.[1]

Bubo virginianus, CASSIN, Baird's B. N. Am., 1858, 49 (part).—BAIRD, Cat. N. Am. B., 1859, No. 48.—COOPER, Orn. Cal., I, 1870, 418.

The Great Horned Owl was found by us in all wooded districts, except-

---

[1] Not of RIDGWAY, in B. B. & R., Hist. N. Am. Birds, which is a northern littoral form, of very dark colors, which appears to be unnamed, and which may be distinguished as *B. virginianus saturatus*, RIDGWAY.

ing the Sacramento Valley, where none were seen, although the species undoubtedly occurs there. In the lower Truckee Valley, near Pyramid Lake, it was abundant in December, and its nocturnal hootings were heard from among the cotton-wood groves every moonlight night, while its feathers, more than those of any other bird, adorned the arrows of the Indians on the reservation. It was also common near Carson City, and a few were startled one morning as we rode through a cedar woods near the "City of Rocks," in southern Idaho. One was also seen on the eastern shore of Pyramid Lake in May, it being chased from rock to rock by a male Falcon (*Falco communis nævius*), who, with his mate, had a nest on the "Pyramid" just off the shore.

The hooting of this Owl is low and hoarse, resembling the distant barking of a large dog; its modulation is something like the syllables *hooh'*, *hoo*, *hoo*, *hoo*—*hooooooo*, the latter portion a subdued trembling echo, as it were, of the more distinctly uttered notes. These notes do not differ in the least from those of the eastern birds of this species.

List of specimens.

504, eggs (3); Carson River, rear Carson City, Nevada, April 21, 1868. Nest about 30 feet from the ground, in a large cotton-wood tree; evidently an abandoned one of the *Buteo swainsoni*.

SPEOTYTO CUNICULARIA.

Burrowing Owl.

γ. *hypogæa*.[1]

Strix hypogæa, BONAP., Am. Orn., I, 1825, 72.

Athene hypogæa, BONAP., Consp., I, 1850, 39.—CASSIN, in Baird's Birds N. Am., 1858, 59.—BAIRD, Cat. N. Am., B., 1859, No. 58.—COOPER, Orn. Cal., I, 440.

Speotyto cunicularia var. *hypogæa*, RIDGWAY, in COUES' Key, 1872, 207; in B. B. & R., Hist. N. Am. Birds, III, 1874, 90.—COUES, Check List, 1873, No. 332; Birds N.W., 1874, 321.—HENSHAW, 1875, 409.

Athene cunicularia, CASSIN, in Baird's Birds N. Am., 1858, 60 (not of MOLINA, 1782). —BAIRD, Cat. N. Am. Birds, 1859, No. 59.—COOPER, Orn. Cal., I, 1870, 437.

Although the "Ground Owl" was found at widely-separated places

---

[1] Races *a* and *β* are, *cunicularia*, Mol., of the Pampas of Paraguay, Buenos Ayres, etc., and *grallaria*, Spix, of Peru and western Brazil. Other geographical forms are δ, *floridana*, Ridgw., of southwestern Florida, and ε, *guadeloupensis*, Ridgw., of the island of Guadeloupe (West Indies).

along our entire route, it was abundant at very few localities. It was most numerous on the dry plains near Sacramento, being even found on the open commons in the outskirts of the city, where it occupied deep excavations which were apparently the result of its own work, as no spermophiles or other burrowing quadrupeds were noticed in the locality. Eastward of the Sierra Nevada we found it only at wide intervals; it was rather rare about Carson City, and in the vicinity of the Steamboat Springs, near Washoe; a single pair was seen on the mesa between the Humboldt River and the West Humboldt Mountains, and a few were noticed in Fairview Valley, while in the neighborhood of Salt Lake City it was more common.

This Owl is as diurnal in its habits as any of the Falconidæ, being habitually found abroad during the brightest hours of day; and its sight is so remarkably acute that it is extremely difficult to approach, even when bushes, banks of earth, or other screens are taken advantage of. Should one be in its burrow, it will almost certainly fly forth at the most noiseless approach of a person, for its sense of hearing is no less remarkable than its sight. When thus disturbed, this Owl flies to a safe distance, and after alighting upon some prominent object, as a hillock or a telegraph-wire, watches attentively every motion of the intruder, while now and then he scolds him with a saucy chattering, at the same time ludicrously bowing.

Near Carson City, we attempted, with the assistance of Mr. Parker, to excavate the burrow of a pair of these Owls. This burrow was situated in a wheat-field, and was guarded by the male bird, who sat at its entrance. As we approached him he flew, but before getting out of range was winged and brought down; he was captured with great difficulty, as he made for the sage-brush fast as his extraordinary leaps could carry him, but when overtaken offered no resistance, merely snapping his bill a little. Having him secured, we then proceeded to our task of excavating to the nest, which was accomplished after digging hard for nearly an hour. The hole terminated about eight feet from the entrance and four beneath the surface of the ground. Before arriving at its extremity our captive was released, when he immediately disappeared into the hole; but when the end was reached he, with his mate (the latter unharmed) was secured. In the chamber, which contained no nest whatever, were found one egg and the remains of a frog, which had probably been carried to the female by her attentive companion.

List of specimens.

60, *ad.;* Sacramento City, California, June 20, 1867. 9½—25⅝—7⅛—5⅝—1¹⅟₁₆—1¹³⁄₁₆—3½—2¼.

315, *ad.;* "near American River, Sacramento County, California, November, 1867." (Presented by Mr. H. G. Parker.)

423, "♀ *ad.;* San Francisco, California, January 23, 1868. 9⅜—24⅝—(?)—5¼. Eyes, bright yellow." (Presented by Mr. Parker.)

525, egg (1); Carson City, Nevada, April 25, 1868.

FAMILY FALCONIDE—HAWKS, EAGLES, KITES, ETC.

FALCO COMMUNIS.

Peregrine Falcon.

β. nævius—American Peregrine; "Duck Hawk."

Falco nævius, GMELIN, Syst. Nat., I, 1788, 271 (*adult*).

Falco anatum, BONAP., Comp. & Geog. List, 1838, 4.—CASSIN, Baird's B. N. Am., 1858, 7.—BAIRD, Cat. N. Am. B., 1859, No. 5.—COOPER, Orn. Cal., I, 457.

Falco communis var. *anatum,* RIDGWAY, Pr. Bost. Soc. Nat. Hist., 1873, 45; in B. B. & R., Hist. N. Am. Birds, III, 1874, 132.—HENSHAW, 1875, 411.

Falco communis. c. anatum, COUES, Birds N.W., 1874, 341.

Falco nigriceps, CASSIN, Illust. Birds of Cal., Tex., &c., 1854, 87; Birds N. Am. (Baird), 1858, 8; ed. 1860, pl. 11.—BAIRD, Cat. N. Am. Birds, 1859, No. 6.— COOPER, Orn. Cal., I, 1870, 456.

Falco communis, COUES, Key, 1872, 213, fig. 141 (not of GMELIN, 1788); Check List, 1873, No. 343.

The Duck Hawk was observed only at Pyramid Lake and along the lower portion of the Truckee River. At the former locality a single pair frequented the rocky eastern shore and the adjacent clusters of pyramidal rocky islands. On the 23d of May, 1868, when we visited the Pyramid, we observed a male of this Falcon, in the blue plumage, flying about this immense pyramidal rock, and from the zealous manner in which he drove away every intruder not to his liking, we concluded the female must be sitting on her eggs or young. The Pyramid was ascended, however, to the very summit, but the nest was not found; but this was not strange, since but one of the three corners of the rock was accessible, while to diverge to either side from the exceedingly difficult path by which we ascended would have been impossible. The location of the nest was afterward definitely ascertained by noticing the male alight on a narrow ledge near the top of one of the vertical sides, about one hundred and fifty feet above the water. A few moments later he was again observed flying around, and while we were watching him he discovered among the rocks a large Horned Owl (*Bubo subarcticus*) which he immediately dislodged and followed a considerable distance along the shore, uttering a whistling note at each assault. The single specimen in our collection was killed under the following circumstances: Having sat down on a log by the edge of the river to rest, as well as to observe the movements of a Killdeer Plover (*Ægialitis vociferus*) which was running back and forth over the gravelly bar forming the opposite shore, we saw the Killdeer suddenly squat and then dodge, and at the same time saw the Falcon check itself in its flight, after having missed its aim. Whether its lack of success was caused by the nimbleness of the intended quarry, or whether the Falcon saw us just as it was about to strike, we know not; but after suddenly checking itself it wheeled immediately about, and would have soon disappeared had we not fired before it got out of range. At the report of our gun, another one, probably the mate of our victim, flew from a cotton-wood tree in the direction from which he came.

List of specimens.

102, ♂ *juv.;* Big Bend of the Truckee, Nevada, July 23, 1857. 16½—39¼—12¾—10—1⅝—1¾—6½—3¾. Weight 1½ pounds. Basal half of the bill, pale bluish-white, terminal portion slate, deepening into black at end; cere, bluish-white, bare orbital space greenish-white; iris, vivid brownish-black; tarsi and toes, lemon-yellow, with a faint greenish tinge; claws, jet black.

FALCO SAKER.

Saker Falcon.

β. polyagrus—Prairie Falcon.

Falco polyagrus, CASSIN, Illustr. Birds Cal., Tex., &c., 1853, 88, pl. 16 (front figure—not the dark one, which = *F. communis pealei*, RIDGWAY, Bull. Essex Inst., V, Dec., 1873, p. 201); in Baird's Birds N. Am., 1858, 12.—BAIRD, Cat. N. Am. Birds, 1859, No. 10.—COOPER, Orn. Cal., I, 458.

Falco lanarius var. *polyagrus*, RIDGWAY, in B. B. & R., Hist. N. Am. Birds, III, 1874, 123.—HENSHAW, 1875, 410.

Falco mexicanus, COUES, Key, 1872, 213; Check List, 1873, No. 342.

Falco mexicanus var. *polyagrus*, COUES, Birds N.W., 1874, 339.

This daring Falcon was a rather common species throughout the Great Basin. It was first observed on the 31st of October, 1867, at the Humboldt Marshes, where we saw one swoop upon a flock of tame pigeons at the stage-station. Late in November, of the same year, it was noticed again among the marshes along the Carson River, near Genoa, where it was observed to watch and follow the Marsh Hawks (*Circus hudsonius*), compelling them to give up their game, which was caught by the Falcon before it reached the ground; this piracy being not an occasional, but a systematic habit. In the Truckee Valley we saw one snatch a young chicken from a door-yard, in the presence of several spectators. The quarry of this Falcon is by no means confined to animals smaller than itself, however, for the specimen in our collection was killed while leisurely eating a Jackass Rabbit (*Lepus callotis*), an animal of nearly twice his weight, and which he had carried to the top of a fence-post by the road-side. He exhibited no alarm at the approach of our buggy, but continued tearing and devouring his prey; we had even passed by him without seeing him, when the quick eye of Mr. Parker detected him in time for a shot.

In the rocky cañons of the more lofty ranges to the eastward it was common during summer, particularly about the limestone cliffs of the Ruby range, where the families of young, accompanied by their parents, made a great clamor, as they flew among the precipitous rocks where they had been bred. They were likewise common in the rocky cañons of the Wahsatch.

List of specimens.

336, ♂ *juv.;* Carson City, Nevada, November 29, 1867.   17—37¾—12¼—10¼—⅞—
1⅞—7½—4½. Weight, 1½ pounds. Bill, very pure bluish-white, shading terminally into
bluish-slaty, the point black ; cere, rictus, and bare orbital region, greenish-white ; iris,
vivid vandyke-brown ; tarsi and toes, very pale yellowish, with a tinge of verdigris-
green.

FALCO COLUMBARIUS.

Pigeon Hawk; American Merlin.

Falco columbarius, LINN., Syst. Nat., I, 1766, 128.—COUES, Key, 1872, 214; Check
    List, 1873, No. 344 ; Birds N.W., 1874, 345.—HENSHAW, 1875, 412.—COOPER,
    Orn. Cal., I, 1870, 460.

Hypotriorchis columbarius, GRAY, Genera of Birds, 184-.—BAIRD, Cat. N. Am.
    Birds, 1859, No. 7.

Falco (Hypotriorchis) columbarius, CASSIN, in Baird's Birds N. Am., 1858, 9.

Falco (Æsalon) lithofalco var. *columbarius,* RIDGW., Pr. Boston Soc., N. H., 1873,
    46; in B. B. & R., Hist. N. Am. Birds, III, 1874, 144.

This little Falcon was seen on but three or four occasions. The specimen in the collection was shot just after it had made an unsuccessful
assault on a flock of black-birds (*Scolecophagus cyanocephalus*) which were
feeding on the ground in a corral. Its success was no doubt thwarted by
the opening of the door of the house near by, for it flew away frightened,
but fortunately came in our direction, and alighted upon a fence-post within
easy gunshot range.

List of specimens.

291, ♀ *ad.;* Truckee Meadows, Nevada, November 18, 1867.   11¼—21—7⅞—6¾—
⁹⁄₁₆—1¼—5½—3¼. Terminal portion of the bill, deep slate-black, basal half very pale
whitish-blue, with a yellowish wash toward the rictus ; cere and rictus, light greenish-
yellow ; eyelids, bright gamboge-yellow, bare orbital region more citreous ; iris, bright
vandyke-brown ; tarsi and toes, deep gamboge-yellow : claws, jet-black.

FALCO SPARVERIUS.

"Sparrow Hawk ;" American Kestril.

Falco sparverius, LINN., Syst. Nat., I, 1766, 128.—COOPER, Orn. Cal., I, 1870,
    462.—COUES, Key, 1872, 214, fig. 142; Check List, 1873, No. 346 ; Birds N.W.,
    1874, 349.—HENSHAW, 1875, 413.

Falco (Tinnunculus) sparverius, CASSIN, Baird's Birds N. Am., 1858, 13.—RIDGW.,
    in B. B. & R., Hist. N. Am. Birds, III, 1874, 169.

Tinnunculus sparverius, VIEILL., Ois. Am. Sept., I, 1807, 40, pl. 12.—BAIRD, Cat.
    N. Am. Birds, 1859, No. 13.

Regarding the western range of this widely-distributed species, nothing more need be said than that it occurs *everywhere*, in suitable places; at the same time, we may remark that it is by far the most abundant of all the birds of prey, although its numbers vary greatly with the locality. At a certain spot along the Carson River, not far from Carson City, stood, in the spring of 1868, a clump of five large cotton-wood trees, the only ones for miles around, and each of these trees was inhabited by a pair of these little Falcons, who had nests in the hollows of the limbs. This is well known to be the favorite location for their nests; but where there were no trees to accommodate them, we found them adapting their nesting-habits to the character of the surroundings. Thus, in the precipitous cañons of the Ruby Mountains, they built among the crevices of the limestone cliffs, in company with the Prairie Falcon (*F. polyagrus*), the Violet-green and Cliff Swallows, and the White-throated Swift; while in some portions of Utah they took possession of the holes dug by the Kingfishers and Red-shafted Flickers in the earthy banks of the ravines. Among the cliffs of Echo Cañon, along the line of the Union Pacific Railroad, in Utah, we noticed these birds in August swarming by hundreds about the brow of the precipice, several hundred feet overhead.

List of specimens.

63, ♂ *ad.;* Sacramento, California, June 20, 1867. $10\frac{5}{8}$—$22\frac{7}{8}$—$7\frac{3}{4}$—$6\frac{3}{8}$—$\frac{9}{16}$—$1\frac{1}{8}$—5—4. Bill, bluish-white, growing slate-black terminally; *cere and angle of the mouth, intense orange-red;* iris, very dark brown; tarsi and toes, deep orange-chrome; claws, jet-black.

107, ♂ *ad.;* Big Bend of the Truckee (Camp 12), Nevada, July 26, 1867. 10—$22\frac{3}{4}$—$7\frac{1}{2}$—$6\frac{3}{8}$—$\frac{7}{16}$—$1\frac{1}{16}$—$5\frac{3}{8}$—$3\frac{1}{8}$. Bill, pale blue basally, slate-black terminally; cere and bare orbital region, pale dull yellow; iris, vandyke-brown; tarsi and toes, dull yellow; claws, black.

108, ♀ *juv.* (young of preceding); Camp 12, July 26, 1867. $10\frac{3}{4}$—23—$7\frac{9}{16}$—$6\frac{7}{16}$—$\frac{1}{2}$—1—$5\frac{1}{2}$—$3\frac{1}{2}$. *Bill, pale fleshy-blue, or lilaceous-white;* cere and orbital region, pale dull yellow; iris dark brown; tarsi and toes, very pale dull yellow.

125, ♂ *ad.;* Camp 12, August 6, 1867. $10\frac{3}{8}$—$22\frac{7}{8}$—$7\frac{5}{8}$—$6\frac{5}{8}$—$\frac{9}{16}$—$\frac{14}{16}$—$5\frac{3}{8}$—$3\frac{11}{16}$. Basal half of the bill, pure pale blue, terminal portion slate-black; cere and bare orbital region, dull yellow; iris, very deep brown; tarsi and toes, deep chrome-yellow; claws, black.

343, ♀ *ad.;* near Fort Churchill, Nevada, December 6, 1867. $11\frac{1}{4}$—24—$8\frac{3}{8}$—7—$\frac{9}{16}$—$1\frac{1}{4}$—$5\frac{1}{2}$—$3\frac{7}{8}$. Same remarks.

419, "♀ *ad.;* San Francisco, California, January 23, 1868. $11\frac{1}{4}$—$24\frac{1}{4}$—(?)—$7\frac{1}{8}$." (Presented by Mr. H. G. Parker.)

420, "♀ *ad.;* San Francisco, January 23, 1868. $11\frac{1}{8}$—$23\frac{7}{8}$—(?)—$6\frac{7}{8}$." (H. G. Parker.)

489, ♀ *ad.;* Carson, Nevada, April 4, 1868. 11—24—$8\frac{1}{4}$—$6\frac{7}{8}$. Cere (entirely surrounding base of the bill), bare orbital region, and tarsi and toes, intense reddish-orange, or orange-chrome.

496, ♂ *ad.;* Carson, April 18, 1868. $10\frac{1}{2}$—$23\frac{7}{8}$—$7\frac{13}{16}$—$6\frac{5}{8}$. Same remarks.

816, egg (1); Fort Churchill, Carson River, June 24, 1868. Egg, with four downy young, deposited in a hollow snag of a cotton-wood tree, about 15 feet from the ground.

CIRCUS HUDSONIUS.

Marsh Hawk.

Falco hudsonius, LINN., Syst. Nat., I, 1766, 128.

Circus hudsonius, VIEILL., Ois. Am. Sept., I, 1807, 36, pl. IX.—CASSIN, Baird's Birds N. Am., 1858, 38.—BAIRD, Cat. N. Am. Birds, 1859, No. 38.—COOPER, Orn. Cal., I, 489.

Circus cyaneus hudsonius, SCHLEG., Mus. Pays-Bas, *Circi*, 1862, 2.

Circus cyaneus var. *hudsonius*, ALLEN, Bull. Mus. Comp. Zool., III, 1872, 181.—COUES, Key, 1872, 210, fig. 159; Check List, 1873, No. 333; Birds N.W., 1874, 327.—B. B. & R., Hist. N. Am. Birds, III, 1874, 214.—HENSHAW, 1875, 416.

No marsh of any extent was visited, either in winter or summer, where this Hawk could not be seen at almost any time during the day skimming over the tules in search of its prey. The latter consists of small birds of all kinds, the young of water-fowl, lizards, and probably small mammals, although the latter were not found in the crop of any of the specimens examined. The stomachs and crops of those killed at Pyramid Lake were filled to their utmost capacity with the remains of small lizards, and nothing else; at the same locality, however, they were often observed to chase small birds, particularly Brewer's and the Black-throated Sparrows, the most numerous species, of which this Hawk appears to be a most dreaded enemy, since its appearance creates perfect consternation among all the Sparrows in its path, who utter distressed cries, and make confused and desperate efforts to escape by plunging precipitately into the thickest bushes.

List of specimens.

129, ♀ *juv.;* eastern shore of Pyramid Lake, August 15, 1867. $19\frac{1}{2}$—$43\frac{1}{2}$—$13\frac{7}{8}$—$11\frac{1}{4}$—$\frac{3}{4}$—$2\frac{3}{8}$—$9\frac{1}{4}$—6. Bill, deep black, more bluish basally; cere and rictus, greenish-gamboge, most yellowish on top; iris, yellowish-gray; tarsi and toes, rich orange-yellow; claws, jet-black.

131, ♂ *juv.;* Big Bend of the Truckee (Camp 12), August 17, 1867. $18\frac{3}{4}$—42—13—11—$\frac{23}{32}$—$2\frac{1}{8}$—9—$6\frac{1}{2}$. Same remarks.

367, ♀ *juv.;* Truckee Reservation, near Pyramid Lake, December 21, 1867. $20\frac{1}{4}$—44—15—$12\frac{1}{2}$. Iris, dull fulvous.

NISUS COOPERI.
Cooper's Hawk.

Falco cooperi, BONAP , Am. Orn., I, 1828, pl. x, fig. 1.

Accipiter cooperi, DE KAY, Zool. N. Y., II, 1844, 18, pl. IV, fig. 5.—CASSIN, in Baird's Birds N. Am., 1858, 16.—BAIRD, Cat. N. Am. Birds, 1859, No. 15.— COOPER, Orn. Cal., I, 464.—COUES, Key, 1872, 212; Check List, 1873, No. 339; Birds N.W., 1874, 334.

Nisus cooperi, SCHLEG., Rev. Acc., 1873, 73.—RIDGWAY, in B. B. & R., Hist. N. Am. Birds, III, 1874, 230.—HENSHAW, 1875, 418.

Accipiter mexicanus, SWAINS., Fauna Bor. Am., II, 1831, 45.—CASSIN, Baird's B. N. Am., 1858, 17.—BAIRD, Cat. N. Am. B., 1859, No. 16.—COOPER, Orn. Cal., I, 1870, 465.

Nisus cooperi var. *mexicanus*, RIDGW., Proc. Boston Soc. Nat. Hist., May, 1873, 19.—B. B. & R., Hist. N. Am. B., III, 1874, 231.

This daring depredator was more or less common in all localities where small birds abounded, but it was far from numerous anywhere. It was most often seen sailing, with the long tail widely expanded, in broad circles over the thickets which sheltered its prey. The specimen in the collection was shot while soaring thus over an aspen copse, and came whirling to the ground; but being merely winged, made for the thicket by vigorous leaps, and would have escaped but for a second charge. In other portions of the country, particularly in the fertile cañons of the East Humboldt Mountains, it was often observed chasing, with its swift, rushing flight, a fleeing Robin or Flicker.

List of specimens.

240, ♂ *juv.;* West Humboldt Mountains (Camp 19), October 8, 1867. 14¾—26⅝— 8¼—6⅞—½—11¾—7—4½. Bill, pale blue on the basal third, dull black terminally; cere and rictus, yellowish-green; iris, light chrome-yellow; tarsi and toes, lemon-yellow, with a slight tinge of green; claws, slate-black.

NISUS FUSCUS.
Sharp-shinned Hawk.

Falco fuscus, GMELIN, Syst. Nat., I, 1788, 283.

Accipiter fuscus, BONAP., Comp. & Geog. List, 1838, 5.—CASSIN, in Baird's B. N. Am., 1858, 18.—BAIRD, Cat. N. Am. B., 1859, No. 17.—COOPER, Orn. Cal., I, 1870, 466.—COUES, Key, 1872, 212; Check List, 1873, No. 338; Birds N.W., 1874, 333.

Nisus fuscus, KAUP, Jardine's Contr. Orn., 1850, 64, 281.—RIDGW., in B. B. & R., Hist. N. Am. B., III, 1874, 224.—HENSHAW, 1875, 417.

This miniature of Cooper's Hawk was observed only in the Upper

Humboldt Valley, where it was common in September along the streams flowing from the Clover Mountains. The specimen obtained had been chasing a small bird through a very dense thicket, but losing sight of the fugitive, alighted upon a twig within a few feet of us.

List of specimens.

917, ♀ *juv.*; Upper Humboldt Valley (Camp 24), September 10, 1868. 13½—24¾—(?)—6⅞. Bill, black, growing gradually pale bluish basally; cere and angle of the mouth, yellowish-green; iris, sulphur-yellow; tarsi and toes, rich lemon-yellow; claws, jet-black.

BUTEO LINEATUS.
Red-shouldered Hawk.
β. elegans—Red-breasted Hawk.

Buteo elegans, CASSIN, Pr. Ac. Nat. Sci. Philad., 1855, 281; Baird's B. N. Am., 1858, 28.—BAIRD, Cat. N. Am. B., 1859, No. 25.—COOPER, Orn. Cal., I, 1870, 477.

Buteo lineatus var. *elegans*, RIDGWAY, in Coues' Check List, 1873, No. 352a; in B. B. & R., Hist. N. Am. B., III, 1874, 277.

Buteo lineatus, COUES, Key, 1872, 216 (part).

This handsome Hawk was seen only in the Sacramento Valley, where it was rather common among the trees near the river.

BUTEO BOREALIS.[1]
Red-tailed Hawk.
β. calurus—Dusky Red-tail.

Buteo calurus, CASSIN, Pr. Ac. Nat. Sci. Philad., 1855, 281; Baird's Birds N. Am., 1858, 22.—BAIRD, Cat. N. Am. B., 1859, No. 20.—COOPER, Orn. Cal., I, 1870, 471.

Buteo borealis var. *calurus*, RIDGWAY, in Coues' Check List, 1873, No. 351a; in B. B. & R., Hist. N. Am. B., III, 1874, 236.—HENSHAW, 1875, 423.

Buteo borealis. b. *calurus*, COUES, B. N.W., 1874, 352.

Buteo montanus, CASSIN, Pr. Ac. Nat. Sci. Philad., 1856, 39; Baird's B. N. Am., 1858, 26 (not of NUTTALL, 1840,=*B. swainsoni*).—BAIRD, Cat. N. Am. B., 1859, No. 24.—COOPER, Orn. Cal., I, 1870, 469.

The Red-tailed Hawk was a very common species in all wooded localities of the Interior. It was especially abundant during the winter among

---

[1] Other western races of this Hawk are *γ. lucasanus*, RIDGW., of Cape St. Lucas, and *δ. krideri*, HOOPES, of the Great Plains, from Minnesota to Texas. *B. harlani*, AUD., and *B. cooperi*, CASS., are allied but apparently distinct species.

the cotton-woods of the Truckee and Carson Valleys, where we found it quite unsuspicious and easily killed. During the summer it was much less abundant in the lower valleys than Swainson's Hawk, but it was more common on the mountains, particularly in the pine forests. On the Wahsatch, we saw several of its nests on tall pine trees or on ledges of the cliffs, most of them being inaccessible, in which respect this species differs conspicuously from the *B. swainsoni*, which in the same region was found to build its nest on the top of the scrub-oaks or in the small aspens, within easy reach.

The series of specimens in the collection exhibits the usual individual variation so remarkable to the western birds of this species, there being examples so light-colored as to be scarcely distinguishable from the typical eastern *B. borealis*, while one is of an almost uniform deep sooty-black, the others being variously intermediate. As was the case with *B. swainsoni*, the light and dark individuals were often found paired.[1]

List of specimens.

132, ♀ ad. *(melanotic, very black);* Big Bend of the Truckee (Camp 12), Nevada, August 17, 1867. 23½—54—16½ (molting). Bill, slate-black, the basal half of the lower mandible bluish-slate; cere, dull yellowish-green, purest on top; rictus, more yellow; iris, muddy naples-yellow; tarsi and toes, dull pale greenish-yellow; claws black.

337, ♀ ad *(melanotic, rufous-breasted style);* Genoa, Nevada, November 29, 1867. 23½—55—17—14—1¾₁₆—2—9¼—5¼. Weight, 3½ pounds. Bill, dull black, passing into pale bluish basally; cere and rictus, light dull ashy-green; iris, deep hazel; tarsi and toes pale dull naples-yellow; claws, black.

347, ♂ ad.; Truckee Reservation, December 19, 1867. 21¾—51¾—16—13¼—1¼—(?)—9—5. Weight, 2 pounds. Bill, dull black, fading into dull light bluish basally; cere and rictus, dull greenish-yellow; iris, deep light hazel; tarsi and toes, very dull light chrome-yellow, deeper beneath.

351, ♂ ad.; same locality, December 11, 1867. 21½—49—15⅝—12¾—1³₁₆—(?)—9⅝—5½. Weight, 2½ pounds. Bill, black, fading basally into light horn-drab; basal half of the lower mandible, pale blue; cere and rictus, clear light yellowish-green; iris,

---

[1] There being many who yet hold the old belief that this dark phase, found in so many species of Falconidæ, is in some manner dependent on *age*, we wish to impress our readers with the fact that it is a *purely individual* condition, *entirely independent of age, sex, or season;* it is properly styled *melanism*, and is analogous to the condition of *erythrism* in certain owls. In every American species which has this fuliginous plumage, the dark birds are dusky *from the nest up;* while those in light plumage never assume the dark dress. This is probably the case with the Old World species also.

naples-yellow, the lower two-thirds with a brownish suffusion; tarsi and toes, dull light naples-yellow, with a slight greenish tinge.

352, ♀ *ad.;* same locality and date. 23—$57\frac{1}{2}$—$17\frac{3}{4}$—$14\frac{1}{2}$—$1\frac{3}{16}$—(?)—10—$5\frac{3}{4}$. Weight, $3\frac{1}{4}$ pounds. Iris, deep light brown, the upper third naples-yellow.

353, ♀ *ad.;* same locality, December 13, 1867. 23—54—17—$13\frac{5}{8}$—$1\frac{3}{16}$—(?)—$9\frac{3}{4}$—$5\frac{1}{2}$. Weight, 3 pounds. Same remarks.

354, ♂ *ad.;* same locality and date. 22—53—$16\frac{1}{2}$—$13\frac{7}{8}$—$1\frac{1}{8}$—(?)—$9\frac{1}{2}$—$5\frac{1}{2}$. Weight, $2\frac{3}{4}$ pounds. Iris, hazel; tarsi and toes, deep light chrome-yellow.

355, ♂ *ad.;* same locality and date. $22\frac{1}{2}$—52—16—13—$1\frac{1}{8}$—(?)-9—$5\frac{1}{8}$. Weight, $2\frac{1}{2}$ pounds. Iris, deep light hazel, naples-yellow above; tarsi and toes, dull greenish naples-yellow.

356, ♀ *ad.;* same locality, December 14, 1867. 24—55—$17\frac{1}{2}$—$14\frac{1}{2}$—$1\frac{9}{32}$—(?)—$10\frac{1}{2}$—6. Weight, 4 pounds. Same remarks as to No. 352.

361, ♂ *ad.;* same locality, December 18, 1867. 22—$50\frac{3}{4}$—16—$13\frac{1}{4}$—$1\frac{1}{16}$—(?)—10—5. Weight, 3 pounds. Same remarks.

418, ♂ *juv.;* San Francisco, California, February 11, 1868. "$20\frac{3}{4}$—$49\frac{3}{4}$—(?)—13. Eye, bright yellow." (Presented by Mr. H. G. Parker.)

1502, ♀ *juv.;* Echo Cañon, Utah, July 29, 1869. ·23—51. Collected by J. C. Olmstead.

BUTEO SWAINSONI.

Swainson's Hawk.

Buteo swainsoni, BONAP., Comp. and Geog. List, 1838, 3.—CASSIN, Baird's Birds N. Am., 1858, 19.—BAIRD, Cat. N. Am. Birds, 1859, No. 18.—COOPER, Orn. Cal., I, 476.—COUES, Key, 1872, 217; Check List, 1873, No. 354; Birds N.W., 1874, 355.—B. B. & R., Hist. N. Am. Birds, III, 1874, 263.—HENSHAW, 1875, 421.

Buteo bairdii, HOY, Pr. Ac. Nat. Sci. Philad., 1853, 451 (*Young*).—CASSIN, Baird's Birds N. Am., 1858, 21.—BAIRD, Cat. N. Am. Birds, 1859, No. 19.

Buteo insignatus, CASSIN, Illustr. Birds Cal., Tex., &c, 1854, 102, 198, pl. XXXI, (*melanotic.*); Baird's Birds N. Am., 1858, 23.—BAIRD, Cat. N. Am. Birds, 1859, No. 21.—COOPER, Orn. Cal., I, 474.

Buteo oxypterus, CASSIN, Pr. Ac. Nat. Sci. Philad., 1855, 283 (*Young*); Baird's Birds N. Am. 1858, 30.—BAIRD, Cat. N. Am. Birds, 1859, No. 28.—COOPER, Orn. Cal., I, 1870, 480.

Buteo swainsoni var. *oxypterus*, RIDGW., in B. B. & R., Hist. N. Am. Birds, III, 1874, 266.

"*Buteo harlani*," BRYANT, Pr. Bost. Soc. N. H., 1861, 116.—COOPER, Orn Cal., I, 1870, 473 (part) [not *B. harlani*, AUD.].

Swainson's Buzzard is one of the most abundant of the large Hawks of the Interior, but it seemed to be less common in winter than in summer. It appeared to be most numerous in the valleys, but it was nevertheless far from rare on the lower slopes of the mountains, as well as in the parks. Our observations in the field tended from the very first to confirm the theory advanced by Dr. Bryant,[1] that the several supposed species described by Mr. Cassin under the names of *B. bairdi*, Hoy, *B. insignatus*, Cassin, and *B. swainsoni*, Bonap., were merely different plumages of one species, the very first specimens obtained by us being a family of four young, with their parents, the former being *B. bairdi*, while of the latter the male was a very light-colored, or extremely typical, *B. swainsoni*, and the female a very extreme example of *B. insignatus!* Similar cases were often observed afterward, the plumage of the adults being sometimes reversed—that is, a male in the plumage of the so-called *insignatus* being sometimes paired with a very light-colored female.

The family mentioned above was first observed on the 26th of July, while we were hunting among the cotton-woods of the lower Truckee Valley. Our attention was attracted by a peculiar squealing cry, not before heard by us, and upon emerging from the willows and looking across the open meadow we observed among the trees on the opposite side several large Hawks, one of which was feeding a young one in a nest in the top of a tall cotton-wood. We then approached this tree under cover of the willows, but upon arriving there found that the old Hawk had gone after more food for its young, three of which were in the trees on the opposite side of a deep and wide slough which we were unable to cross. We then shot the one in the nest, as it looked over the edge at us; but, as it did not fall, found it necessary to ascend the tree, which was easily done. The nest was very similar to that of other Buteones, being composed almost entirely of sticks, but appeared rather small for the size of the bird, measuring but about two feet in diameter by one foot in thickness. We found it so filled with the accumulated remains of animals carried to the young that scarcely any depression was noticeable on the top, the decomposing rubbish consisting of bones and other remnants of small hares (*Lepus artemisia*), ground squirrels (*Spermophilus lateralis*, *S. harrisi*, and *Tamias quadrivittatus*), and, strange to say, a full-grown young Sparrow Hawk (*Falco sparverius*). We had scarcely reached the nest before the male arrived, and flying about us uttered plaintive cries, of a mewing character, somewhat like the

---

[1] "Remarks on the Variations of Plumage of *Buteo borealis*, AUCT., and *Buteo harlani*, AUD." Proc. Bost. Soc. Nat. Hist., VIII, 1861, pp. 107–119.

notes of *B. lineatus,* but less loud and more monotonous. Three days afterward this family was again met with, and the three remaining young immediately secured; but the parent birds were not so easily killed, for, although they received several charges of dust shot, as they courageously flew about us, they were far tougher than their young. The female was brought down first, when the male only increased in courage and clamor, until he, too, was killed.

On the Truckee Reservation a nest of this species was found in a large cotton-wood tree, and the female (No. 771) shot from it. This nest was built near the extremity of a large drooping branch, and was consequently inaccessible; by climbing above it, however, the eggs, two in number, could be seen, but it was found impossible, under the circumstances, to secure them. Many other nests were discovered in this locality, but they were in the ordinary position, viz. in a fork of a tall tree. In Parley's Park, on the Wahsatch Mountains, Swainson's Hawk was common, and many nests were found among the scrub-oaks on the slopes or on small aspens on the sides of the ravines. Their position was always low down, often merely a few feet from the ground, and easily reached without climbing. In one of these nests, found July 2d, was a single young one, which, although yet covered with snow-white cottony down, was savagely tearing at a dead weasel which had been carried to the nest by the old birds, both of which were killed; of these, the male is a remarkably light-colored example, the entire lower parts, including the under side of the wings, being pure white, the breast covered by a broad patch of uniform cinnamon-rufous, while the female, on the other hand, is one of the darkest examples of the species we ever saw, being of a uniform sooty-black, only the under tail coverts being slightly barred with whitish.

The food of this Hawk is by no means confined to small mammals and birds, but during the flights of the grasshoppers, which so often devastate the fields of Utah and other portions of the West, they keep continually gorged on these insects; and at one season we found them living chiefly on the large cricket so common in the Salt Lake Valley. On the 31st of May, 1869, at Salt Lake City, we noticed a number of these Hawks on the ground, where they remained most of the time quiet, but every now and then they would raise their wings and hop briskly in pursuit of some object, which, at the distance, we could not distinguish. Cautiously approaching them, four were shot during the forenoon; they would not allow us to walk to within gunshot, but after flying for a few minutes would sometimes return toward us, and, passing by, give us a fair opportunity for wing-shots. Upon dissection, the stomachs of these specimens were found to be filled entirely with the large crickets mentioned above.

At our camp in Parley Park we reared four young birds of this species, which were taken from their nests while in the downy state. As they grew up under our care they became very pleasing pets, being exceedingly docile, and much attached to those who fed them. When sufficiently old to use their wings they showed no disposition to leave, although they were allowed full liberty all the while; and though they made frequent tours of inspection over the neighboring meadows, and occasional foraging excursions among the flocks of Blackbirds (*Scolecophagus cyanocephalus*) which frequented the vicinity, they seldom went far away, and always returned after a short absence. They were fed principally upon bits of fresh beef and mutton, varied occasionally by the carcasses of birds we had skinned. Their chief amusement about camp consisted in chasing grasshoppers over the ground, which they pursued by leaping after them, with the wings extended; but when not engaged in this occupation they usually perched quietly upon the fence near by or upon the tents.

List of specimens.

109, ♀ *juv*; Big Bend of the Truckee (Camp 12), Nevada, July 26, 1867. $16\frac{1}{2}$—45—13—$10\frac{1}{8}$—1—$1\frac{5}{8}$—$6\frac{7}{8}$—3. Bill, dull black, inclining to pale blue on the rictus and on the basal half of the lower mandible; cere, pale yellowish-green; iris, cinereous, with a brownish outer wash; tarsi and toes, very pale ashy-green.

113, ♀ *ad.* (*fuliginous plumage, parent* of Nos. 109, 115, 116, and 117); Camp 12, July 29, 1867. $21\frac{1}{2}$—53—17—14—1—2—$8\frac{5}{8}$—5. Weight, $2\frac{1}{4}$ pounds. Bill, slate-black, light blue basally; cere and rictus, pure light yellow; iris, deep hazel; tarsi and toes, light chrome-yellow; claws, black.

114, ♂ *ad.* (*normal plumage, mate of the preceding*); Camp 12, July 29, 1867. $19\frac{3}{4}$—48—16—$12\frac{7}{8}$—$1\frac{1}{16}$—$1\frac{5}{8}$—$7\frac{3}{4}$—$4\frac{1}{2}$. Weight, $1\frac{1}{2}$ pounds. Cere and rictus, light dull lemon-yellow; tarsi and toes, deep chrome-yellow; iris, deep hazel.

115, ♀ *juv.*; Camp 12, July 29, 1867. $19\frac{3}{4}$—47—14—11—$1\frac{5}{16}$—$1\frac{3}{4}$—$7\frac{1}{2}$—$3\frac{3}{4}$. Weight, 2 pounds. Same remarks as to No. 109.

116, ♂ *juv.*; Camp 12, July 29, 1867. $19\frac{3}{8}$—$45\frac{1}{2}$—$13\frac{3}{4}$—$10\frac{3}{4}$—$\frac{31}{32}$—$1\frac{1}{2}$—7—$3\frac{3}{4}$. Weight, $1\frac{3}{8}$ pounds. Same remarks.

117, ♂ *juv.*, Camp 12, July 29, 1867. $18\frac{1}{4}$—$43\frac{3}{4}$—$12\frac{1}{4}$—$9\frac{3}{4}$—$\frac{37}{32}$—$1\frac{1}{2}$—$6\frac{3}{4}$—$4\frac{1}{8}$. Weight, $1\frac{1}{2}$ pounds. Same remarks.

771, ♀ *ad.* (*intermediate plumage, barred ochraceous belly*); Truckee Reservation, May 29, 1868. (*Shot from nest.*) $21\frac{1}{2}$—52—$16\frac{1}{2}$—$13\frac{1}{2}$. Weight, 3 pounds. Bill, deep black, the upper mandible scarcely paler basally; lower with the basal third pale blue; cere and rictus, greenish-gamboge; iris, burnt-sienna; tarsi and toes, deep gamboge, with a greenish tinge.

1072, ♀ *ad.* (*normal plumage, immaculate white belly*); Salt Lake City, Utah, May 31, 1869. 21—53. Weight, $2\frac{1}{2}$ pounds. Bill, slate-black, becoming light slate-blue basally; cere and rictus, greenish-gamboge; naked eyebrow, olive-yellow; iris, deep fine hazel; tarsi and toes, deep chrome-yellow. (Stomach filled with grasshoppers.)

1073, ♀ *ad.* (*normal plumage, immaculate white belly*); same locality and date. $21\frac{1}{2}$—53. Weight, $2\frac{1}{2}$ pounds. Same remarks.

1074, ♀ *ad.* (*normal plumage, immaculate white belly*); same locality and date. 22—$53\frac{1}{2}$. Weight, $2\frac{3}{4}$ pounds. Same remarks.

1075, ♀ *ad.* (*normal plumage, immaculate white belly*); same locality and date. $21\frac{1}{2}$—54. Weight, $2\frac{3}{4}$ pounds. Same remarks.

1291, ♂ *ad.* (*normal plumage*); Parley's Park, Utah, June 25, 1869. 20—50. Weight, $2\frac{1}{4}$ pounds. Upper mandible, deep black, scarcely bluish basally; lower, with basal third, light blue; cere and rictus, greenish-gamboge; iris, burnt-sienna, yellowish on top; eyebrow, olivaceous; tarsi and toes, deep light chrome-yellow.

1310, ♂ *ad.* (*normal plumage*); Parley's Park, June 26, 1869. $19\frac{1}{2}$—48. Same remarks.

1322, fragment of egg. Parley's Park, June 27, 1869.

1335, ♀ *ad.* (*fuliginous plumage*); Parley's Park, June 28, 1869. 22—56—17. Weight, $3\frac{1}{2}$ pounds. Bill, black, pale blue basally; cere and rictus, greenish lemon-yellow; iris, deep brown; tarsi and toes, chrome-yellow.

1359, ♂ *ad.* (*normal plumage, very white*); Parley's Park, July 2, 1869. 20—$50\frac{1}{4}$. Same remarks.

1360, ♀ *ad.* (*fuliginous plumage, very black; mate of the preceding!*); Parley's Park, July 2, 1869. 21—$51\frac{1}{2}$. Weight, $2\frac{1}{2}$ pounds. Same remarks.

1501, ♀ *juv.*; Parley's Park, August 10, 1869. 21—$50\frac{3}{4}$. Bill, black, becoming pale blue basally; cere and rictus, fine yellowish-green; iris, yellowish-brown; tarsi and toes, light chrome-yellow.

ARCHIBUTEO LAGOPUS.

Rough-legged Hawk.

β. sancti-johannis.

(*Ma'-hoo-chk* and *Ma'-ede-kan-ah'-chk* of the Washoes; *Assut'te-Queh-nah'*
of the Paiutes; *Pe'ah-Gueh-nah'* of the Shoshones)

Falco sancti-johannis, GMELIN, Syst. Nat., I, 1788, 273.

Archibuteo sancti-johannis, GRAY, Genera of Birds, ——.—CASSIN, Baird's Birds
N. Am., 1858, 33.—BAIRD, Cat. N. Am. Birds, 1859, No. 31.—COOPER, Orn.
Cal., I, 1870, 485.

Archibuteo lagopus var. *sancti-johannis,* RIDGWAY, Pr. Ac. Nat. Sci. Philad., 1870,
142.—COUES, Key, 1872, 218; Check List, 1873, No. 356; Birds N.W., 1874,
361.—B. B. & R., Hist. N. Am. Birds, III, 1874, 304.—HENSHAW, 1875, 425.

Archibuteo lagopus, CASSIN, Baird's Birds N. Am., 1858, 32 (not of GRAY, *ex*
BRUNN, 1764).—BAIRD, Cat. N. Am. Birds, 1859, No. 30.—COOPER, Orn. Cal.,
I. 1870, 483.

This common species was observed nearly everywhere in the vicinity
of the fertile valleys. It appears to be resident in western Nevada, for it
was extremely abundant in July at the Truckee Meadows, where during
the day half a dozen or more were often noticed at one time sailing in broad
circles over the meadows. The flight of this Hawk is extremely similar
to that of the Golden Eagle, a fact which probably explains why the
Indians class it with the Eagles instead of with the Hen Hawks (*Buteo*).[1]
Most of those seen were in the light-colored, or normal, phase of plumage ;
in fact, but one individual was seen which might have been the black phase
of this species, although it is by no means certain it was not an adult specimen of *Buteo abbreviatus*.[2] This specimen was seen in the latter part of
February, high overhead, sailing in a direct line from the eastward toward
the Sierra Nevada. Its color was an intense black, relieved by a conspicuous white patch under the primaries and several distinct bands of the same
across the tail.

List of specimens.

348, ♀ *juv.*: Truckee Reservation, near Pyramid Lake, December 9, 1867. 23½—
56—18¼—15—1³⁄₁₆—(?)—10—5⅜. Bill, deep black, becoming pale blue on the basal half

---

[1] See Indian names above, and compare with those of *Aquila canadensis* (page 590).
[2] *Buteo zonocercus*, SCL., B. B. & R., Hist. N. Am. Birds, III, p. 272.

of the lower mandible, and on the base of the upper, below the cere; cere and rictus, light yellowish-green; naked eyebrow, plumbeous; iris, deep light-hazel; toes, pure light lemon-yellow; claws, deep black.

ARCHIBUTEO FERRUGINEUS.

Squirrel Hawk.

Buteo ferrugineus, LICHT., Tr. Berlin Acad., 1838, 429.

Archibuteo ferrugineus, GRAY, Genera of Birds, ——, —, pl. VI (name *A. regalis* on plate).—CASSIN, Baird's Birds N. Am., 1858, 34.—BAIRD, Cat. N. Am. Birds, 1859, No. 32.—COOPER, Orn. Cal., I, 1870, 482.—COUES, Key, 1872, 218; Check List, 1873, No. 357; Birds N.W., 1874, 363.—B. B. & R., Hist. N. Am. Birds, III, 1874, 300.—HENSHAW, 1875, 425.

This magnificent Hawk, which Dr. Coues justly calls the "handsomest of the North American Falconidæ," was much less frequently seen than its relative, the common Rough-leg (*A. sancti-johannis*). The few observed were sailing majestically overhead, describing broad circles, and resembling the Golden Eagle in the manner of their flight. At such times it may be immediately distinguished from *A. sancti-johannis* by the snowy white of its lower plumage, which, as seen from below, is the predominating color of the bird.

AQUILA CHRYSAËTOS.

Golden Eagle.

β. canadensis.

(*Poh-tahl'-ing-ehk* of the Washoes; *Queh-nah'* of the Paiutes; *Gueh'-nah* of the Shoshones.)

Falco canadensis, LINN., Syst. Nat., I, 1753, 88.

Aquila canadensis, CASSIN, Baird's Birds N. Am., 1858, 41.—BAIRD, Cat. N. Am. Birds, 1859, No. 39.—COOPER, Orn. Cal., I, 1870, 449.

Aquila chrysaëtos var. *canadensis*, RIDGWAY, B. B. & R., Hist. N. Am. B., III, 1874, 314.—HENSHAW, 1875, 426.

Aquila chrysaëtos, COUES, Key, 1872, 219; Check List, 1873, No. 361; Birds N.W., 1874, 368.

The magnificent Golden Eagle is an almost daily sight in the mountain-regions of the Interior. At Carson City we scarcely ever went among the hills without seeing it, soaring about, generally in pairs, overhead. We first met with it in July, 1867, near the summit of the western slope of the

Sierra Nevada; afterward, it was continually observed on all the high ranges to the eastward, such as the Toyabe and the West and East Humboldt, being particularly common among the rocky heights of the latter. At Camp 19, on the last-named mountains, on the 29th of July, we were so fortunate as to witness the chase and capture of a Sage-Hen (*Centrocercus urophasianus*) by a pair of these Eagles. We were standing a few yards in the rear of a tent, when our attention was arrested by a rushing noise, and upon looking up the slope of the mountain we saw flying down its wooded side, with the rapidity of an arrow, a Sage-Hen, pursued by two Eagles. The Hen was about twenty yards in advance of her pursuers, exerting herself to the utmost to escape; her wings, from their rapid motion, being scarcely visible. The Eagles in hot pursuit (the larger of the two leading), followed every undulation of the fugitive's course, steadily lessening the distance between them and the object of their pursuit; their wings not moving, except when a slight inclination was necessary to enable them to follow a curve in the course of the fugitive. So intent were they in the chase that they passed within twenty yards of us. They had scarcely gone by, however, when the Sage-Hen, wearied by her continued exertion, and hoping, probably, to conceal herself among the bushes, dropped to the ground; but no sooner had she touched it than she was immediately snatched up by the foremost of her relentless pursuers, who, not stopping in its flight, bore the prize rapidly toward the rocky summits of the higher peaks, accompanied by its mate. Some moments later, we again saw them soaring overhead, describing circles as they rose higher and higher, when, taking a direct course for some distant range, they disappeared from view. At the Overland Ranche, in Ruby Valley, one of these powerful birds was in captivity; he was one of the largest size, and a truly noble-looking creature. He was kept tied to a horizontal pole, which served him for a perch, in a kind of bower constructed of green branches; none but his keeper could handle him, and every motion of a person who approached was followed by the quick fiery glance of his watchful eye, which did not permit even the slightest movement to pass unobserved. Specimens of the "Mountain-Eagle," as this bird is there called, may be found in captivity in almost any settlement in the mountain-regions of the West.

HALIAËTUS LEUCOCEPHALUS.

Bald Eagle.

Falco leucocephalus, LINN., Syst. Nat., I, 1766, 124.

Haliaëtus leucocephalus, SAVIGNY.—CUV., Règ. An., ed. 2, I, 1817, 326.—CASSIN
  Baird's Birds N. Am., 1858, 43.—BAIRD, Cat. N. Am. Birds, 1859, No. 43.—
  COOPER, Orn. Cal., I, 1870, 451.—COUES, Key, 1872, 219; Check List, 1873,
  No. 362; Birds N.W., 1874, 369.—B. B. & R., Hist. N. Am. Birds, III, 1874,
  326.—HENSHAW, 1875, 427.

The Bald Eagle was met with only in the neighborhood of Pyramid
Lake, where it was rare.   One individual was seen some thirty or forty
miles from the lake, in the pass of the Truckee River through the Virginia
Mountains; it was an adult, and was flying along the stream.   In August,
1867, when we visited the main island in Pyramid Lake, Mr. H. G. Parker
pointed out to us the nest of a pair of these Eagles which had been occupied
the preceding season.   This nest was placed inside an oven-like cave about
half-way up the side of the perpendicular rocks which formed this portion
of the shore.   The entrance was about fifteen feet from the top of the rock,
and the same distance from the water, so it was inaccessible by any means
then at command; but it could be plainly seen by looking through a crevice
in the top of the rock.   This nest was a huge bed of coarse sticks laid on
the floor of the cave, and scattered about were the bones of numerous
animals which were carried as food to the young.   Mr. Parker remarked
that on a former visit to the island the nest was occupied, and that he had
seen the owners destroy the nest of a pair of wild geese (*Branta canadensis*)
which had been established on the ground near by.   The nest had doubtless
been abandoned in consequence of frequent visits to the island by persons
who came after Gull's eggs.

ELANUS LEUCURUS.

White-tailed Kite.

Milvus leucurus, VIEILLOT, Nouv. Dict. d'Hist. Nat., XX, 1816, 556.

Elanus leucurus, BONAP., Comp. & Geog. List, 1838, 4.—CASSIN, Baird's Birds
  N. Am., 1858, 37.—BAIRD, Cat. N. Am. Birds, 1859, No. 35.—COOPER, Orn.
  Cal., I, 1870, 488,   COUES, Key, 1872, 211; Check List, 1873, No. 336.—B. B.
  & R., Hist. N. Am. Birds, III, 1874, 198.

We did not see this species, but it is represented in the collection by a fine specimen presented by Mr. Parker, and obtained by that gentleman in the neighborhood of San Francisco, California, where it is said to be a common bird in the marshy tracts.

List of specimens.

421, " ♀ *ad.;* San Francisco, February 11, 1868. 16¾—42—?—11¼. Bill, black; eyes, orange-red; tarsi and toes, yellow." (Presented by Mr. H. G. Parker.)

PANDION HALIAËTUS.

Osprey: Fish-Hawk.

β. carolinensis.

Falco carolinensis, GMELIN, Syst. Nat., I, 1788, 263.
Pandion carolinensis, BONAP., Comp. and Geog. List, 1838, 3.—CASSIN, Baird's B. N. Am., 1858, 44.—BAIRD, Cat. N. Am. Birds, 1859, No. 44.—COOPER, Orn. Cal., I. 1870, 454.
Pandion haliaëtus var. *carolinensis,* RIDGW., Pr. Ac. Nat. Sci. Philad., 1870, 143; in B. B. & R., Hist. N. Am. B., III, 1874, 184.—HENSHAW, 1875, 415.
Pandion haliaëtus, COUES, Key, 1872, 219; Check List, 1873, No. 360; B. N.W., 1874, 367.

The Fish-Hawk, like the Bald Eagle, was seen only along the lower portion of the Truckee River, near Pyramid Lake, where it was rather common in May. It no doubt bred in that locality, since it was often observed flying up the river, bearing fish in its talons, as if going to its nest.

FAMILY CATHARTIDÆ—AMERICAN VULTURES.

RHINOGRYPHUS AURA.

Turkey-Buzzard.

(*Ho'-shim* of the Washoes.)

Vultur aura, LINN., Syst. Nat., I, 1766, 122.
Cathartes aura, ILLIGER, Prodomus, 1811, 236.—CASSIN, in Baird's B. N. Am., 1858, 4.—BAIRD, Cat. N. Am. B., 1859, No. 1.—COOPER, Orn. Cal., I, 1870, 502.—COUES, Key, 1872, 222; Check List, 1873, No. 365; B. N.W., 1874, 379.
Rhinogryphus aura, RIDGWAY, in B. B. & R., Hist. N. Am. B., III, 1874, 344.—HENSHAW, 1875, 428.

In the Sacramento Valley, the Turkey-Buzzard was so rare that not more than three or four individuals were seen during the entire month of

June, these being observed sailing over the plains toward the foot-hills of
the Sierra Nevada. In the Interior, however, it was abundant throughout
the summer, when it was found in nearly all localities; but during the
winter months they seemed to have all retired to the southward, none
having been seen in the latitude of Carson City earlier than the middle
of March. It was more numerous in the vicinity of Pyramid Lake than
anywhere else, for there the surf cast up many dead fish, thus affording
them a plentiful supply of food. At this place they were almost constantly
seen sailing quite low along the shore of the lake searching for their food.
During rainy weather we frequently observed them perched among the
cotton-wood trees along the river in such numbers as to completely cover
the branches. Throughout the Interior the distribution of the Turkey-
Buzzard was so general that it might be met with in any sort of locality;
thus, on the 19th of April we shot a fine specimen from the top of a dead
pine in a ravine of the Sierra Nevada, near Carson City, the spot being in
the midst of a dense forest, while on the 29th of June a group, consisting
of about a dozen individuals, was seen near "Sand Springs" Station, on the
Carson Desert, and one of them killed with a rifle. They had collected
about a small pool of putrid water in a portion of the desert so completely
sterile as to be almost devoid of even the usual alkaline shrubs. Throughout the country to the eastward, the Turkey Buzzard was continually met
with, both in the valleys and on the mountains, and at all elevations, the
latest individual of the season being seen October 3d, at the "City of
Rocks," in southern Idaho (latitude about 42°). In securing No. 130 of
the collection, we went to an amount of trouble worthy of a better result.
It was perched upon a high crag of the northern peak of the island, several
hundred feet above us, but even at this distance its head appeared to be
partly *white*, as if there might be a ruff of feathers of this color across the
occiput; this appearance was only more distinct as we scanned it closely
through a field-glass, so it was determined to secure the specimen if it were
possible to do so. We accordingly began climbing cautiously toward it,
but long before getting within range it flew. We kept on, however, until
arrived nearly to the spot where it had been perched, and sitting down to
rest, had remained there but a few moments when it was observed sailing

slowly back again, and approaching within gunshot, was fired at, when it fell with a thump on the rocks below. Other individuals similar to this one were seen as they soared majestically, in broad circles, about the higher cliffs, but none of them came within range. Upon descending to where our supposed prize lay, we were considerably disappointed to find it but the young of the common species, its peculiar appearance being caused by a patch of dense white down which still covered the occiput. Upon dissection, this specimen was found to have been last feeding entirely on dead fish.

List of specimens.

128, ♂ *ad.;* eastern shore of Pyramid Lake, August 16, 1867. 27¼—69—20½—16¼—1⅜—2—11½—7¼. Bill, chalk-white; iris, raw-umber; head and naked portion of the neck, livid crimson, deepest on the forehead and occiput; across the vertex, from eye to eye, a broad band of livid whitish papillæ; tarsi and toes, dirty livid yellowish-white.

130, ♀ *juv.;* island in Pyramid Lake, August 16, 1867. 27⅞—70½—21½—17—1⅛—2—11½—7½. Bill, dull black; iris, light yellowish-brown; head and naked portion of the neck, livid brownish-black; tarsi and toes, dirty livid ashy-white.

FAMILY COLUMBIDÆ—PIGEONS OR DOVES.

COLUMBA FASCIATA.

Band-tailed Pigeon.

Columba fasciata, SAY, Long's Exped., II, 1823, 10.—BAIRD, Birds N. Am., 1858, 597; Cat. N. Am. Birds, 1859, No. 445.—COOPER, Orn. Cal., I, 1870, 506.—COUES, Key, 1872, 225; Check List, 1873, No. 367; Birds N.W., 1874, 385.—B. B. & R., Hist. N. Am. Birds, III, 1874, 360, pl. LVII, fig. 2.—HENSHAW, 1875, 429.

On the 19th of November, 1867, we saw a single individual of what must have been this species, flying to the southward over the Truckee Meadows. Its appearance and size was very much that of the common House-Pigeon, but, from the manner of its flight, it was evidently a wild bird. The specimens in our collection were presented by Mr. Parker, who obtained them in the neighborhood of San Francisco.

List of specimens.

426, "♀" *ad.;* "San Francisco, California, January 31, 1868. 16—26¾—(?)—7 3/16. Bill, yellow, the tip black; eye, pink-red; lids, vermilion-red; feet, yellow."

427, "♂" (?) *ad.;* "San Francisco, January 31, 1868. 15¾—26½—(?)—7¼." Same remarks.

ECTOPISTES MIGRATORIA.

Passenger Pigeon.

Columba migratoria, LINN., Syst. Nat., I. 1766, 285.

Ectopistes migratoria, SWAINS., Zool. Jour., III, 1827, 355.—BAIRD, Birds N. Am.,
1858, 600; Cat. N. Am. Birds, 1859, No. 448.—COOPER, Orn. Cal., I, 1870,
509.—COUES, Key, 1872, 225, fig. 145; Check List, 1873, No. 370; Birds
N.W., 1874, 387.—B. B. & R., Hist. N. Am. Birds, III, 1874, 308, pl. LVII,
fig. 4.

Only a stray individual of this species was met with by us, and it
cannot be considered as more than an occasional straggler in the country
west of the Rocky Mountains. The specimen obtained flew rapidly past
one morning, and alighted a short distance from us, upon a stick by the
edge of a stream, whither it had probably come for water. Upon dissection it was found to have been feeding upon the berries of a small cornel
(*Cornus pubescens*), which grew abundantly in the mountains.

List of specimens.

179, ♀ *juv.;* West Humboldt Mountains (Camp 18), Nevada, September 10, 1867.
$13\frac{1}{2}$—$21\frac{5}{8}$—$7\frac{3}{8}$—$6\frac{1}{4}$—$\frac{5}{8}$—$\frac{7}{8}$—$5\frac{1}{16}$—3. Bill, black, the rictus pinkish; iris, brownish, with
a narrow outer ring of carmine; tarsi and toes, pale livid salmon-color, the scutellæ
more brownish; claws, blackish.

ZENÆDURA CAROLINENSIS.

Mourning Dove.

(*Hung'-o-ho'-ah* of the Washoes; *We-ho-pe* of the Paiutes.)

Columba carolinensis, LINN., Syst. Nat., I, 1766, 286.

Zenaidura carolinensis, BONAP., Consp., II, 1854, 84.—BAIRD, Birds N. Am., 1858,
604; Cat. N. Am. Birds, 1859, No. 451.—COOPER, Orn. Cal., I, 1870, 512.—
COUES, Key, 1872, 226, fig. 146; Check List, 1873, No. 371; Birds N.W.,
1874, 389.—B. B. & R., Hist. N. Am. Birds, III, 1874, 383, pl. LVIII, fig. 2.—
HENSHAW, 1875, 431.

Perhaps no bird, not even the Raven, is more universally distributed
through the Interior, without regard to the nature of the country, than the
common Mourning Dove, and certainly none is more abundant. It occurred
about the corrals of the stage-stations in the midst of the most extensive
deserts, many miles from any cultivated or wooded district, or natural

water-courses, while it was also met with on the equally barren mountains and plains far from the abode of man. In the arid portions of the country, however, it is far less common than in the fertile localities, where it sometimes literally abounds. Such was particularly the case at the Truckee Meadows, where one November evening, after supper, we killed over thirty specimens for the "pot," in the immediate vicinity of our camp. In the Sacramento Valley it was no less abundant than in the Interior.

List of specimens.

31, nest and eggs (2); Sacramento, California, June 11, 1867. Nest about six feet from ground, in small aspen. in copse.

53, nest and eggs (2); Sacramento, June 18, 1867. Nest in oak-tree, in grove, about fifteen feet from ground.

110, nest and eggs (2); Big Bend of Truckee (Camp 12), Nevada, July 26, 1867. Nest on the arid mesa, *two miles from water*, on the ground, beneath a sage-bush.

112, nest and eggs (2); Camp 12, July 29, 1867. Same locality and situation as No. 110.

192, ♀ *juv.;* West Humboldt Mountains (Camp 19), September 18, 1867. $10\frac{5}{16}$—17—6—5—$\frac{1}{2}$—$1\frac{3}{16}$—$4\frac{1}{2}$—$2\frac{1}{4}$. Bill, slate-black, bluish-slate at base; rictus, pinkish; iris, hazel; bare eyelids, bluish; tarsi and toes, pale lake-red; claws, blackish.

516, ♂ *ad.;* Carson City, April 23, 1868. $12\frac{3}{4}$—$17\frac{1}{2}$—6—$4\frac{7}{8}$. Bill, deep black, becoming slaty-bluish on the soft nasal membrane; rictus and interior of mouth, deep lake-red; bare orbital region, delicate pale blue, with a greenish tinge beneath the eye; iris, deep sepia; tarsi and toes, deep lake or coral-red; claws, deep black.

786, eggs (2); Virginia Mountains, near Pyramid Lake, June 3, 1868. Nest on ground, beneath sage-bush, on side of ravine.

1170, eggs (2); Salt Lake City, June 16, 1869. Nest on ground, beneath sage-bush.

1184, nest and eggs (2); near Salt Lake City (City Creek Cañon), June 18, 1869. Nest on mountain-mahogany tree.

1293, eggs (2); Parley's Park, Utah, June 26, 1869. Nest in aspen tree.

1294, eggs (2); Parley's Park, June 26, 1869. Same remarks.

1340, eggs (2); Parley's Park, June 28, 1869. Same remarks.

1341, eggs (2); Parley's Park, June 28, 1869. Same remarks.

1385, nest and egg (1); Provo River, July 10, 1869. Nest on bush leaning over river-bank.

1386, nest and egg (1); Provo River, July 10, 1869. Nest on bush on river-bank.

1417, eggs (2); Parley's Park, July 16, 1869. Nest among willows, along stream.

1522, egg (1); Cash Valley, Utah, July, 1869. [Collected by J. C. Olmstead.]

Family TETRAONIDÆ—Grouse.

Canace obscura.

Dusky Grouse.

Tetrao obscurus, Say, Long's Exped., II, 1823, 14, 202.—Baird, Birds N. Am.,
    1858, 620; Cat. N. Am. Birds, 1859, No. 459.—Cooper, Orn. Cal., I, 1870,
    526.—Coues, Key, 1872, 233; Check List, 1873, No. 381; Birds N.W., 1874, 395.
Canace obscura, Bonap., Comp. Rend., XLV, 1857, 428.—B. B. & R., Hist. N. Am.
    Birds, III, 1874, 422, pl. LIX, figs. 1, 2.

The "Mountain Grouse," or "Blue Grouse," was a more or less common
species on all the ranges clothed with a sufficient extent of pine forests, the
existence of which seemed to strictly govern its distribution. It was found
on the Sierra Nevada, near Carson City, and on several of the higher
ranges of the Great Basin; but it did not occur in abundance until we
arrived at the Wahsatch and Uintah Mountains, where it literally abounded
in certain localities, particularly on the latter range.

Although seldom seen in the dense pine forests, we always found
these Grouse in their vicinity, usually in the open glades with scattered
trees and brush, with thicker woods on either side. Our acquaintance with
this species being made wholly in the fall and latter part of summer, we
did not learn much regarding its habits. We can testify, however, to the
excellence of its flesh, which is white and tender as that of a partridge.

List of specimens.

891, ♂ *ad.;* East Humboldt Mountains (near Camp 22), September 4, 1868. 21—
31½—7½. Weight, 2¾ lbs. Bill black, the lower mandible slightly variegated with
whitish at the base; iris, raw-umber; bare space over eye, orange-yellow; toes,
brownish-gray; claws, black.

954, ♀ *ad.;* Wahsatch Mountains, near Salt Lake City, October, 1868.

1290, ♂ *ad.;* Parley's Park, June 25, 1869. 22—31½. Weight, 3¼ lbs. Bill, black;
iris, raw-umber; naked superciliary space, orange; toes, lilaceous-gray.

1370, ♀ *ad.;* Pack's Cañon, Uintah Mountains, July 5, 1869. 19—29. Bill, black;
iris, raw-umber; toes, ashy.

1371, ♀ *ad.;* Pack's Cañon, July 5, 1869. Same remarks.

1372, *juv.;* same date and locality.

1382, *juv.;* Pack's Cañon, July 8.

1444, ♂ *juv.;* Parley's Park, July 23.

BONASA UMBELLUS.

Ruffed Grouse.

β. umbelloides—Gray Ruffed Grouse.

Tetrao umbelloides, DOUGLAS, Trans. Linn. Soc., XVI, 1829, 148.
Bonasa umbellus var. *umbelloides,* BAIRD, Birds N. Am., 1858, 925; Cat. N. Am.
  Birds, 1859, No. 465.—COUES, Key, 1872, 235; Check List, 1873, No. 385a;
  Birds N.W., 1874, 425.—B. B. & R., Hist. N. Am. Birds, III, 1874, 453, pl.
  LXI, fig. 10.

This bird we did not see alive, but dead specimens were occasionally
seen in the hands of hunters. It was said to be common in the pine forests
of the Wahsatch, where it is known as the " Pine-Hen."

List of specimens.

955, ♂ ad.; Wahsatch Mountains, near Salt Lake City, October, 1868.

PEDIŒCETES PHASIANELLUS.

Sharp-tailed Grouse.

β. columbianus—Western Prairie Chicken.

Phasianus columbianus, ORD, Guthrie's Geog., 2d Am. ed., 1815, 317.
Pediœcetes columbianus, ELLIOT, Pr. Philad. Acad., 1862, 403.—COOPER, Orn.
  Cal., I, 1870, 532.
Pediœcetes phasianellus var. *columbianus,* COUES, Key, 1872, 234; Check List, 1873,
  No. 383a; Birds N.W., 1874, 407.—B. B. & R., Hist. N. Am. Birds, III, 1874,
  436, pl. LX, fig. 1.
Pediœcetes phasianellus, BAIRD, Birds N. Am., 1858, 626 (not *Tetrao phasianellus,*
  LINN., 1758, = *Pediœcetes*); Cat. N. Am. Birds, 1859, No. 463.

This Grouse, known universally among the western people as the
Prairie Chicken," we found only in the Upper Humboldt Valley, near
Trout Creek, where it was abundant in the rye-grass meadows at the base
of the Clover Mountains, and in a very few similar localities in the Wahsatch district.

List of specimens.

927, ♀ ad.; Upper Humboldt Valley (Camp 25), September 16, 1868.   15—25—
6.—6. Bill, black, the lower mandible more ashy basally; iris, raw-sienna; toes, ashy
horn-color.

CENTROCERCUS UROPHASIANUS.

Sage-Hen.

(*See-yuh'* of the Washoes.)

Tetrao urophasianus, BONAP., Zool. Journ., III, 1828, 214.
Tetrao (Centrocercus) urophasianus, SWAINS., Fauna Bor.-Am., II, 1831, 358, pl. 58.
Centrocercus urophasianus, JARDINE, Nat. Lib. Birds, —, 1840, pl. XVII.—BAIRD,
    B. N. Am., 1858, 624; Cat. N. Am. B., 1859, No. 462.—COOPER, Orn. Cal., I,
    1870, 536.—COUES, Key, 1872, 233; Check List, 1873, No. 382; Birds N.W.,
    1874, 400.—B. B. & R., Hist. N. Am. Birds, III, 1874, 429, pl. LX, figs. 2, 4.

Although this large and well-known Grouse was met with throughout the sage-brush country between the Sierra Nevada and the Wahsatch, we saw it so seldom that little was learned of its habits, particularly during the breeding-season. It came under our notice only late in summer and during the autumn, when it was found to be abundant in certain localities, but by no means uniformly distributed. When startled, the Sage-Hen rises with a noisy and apparently laborious fluttering, and then flies off, with a heavy but well-sustained flight, a few yards above the ground, and usually goes a long way before alighting; indeed, if allowed to escape after being once flushed there is generally little hope of getting a second opportunity for a shot. As an article of food the Sage-Hen cannot be recommended, unless the precaution is taken to flay it immediately, for its flesh soon becomes permeated with the disagreeable odor of the sage-brush, the leaves of which form its principal food. In fact, it is often found necessary to soak the carcase in salt-water over night before the flesh becomes palatable. The leaves of the *Artemisia* do not form the exclusive food of this species, however, but during the season when grasshoppers abound it feeds largely on these insects, several specimens killed in Parley's Park during a flight of these pests in August having nothing else in their crops. It is a well-known fact among western hunters that the Sage-Hen "has no gizzard," and the truth of this statement, which was often told us, we confirmed by the dissection of numerous specimens; the stomach being merely membraneous, or at most but slightly muscular, like that of a bird of prey, and nothing like the thick and powerful grinding machine of other *Gallinæ*.[1]

---

[1] See *American Naturalist*, April, 1874, p. 240, where this remarkable peculiarity of the Sage-Hen is referred to, by the writer.

List of specimens.

214, ♂ *ad.;* West Humboldt Mountains (Camp 19), September 23, 1867. 29—40½—12¾—10—1½—2¼—11½—3⅛. Weight, 4½ pounds. Bill, deep black; iris, light hazel; cervical sac, light leaden-blue; toes, grayish-olive.

311, ♀ *ad.;* Pea-Vine district, Western Nevada, November 21, 1867. 23—36½—12¾—8½—1½—1¾—7¾—2¾. Bill, deep black; iris, light brown; toes, blackish horn-color.

312, ♀ *ad.;* same locality and date. 21⅝—34—10½—8—1¼—1⅝—7¼—3. Same remarks.

313, ♀ *ad.;* same locality and date. 21½—34—10¾—8—1½—1¾—7⅛—2⅛. Same remarks.

943, ♀ *ad.;* City of Rocks, Idaho, October 3, 1868. 22—35—(?)—8¼. Same remarks.

FAMILY PERDICIDÆ—PARTRIDGES and QUAILS.

OREORTYX PICTUS.

Mountain Quail or Partridge.

β. plumiferus.

(*Mah'-tem-ah'-tek* and *Tu-ehk'-tuddle* of the Washoes; *Kih'-hik* of the Paiutes.)

Ortyx plumifera, GOULD, Proc. Zool. Soc. Lond., V, 1837, 42.

Oreortyx pictus var. *plumiferus*, B. B. & R., Hist. N. Am. Birds, III, 1874, p. 476.

Oreortyx pictus, AUCT. (part).

This superb bird occurred rather sparingly among the mountains and hills immediately adjacent to the eastern base of the Sierra Nevada, as well as on the eastern slope of that range itself. It was so rare, however, or at least so difficult to find, that we could learn but little concerning its habits. We first met with it in a broad cañon of the Virginia Mountains fronting on Pyramid Lake, where the slopes were covered, more or less, by the tall rye-grass, interspersed with scattered cedars. Here a flock of perhaps a

---

[1] The typical form, which inhabits the *coast districts* of California and Oregon (the present one inhabiting the Sierra Nevada and the peninsula of Lower California), differs in darker, browner colors. Its synonymy is as follows:—

Ortyx picta, DOUGLAS, Trans. Linn. Soc., XVI, 1829, 143.

Oreortyx pictus, BAIRD, Birds N. Am., 1858, 642; Cat. N. Am. Birds, 1859, No. 473.—COOPER, Orn. Cal., I, 1870, 546 (part).—COUES, Key, 1872, 237; Check List, 1873, No. 390; Birds N.W., 1874, 440.—B. B. & R., Hist. N. Am. Birds, III, 1874, 475, pl. LXIII, fig. 5 (part).

dozen individuals was flushed on the 27th of December, 1867, and one of them secured. Before they rose they uttered a confused chuckling, somewhat like the alarm-notes of the eastern Bob-White (*Ortyx virginianus*), and after they had been separated for some time, commenced calling to one another in a manner exactly similar to young Turkeys (*Meleagris*) under the same circumstances. Its love-notes we have never heard.

In western Nevada, where the statement seems to be generally believed, we were informed that the Mountain Quail was not an inhabitant of the country eastward of the summit of the Sierra Nevada until after the settlement of that country by the whites, when they began following the wagon-roads over the mountains for the purpose of picking up the grain scattered along the way. This may possibly be true; but judging from the fact that a number of essentially Californian birds and mammals, and even plants, occur plentifully along the eastern base of the Sierra Nevada, in an exactly similar manner, we rather incline to the opinion that it is a true native, in support of which view of the case, we were informed by the Indians at the Truckee Reservation that it had always been found on the neighboring mountains.

List of specimens.

319, ♂ ad.; Carson City, Nevada, November, 1867. (Presented by Mr. H. G. Parker.)

386, ♂ ad.; Virginia Mountains, near Pyramid Like, December 27, 1867. 11¼—17—5¾—1⅞—₁₆⁹—1₁₆³—3½—¼. Bill, dull black, more brownish terminally; iris, deep brown; tarsi and toes, dilute brownish.

440, ♂ ad.; Carson City, Nevada, March 10, 1868. (Cedar-groves.) 11¾—16¾—5¾—4¼. Bill, black, slightly brownish terminally; iris, vandyke-brown; tarsi and toes, dilute sepia.

441, ♀ ad. (mate of No. 440); same locality and date. 11¼—16⅝—5½—4¼. Same remarks.

LOPHORTYX CALIFORNICUS

California Valley Quail.

Tetrao californicus, SHAW, Nat. Misc., —, pl. 345.

Lophortyx californicus, BONAP., Comp. & Geog. List, 1838, 42.—BAIRD, Birds N. Am., 1858, 644; Cat. N. Am. Birds, 1859, No. 474.—COOPER, Orn. Cal., I, 1870, 549.—COUES, Key, 1872, 238; Check List, 1873, No. 391; Birds N.W., 1874, 439.—B. B. & R., Hist. N. Am. Birds, III, 1874, 479, pl. XLIV, figs. 1, 2.

The "Valley Quail" of California was met with only among the western foot-hills of the Sierra Nevada, where it seemed to be an abundant species. It continued along our route up to the beginning of the continuous pine forest, or to an altitude of about 5,000 feet, where a specimen, a fine adult male, was killed among the brushwood of a ravine by the roadside. There were evidently others in the locality, since the one killed was in a small tree, anxiously calling, his note being a sharp *chip*, almost exactly like the common note of the Cardinal Grosbeak (*Cardinalis virginianus*). We unfortunately had little opportunity to observe the habits of this beautiful species.

List of specimens.

316, ♂ *ad.*; 317, ♂ *ad.*; 318, ♀ *ad.*; "Coast of California, near San Francisco." (H. G. Parker.)

FAMILY CHARADRIIDÆ—PLOVERS.

ÆGIALITIS VOCIFERUS.

Kill-deer.

Charadrius vociferus, LINN., Syst. Nat., I, 1766. 253.
Ægialitis vociferus, BONAP., Comp. & Geog. List, 1838, 45.—CASSIN, in Baird's Birds N. Am., 1858, 692.—BAIRD, Cat. N. Am. Birds, 1859, No. 504.—COUES, Key, 1872, 244, fig. 156; Check List, 1873, No. 397; Birds N.W., 1874, 452 (*vocifera*).—HENSHAW, 1875, 445.

The common Kill-deer was found to be by far the most abundant and generally distributed bird of the order, since it was found about every stream or other body of water, while it was common wherever it occurred. It was also resident, but more numerous in summer than in winter.

List of specimens.

431, ♂ *ad.*; Carson City, Nevada, March 7, 1868. 10⅛—20¼—7—5⅝. Bill, black; iris, bister: eyelids, orange-red; tarsi and toes, pale ashy naples-yellow.
472, ♂ *ad.*; Carson City, March 28, 1868. 10—20½—6¹⁵⁄₁₆—5⅝. Same remarks.
1154, eggs (4); Antelope Island, Great Salt Lake, June 9, 1869. Eggs deposited on the bare sand, in a slight depression, near the shore.

ÆGIALITIS CANTIANUS.

Kentish Plover.

β. nivosus—Snowy Plover.

Ægialitis (Leucopolius) nivosus, CASSIN, in Baird's Birds N. Am., 1858, 696.
Ægialitis nivosus, BAIRD, Cat. N. Am. Birds, 1859, No. 509.
Ægialitis cantianus, COUES, Key, 1872, 245 (not of LATHAM); Check List, 1873.
   No. 401.
Ægialitis cantianus var. *nivosus*, RIDGWAY, Am. Nat., VIII, 1874, 109.—COUES,
   Check List, App., No. 401.
Ægialitis cantiana var. *nivosa*, COUES, Birds N.W., 1874, 456.

This handsome and graceful little Plover was exceedingly numerous in
May on the bare mud-flats around Warm Spring Lake, near Salt Lake
City. It kept in flocks, running nimbly and very swiftly over the ground,
all the while uttering a soft and rather musical whistling note.

List of specimens.

969, ♂ ad ; Salt Lake City, Utah, May 21, 1869. 7—13¼. Bill, deep black; iris,
burnt-sienna; eyelids, deep black; interior of mouth, fleshy-white; tarsi, slate-color;
toes, black.

1026, ♂ ad.; near Salt Lake City, Utah, May 22, 1869. 7—13⅜ Bill, deep black;
eyelids, black ; iris, deep brown ; tarsi, dull slate; toes, black.

1027, ♂ ad.; same locality and date. 6½—13¼. Same remarks.
1028, ♀ ad.; same locality and date. 6¼—12⅛. Same remarks.
1029, ♂ ad.; same locality and date. 6½—13. Same remarks.
1030, ♂ ad.; same locality and date. 6¼—14¾. Same remarks.
1031, ♀ ad.; same locality and date. 6⅔—13¼. Same remarks.

FAMILY PHALAROPODIDÆ—PHALAROPES.

STEGANOPUS WILSONI.

Wilson's Phalarope.

Phalaropus wilsoni, SABINE, App. Franklin's Journal, 1823, 691.—CASSIN, in
   Baird's B. N. Am., 1858, 705.—BAIRD, Cat. N. Am. B., 1859, No. 519.
Phalaropus (Steganopus) wilsoni, GRAY, Hand List, III, 1871, 55, No. 10,362.
Steganopus wilsoni, COUES, Ibis, April, 1865, —; Key, 1872, 248, fig. 161; Check
   List, 1873, No. 409; Birds N.W., 1874, 467.—HENSHAW, 1875, 451.

This species was shot from a flock of Sandpipers (*Tringa alpina americana, T. minutilla, T. bairdi*, and *Ereunetes pusillus*), at Pyramid Lake, in

May, 1868, and was again seen swimming in the alkaline ponds along the southern shore of Great Salt Lake, in June, 1869.

FAMILY RECURVIROSTRIDÆ—AVOCETS and STILTS.

RECURVIROSTRA AMERICANA.

American Avocet.

Recurvirostra americana, GMELIN, Syst. Nat., I, 1788, 693.—CASSIN, in Baird's B. N. Am., 1858, 703.—BAIRD, Cat. N. Am. B., 1859, No. 517.—COUES, Key, 1872, 147, fig. 159; Check List, 1873, No. 407; Birds N.W., 1874, 460.—HENSHAW, 1875, 448.

This abundant bird is confined chiefly to the vicinity of the alkaline ponds or lakes, where it is usually found in the most barren places, or where the bare earth is covered chiefly with an alkaline efflorescence. At the Soda Lakes, on the Carson Desert, it was particularly abundant, and appeared to be feeding on a kind of insect thrown by the surf upon the beach. It was not met with in the Sacramento Valley, but was first seen at the Truckee Meadows, where it was abundant in July in some alkaline marshes. Its local names are "Lawyer" and "Yelper" in most localities where it is known.

List of specimens.

811, ♂ ad.; Soda Lake, Carson Desert, Nevada, June 28, 1868. 18—29¾—(?)—7. Bill deep black; iris, burnt-umber; tarsi and toes, ashy-blue.

812, eggs (4); 813, eggs (3); 814, egg (1). Same locality and date. Eggs deposited in depressions in the alkaline deposit.

1071, ♂ ad.; near Salt Lake City, May 29, 1869. 18¾—36½. Bill, deep black; iris, brown; legs and feet, plumbeous-blue.

1107, ♂ ad.; Antelope Island, Salt Lake, June 5, 1869. 18½—31. Same remarks.

1218, 1219, 1220, 1221 (eggs); Carrington Island, Salt Lake, June 17, 1869. (Collected by Mr. R. N. Davis and Mr. S. Watson.)

HIMANTOPUS MEXICANUS.

American Stilt.

(*Pahn-tuy'-he* of the Shoshones.)

Charadrius mexicanus, MÜLLER, Syst. Nat., 1776, 117.
Himantopus mexicanus, ORD (ed. Wils.), Am. Orn., VII, 1824, 52.
Himantopus nigricollis, VIEILLOT, Nouv. Dict. d'Hist. Nat., X, 1817, 42.—CASSIN,
    in Baird's Birds N. Am. 1858, 704.—BAIRD, Cat. N. Am. Birds, 1859, No. 518.
    —COUES, Key, 1872, 247, fig. 160; Check List, 1873, No. 408; Birds N.W.,
    1874, 462.—HENSHAW, 1875, 450.

This species was almost invariably found in the same localities with
the Avocet (*Recurvirostra*), but it was everywhere less abundant than that
species. It was more numerous about the southeastern portion of the Great
Salt Lake than at any other locality visited by us.

List of specimens.

815, ♂ *ad.*; Soda Lake, Carson Desert, June 28, 1868. 15—29¼—(?)—7¾. Bill, deep
black; iris, grayish-brown next the pupil, with a wide outer ring of clear rosy-car-
mine; legs and feet, deep light rose-pink or lake-red.

1018, eggs (4); near Salt Lake City, May 22, 1869. Nest on the ground, on small
grassy island in Warm Spring Lake.

1072, ♀ *ad.*; near Salt Lake City, May 29, 1869. 14⅜—27½. Same remarks as to
No. 815.

1084, ♂ *ad.*; mouth of Jordan River, Utah, June 2, 1869. 15½—30. Iris, rich
fine carmine.

FAMILY SCOLOPACIDÆ—SNIPE, SANDPIPERS, ETC.

GALLINAGO WILSONI.

Wilson's Snipe.

(*Tuttoo-hoy'-ehk* and *Kay'-lehk* of the Washoes; *Si'-yeheh* of the Shoshones.)

Scolopax wilsonii, TEMM., Pl. Col. V, *livr.* LXVIII (in text).
Gallinago wilsoni, BONAP., Comp. & Geog. List, 1838, 52.—CASSIN, in Baird's Birds
    N. Am., 1858, 710.—BAIRD, Cat. N. Am. Birds, 1859, No. 523.—COUES, Key,
    1872, 262, fig. 163; Check List, 1873, No. 414; Birds N.W., 1874, 475.—HEN-
    SHAW, 1875, 452.
Gallinago gallinaria var. *wilsoni*, RIDGWAY, Ann. Lyc. N. Y., X, 1874, 383.

The Common Snipe was an abundant species during the spring and autumn, in all wet and grassy places. In Parley's Park, either this species or *Macrorhamphus griseus* was breeding, but we found it impossible to positively determine the species. In the lower portion of the park, about a quarter of a mile from our camp, was an extensive meadow, portions of which were quite wet or marshy; and in this direction we would hear every evening a peculiar hollow gurgling sound, somewhat like the noise produced by water escaping from a nearly full jug. This was heard only just before dark, and, as we soon ascertained, was produced by a kind of "Snipe," as it pitched downward from a great height. We found it impossible to obtain a specimen, but conclude that the bird must have been this species, since we shot specimens along a brook in the same locality at about the same time.

List of specimens.

259, ♀ *ad.;* Truckee Meadows (Camp 26), Nevada, November 7, 1867. $11\frac{3}{8}$—$17\frac{1}{2}$—$5\frac{5}{8}$—$4\frac{1}{2}$—$2\frac{11}{16}$—$1\frac{3}{16}$—$2\frac{1}{2}$—$\frac{9}{16}$. Bill, blackish for terminal third, greenish-ashy basally, the lower mandible rather paler than the upper; iris, bister; tarsi and toes, pale greenish-ashy; claws, black.

260, ♂ *ad.;* Camp 12, November 7, 1867. $11\frac{1}{8}$—$17\frac{1}{2}$—$5\frac{5}{8}$—$4\frac{1}{2}$—$2\frac{9}{16}$—$1\frac{3}{16}$—$2\frac{1}{2}$—$\frac{9}{16}$. Same remarks.

261, ♂ *ad.;* same locality and date. $10\frac{13}{16}$—$16\frac{7}{8}$—$5\frac{1}{2}$—$4\frac{7}{16}$—$2\frac{7}{16}$—$1\frac{1}{16}$—$2\frac{3}{8}$—(?). Same remarks.

262, ♂ *ad.;* same locality and date. $10\frac{1}{2}$—$16\frac{5}{8}$—$5\frac{1}{4}$—$4\frac{3}{16}$—$2\frac{3}{8}$—$1\frac{1}{8}$—$2\frac{1}{2}$—$\frac{3}{8}$. Same remarks.

1453, ♀ *ad.;* Parley's Park, Utah, July 26, 1869. $11\frac{1}{8}$—$17\frac{1}{4}$. Bill, black, growing gradually greenish horn-color basally; iris, dark brown; tarsi and toes, light ashy, with distinct yellowish-green wash on the scutellæ.

1454, ♀ *ad.;* same locality and date. $10\frac{3}{4}$—$16\frac{3}{4}$. Same remarks.

1455, ♀ *ad.;* same locality and date. 11—$16\frac{3}{4}$. Same remarks.

TRINGA ALPINA.

Red-backed Sandpiper.

β. americana.

Tringa (Schœniclus) alpina var. *americana*, CASSIN, in Baird's Birds N. Am., 1858, 719.

Tringa alpina var. *americana*, BAIRD, Cat. N. Am. Birds, 1859, No. 530.—COUES, Key, 1872, 256, fig. 166; Check List, 1873, No. 424; Birds N.W., 1874, 489.

This species occurred among the large flocks of Sandpipers and other

small waders found in the vicinity of Pyramid Lake in May, along with
Steganopus wilsoni, Tringa bairdi, T. minutilla, and *Ereunetes pusillus,* all of
which were killed at a single shot.

TRINGA BAIRDI.

Baird's Sandpiper.

Actodromus bairdii, COUES, Pr. Ac. Nat. Sci. Philad., 1861, 194.—HENSHAW,
1875, 455.
Tringa bairdii, SCL., Proc. Zool. Soc. Lond., 1867, 332.—COUES, Key, 1872, 255;
Check List, 1873, No. 419; Birds N.W., 1874, 484.

Found about Pyramid Lake in May, and at the Humboldt Marshes in
August.

List of specimens.

133, ♀ *juv.;* Humboldt Marshes (Camp 15), August 26. 1867. $7\frac{9}{16}$—15—$5\frac{1}{3}$—$4\frac{5}{16}$—
1—$1\frac{3}{16}$—$2\frac{1}{16}$—$\frac{5}{8}$.   Bill, black; iris, brown; tarsi and toes, slate-black

TRINGA MINUTILLA.

Least Sandpiper.

Tringa minutilla, VIEILLOT, Nouv. Dict. d'Hist. Nat., XXXIV, 1819, 452.—COUES,
Key, 1872, 254; Check List, 1873, No. 418; Birds N.W., 1874, 482.
Actodromus minutilla, COUES, Pr. Phil. Ac., 1861, 194, 230.—HENSHAW, 1875, 455.
Tringa wilsonii, NUTTALL, Man. Orn., II, 1834, 121.—CASSIN, in Baird's Birds N.
Am., 1858, 721.—BAIRD, Cat. N. Am. B., 1859, No. 532.

Vicinity of Pyramid Lake in May, about Salt Lake throughout the
summer, and at the Humboldt Marshes in August.

List of specimens.

134, ♂ *juv.;* Camp 15, August 26, 1867. $6\frac{5}{16}$—$11\frac{3}{4}$—$3\frac{3}{8}$—$3\frac{2}{16}$—$1\frac{3}{16}$—$1\frac{3}{4}$—$1\frac{3}{16}$—$\frac{7}{16}$.
Bill, black; iris, brown; tarsi and toes, slate-black.
135, ♀ *juv.;* same locality and date. $6\frac{3}{8}$—$12\frac{7}{16}$—$4\frac{1}{16}$—$3\frac{7}{16}$—$1\frac{3}{16}$—$1\frac{3}{4}$—$1\frac{5}{8}$—$\frac{11}{16}$.   Same
remarks.
136, ♀ *juv.;* same locality and date. $5\frac{3}{4}$—11—$3\frac{11}{16}$—3—$1\frac{1}{16}$—$\frac{3}{4}$—$1\frac{1}{3}$—$\frac{1}{2}$.   Bill, dull
black; iris, hazel; tarsi and toes, grayish-olive.

EREUNETES PUSILLUS.

Semipalmated Sandpiper.

Tringa pusilla, LINN., Syst. Nat., I, 1766, 252.

Ereunctus pusillus, CASSIN, Pr. Ac. Nat. Sci. Philad., XIII, 1860, 195.—COUES,
    Key, 1872, 254, fig. 165; Check List, 1873, No. 417; Birds N.W., 1874, 481.
    —HENSHAW, 1875, 454.

Ereunetes petrificatus, ILLIGER, Prodromus, 1811, 262.—CASSIN, in Baird's Birds
    N. Am., 1858, 724.—BAIRD, Cat. N. Am. B., 1859, No. 535.

Ereunetes occidentalis, LAWR., Pr. Philad. Acad., 1864, 107.

Ereunetes pusillus var. *occidentalis*, COUES, Key, 1872, 254; Check List, 1873, No.
    417a.

Vicinity of Pyramid Lake in May, and Humboldt Marshes in August,
in flocks with *Tringa bairdi* and *T. minutilla*. [All the specimens of these
three species shot from one flock at a single discharge.]

List of specimens.

137, ♂ *juv.;* Camp 15, August 26, 1867. $5\frac{3}{4}$—$11\frac{1}{4}$—$3\frac{5}{8}$—3—$\frac{11}{16}$—$\frac{13}{16}$—$1\frac{1}{2}$—$\frac{7}{16}$. Bill,
black, becoming greenish-olive on base of lower mandible; iris, brown; tarsi and toes,
greenish-olive.

138, ♀ *juv.;* same locality and date. $5\frac{7}{8}$—11—$3\frac{9}{16}$—$2\frac{15}{16}$—$\frac{3}{4}$—$\frac{3}{4}$—$1\frac{9}{16}$—$\frac{7}{16}$. Same
remarks.

139, ♀ *juv.;* same locality and date. $6\frac{1}{4}$—$11\frac{1}{2}$—$3\frac{3}{4}$—$3\frac{1}{4}$—$\frac{13}{16}$—$\frac{13}{16}$—$1\frac{11}{16}$—$\frac{7}{16}$. Same
remarks.

SYMPHEMIA SEMIPALMATA.

Willet.

Scolopax semipalmata, GMELIN, Syst. Nat., I, 1788, 659.

Totanus semipalmatus, TEMM., Man. Orn., II, ——, 637.—COUES, Key, 1872, 258;
    Check List, 1873, No. 431; Birds N.W., 1874, 494.—HENSHAW, 1875, 457.

Symphemia semipalmata, HARTLAUB, Rev. Zool., 1845, 342.—CASSIN, in Baird's
    Birds N. Am., 1858, 729.—BAIRD, Cat. N. Am. Birds, 1859, No. 537.

This large and conspicuous Snipe, readily distinguished at sight from
other species by the conspicuous white patch on the wings, was found
breeding in nearly all marshy localities.   It was particularly numerous on
the grassy flats along the southern shore of the Great Salt Lake, near the
mouth of the Jordan River, where it was found in company with the Long-
billed Curlew (*Numenius longirostris*) and various species of Ducks.

List of specimens.

1160, ♀ *ad.;* southern shore of Great Salt Lake, Utah, June 11, 1869.   16—$29\frac{1}{2}$.
Bill, black; iris, brown; tarsi and toes, slate-color.

   39 P R

RHYACOPHILUS SOLITARIUS.

Solitary Sandpiper.

Tringa solitaria, WILSON, Am. Orn., VII, 1813, 53, pl. 58, fig. 3.
Totanus solitarius, AUDUBON, Synop., 1839, 242.—COUES, Key, 1872, 259; Check List, 1873, No. 435; Birds N.W., 1874, 498.—HENSHAW, 1875, 459.
Rhyacophilus solitarius, CASSIN, Baird's Birds N. Am., 1858, 733.—BAIRD, Cat. N. Am. B., 1859, No. 541.

This species seemed to be exceedingly rare in the Interior, since it was seen on but two or three occasions; it was noticed in the Truckee Valley, May 13, 1868, while a pair were observed at the Glendale Meadows in July, 1867; a single individual was also observed in Parley's Park, in August. It was not met with in the Sacramento Valley.

TRINGOIDES MACULARIUS.

Spotted Sandpiper.

Tringa macularia, LINN., Syst. Nat., I, 1766, 249.
Tringoides macularius, GRAY, Genera of Birds, III, 1849, 574.—CASSIN, in Baird's Birds N. Am., 1858, 735.—BAIRD, Cat. N. Am. Birds, 1859, No. 543.—COUES, Key, 1872, 260; Check List, 1873, No. 436; Birds N.W., 1874, 501.—HENSHAW, 1875, 460.

Next to the Kill-deer (*Ægialitis vociferus*), the Spotted Sandpiper is probably the most abundant and generally-distributed of the small waders in the Great Basin. It was found breeding from the lowest valleys up to an altitude of more than 7,000 feet, its favorite haunts being the gravelly banks of running streams rather than the vicinity of ponds or lakes. Its first arrival at Carson City was noted on the 29th of April, 1868.

List of specimens.

562, ♂ ad.; Carson City, April 29, 1868. 7¾—13⅝—4⅜—3⅝. Commissure and whole of the lower mandible, dilute wax-yellow; rest of the bill, black; iris, vandyke-brown; tarsi and toes, dilute ashy-olive.

1362, eggs (2); Pack's Cañon, Uintah Mountains, July 3, 1869. Nest, a very neat one of sticks, in a slight depression on the gravelly bank of a brook. Eggs nearly hatched.

1468, *juv.*; Parley's Park, July 28, 1869. Bill, black, lower mandible purplish basally; iris, dark brown; tarsi and toes, olive.

ACTITURUS BARTRAMIUS.
Bartram's Tatler.

Tringa bartramia, WILSON, Am. Orn., VII, 1813, 63, pl. 59, fig. 2.
Actiturus bartramius, BONAP., Saggio, 1831, —.—CASSIN, in Baird's Birds N. Am.,
1858, 737.—BAIRD, Cat. N. Am. Birds, 1859, No. 545.—COUES, Key, 1872,
260; Check List, 1873, No. 438; Birds N.W., 1874, 502.

This eastern species was rather common in July in the grassy fields
of Kamas Prairie, Utah, but none were seen anywhere else.

NUMENIUS LONGIROSTRIS.
Long-billed Curlew.

Numenius longirostris, WILSON, Am. Orn., VIII, 1814, 24, pl. 64, fig. 4.—CASSIN, in
Baird's Birds N. Am., 1858, 743.—BAIRD, Cat. N. Am. Birds, 1859, No. 549.
—COUES, Key, 1872, 262, fig. 174; Check List, 1873, No. 441; Birds N.W.,
1874, 508.—HENSHAW, 1875, 461.

This large Curlew, called "Snipe" by the people of the Salt Lake
Valley, was distributed in summer throughout the Interior in the vicinity
of marshes, the wet meadows near the shores of the larger lakes being
its favorite resort. It was particularly abundant along the southern shore
of the Great Salt Lake, and on some of the larger islands.

List of specimens.

1088, ♂ *ad.*; Antelope Island, Great Salt Lake, June 4, 1869. 22½—39. Bill, black,
becoming dull lilaceous on the basal half of the lower mandible; iris, vandyke-brown;
legs and feet, ashy.

1110, ♂ *ad.*; Antelope Island, June 5, 1869. 23½—39. Same remarks.

1111, *pullus*; 1112, *pullus*; same locality and date.

1159, ♀; south shore of Great Salt Lake, June 11, 1869. 26—41¾. Same remarks
as to No. 1088.

FAMILY GRUIDÆ—CRANES.
GRUS CANADENSIS.
Sand-hill Crane.

Ardea canadensis, LINN., Syst. Nat., I, 1766, 234.
Grus canadensis, TEMM., Anal. p. c.—BAIRD, Birds N. Am., 1858, 655; Cat. N.
Am. Birds, 1859, No. 479.—COUES, Key, 1872, 271; Check List, 1873, No.
463; Birds N. W., 1874, 532.—HENSHAW, 1875, 467.

The Sand-hill Crane was an abundant species in nearly all localities
where extensive grassy marshes or wet meadows existed. A friend living

in Carson Valley had a tame bird of this species which had been caught in an adjoining meadow when very young.   Our introduction to this remarkable pet was somewhat amusing, the circumstances being as follows: Just before coming to the house we had shot a Snow-bird (*Junco oregonus*), and hastily thrust it into our coat pocket, before opening the gate of the front yard to walk in.   We had scarcely entered, when his craneship, having seen the movement, walked familiarly up, and deliberately snatching the bird, proceeded, without further ceremony, to beat it upon the ground until nearly denuded of its feathers, when he swallowed it whole; he then carefully examined our person for more birds.   Not finding any, however, he turned away and with stately steps walked off across the yard.   This bird was a great friend of the children belonging to the family, and would frequently join them in their sports.   Often, while they were indoors, he would walk upon the porch, and going to the window would look inside, and if the young folks took the least notice of him he would show his pleasure by amusing gesticulations

FAMILY RALLIDÆ—RAILS, GALLINULES, and COOTS.

RALLUS VIRGINIANUS.

Virginia Rail.

Rallus virginianus, LINN., Syst. Nat., I, 1766, 263.—CASSIN, in Baird's Birds N. Am., 1858, 748.—BAIRD, Cat. N. Am. Birds, 1859, No. 554.—COUES, Key, 1872, 273; Check List, 1873, No. 467; Birds N.W., 1874, 536.—HENSHAW, 1875, 468.

Two or three specimens of this Rail were seen in May, among the sedges bordering a pond near Pyramid Lake.

PORZANA CAROLINA.

Sora Rail.

Rallus carolinus, LINN., Syst. Nat., I, 1766, 263.

Porzana carolina, CASSIN, in Baird's Birds N. Am., 1858, 749.—BAIRD, Cat. N. Am. Birds, 1859, No. 555.—COUES, Key, 1872, 273; Check List, 1873, No. 468; Birds N.W., 1874, 538.—HENSHAW, 1875, 468.

The Common Rail was constantly met with in all suitable localities in the Interior; it was not identified at Sacramento, where, however, it no doubt occurs also.

List of specimens.

1019, nest and eggs (6); near Salt Lake City, May 22, 1869. Nest in the coarse grass and sedges of a pond, near Warm Spring Lake.

1456, ♂ ad.; Parley's Park, Wahsatch Mountains, July 26, 1869. 9—13⅞. Bill yellow, the upper mandible chiefly greenish-olive; iris, brown; tarsi and toes, olive, deepening into yellow on the scutellæ.

? PORZANA JAMAICENSIS.

Little Black Rail.

Rallus jamaicensis, GMELIN, Syst. Nat., I, 1788, 718.

Porzana jamaicensis, CASSIN, in Baird's Birds N. Am., 1858, 749.—BAIRD, Cat. N. Am. Birds, 1859, 556.—COUES, Key, 1872, 274; Check List, 1873, No. 470; Birds N.W., 1874, 540.

On several occasions, and at widely-distant localities, we met with a small Rail of a black color, which must have been this species, unless it should prove to be one at present undescribed. It was first seen on the 5th of September, 1868, in Ruby Valley. We happened to be riding horseback through a wet meadow, when the bird sprang up before us, but suddenly dropped into the grass at the edge of a dense willow thicket. We dismounted and attempted to flush it, but without success, for it had evidently escaped into the densest portion of the thicket where it could not be found. This bird appeared to be of about the size of *Porzana carolina*, though it may have been smaller, and was of a uniform blackish color, with white along the hinder edge of the wing, showing conspicuously as it flew. The same species was again met with in Parley's Park, in June, July, and August, where several were killed, but all lost in the tall grass and sedges among which they fell. We are well aware that the above description does not correspond with *Porzana jamaicensis*, but it could have been no other species at present known.

GALLINULA GALEATA

American Gallinule.

Crex galeata, LICHTENSTEIN, Verz. Doubl., 1823, 80, No. 826.

Gallinula galeata, BONAP., Am. Orn., IV, 1832, 128.—CASSIN, in Baird's Birds N. Am., 1858, 752.—BAIRD, Cat. N. Am. Birds, 1859, No. 560.—COUES, Key, 1872, 275; Check List, 1873, No. 472; Birds N.W., 1874, 540.

The "Red-billed Mud-hen" was a very abundant species in the *tule* sloughs near Sacramento, where it was found in company with the Coot, or "White-billed Mud-hen" (*Fulica americana*). It was not seen in the Interior, where the latter bird was extremely numerous.

List of specimens.

40, ♀ *ad.;* Sacramento, California, June 13, 1867. 13—21—6⅜—5¼—1½—1¹⁄₁₆' 1⅞—2¾—1¼. Bill and frontal plate, bright veinous-scarlet; tip of bill, abruptly, yellowish-green; iris, *brown;* tarsal scutellæ, bright yellowish-green, scutellæ of the toes, deeper green; knees, and joints of toes, fine ashy-blue; upper half of tibia, all round, bright scarlet.

FULICA AMERICANA.

American Coot.

(*Sï-yeh-eh* of the Shoshones.)

Fulica americana, GMELIN, Syst. Nat., I, 1788, 704.—CASSIN, in Baird's Birds N. Am., 1858, 751.—BAIRD, Cat. N. Am. Birds, 1859, No. 559.—COUES, Key, 1872, 275; Check List, 1873, No. 474; Birds N.W., 1874, 541.—HENSHAW, 1875, 469.

The Coot, or "White-billed Mud-hen," as it is sometimes called, was extremely numerous in all extensive marshes, both in the Sacramento Valley and eastward of the Sierra Nevada. In the latter region it was resident, though most abundant in summer.

List of specimens.

841, ♀ *ad.;* Camp 19, Ruby Valley, Nevada, July 15, 1868. 15¾—26⅝—(?)—6. Bill, opaque milk-white (purest basally), with a very faint lilaceous glow in the middle portion, assuming terminally a pale bluish-cast; spot at base of frontal plate, and near tip of each mandible, dark hepatic-sepia, each spot bordered anteriorly with dragon's-blood-red; iris, *carmine;* prevailing hue of tibia, tarsi, and toes, delicate pale ashy-blue, but this overlaid on tarsi (all round) and on upper surface of toes (except on joints) with bright yellowish-green; claws, black.

---

[1] To posterior end of frontal plate.

FAMILY TANTALIDÆ—IBISES.

FALCINELLUS GUARAUNA.

Bronzed Ibis.

Scolopax guarauna, LINN., Syst. Nat., I, 1766, 242.

Ibis guarauna, RIDGWAY, Am. Nat., Feb., 1874, 110, 111.—COUES, Check List, App., No. 445 bis.—HENSHAW, 1875, 463.

"*Ibis ordii*, BONAP."—BAIRD, Birds N. Am., 1858, 685 (excl. syn.); Cat. N. Am. B., 1859, No. 500.

Ibis falcinellus var. *ordii* (part), COUES, Key, 1872, 263; Check List, 1873, No. 445.

The Bronzed Ibis was an abundant bird at Franklin Lake, in August and September, but being without a boat we were unable to obtain specimens; a few were also seen at the Great Salt Lake in May and June. Like the following species, from which it may possibly not be distinct, it is known to the inhabitants of the country as the "Black Curlew," or "Black Snipe."

FALCINELLUS THALASSINUS.

Green Ibis.

"*Ibis guarauna*, LINN."—BAIRD, Birds N. Am., ed. 1860, pl. LXXXVII; Cat. N. Am. Birds, 1859, No. 500a.

Ibis thalassinus, RIDGWAY, Am. Nat., Feb., 1874, 110, 111.—COUES, Check List, 1873, App., No. 445, ter.—HENSHAW, 1875, 464.

This bird, known locally as the "Black Curlew," or "Black Snipe," was first observed in September, at the Humboldt Marshes, where it was one of the most abundant of the water-birds, since it sometimes occurred in flocks composed of hundreds of individuals. They were generally seen about the margin of the pools, standing in a single line along the edge of the water. At Oreana, about forty miles farther up the river, they were almost constantly seen passing back and forth over our camp by the river, the flocks usually formed with a widely-extended front, but oftener arranged in a V-shaped form. They flew quite low, rarely higher than fifty yards, and quite swiftly; and at this distance appeared of a uniform black color, and much like *Numenius longirostris* in size and form, whence their common name. Only once was a flock seen to alight at this locality, and from this we obtained the three specimens enumerated below, killing them all at a single shot. We approached them under cover of the willows along the river, and found them busily engaged in feeding among the aquatic plants in a slough entirely hemmed in by a dense growth of willows, each individual uttering a hoarse, but low, croaking note, as it waded about. It is still an unsettled question whether this bird is not merely the first plumage of the *I. guarauna*; but there are important considerations, geographical and otherwise, which induce us to consider it a distinct species until future developments prove the contrary

List of specimens.

159, ♂ *ad.*; Humboldt River, Nevada (Camp 17), September 3, 1867. 23—38¾—11—8⅜—5$\frac{3}{16}$—4—4—2¼. Bill, pale greenish horn-blue, becoming blackish terminally and basally; iris, hazel; tarsi and toes, deep black.

160, ♀ *ad.*; same locality and date. 21—37—10¾—8$\frac{1}{16}$—4$\frac{7}{16}$—3$\frac{5}{16}$—3¾—1$\frac{5}{16}$. Same remarks.

161, ♀ *juv.*; same locality and date. 19¾—34¼—10—7⅞—4—2⅞—3¼—1¾. Same remarks.

FAMILY ARDEIDÆ—HERONS.

ARDEA HERODIAS.

Great Blue Heron.

Ardea herodias, LINN., Syst. Nat., I, 1766, 237.—BAIRD, Birds N. Am., 1858, 667; Cat. N. Am. Birds, 1859, No. 487.—COUES, Key, 1872, 267; Check List, 1873, No. 449; Birds N.W., 1874, 517.—HENSHAW, 1875, 464.

The Great Blue Heron was abundant about all bodies of water affording it a plentiful supply of food. It was particularly numerous at Pyramid Lake, where it built upon the rocky islands. One colony had their nests on the large grease-wood bushes on the southern portion of the main island, each nest being placed directly on top of the bush, at a height of about five or six feet from the ground. These nests were very bulky, being several feet in diameter and of proportionate depth, but they were elaborately made; each contained from three to four young, about half-fledged, but very active and saucy, who, when disturbed, opened wide their bills and made spiteful thrusts, at the same time uttering an admonishing hiss. On the Pyramid were several other nests, placed among the naked rocks at varying heights from the water.

List of specimens.

763, eggs (4); Pyramid Lake, Nevada, May 23, 1868. Nest on the "Pyramid," among the rocks, about 150 feet above the surface of the lake.

HERODIAS EGRETTA.

Great White Heron.

Ardea egretta, GMELIN, Syst. Nat., I, 1788, 629.—COUES, Key, 1872, 267; Check List, 1873, No. 452; Birds N.W., 1874, 519.

Herodias egretta, GRAY, Genera of Birds, III, 1849,—.—BAIRD, Birds N. Am., 1858, 666; Cat. N. Am. B'ds, 1859, No. 486.—HENSHAW, 1875, 465.

Herodias egretta var. *californica,* BAIRD, Birds N. Am., 1858, 667; Cat. N. Am. Birds, 1859, No. 486a.

This handsome Heron we saw at Sacramento in June, and along the lower Truckee in May, a single individual only having been observed at each place.

BUTORIDES VIRESCENS.

Green Heron.

Ardea virescens, LINN., Syst. Nat., I, 1766, 238.—COUES, Key, 1872, 268; Check List, 1873, No. 457; Birds N.W., 1874, 522.

Butorides virescens, BONAP., Conspectus Avium, II, 1855, 128.—BAIRD, Birds N. Am., 1858, 676; Cat. N. Am. Birds, 1859, No. 493.—HENSHAW, 1875, 465.

This common bird was observed only in the vicinity of Sacramento, where it was abundant, as it usually is in all parts of its range. It appeared to be entirely wanting in the Great Basin—at least we could never find it, even in localities where other species of the family were found in the usual numbers.[1]

List of specimens.

14, ♀ ad.; Sacramento, California, June 10, 1867. Shallow pond along edge of oak-grove. 18½—27½—7¾—6¼—2⁷⁄₁₆—2—3—1. Bill, deep black, pale greenish-yellow along gonys; naked loral and orbital space, greenish-yellow; iris, gamboge-yellow; tarsi and toes, dull olivaceous-yellow, olive-greenish on scutellæ.

58, ♂ ad.; Sacramento, June 19, 1867. Willows along slough near river. 18½—27¼—8—6¾—2¼—1⅛—3—1¼. Same remarks.

---

[1] A parallel case is apparently afforded in *Gallinula galeata,* which we found abundant at Sacramento, in company with *Fulica americana,* but which we did not detect in the Interior, where the latter was everywhere exceedingly numerous, in suitable localities.

ARDETTA EXILIS.

Least Bittern.

Ardea exilis, GMELIN, Syst. Nat., I, 1788, 645.

Ardetta exilis, GRAY, Genera of Birds, III, 1849, —.—BAIRD, Birds N. Am., 1858, 673; Cat. N. Am. Birds, 1859, No. 491.—COUES, Key, 1872, 270; Check List, 1873, No. 461; Birds N.W., 1874, 528.

One individual of this diminutive Heron was seen in May, among the willows along the lower Truckee, the one in question being startled by the approach of our boat.

NYCTIARDEA GRISEA.

Night Heron.

β. nœvia.

Ardea nœvia, BODDAERT, Planch. Enl. Tabl., 1784, pl. 939.

Nyctiardea nœvia, GRAY, Genera of Birds, III, 1849, 558.

Nyctiardea grisea var. *nœvia*, ALLEN, Bull. Mus. Comp. Zool., III, 1872, 182.— COUES, Key, 1872, 269; Check List, 1873, No. 458; Birds N.W., 1874, 523.— HENSHAW, 1875, 466.

Ardea gardeni, GMELIN, Syst. Nat., I, 1788, 645.

Nyctiardea gardeni, BAIRD, Birds N. Am., 1858, 678; Cat. N. Am. Birds, 1859, No. 495.

This Heron was common both in the vicinity of Sacramento and in the wooded river-valleys of the Interior. Near our camp at the former place was a small pond, where, just at dusk, one of these birds alighted regularly to feed.

BOTAURUS MINOR.

American Bittern.

(*Loo'-kem-o* of the Washoes; *Tah'-bah-bo-ne-kah'-bah* of the Paiutes.)

Ardea stellaris var. *β. minor*, GMELIN, Syst. Nat., I, 1788, 635.

Ardea minor, WILSON, Am. Orn., VIII, 1814, 35, pl. 65, fig. 3.

Botaurus minor, BOIE, Isis, 1826, 979.—COUES, Key, 1872, 269; Check List, 1873, No. 460; Birds N.W., 1874, 523.—HENSHAW, 1875, 466.

Ardea lentiginosa, MONTAGUE, Orn. Dict., Suppl., 1813, —.

Botaurus lentiginosus, STEPHENS, Shaw's Gen. Zool., XI, 1819, 596.—BAIRD, Birds N. Am., 1858, 674; Cat. N. Am. Birds, 1859, No. 492.

The common Bittern was constantly found in all marshy situations in the Interior, where it appeared to be resident all the year.

List of specimens.

288, ♂ *ad.*; Camp 26, Truckee Meadows, Nevada, November 18, 1867. Wet meadow. 28—43⅜—12½—9⅜—3½—3½—4½—1¼. Upper half of upper mandible, brownish olivaceous-black, growing more brownish basally, this color continuing in a broad stripe over the lore to the eye; sharply-defined stripe of pure lemon-yellow above this, on upper edge of bare loral space, and involving upper eyelid; stripe of same on lower edge of bare loral space, along angle of mouth, and continuing in a well-defined stripe along the commissure, terminally blending into the brownish of the mandible. Lower mandible, pale lemon-yellow, deepest basally; stripe of dusky brownish along upper posterior portion. Iris, clear light sulphur-yellow next the pupil, shading exteriorly into orange-brownish, this encircled narrowly with black. Tarsi and toes, bright yellowish-green. Claws, pale brown, dusky toward point.

350, ♀ *ad.*; salt marshes, shore of Pyramid Lake, near mouth of Truckee, December 11, 1867. 24¼—37—11—8¼—2⅝—3¼—3½—1¼. Same remarks.

FAMILY ANATIDÆ—SWANS, GEESE, and DUCKS.

CYGNUS BUCCINATOR.?

Trumpeter Swan.

Cygnus buccinator, RICHARDSON, Fauna Bor. Am., II, 1831, 464.—BAIRD, Birds N. Am., 1858, 758; Cat. N. Am. Birds, 1859, No. 562.—COUES, Key, 1872, 281; Check List, 1873, No. 476; Birds N.W., 1874, 544.

In December, 1867, Swans were exceedingly numerous in the vicinity of Pyramid Lake, but as no specimens were obtained, we do not know certainly whether they were the Trumpeter or Whistler (*C. americanus*). Their note was almost exactly like that of the Sand-hill Crane (*Grus canadensis*).

ANSER ALBATUS.

Lesser Snow-Goose.

Anser albatus, CASSIN, Pr. Ac. Nat. Sci. Philad., 1856, 41.—BAIRD, Birds N. Am., 1858, 925; Cat. N. Am. Birds, 1859, No. 563a.

Anser hyperboreus var. *albatus*, COUES, Key, 1872, 282; Check List, 1873, No. 480a.

Anser hyperboreus. b. *albatus*, COUES, Birds N.W., 1874, 549.

Anser hyperboreus, HENSHAW, 1875, 470 (?).

This Goose, almost universally known as the "White Brant," was an abundant winter visitant to the lakes of the Great Basin.

---

[1] Our notes on many of the Anatidæ are necessarily very brief, from the fact that they are more difficult to observe than most other birds, except at certain times, when the habits of all the species appear much the same. Many of them are also migratory, and thus were seen only for a brief season. We must therefore pass by certain species without further remarks than to note the season when observed, or a few similar facts.

List of specimens.

255, *jur.;* Humboldt Marshes (Camp 22), October 31, 1867. Bill, blackish dusky, greenish-slate on upper basal portion; iris, brown; tarsi and toes, greenish-slate.

388, ♂ *ad.;* eastern shore of Pyramid Lake, December 28, 1867. 28—(?)—17½—13¾—2⁵⁄₁₆—2¾—(?)—(?). Weight, 5 pounds. Bill, dull light salmon-purple, becoming whitish terminally; deepest salmon-color on the culmen, and most purplish basally; commissure deep black, separated from the general purplish hue by a backward continuation of the white of the nail; eyelids, flesh-color; iris, vandyke-brown; tarsi and toes, deep salmon-purple; claws, black.

BRANTA CANADENSIS.

Canada Goose.

Anas canadensis, LINN., Syst. Nat., I, 1766, 198.

Bernicla canadensis, BOIE, Isis, 1826, 921.—BAIRD, Cat. N. Am. Birds, 1859, No. 567.

Bernicla (Leucoblepharon) canadensis, BAIRD, Birds N. Am., 1858, 764.

Branta canadensis, BANNISTER, Proc. Ac. Nat. Sci., Phila., 1870, 131.—COUES, Key, 1872, 283, fig. 185a; Check List, 1873, No. 485; Birds N.W., 1874, 554.—HENSHAW, 1875, 471.

This species was the only one of the genus found breeding in the Great Basin, where it remained throughout the year about all the larger lakes. Several goslings were caught in May, at Pyramid Lake, and their parents likewise secured; the latter were unable to fly, having molted their quill-feathers, but it required strong rowing far out into the lake to get within gunshot of them, for they were fast swimmers, and took to the open water when pursued. This species was also breeding at Great Salt Lake.

List of specimens.

1222, egg; Carrington Island, Great Salt Lake, June 17, 1869. Collected by Mr. R. N. Davis.

BRANTA HUTCHINSI.

Hutchins's Goose.

Anser hutchinsii, SWAINS. & RICH., Fauna Bor.-Am., II, 1831, 470.

Bernicla hutchinsii, WOODHOUSE, Sitgreave's Exped., 1823, 102.—BAIRD, Cat. N. Am. Birds, 1859, No. 569.

Bernicla (Leucoblepharon) hutchinsi, BAIRD, Birds N. Am., 1858, pp. XLIX, 766.

Branta hutchinsii, BANNISTER, Pr. Ac. Nat. Sci. Philad., 1870, 131.

Branta canadensis var. hutchinsii, COUES, Key, 1872, 284; Check List, 1873, No. 485b.

Branta canadensis. c hutchinsii, COUES, Birds N.W., 1874, 554.

This miniature of the Canada Goose was an abundant winter visitant in western Nevada, but it was not seen anywhere in summer, when all had gone northward to breed.

257, ♂ ad.; Truckee Meadows (Camp 26), Nevada, November 5, 1867. 34¼—60—18—13¾—1¹³⁄₁₆—2⅔—6—3¼. Bill, deep black; iris, vandyke-brown; tarsi and toes, dull brownish slaty-black.

258, ♂ ad.; Camp 26, November 6, 1867. 30¾—61½—18—14—1¾—2½—6—2¼. Same remarks.

BRANTA NIGRICANS.

Black Brant.

Anser nigricans, LAWRENCE. Ann. Lyc. Nat. Hist. N. Y., IV, 1846, 171, pl. —.

Bernicla nigricans, CASSIN, Illust. Birds Cal., Tex., &c., 1853, 53, pl. 10.—BAIRD, Birds N. Am., 1858, 767; Cat. N. Am. Birds, 1859, No. 571.

Branta nigricans, BANNISTER, Pr. Ac. Nat. Sci. Philad., 1870, 131.

Branta bernicla var. *nigricans*, COUES, Key, 1872, 284, fig. 184b.—HENSHAW, 1875, 472.

Branta bernicla. b. nigricans, COUES, Birds N.W., 1874, 557.

The Black Brant was a rare winter visitant to Pyramid Lake, where we noticed it in December, 1867, but did not obtain specimens.

ANAS BOSCHAS

Mallard.

(*Té-lehk* of the Washoes.)

Anas boschas, LINN.. Syst. Nat., I, 1766, 205.—BAIRD, Birds N. Am., 1858, 774; Cat. N. Am. Birds, 1859, No. 576.—COUES, Key, 1872, 285; Check List, 1873, No. 488; Birds N.W., 1874, 559.—HENSHAW, 1875, 472.

The "Green-head" is one of the most abundant ducks of the Interior; it is likewise a resident, though most numerous in summer. In July, this species, with several others, particularly the Cinnamon Teal (*Querquedula cyanoptera*) and Gadwall, were found in great abundance at the Glendale Meadows, where they were breeding; at that time they were molting, and having lost their quill-feathers, many were run down and killed with sticks; thirteen, including the several species, being thus obtained in a single forenoon.

119, ♀ ad.; Big Bend of the Truckee (Camp 12), August 4, 1867. 21¼—23⅛—9½—7⅛—2—1⁹⁄₁₆—(?)—(?). Bill, dark greenish, becoming olivaceous-yellow along the commissure; iris, brown; tarsi and toes, fine orange-chrome.

1161, eggs (8); south shore of Great Salt Lake, June 11, 1869. Nest in the grass, about a rod from the shore.

CHAULELASMUS STREPERUS.

Gadwall.

Anas strepera, LINN., Syst. Nat., I, 1766, 200.

Chaulelasmus streperus, GRAY, 1838.—BAIRD, Birds N. Am., 1858, 782; Cat. N. Am. Birds, 1859, No. 584.—COUES, Key, 1872, 286; Check List, 1873, No. 491; Birds N.W., 1874, 563.—HENSHAW, 1875, 474.

During the breeding-season this was by far the most abundant of the Ducks in the Lower Truckee Valley, where in May it outnumbered all other species together. The specimens killed were in fine condition and of excellent flavor, affording a delicious addition to our larder.

List of specimens.

770, eggs (9); Truckee Reservation, near Pyramid Lake, May 29, 1868. Nest of down, placed on top of a dilapidated nest of a Magpie, *in a willow-tree, about 8 feet from the ground.*

MARECA AMERICANA.

Bald-pate.

Anas americana, GMELIN, Syst. Nat., I, 1788, 526.

Mareca americana, STEPHENS, Shaw's Gen. Zool., XII, 1824, 135.—BAIRD, Birds N. Am., 1858, 783; Cat. N. Am. Birds, 1859, No. 585.—COUES, Key, 1872, 286; Check List, 1873, No. 493; Birds N.W., 1874, 564.—HENSHAW, 1875, 475.

A rather common summer resident.

List of specimens.

1162, eggs (10); Rabbit Island, Great Salt Lake, June 11, 1869. Nest of down under a grease-wood bush, near the shore.

DAFILA ACUTA.

Pin-tail.

Anas acuta, LINN., Syst. Nat., I, 1766, 202.

Dafila acuta, BONAP., Comp. & Geog. List, 1838, 56.—BAIRD, Birds N. Am., 1858, 776; Cat. N. Am. Birds, 1859, No. 578.—COUES, Key, 1872, 286, fig. 186; Check List, 1873, No. 490; Birds N.W., 1874, 561.—HENSHAW, 1875, 473.

Not abundant, but observed in November at the Truckee Meadows, and in December near Pyramid Lake. Not seen during the breeding-season.

NETTION CAROLINENSIS
Green-winged Teal.

Anas carolinensis. GMELIN, Syst. Nat., I, 1788, 533.

Querquedula carolinensis, STEPHENS, Shaw's Gen. Zool., XII, 1824, 128.—COUES, Key, 1872, 287; Check List, 1873, No. 495; Birds N.W., 1874, 565.—HENSHAW, 1875, 475.

Nettion carolinensis, BAIRD, Birds N. Am., 1858, 777; Cat. N. Am. Birds, 1859, No. 579.

Not common, but shot in June on Antelope Island, Great Salt Lake.

QUERQUEDULA DISCORS.
Blue-winged Teal.

Anas discors, LINN., Syst. Nat., I, 1766, 205.

Querquedula discors, STEPHENS, Shaw's Gen. Zool., XII, 1824, 149.—BAIRD, Birds N. Am., 1858, 779; Cat. N. Am. Birds, 1859, No. 581.—COUES, Key, 1872, 287; Check List, 1873, No. 496; Birds N.W., 1874, 566.—HENSHAW, 1875, 476.

Rather common in May at Pyramid Lake, where breeding in the meadows.

QUERQUEDULA CYANOPTERA.
Cinnamon Teal.

Anas cyanoptera, VIEILLOT, Nonv. Dict. d'Hist. Nat., V, 1816, 104.

Querquedula cyanoptera, CASSIN, U. S. N. (Gilliss') Astron. Exp., II, 1855, 202.—BAIRD, Birds N. Am., 1858, 780; Cat. N. Am. Birds, 1859, No. 582.—COUES, Key, 1872, 288; Check List, 1873, No. 497; Birds N.W., 1874, 567.—HENSHAW, 1875, 477.

This handsome species was common, though not abundant, throughout the West, both in the Sacramento Valley and in the Interior.

List of specimens.

100, nest and eggs (8); Truckee Meadows, Nevada, July 16, 1867. Nest in tuft of grass in meadow, about two rods from the river.

775, eggs (9); Truckee Reservation, June 1, 1868. Nest in a grease-wood bush, near the water.

1086. ♂ ad.; mouth of Jordan River, Utah, June 3, 1869. 16½—24½. Bill, black; iris, orange; tarsi and toes, orange, joints and webs blackish.

1087. ♀ ad.; same locality and date. 15½—24. Bill, dusky, paler along edge and beneath; iris, brown; tarsi and toes, ochraceous-drab.

SPATULA CLYPEATA.

Shoveller.

Anas clypeata, LINN., Syst. Nat., I. 1766, 200.
Spatula clypeata, BOIE, Isis, 1822, 564.—BAIRD, Birds N. Am., 1858, 781; Cat. N.
Am. Birds, 1859, No. 583.—COUES, Key. 1872, 288; Check List, 1873, No. 498;
Birds N.W., 1874, 570.—HENSHAW, 1875, 478.

Common at Pyramid Lake in May

AIX SPONSA.

Wood Duck.

Anas sponsa, LINN., Syst. Nat., I, 1766, 207.
Aix sponsa, BOIE, Isis, 1826, 329.—BAIRD, Birds N. Am., 1858, 785; Cat. N. Am.
Birds, 1859, No. 587.—COUES, Key, 1872, 288; Check List, 1873, No. 499;
Birds N. W., 1874, 571.

One pair of this superb Duck was seen in July, among the cotton-
woods of the Truckee.

AYTHYA AMERICANA.

Red-head.

Fuligula americana, EYTON, Monograph Anatidæ, 1838, 155.
Aythya americana, BONAP., Comp. Rend., 1856, —.—BAIRD, Birds N. Am., 1858,
793; Cat. N. Am. Birds, 1859. No. 591.
Aythya ferina var. *americana*, ALLEN, Bull. Mus. Comp. Zool., III, 1872, 183.
Fuligula ferina var. *americana*, COUES, Key, 1872, 289; Check List, 1873, No.
503; Birds N.W., 1874, 575.—HENSHAW, 1875, 480.

In winter this is an abundant species on the lakes of the Great Basin.
It and the succeeding species are frequently used by the Paiute Indians in
making very artistic and elaborate decoys, which have a body of bent and
twisted dry *tules* (*Scirpus*), with the skin stretched over it, the head prepared
and poised in a style equal to that of the most accomplished taxidermist.
The floating decoy is anchored by a stone tied to a string, the other end of
which is fastened to the bill.

AYTHYA VALLISNERIA.

Canvas-back.

Anas vallisneria, WILSON, Am. Orn., VIII, 1814, 103, pl. 7, fig. 3.
Fuligula vallisneria, STEPHENS, Shaw's Gen. Zool., XII, pt. II, 1824, 196.—COUES, Key, 1872, 290; Check List, 1873, No. 504; Birds N.W., 1874, 575.
Aythya vallisneria, BOIE, Isis, 1826, 980.—BAIRD, Cat. N. Am. Birds, 1859, No. 592.

The Canvas-back was abundant in winter at the lakes and marshes of the Great Basin, and it was also shot in May at Pyramid Lake, when other species were breeding. In June, either this species or the Red-head was very abundant in the tule-sloughs in the vicinity of Sacramento, where they were undoubtedly breeding. We could obtain no specimens, however, although numbers were seen, and are consequently doubtful as to the species.

FULIX MARILA.

Big Black-head.

Anas marila, LINN., Syst. Nat., I, 1766, 196.
Fuligula marila, STEPHENS, Shaw's Gen. Zool., XII, pt. II, 1824, 198.—COUES, Key, 1872, 289; Check List, 1873, No. 500; Birds N.W., 1874, 573.—HENSHAW, 1875, 479.
Fulix marila, BAIRD, Birds N. Am., 1858, 791; Cat. N. Am. Birds, 1859, No. 588.

Winter visitant to Pyramid Lake.

FULIX AFFINIS.

Little Black-head.

Fuligula affinis, EYTON, Monograph Anatidæ, 1838, 157.—COUES, Key, 1872, 289; Check List, 1873, No. 501; Birds N.W., 1874, 573.
Fulix affinis, BAIRD, Birds N. Am., 1858, 791; Cat. N. Am. Birds, 1859, No. 589.

Winter visitant to Pyramid Lake.

FULIX COLLARIS.

Ring-bill.

Anas collaris, DONOVAN, British Birds, VI, 1809, pl. 147.
Fuligula collaris, BONAP., List Birds Eur., 1842, —.—COUES, Key, 1872, 289; Check List, 1873, No. 502; Birds N.W., 1874, 574.—HENSHAW, 1875, 479.
Fulix collaris, BAIRD, Birds N. Am., 1858, 792; Cat. N. Am. Birds, 1859, No. 590.

Pyramid Lake, in December.

BUCEPHALA CLANGULA.

Golden-eye.

β. americana.

Clangula americana, BONAP., Comp. & Geog. List, 1838, 53.

Bucephala americana, BAIRD, Birds N. Am., 1858, 796; Cat. N. Am. Birds, 1859,
No. 593.

Bucephala clangula, COUES, Key, 1872, 290 (not *Anas clangula*, LINN., = *Bucephala*); Check List, 1873, No. 505; Birds N.W., 1874, 576.—HENSHAW, 1875,
480.

Pyramid Lake, in December.

BUCEPHALA ALBEOLA.

Butter-ball.

Anas albeola, LINN., Syst. Nat., I, 1766, 199.

Bucephala albeola, BAIRD, Birds N. Am., 1858, 797; Cat. N. Am. Birds, 1859, No.
595.—COUES, Key, 1872, 290; Check List, 1873, No. 507; Birds N.W., 1874,
577.—HENSHAW, 1875, 482.

Winter resident on the lakes and larger rivers of the Interior.

List of specimens.

387, ♂ *ad.*; Pyramid Lake, December 27, 1867. $14\frac{1}{4}$—$24\frac{1}{2}$—$7\frac{1}{4}$—$5\frac{9}{16}$—$1\frac{3}{16}$—$1\frac{1}{8}$—
3—$1\frac{1}{2}$.   Bill, deep leaden-blue, dusky on the nail, on the basal portion of the culmen,
and behind the nostril; *iris, dark vandyke-brown;* tarsi and feet, clear pinkish-white,
with a slight lilac tinge.

ERISMATURA RUBIDA.

Ruddy Duck.

Anas rubida, WILSON, Am. Orn., VIII, 1814, 128, 130, pl. 71, figs. 5, 6.

Erismatura rubida, BONAP., Comp. & Geog. List, 1838, 59.—BAIRD, Birds N. Am.,
1858, 811; Cat. N. Am. Birds, 1859, No. 609.—COUES, Key, 1872, 295; Check
List, 1873, No. 519; Birds N.W., 1874, 583.—HENSHAW, 1875, 483.

This Duck, the adult male of which is very conspicuous from its
peculiar markings, was abundant in the lagoons near Sacramento. In the
Interior it seemed to be rare, a female killed at Pyramid Lake, in December, being about the only one seen.

MERGUS MERGANSER.

Buff-breasted Sheldrake.

β. americanus.

Mergus castor var. *americanus,* BONAP., Comp. Rend., XLIII, 1856, —.

Mergus americanus, CASSIN, Pr. Acad. Nat. Sci. Philad., 1853, 187.—BAIRD, Birds
N. Am., 1858, 813; Cat. N. Am. Birds, 1859, No. 611.

Mergus merganser, COUES, Key, 1872, 296; Check List, 1873, No. 521; Birds N.
W., 1874, 583 (not of LINN.).—HENSHAW, 1875, 483.

Truckee and Carson Rivers, during the winter.

MERGUS SERRATOR.

Red-breasted Sheldrake.

Mergus serrator, LINN., Syst. Nat., I, 1766, 208.—BAIRD, Birds N. Am., 1858, 814;
Cat. N. Am. Birds, 1859, No. 612.—COUES, Key, 1872, 296; Check List, 1873,
No. 522; Birds N.W., 1874, 584.—HENSHAW, 1875, 484.

Truckee River and Pyramid Lake, in December.

LOPHODYTES CUCULLATUS.

Hooded Sheldrake.

Mergus cucullatus, LINN., Syst. Nat., I, 1766, 207.—COUES, Key, 1872, 296; Check
List, 1873, No. 523; Birds N.W., 1874, 584.—HENSHAW, 1875, 484.

Lophodytes cucullatus, REICH., Syst. Av., 1852, IX.—BAIRD, Birds N. Am., 1858,
816; Cat. N. Am. Birds, 1859, No. 613.

This handsome species was occasionally met with in summer in the
wooded valleys of the Truckee and Carson Rivers, but it seemed to be
very rare

FAMILY PELECANIDÆ—PELICANS

PELECANUS ERYTHRORHYNCHUS.

American Pelican.

(*Bahns* or *Bah'-nus* of the Paiutes.)

Pelecanus erythrorhynchus, GMELIN, Syst. Nat., I, 1788, 571.—BAIRD, Birds N. Am.,
1858, 868; Cat. N. Am. Birds, 1859, No. 615.

Pelecanus trachyrhynchus, LATHAM, Index Orn., II, 1790, 884.—COUES, Key, 1872,
300; Check List, 1873, No. 526; Birds N.W., 1874, 586.—HENSHAW, 1875, 484.

Pelecanus occipitalis, RIDGWAY, American Sportsman, Vol. IV, No. 19, Aug. 8, 1874, p. 297. [Name proposed in case the western birds prove distinct from the eastern.[1]]

In July, 1867, when encamped at the Big Bend of the Truckee River, about fifteen miles from Pyramid Lake, our first opportunity was afforded to observe the habits of the White Pelican. At that time few

[1] In the author's paper, above cited ["Breeding-ground of White Pelicans at Pyramid Lake, Nevada"], certain discrepancies between the descriptions given by various authors, of the breeding plumage, and form of the mandibular crest, of the White Pelicans of the northern and eastern portions of the continent, and the characters of those observed at Pyramid Lake, are noted; these consisting, in brief, of the possession by the latter of a conspicuous patch of dusky-grayish on the occiput, which is wanting in the former, the absence of a yellowish occipital crest and a rosy tint to the plumage, which is mentioned in nearly all descriptions, the smaller general size, and other minor points of difference. Captain Bendire, however, who found these birds breeding at Lake Milheur, southeastern Oregon (see *Rod and Gun*, June 19, 1875, p. 194), says that those observed by him had a *white* occipital crest, while he does not mention any dusky occipital spot. This apparent difference between the birds of two quite adjacent localities is explained, however, by Mr. C. J. Maynard, who from observations on a specimen kept in confinement, ascertained that this dusky spot appears *only after the occipital crest is dropped;* and that this takes place just at the close of the breeding-season is proven by the fact that our visit to Pyramid Lake was in the latter part of May, when these birds had just made their *second* attempt to raise a brood of young, the first effort having been foiled by the gulls, who had broken and eaten the eggs. It is a notable fact, in this connection, that our birds possessing the dusky occipital spot *had dropped the mandibular excrescence.* Mr. Maynard's bird was obtained in Florida (the date of capture is not mentioned), and had then the mandibular excrescence and an occipital crest; these were both thrown off early in May, *when the dusky spot on the occiput made its appearance*, the general plumage and the colors of the soft parts at the same time undergoing certain changes—the brilliant orange of the gular sac and orbital region fading to yellow. At the same time, however, Mr. Maynard's specimen differed in certain respects from all western examples which we have seen, which still renders it likely that, as we suggested, the eastern and western birds of this species may prove to be different races. As to this, Mr. Maynard, in the article cited above, says: "When captured he [the Florida specimen] had a fine occipital crest three or four inches in length, *of a pale straw-color* [italics our own].   *   *   The feathers of the back, usually the tertiaries, had *an elongated central spot of pale roseate. The center of the tail-feathers were also of a beautiful roseate tinge. Others shot at the same time agreed with the description given above.*" Mr. Maynard also states that his bird had *hazel* eyes instead of *white*, and that the eyelids were yellow instead of red; and that "although Audubon and Mr. Ridgway state that Pelicans have white eyes, all that I have examined have hazel." It may yet be ascertained, however, that at the proper season (the height of the pairing-season) the western White Pelicans may also possess the rosy tinge to the plumage, the yellow crest, etc., and that the color of the iris may be to a certain extent dependent on age.

of these birds were seen, only a solitary individual being now and then startled from a bed of driftwood in the river or noticed flying overhead. In August, a portion of the party, accompanied by Mr. H. G. Parker, United States Superintendent of Indian Affairs for Nevada, started on an excursion to explore the lake and visit the abode of the Pelicans on the island therein. As we descended the river the number of Pelicans seen increased hourly, and when we reached the large open sheets of water protected from the gales and swells of the lake by the intervening areas of rushes and reeds (*tules*), bodies of hundreds of these melancholy-looking birds were seen floating quietly upon the surface. They were exceedingly unsuspicious, and so unmindful of our approach that when we stopped our boat one old fellow swam slowly toward it until his curiosity brought him within gunshot and to his death. Upon reaching the lake we encamped on the sandy-shore about three quarters of a mile from the mouth of the river. There we could see during the day thousands of Pelicans, as they dotted the bosom of the lake, and in the morning, about sunrise, "strings" of several hundreds were observed flying from the island, about twelve miles distant, where they had passed the night, to their feeding-grounds at the mouth of the river. At such times they flew single-file, their manner of flight being a succession of slow regular flaps of the wings, which at intervals were extended to their full length, the birds sailing thus for a few rods, when the flapping was resumed. In their flight, the line preserved the utmost order and method; the leader being invariably the first to beat or extend his wings, each one of the line following in succession. Occasionally an individual would break the rank and alight upon the water, often remaining in one spot for hours, and appearing in the distance like a white boat at anchor. We remained here at our shore-camp about three days, when, two more of the party joining us, we started about ten o'clock one moonlight night for the island, which we reached after a hard row of about three hours. Our arrival at the island startled the thousands of Pelicans which were slumbering on the beach, and as they rose into the air the noise caused by their confusion was so great that we could scarcely hear one another's voices. When we landed they had all flown save a few sick or old birds, that swam silently away from the shore; they could be plainly seen, however, in the bright moonlight, floating as a mass some distance out upon the water; and no sooner had we left the boat than they turned and swam slowly back again. Our blankets were spread upon the higher ground, some distance from the boat, in order to avoid the offensive smell of the roosting-ground. No sooner had we retired than the Pelicans all returned, and in the morning, when we awoke, the whole beach about fifty yards distant was covered with a dense crowd of these gigantic snow-white creatures, who scarcely heeded us as we arose from our blankets; as we approached them, however, they pushed one another awkwardly into the water, or rose heavily and confusedly from the ground, and flying some distance out upon the lake, alighted on the water. Now and then, one swimming from the shore would turn its head and gaze upon us with a melancholy look; but the majority of the flock remained upon the water only a short time, when they arose and flew over us, divided into battalions, each turning its head and looking down upon us as it went by.

In this connection, it may perhaps be well to remark that of the many individuals killed, including old and young of both sexes, and of the thousands seen, not one possessed at this time the horny appendage to the culmen of the upper mandible, so characteristic of the species during the breeding-season. Three specimens, an adult male and female and a full-grown young bird of the year, were prepared; but our return to camp being attended by many difficulties, they were lost.

The next visit to the lake was made in December, following, when Mr. Parker extended us an invitation to accompany him to the agency of the reservation; but during our stay of about a month we did not see a single Pelican, all having retired to the southward. Their return was first observed about the twentieth of the following March, when we noticed, at Carson City, immense flocks of them passing northward, in the direction of the lake. They flew at a great height, and at times appeared bewildered, moving in circles and deviating from the course they had pursued, as if uncertain of their way.

In May, 1868, the lake was again repaired to, and at this time we found the Pelicans in as great abundance as during our visit the summer previous; they appeared to be much more active, however, pairs, small companies, or single birds flying up and down the river, quite near the ground; and it was noticed that only a portion of them possessed the "center-board," although all exhibited the high-colors of the feet and pouch found only in the fully adult birds in the breeding-season.

A few days after our arrival, we visited the island before mentioned. This island is situated about twelve miles from the mouth of the river, on the southeastern shore, and about three miles from the nearest point on the eastern side, just off which is the remarkable "Pyramid," from which the lake receives its name—a wonderfully regular pyramidal rock about three hundred feet high, with a triangular base. The island itself is about three miles in circuit; its central portion culminates in two peaks having a height of about five hundred feet above the surface of the lake, while the northern and southern extremities run out in long, pointed beaches, the intervening eastern shore being a sloping plateau, with a water-front of perpendicular though broken rocks. In a cave on this rocky shore was the eyrie of a Bald Eagle, which was inaccessible from any point, although it could be plainly seen from above through a crevice in the rocks. The southern point of the island was overgrown by grease-wood bushes of an unusually large size, and on the top of each of these was the nest of a pair of Great Blue Herons (*Ardea herodias*); the more elevated and rocky northern shore was covered by the nests of an immense colony of Gulls (*Larus californicus*), while the northeastern point, a long strip of low gravelly beach, extending for a hundred yards or more out into the lake from the main shore, was the portion of the island which had been selected by the Pelicans as their breeding-ground. This drove of Pelicans, which comprised several hundred pairs, had previously, during the same season, laid their eggs on the highest part of the eastern plateau, where we found the fragments of their eggs, which had been destroyed by their incessant enemies, the Gulls, strewn over an area of about two acres' extent. This old breeding-ground was discovered by us during our first exploration of the island, and it was not until a week or so later that we found the new settlement. The site of the latter was a low gravelly point extending a hundred yards or more beyond the main beach, and when first discovered was covered by a compact body of Pelicans, which to all appearance were merely resting, since many of them were standing. Upon proceeding to the spot, however, it was found that the latter were male birds, standing beside their mates, who were, themselves, sitting on their eggs. At our approach all of them flew, and alighted some distance out upon the water. The ground was then found to be literally covered with their nests, which occupied nearly if not quite one-half of the surface, each nest consisting merely of a heap of gravel raked into a pile and flattened on top, and without any additional material, such as sticks and feathers, like those of the Gulls. No nest contained more than a single egg, which is no doubt explained by the fact that they had laid once before that season. One hundred and nine, altogether, were picked up, and when blown were found to be perfectly fresh. Many nests were empty, so that it is altogether likely some of the birds had not laid yet. These eggs were, with scarcely an exception, conspicuously blood-stained, caused in part by their large size, but chiefly by the roughness of their calcareous coating; the hæmorrhage being in some instances so copious that half the surface was discolored.

It was during this visit to Pyramid Lake that the fact that the man-dibular excrescence characteristic of this species is deciduous was confirmed, it having been first ascertained, so far as we know, several years previous, by Mr. H. G. Parker, of Carson City, a very careful and intelligent observer, at that time United State Superintendent of Indian Affairs for Nevada, who accompanied us upon our several visits to the lake. Upon our arrival there, early in May, it was noticed that quite a number of the Pelicans did not possess this appendage, but it was supposed that these were females; and it was also observed that there was a very perceptible daily increase in the number of such individuals. When we first visited the island none of these curious appendages, appropriately styled by Mr. Parker "center-boards," were noticed; but in the course of a few days they became so numerous that a bushel of them could have been picked up in a short time. Some had been recently dropped, as was readily detected from the soft texture of the surface where they had been joined to the culmen, while others were dried and warped by the sun, having been cast for some time. Among the large number examined, we found none corresponding in shape with that figured and described by Mr. Audubon, namely, "about one inch high   *   * and about three inches in length, in some specimens as much as five inches," and "continued forward, of less elevation, to the extent of an inch farther"[1] —all being of quite regular and firm outline, the top convex or arched, the width at the base greater than that through the middle; they were also without anterior or posterior continuations. The usual size was about two and a half inches in vertical length, and the same in width at the base, the largest specimen found being three and a half inches high by three wide. Of two now before us, one measures two and a half inches from the center of the top to the posterior lower angle, three and a quarter from the same point to the anterior lower corner, and a little more than two and a half inches along its base, its transverse thickness being three-tenths of an inch. The other measures one inch and eight-tenths in height (the fibers running perpendicularly, instead of very obliquely backward, toward the top) by two inches and seven-tenths in width at the base. In some examples the two edges were nearly parallel, the general form being thus very nearly semi-elliptical; but such specimens were rare, the usual form being an irregular arch.

In a former account of the habits of the White Pelican as observed at Pyramid Lake, published in the *American Sportsman* (Vol. IV, No. 19, pp. 289 and 297), we stated that the horny excrescence, characteristic of this species in the breeding-season, was peculiar to the male. We were led to make this statement by the fact that of the several specimens dissected every one possessed of this appendage proved to be a male, while nearly all those in which it was absent were females. We did not, unfortunately, take into consideration the circumstance that the breeding-season was nearly over, and that, as a consequence, a very large proportion (a considerable majority, in fact) of these birds had shed, or cast, this curious deciduous growth. We are glad, however, to have our error corrected, as has been done by several observers having opportunities which were not afforded ourselves for deciding the point, and who furnish satisfactory evidence that both sexes possess the so-called "center-board." According to Dr. T. M. Brewer (*Rod and Gun*, June 19, 1875, p. 194), the error of our statement was perhaps first ascertained by Captain Charles Bendire, U. S. A.,

---

[1] *Birds of America*, Oct. ed., Vol. VII, p. 20, pl. 422.

who found these birds breeding in immense numbers at Lake Malheur, in southeastern Oregon, on the 16th of April, 1865; but we had been previously corrected by Professor F. S. Snow, in the *Observer of Nature* (Lawrence, Kansas), June 4, 1875, and by Mr. N. S. Goss, of Neosho Falls, Kansas, in the *Rod and Gun* for June 12, 1875 (page 167). That the mandibular crest of this species is really deciduous, however, has been fully confirmed by recent observers; and regarding this remarkable fact, it may be proper to state here, that it was first discovered by Mr. H. G. Parker, of Carson City, Nevada (in about 1865), and first published by us, through Professor Baird, in *The Ibis* (London), in 1869 (p. 350).

The length of time required for the perfect development of this appendage is not known. From the articles cited above, however, we know that it is to be found from the 16th of April until June 3d, so that it may therefore fairly be presumed that its growth commences early in the spring or late in winter; and we have also positive proof that it falls off of many individuals as soon as the beginning of May, and that by the end of the latter month exceedingly few which possess it are to be found; while it is also certain that it does not exist on any specimens during the latter part of summer, in fall, or in the early part of winter. As to the use of this appendage, no plausible theory has yet been proposed, so far as we know; it certainly is not a weapon of defense or offense, since in that case it would hardly be possessed by both sexes, while it is also well known that few birds are less combative than the Pelican.

There are many seasonal changes of plumage in this species which are, as yet, only very imperfectly understood, but which we hope soon to see made clear by the observations of those who have the opportunity to study these birds in nature during different times of the year. These problems have been fully discussed by us in the paper in the *American Sportsman*, alluded to above, to which the reader is referred for information on this point.

List of specimens.

749, ♀ *ad.*; Pyramid Lake, Nevada, May 19, 1868. 62—106—25½—19. Weight, 15 pounds. General hue of the bill, reddish salmon color, the culmen dirty whitish, the reddish deepening on the nail and edges of the mandibles into orange-red; lower mandible deeper reddish than the upper, and growing more intense, or brick-red, basally; gular pouch, passing from nearly white anteriorly, through rich yellow and then orange, into intense dragon's-blood- or brick-red at the base, and with a blackish suffusion anteriorly; loose, flabby skin of the lores and orbital region, rich orange-yellow; eyelids, dark dragon's-blood-red; iris, clear pearl-white; naked portion of the tibia, tarsi, and feet, intense orange-red, so deep as to have the appearance of having been dyed. [*Without the mandibular process.*]

766, ♂ ad.; Pyramid Lake, May 28, 1868. 62—101—24½—18½. Weight, 17 pounds. Same remarks. [*Without the mandibular process.*]

570–679, eggs; island in Pyramid Lake, May 16, 1868. One hundred and nine eggs, *from as many nests.* Nests, mere heaps of gravel, with a slight depression on top, crowded together on a narrow point of the island, only a few feet above the surface of the lake.

Family GRACULIDÆ—Cormorants.

Graculus dilophus.

Double-crested Cormorant.

β. floridanus.

(*Pah-tsik'-wy-he* or *Pah-tsik'-we* of the Paiutes.)

Phalacrocorax floridanus, Audubon, Orn. Biog., III, 1835, 387; B. Am., oct. ed., VI, 430, pl. 417.

Graculus floridanus, Bonap., Consp. Av., II, 1855, 172.—Lawrence, in Baird's Birds N. Am., 1858, 879.—Baird, Cat. N. Am. Birds, 1859, No. 624.

Graculus dilophus var. *floridanus,* Coues, Key, 1872, 303; Check List, 1873, No. 530a.

Graculus dilophus. b. *floridanus,* Coues, Birds N.W., 1874, 587.

This Cormorant was very abundant at Pyramid Lake and along the lower portion of the Truckee River, being the only species of the family occurring in that vicinity. It was found from May until August, but in December none were observed. Small congregations were frequently to be seen during the summer-time, perched upon the snags far out in the lake, the latter being nearly submerged cotton-wood trees which marked, at that time, the former course of the river when the lake occupied more restricted limits.[1]

---

[1] As is the case with the Great Salt Lake, Pyramid Lake has risen many feet within the last few years, the principal encroachment being on the low land adjacent to the mouth of the Truckee River, which at the time of our last visit was thrown a mile or more back from its former location, as marked by the line of partly-submerged trees alluded to above.

On these tree-tops many of their nests were found, these being composed of sticks, and containing one to three eggs each.

Besides the specimen in our collection, an adult, in the nuptial plumage, was killed in May, but was not preserved; in this specimen the following differences were noted in the colors of the soft parts: Iris, brilliant green; eyelids, and whole interior of the mouth, bright cobalt-blue; gular sac, deep orange.

List of specimens.

127, ♀ *juv.;* Pyramid Lake, August 13, 1867. 33½—52½. Bill, dull brownish-yellow, nearly black on the culmen; gular sac, dull chrome-yellow; iris, greenish-gray; tarsi and toes, deep black.

735, egg (1); Pyramid Lake, May 17, 1868. Nest in top of cotton-wood tree, at mouth of the river.

751, egg (1); Pyramid Lake, May 20, 1868. Same remarks.

FAMILY LARIDÆ—GULLS and TERNS.

BLASIPUS HEERMANNI.

Heermann's Gull.

Larus heermanni, CASSIN, Pr. Ac. Nat. Sci. Philad., VI, 1852, 187.

Blasipus heermanni, BONAP., Consp. Av., II, 1856, 211.—LAWRENCE, in Baird's Birds N. Am., 1858, 848.—BAIRD, Cat. N. Am. Birds, 1859, No. 666.

Larus (Blasipus) heermanni, SCL. & SALV., Proc. Zool. Soc. Lond., 1875, 574 (fig.).—COUES, Birds N.W., 1874, 641.

Larus belcheri, SCHLEG., Mus. Pays-Bas, *Lari,* 9 (part).—COUES, Check List, 1873, No. 531.

Larus (Blasipus) belcheri, COUES, Key, 1872, 314.

Found only along the Pacific coast. Represented in our collection by a specimen presented by Mr. Parker.

List of specimens.

429, " ♂ *juv.;* Bay of San Francisco, February 20, 1863. 17¾—42—(?)—10." (Presented by H. G. Parker.)

LARUS CALIFORNICUS.

California Gull.

(*Que-nahk'-et* or *Gui-ni'-heet* of the Paiutes.)

? *Larus argentatoides*, BONAP., Synop., 1828, 360.

Larus californicus, LAWRENCE, Ann. Lyc. Nat. Hist. N. Y., VI, 1854, 79; in Baird's
Birds N. Am., 1858, 846.—BAIRD, Cat. N. Am. Birds, 1859, No. 663.—COUES,
Birds N.W., 1874, 634.

Larus delawarensis var. *californicus*, COUES, Key, 1872, 313; Check List, 1873,
No. 548a.

This species was the only Gull found in the Great Basin during summer, but it was apparently entirely absent in winter, when its place was
supplied by *L. delawarensis*. It was abundant both at Pyramid Lake and
Great Salt Lake, on the rocky islands of which it nested in immense
colonies. At the former locality, many hundred pairs occupied a portion of
the northern shore of the main island, where the ground was elevated many
feet above the lake, with a broken ledge of rock along the shore as well as
above their breeding-ground. Here their nests covered several acres of
ground, and were thickly strewn over the surface; each consisted of an
external rim of gravel and other rubbish raked into a pile, the center hol-
lowed out and lined with a few feathers and sticks; the number of eggs, of
which many bushels were gathered for food, varied from one to four in a
nest, and among this immense quantity we noticed very remarkable ex-
tremes of form, size, and colors, the series selected for preservation illustra-
ting the principal of these variations. While their nests were being despoiled,
the Gulls kept up a constant clamor, some hovering over our heads, but most
of them perched in rows on the ledge of rocks back from the breeding-
ground. Over fifty specimens were shot, and among these slight individual
discrepancies were noted, the principal one being in the distinctness of the
black spots near the end of the bill, which in a few were entirely obsolete,
in some distinct on both mandibles, and in others of intermediate development. The examples in the collection, enumerated below, were selected
with a view to represent the extreme variations detected in the large series
examined.

List of specimens.

111, ♂ *ad.;* Truckee River, at Big Bend, July 29, 1867. $21\frac{5}{8}$—53—$15\frac{3}{4}$—12—$2\frac{1}{4}$—$2\frac{1}{8}$—$6\frac{1}{8}$—$2\frac{1}{4}$. Bill, greenish lemon-yellow, the terminal third of the lower mandible bright orange-red, tinged with carmine, the tip again yellow; a distinct dusky spot in the middle of the red, and one immediately above it, near end of upper mandible; rictus and eyelids, vermilion-red; *iris, dark hazel; tarsi and toes, light ashy pea-green;* claws, black.

680–734, eggs; island in Pyramid Lake, May 16, 1868.

739–747, eggs; same locality, May 18, 1868.

752, ♂ *ad.;* island in Pyramid Lake, May 20, 1868. 22—54—$13\frac{1}{8}$. Bill, deep naples-yellow, tinged with chrome, and having a distinct band of dusky near the end, which is grayish-white; the dusky spot on the lower mandible followed posteriorly by a spot of deep orange-red; rictus and eyelids, vermilion; *iris, vandyke brown; tarsi and toes, pale pea-green.* [Compare with notes on *L. delawarensis*, as given below.]

753–760, eggs; same locality, May 22, 1868.

800, ♂ *ad.;* same locality, May 25, 1868. $22\frac{3}{4}$—$55\frac{1}{2}$—(?)—$13\frac{1}{2}$. Same remarks as to No. 111, but black spots of the bill obsolete.

801, ♂ *ad.;* same locality and date. $22\frac{1}{2}$—$55\frac{1}{2}$—(?)—$13\frac{1}{2}$. Same remarks; black spots distinct.

802, ♀ *ad.;* same locality and date. $21\frac{1}{2}$—$51\frac{1}{4}$—(?)—$12\frac{3}{4}$. Black spots obsolete.

1199–1217, eggs; Carrington Island, Great Salt Lake, June 17, 1869. (Collected by R. N. Davis and S. Watson.)

LARUS DELAWARENSIS.

Ring-billed Gull.

(*Que-nahk'-et* of the Paiutes.)

Larus delawarensis, ORD, Guthrie's Geog., 2d Am. ed., II, 1815, 319.—LAWR., in Baird's Birds N. Am., 1858, 846.—BAIRD, Cat. N. Am. Birds, 1859, No. 664.—COUES, Key, 1872, 313; Check List, 1873, No. 548; Birds N.W., 1874, 636.—HENSHAW, 1875, 485.

This Gull was observed only as a winter sojourner at Pyramid Lake, being entirely absent from there in summer.

List of specimens.

365, ♀ *ad.;* Pyramid Lake, Nevada, December 21, 1867. 18—45—$14\frac{1}{2}$—$12\frac{1}{4}$—$1\frac{1}{2}$—$1\frac{7}{8}$—$5\frac{3}{4}$—$2\frac{1}{8}$. Bill, greenish naples-yellow, with a transverse band of deep black near the end; rictus and eyelids, vermilion-red; interior of the mouth, deep orange-red, growing more intense posteriorly; *iris, light naples-yellow; tarsi and feet, deep, light, naples-yellow.* [Compare with notes on *L. californicus*, given above.]

CHRŒCOCEPHALUS PHILADELPHIA.

Bonaparte's Gull.

Sterna philadelphia, ORD, Guthrie's Geog., 2d Am. ed., II, 1815, 319.

Chrœcocephalus philadelphia, LAWR., in Baird's Birds N. Am. 1858, 852.—BAIRD, Cat. N. Am. Birds, 1859, No. 670.

Larus philade'phia. GRAY, List. Br. Birds, 1863, 235.—COUES, Key, 1872, 316; Check List, 1873, No. 556.

Larus (Chrœcocephalus) philadelphia, COUES, Birds N.W., 1874, 655.

Not seen by us.

List of specimens.

430, " ♀ *ad.;* Bay of San Francisco, February 1, 1868. 13¼—31⅜—(?)—8¼." (Presented by H. G. Parker.)

STERNA REGIA.

Royal Tern.

Sterna regia, GAMBEL, Pr. Ac. Nat. Sci. Philad., IV, 1848, 228.—LAWR., in Baird's Birds N. Am., 1858, 859.—BAIRD, Cat. N. Am., B., 1859, No. 683.—COUES, Key, 1872, 319; Check List, 1873, No. 562.

Thalasseus regius, GAMBEL, Jour. Ac. Nat. Sci. Philad., I, 2d ser., 1849, 228.

Sterna (Thalasseus) regia, COUES, Birds N.W., 1874, 669.

This powerful Tern was more or less common in May at Washoe Lake and near Pyramid Lake, in September at the Humboldt Marshes, and among the marshes near Salt Lake City in June and July.

STERNA FORSTERI.

Forster's Tern.

Sterna forsteri, NUTTALL, Man. Orn., II, 1834, 274 (foot-note).—LAWR., in Baird's Birds N. Am., 1858, 862.—BAIRD, Cat. N. Am. Birds, 1859, No. 691.—COUES, Key, 1872, 321; Check List, 1873, No. 566; Birds N.W., 1874, 676.—HENSHAW, 1875, 486.

Sterna havelli, AUDUBON, Orn. Biog., V, 1839, 122, pl. 409, fig. 1 (= *young*).—LAWR., in Baird's Birds N. Am., 1858, 861.—BAIRD, Cat. N. Am. Birds, 1859, No. 686.

Forster's Tern was very common in June at Sacramento, and throughout the summer in the vicinity of Pyramid, Ruby, and Franklin Lakes, and the Humboldt Marshes. It was met with afterward at Great Salt Lake, where it was the most abundant species, far exceeding in numbers even the *Hydrochelidon lariformis.*

List of specimens.

1085, ♂ *juv.;* Salt Lake City, Utah, June 2, 1869. 14½—30¼. Terminal half of bill, black; basal half, dull orange-red; iris, brown; tarsi and toes, beautiful rich orange-red.

HYDROCHELIDON LARIFORMIS.

Black Tern.

Rallus lariformis, LINN., Syst. Nat., I, ed. 10, 1758, 153 (*European*).

Hydrochelidon lariformis, COUES, Birds N.W., 1874, 704.—HENSHAW, 1875, 487.

Sterna fissipes, LINN., Syst. Nat., I, 1766, 228 (*European*).

Hydrochelidon fissipes, GRAY, Genera of Birds, III, 1849, 660 (*European*).—COUES, Pr. Ac. Nat. Sci. Philad., 1862, 554; Key, 1872, 323; Check List, 1873, No. 575 (*American*).

Sterna plumbea, WILSON, Am. Orn., VII, 1813, 83, pl. LXIX, fig. —(*American*).

Hydrochelidon plumbea, LAWR., in Baird's Birds N. Am., 1858, 864.—BAIRD, Cat. N. Am. Birds, 1859, No. 695.

This lively and interesting Tern was an exceedingly numerous species at Sacramento, as well as about the extensive marshes of the Interior. At the former locality they were seen about every pool in the outskirts of the city, flitting over the surface of the water, and across the meadows, uttering their harsh note of *krik, krik, krik,* as they flew. They were so unsuspicious that the town boys often killed them with stones or clubs thrown at them when flying.

List of specimens.

59 ♂ *ad.;* Sacramento City, California, June 19, 1867. 9⅝—24¼—8½—6¾—1⅛— 1⅜₆—3¼—1½. Bill, deep black; rictus, purplish lake-red; interior of mouth, lavender-pink; iris, hazel; tarsi and toes, dark purple; claws, black.

FAMILY PODICIPIDÆ—GREBES.

PODICEPS OCCIDENTALIS.

Western Grebe.

Podiceps occidentalis, LAWRENCE. in Baird's Birds N. Am., 1858, 894.—BAIRD, Cat.
N. Am. Birds, 1859, No. 704.—COUES, Key, 1872, 336; Check List, 1873, No.
608.—HENSHAW, 1875, 458.

Æchmophorus occidentalis, COUES. Pr. Ac. Nat. Sci. Philad., 1862, 229.

Podiceps (Æchmophorus) occidentalis. a. occidentalis, COUES, Birds N.W., 1874,
727.

This large Grebe was very abundant in Pyramid Lake, where it
appeared to be a permanent resident. The specimen in the collection was
found "snow-bound" in the sage-brush near Carson City, being discovered
by its tracks in the deep snow, where it had scrambled along for a hundred
yards or more. It was headed toward the Carson River, and had evidently
come from Washoe Lake, about five miles distant, and becoming exhausted
by the long flight had fallen to the ground. In Pyramid Lake, these Grebes
were exceedingly abundant in May, and were constantly in sight from our
boat. When fired at with a rifle they would dive at the report, and upon
their reappearance generally showed only the head or head and neck above
the surface; but they swam so low in the water that we found it exceedingly difficult to kill them; one was shot, however, and was found to agree
exactly in colors and other respects with the specimen in our collection.[1]

List of specimens.

402, ♂ ad.; Carson City, Nevada, January 13, 1868. 26—40—8—5½—3—2¾—(?)
—(?). Bill, dull, rather light yellow, the lower mandible deepening into orange terminally; culmen and broad longitudinal space on the side of the basal two-thirds of the
lower mandible, dark olive-green, the former nearly black; iris, pure carmine (having
much the appearance of a red currant), growing narrowly whitish around the pupil;
tarsi and toes, dull olivaceous-yellow, the outer side of the tarsus and joints of the
toes nearly black.

---

[1] The seasonal changes of plumage, so remarkable in most Grebes, do not manifest
themselves in the species of this group (*P. occidentalis* and *P. clarki*), the colors and
markings being identical in winter and in the breeding-season. Even the young do not
differ appreciably from the adult, as is seen from a specimen collected the past season
in Nevada, by Mr. HENSHAW. In view of these facts, as well as in justice to important
peculiarities of form, we should now use the generic name *Æchmophorus*, proposed by
Dr. COUES, for this group.

41 P R

PODICEPS CRISTATUS.

Crested Grebe.

Colymbus cristatus, LINN., Syst. Nat., I, 1766, 222.

Podiceps cristatus, LATHAM, Ind. Orn., II, 1790, 780.—LAWR., in Baird's Birds
N. Am., 1858, 893.—BAIRD, Cat. N. Am. Birds, 1859, No. 703.—COUES, Key,
1872, 336; Check List, 1873, No. 609; Birds N.W., 1874, 729.

This species was quite numerous in August and September in Franklin
Lake, but no specimens could be obtained. It is no doubt a summer-resident in suitable localities throughout the Basin.

PODICEPS AURITUS.

Eared Grebe.

β. *californicus—California Grebe.*

Podiceps californicus, HEERMANN, Pr. Ac. Nat. Sci. Philad., 1854, 179.—LAWR.,
in Baird's Birds N. Am., 1858, 895.—BAIRD, Cat. N. Am. Birds, 1859, No. 707.

Podiceps auritus var. *californicus*, COUES, Key, 1872, 337; Check List, 1873, No.
612; Birds N.W., 1874, 733.—HENSHAW, 1875, 489.

This little Grebe was usually found in the same localities with *P. occidentalis*, and like it was a constant resident. In Soda Lake, on the Carson
Desert, we observed a very large flock of what was probably this species,
but they kept so far from the shore that the species could not be determined beyond doubt. They were exceedingly clamorous.

List of specimens.

366, ♂ ad.; Pyramid Lake (mouth of the Truckee River), December 21, 1867. 12
—21—5—3¾. Upper mandible, greenish-black, growing pale ashy olive-green on basal
third of the commissure (broadly) and on the culmen; lower mandible, ashy olive-
green, paler below, and more yellowish basally; iris, bright orange-red, more scarlet
outwardly, and with a fine thread-like white ring around the pupil; tarsi and toes,
dull blackish on outer side, passing on the edges into olive green; inner side, dull light
yellowish-green; inner toe, apple-green. [*In winter plumage.*]

PODILYMBUS PODICEPS

Thick-billed Grebe.

Colymbus podiceps, LINN., Syst. Nat., I, 1766, 223.

Podilymbus podiceps, LAWRENCE, Baird's Birds N. Am., 1858, 898.—BAIRD, Cat. N. Am. Birds, 1859, No. 709.—COUES, Key, 1872, 338; Check List, 1873, No. 614; Birds N.W., 1874, 737.—HENSHAW, 1875, 490.

This common Grebe was a resident species in all suitable localities.

List of specimens.

264, *jur.;* Truckee River (Camp 26), November 18, 1867. 15—22—5½—4—1⁵⁄₁₆—1³⁄₈—(?)—(?). Bill, horn-color, becoming blackish basally and on the culmen; lower mandible, more lilaceous, with a dusky lateral stripe; iris, of three distinct colors, disposed in concentric rings, the first (around the pupil) clear milk-white, the next dark olive-brown, the outer pale ochraceous-brown, the dark ring reticulated into the lighter; tarsi and toes, greenish-slate, the joints darker.

454, ♀ *ad.;* Carson City, March 24, 1868. 13¼—21¾—5—3½. Bill, clear opaque white, or milk-white, purest posterior to a black band across its terminal third, the anterior portion with a strong tinge of slaty-blue; eyelids, pure white; lores, more bluish; iris, rich dark brown, with a narrow outer ring of ochraceous-white, the two colors reticulated together; next the pupil, a fine thread-like ring of white; tarsi and toes, greenish slate-black on the outer side, plumbeous on the inner side.

INDEX TO PART III.

SCIENTIFIC NAMES.

[Names not in italics are synonyms.]

INDEX TO PART III.

INDEX TO PART III.

INDEX TO PART III.

POPULAR NAMES.

INDEX TO PART III.

INDEX TO PART III.

INDEX TO PART III.

INDEX TO PART III.

INDEX TO PART III.

INDIAN NAMES.

The letter annexed to a name is the tribe initial: P., denoting Paiute (or Pah-Ute), S., Shoshone, and and W., Washoe,—the tribes whose vocabularies were, in part, noted.

INDEX TO PART III

LOCALITIES DESCRIBED OR SPECIALLY REFERRED TO.

NATURAL SCIENCES IN AMERICA

An Arno Press Collection

Allen, J[oel] A[saph]. **The American Bisons,** Living and Extinct. 1876

Allen, Joel Asaph. **History of the North American Pinnipeds:** A Monograph of the Walruses, Sea-Lions, Sea-Bears and Seals of North America. 1880

American Natural History Studies: The Bairdian Period. 1974

American Ornithological Bibliography. 1974

Anker, Jean. **Bird Books and Bird Art.** 1938

Audubon, John James and John Bachman. **The Quadrupeds of North America.** Three vols. 1854

Baird, Spencer F[ullerton]. **Mammals of North America.** 1859

Baird, S[pencer] F[ullerton], T[homas] M. Brewer and R[obert] Ridgway. **A History of North American Birds:** Land Birds. Three vols., 1874

Baird, Spencer F[ullerton], John Cassin and George N. Lawrence. **The Birds of North America.** 1860. Two vols. in one.

Baird, S[pencer] F[ullerton], T[homas] M. Brewer, and R[obert] Ridgway. **The Water Birds of North America.** 1884. Two vols. in one.

Barton, Benjamin Smith. **Notes on the Animals of North America.** Edited, with an Introduction by Keir B. Sterling. 1792

Bendire, Charles [Emil]. **Life Histories of North American Birds** With Special Reference to Their Breeding Habits and Eggs. 1892/1895. Two vols. in one.

Bonaparte, Charles Lucian [Jules Laurent]. **American Ornithology:** Or The Natural History of Birds Inhabiting the United States, Not Given by Wilson. 1825/1828/1833. Four vols. in one.

Cameron, Jenks. **The Bureau of Biological Survey:** Its History, Activities, and Organization. 1929

Caton, John Dean. **The Antelope and Deer of America:** A Comprehensive Scientific Treatise Upon the Natural History, Including the Characteristics, Habits, Affinities, and Capacity for Domestication of the Antilocapra and Cervidae of North America. 1877

Contributions to American Systematics. 1974

Contributions to the Bibliographical Literature of American Mammals. 1974

Contributions to the History of American Natural History. 1974

Contributions to the History of American Ornithology. 1974

Cooper, J[ames] G[raham]. **Ornithology.** Volume I, Land Birds. 1870

Cope, E[dward] D[rinker]. **The Origin of the Fittest:** Essays on Evolution and **The Primary Factors of Organic Evolution.** 1887/1896. Two vols. in one.

Coues, Elliott. **Birds of the Colorado Valley.** 1878

Coues, Elliott. **Birds of the Northwest.** 1874

Coues, Elliott. **Key To North American Birds.** Two vols. 1903

Early Nineteenth-Century Studies and Surveys. 1974

Emmons, Ebenezer. **American Geology:** Containing a Statement of the Principles of the Science. 1855. Two vols. in one.

Fauna Americana. 1825-1826

Fisher, A[lbert] K[enrick]. **The Hawks and Owls of the United States in Their Relation to Agriculture.** 1893

Godman, John D. **American Natural History:** Part I — Mastology and **Rambles of a Naturalist.** 1826-28/1833. Three vols. in one.

Gregory, William King. **Evolution Emerging:** A Survey of Changing Patterns from Primeval Life to Man. Two vols. 1951

Hay, Oliver Perry. **Bibliography and Catalogue of the Fossil Vertebrata of North America.** 1902

Heilprin, Angelo. **The Geographical and Geological Distribution of Animals.** 1887

Hitchcock, Edward. **A Report on the Sandstone of the Connecticut Valley,** Especially Its Fossil Footmarks. 1858

Hubbs, Carl L., editor. **Zoogeography.** 1958

[Kessel, Edward L., editor]. **A Century of Progress in the Natural Sciences: 1853-1953.** 1955

Leidy, Joseph. **The Extinct Mammalian Fauna of Dakota and Nebraska,** Including an Account of Some Allied Forms from Other Localities, Together with a Synopsis of the Mammalian Remains of North America. 1869

Lyon, Marcus Ward, Jr. **Mammals of Indiana.** 1936

Matthew, W[illiam] D[iller]. **Climate and Evolution.** 1915

Mayr, Ernst, editor. **The Species Problem.** 1957

Mearns, Edgar Alexander. **Mammals of the Mexican Boundary of the United States.** Part I: Families Didelphiidae to Muridae. 1907

Merriam, Clinton Hart. **The Mammals of the Adirondack Region,** Northeastern New York. 1884

Nuttall, Thomas. **A Manual of the Ornithology of the United States and of Canada.** Two vols. 1832-1834

Nuttall Ornithological Club. **Bulletin of the Nuttall Ornithological Club:** A Quarterly Journal of Ornithology. 1876-1883. Eight vols. in three.

[Pennant, Thomas]. **Arctic Zoology.** 1784-1787. Two vols. in one.

Richardson, John. **Fauna Boreali-Americana;** Or the Zoology of the Northern Parts of British America, Containing Descriptions of the Objects of Natural History Collected on the Late Northern Land Expeditions Under Command of Captain Sir John Franklin, R. N. Part I: Quadrupeds. 1829

Richardson, John and William Swainson. **Fauna Boreali-Americana:** Or the Zoology of the Northern Parts of British America, Containing Descriptions of the Objects of Natural History Collected by the Late Northern Land Expeditions Under Command of Captain Sir John Franklin, R. N. Part II: The Birds. 1831

Ridgway, Robert. **Ornithology.** 1877

Selected Works By Eighteenth-Century Naturalists and Travellers. 1974

Selected Works in Nineteenth-Century North American Paleontology. 1974

Selected Works of Clinton Hart Merriam. 1974

Selected Works of Joel Asaph Allen. 1974

Selections From the Literature of American Biogeography. 1974

Seton, Ernest Thompson. **Life-Histories of Northern Animals: An Account of the Mammals of Manitoba.** Two vols. 1909

Sterling, Keir Brooks. **Last of the Naturalists:** The Career of C. Hart Merriam. 1974

Vieillot, L. P. **Histoire Naturelle Des Oiseaux de L'Amerique Septentrionale,** Contenant Un Grand Nombre D'Especes Decrites ou Figurees Pour La Premiere Fois. 1807. Two vols. in one.

Wilson, Scott B., assisted by A. H. Evans. **Aves Hawaiienses:** The Birds of the Sandwich Islands. 1890-99

Wood, Casey A., editor. **An Introduction to the Literature of Vertebrate Zoology.** 1931

Zimmer, John Todd. **Catalogue of the Edward E. Ayer Ornithological Library.** 1926